The Sword of the Lord

Visit www.swordofthelordbook.com.

The Sword of the Lord

The Roots of Fundamentalism in an American Family

Andrew Himes

Contents

Acknowledgments

I am deeply indebted to friends, volunteer editors, feedback artists, family members, and co-conspirators who have helped me through the long adventure of this book, as advisors, conversation partners, manuscript readers, and helpful critics. Much of its virtue is due to the many who have helped me in so many ways, and all of its faults may be laid at my doorstep.

Parker Palmer helped me to figure out who I was supposed to be when I grew up, and then inspired me to begin writing and continue through many drafts, believing I had something of value to offer. Robin Romeo and Cambrea Ezell provided critical feedback, continual encouragement, and amazing friendship. Jim Henderson gave me a new vision of evangelical Christianity and a redefinition of revival. Daniel Roberts inspired me with his faith and opened my understanding of how book marketing is a conversation. Charles Baker gave the gift of many hours of painstaking copyediting, along with frequent links to silly videos and admonishment not to take myself so seriously. Kat Linehan jolted me into rethinking and expanding my understanding of Christianity. My son-in-law Dave Cornell enlarged my concepts of fatherhood, partnership, Catholicism, and devoted friendship. Sheryl Fullerton helped me understand the vitality of 21st century Christianity, and provided me with early, invaluable feedback and wise advice. Rodney Clapp helped me believe the book had a compelling mission and could find an important audience. Alan and Andrea Rabinowitz helped me understand the story the book needed to tell and offered some great advice about the book's organization. Hannah Adams did an amazing job designing the book cover and the banner of the web site. Rebecca Gleason was the world's best book editor: passionate, disciplined, and professional.

The daughters of John R. Rice—my aunts Libby Handford, Joanna Rice, Joy Martin, Jessie Sandberg, and my mom Mary Lloys Himes—were unstinting with critical help, careful reviews of the manuscript, patience, and compassionate love. My nephew Stephen Lamb gave me several new leases on life with his support, critical insights, and enthusiasm. My nephew Andrew Lamb challenged me with his faith, his humor, and his passion for me to learn about and express our family's legacy so that it could be useful to others. My siblings—Lloys Jean Grace, Faith Lamb, John Himes, and Joanna Murphy—all gave me gracious love and timely feedback, along with occasional necessary corrections to my memory and my attitude. Teresa Posakony gave generously of her time, spirit, advocacy, and wisdom from the first draft to the final manuscript over many cups of coffee. Marilyn Turkovich has been my incredibly prolific and creative partner over the years in creating the Voices Education Project. Lin Carlson, Gary Ikeda, Raj Manhas, and Mike Schaefer (my running partners) all kept me humble and helped me delight in life. Chiara Guerrieri gifted me with hope, ridiculous puns, and the quality of fashion advice that can only be tendered by an Italian. Judy Pigott offered careful review, astute advice and deep friendship throughout my writing process.

In addition, the following have been patient, enthusiastic, and loving friends, providing feedback, advice, and provocative conversation to spur my research, development, and writing: Abdi Sami, Adam Kahane, Amy Studer, Andrew Lamb, Anne Howard, Clara Jong, Anne Stadler, Berit Anderson, Bill Rice, Channapha Khamvongsa, Chris Fordyce, Diane Stielstra, Donn Fry, Don Sandberg, Doug Tanner, Freddie Helmiere, Kathy Gille, Ed Tick, Genessa Krasnow, Jag Bhalla, James D. Price, Jan Bultmann, Jane Posakony, Jeremy Wilber, John and Frederica Helmiere, Jon Ramer, Karl Bischoff, Kathy Gille, Keith Campbell, Kim Corrigan, Larry Winters, Lora-Ellen McKinney, Lori Walls, Mark Anderson, Michele Byrd, Michele Corey, Michael Wolfe, Otts Bolisay, Pam Eakes, Paul Himes, Paul Loeb, Peter Morgan, Phil Klein, Randy Stocki, Rick and Marcy Jackson, Roger Martin Jr., Roger Martin, Sr., Sally Anderson, Stephen Friedrich, Richard Woo, Rich Moniak, Rick and Marcy Jackson, Tim Harris, Valerie Tarico, Walt Handford, Will Poole, and Yaffa Maritz.

Finally, my daughter Amber Himes-Cornell provided powerful emotional and intellectual support through the many years in which I've struggled with the meaning of this book. My baby granddaughter Chiara, who shares my love of avocados, was generous with chortles, shouts, nose-yanks, and grins. And more than anyone else, my wife Alix Wilber has been unfailingly generous, heroically patient, unstintingly supportive, and amazingly good-hearted through all of my struggles to get this book from my head and heart onto the page, and I am more grateful to Alix, my life's love, than I can express.

Foreword

In this book, my intention is to explore the roots of fundamentalism in America in a critical, thoughtful, and honest way, using the history of my own family of Baptist fundamentalists as a rich source of insights.

On my mother's side, my family history has embodied the narrative arc of American fundamentalism for almost three centuries. My maternal ancestors, the Rice clan, arrived on American shores as part of a wave of Scots-Irish immigrants during the early half of the 18th century. They came from Wales originally, and joined the stream of Welsh, Scottish, English, and Irish settlers who became known as the "Scots-Irish." These Scots-Irish had been uprooted before: in the 17th century King James transported the Borderers, a motley but largely Presbyterian assortment of combative Scots, Irish, Welsh and English yeomen, to the northern counties of Ireland to solidify his conquest of that land. Their Irish sojourn was threatened by famine, made difficult by the violent opposition of their Catholic neighbors, and impeded by conflict within their own community. Over the next century the Scots-Irish, my ancestors among them, then re-migrated in sizable waves to colonial America, where they settled at first in the foothills of Appalachia and then spread across the mountains and throughout the South. They carried with them their distinctive culture, shaped by centuries of marginal existence, deep insecurity, and the trauma that results from almost constant war or violent conflict.

The traumatic history of the Scots-Irish helped to shape their religion, combining Calvinist fatalism with combative self-assertion, melding a literal reading of the Bible with a profound regard for democracy and the rights of the individual. The Scots-Irish were quick to wrath, radical in their righteousness, and also profoundly moved by love for their families, their communities, and their new American home.

My own Rice ancestors were Calvinists and Presbyterians[*], and they settled at first in the Carolina foothills of the Appalachians, and then traveled over the mountains to plant small farms in the lush valleys and broad plains beyond the Smoky Mountains.

In the early 19th century, the Rice clan joined yet another migration, this time west to the rich Missouri River Valley, where they could benefit from cheap land and the cheap slave labor necessary to farm it. Like their neighbors, they built large-scale hemp plantations farmed by numerous Negro slaves, and the hemp they produced turned into rope for binding cotton bales—and, through slavery, Negroes—in the deeper South.

Their successful life in Missouri was destroyed by the Civil War. Missouri in particular was the scene of the most violent conflict, with siblings and parents, close friends and neighbors pitted against each other in a vicious and bloody series of fights. It is estimated that over a thousand battles between organized military forces took place in Missouri during the Civil War—more than any other state—in addition to many more thousands of acts of murder, mayhem, and simple criminality committed by individuals and small groups. In the midst of the war thousands of desperate refugees fled the bitter fighting and devastation in Border States such as Missouri. Those who were die-hard supporters of the Confederacy, including many slaveholders, fled farther south to Texas, where they settled down to rebuild their lives and communities after the war. My own Rice family was among them.

The traumatic experience of the Civil War and its aftermath in the 19th century was the incubator of Christian fundamentalism in 20th century America. The agony of the Civil War had a devastating impact on subsequent generations of Southerners, many of whom carried the burden and promise of their Scots-Irish heritage.

By contrast with the rest of the South, Union armies never invaded Texas during the Civil War and Texas suffered relatively little damage to its economic infrastructure. Moreover, many Texans thrived as the state became a hub of trade and agriculture, and Texas ports became the goal of ships seeking to run the Union blockade and win lucrative profits supplying the armies, industries, and civilian markets of the South.

The white population of Texas from before the war, then, was never truly beaten, never truly surrendered, and was never brought violently to terms with the new realities. However, many of the new refugees from the former slave-owning states to the north and east of Texas had been

---

[*] See the Glossary for definitions of the many different religions, sects, and schools of theological thought referred to in this book.

beaten most violently and decisively. Many of them remained in Texas because they refused to acknowledge their defeat or accept their losses. It was in Texas that the myth of the Lost Cause would resonate most powerfully. And it was Texas that turned out to be especially congenial to the development of Christian fundamentalism in America.

My great-grandfather Will Rice was born in Missouri on the eve of the Civil War, grew up in post-war Texas, and worked as a cowboy, a farmer and rancher, a horse trader and a land speculator. He was saved and felt the call to become a preacher, went off to attend the Baptist Theological Seminary in Louisville and then returned to Texas to raise his family. He became involved in politics, joined fraternal societies, including the Ku Klux Klan, and was elected to the Texas State Senate in 1921, the year the Klan took over control of both houses of the Texas Legislature and elected one of their own to the U.S. Senate.

Will Rice's son, my granddad John R. Rice, also became a preacher and evangelist. Although he disagreed with his dad about the Klan, he was nonetheless deeply conservative in his religion and his politics. Granddad locked horns with the local religious establishment over his criticism of the Southern Baptist Convention and its "compromises" with liberalism and modernism, and then helped lead an exodus of fundamentalists from the Southern Baptist denomination in Texas. He started a fundamentalist newspaper in Dallas in 1934 called *The Sword of the Lord*, and spent the next several decades helping develop a national fundamentalist network of churches, denominations, conferences, publishing houses, schools and institutes, and other institutions. He wrote and published over 200 books and pamphlets during his lifetime with a combined circulation of over 60 million copies, with such provocative titles as *All Satan's Apples Have Worms*; *Predestined for Hell?*; *Bobbed Hair, Bossy Wives, and Women Preachers*; *The Dance: Child of the Brothel, Sister of Gambling and Drunkenness, Mother of Lust—Road to Hell!*; *Bible Facts About Heaven*; *The Home*; and *Is God A Dirty Bully?* Famously, he wrote a small pamphlet titled *What Must I Do to Be Saved?* that was published in over 30 languages with over 40 million copies distributed.

The *Sword* developed into the largest and most influential fundamentalist newspaper in the world, with a readership of several hundred thousand preachers, deacons, evangelists, missionaries, Sunday School teachers, and various other soul-winners. Granddad mentored and encouraged hundreds or thousands of other and younger fundamentalist and evangelical leaders such as Billy Graham, Jerry Falwell, Bob Jones Jr., and W. A. Criswell, a fellow Texan who became the most prominent Southern Baptist of his generation and helped lead the Southern Baptist

Convention's return to its fundamentalist roots in the last third of the 20th Century.

Granddad wrote and published thousands of editorials and sermons in *The Sword of the Lord*. Over several decades, through his battles to define both the principles and acceptable limits of fundamentalism and the acceptable behavior of fundamentalists themselves, he helped to lay the basis for the rise of the Religious Right in America. He died in 1980, when I was 30 years old, a few months after the election of Ronald Reagan to the presidency. For many, that election marked the beginning of an era.

The entire history of Protestant fundamentalism is a topic beyond my ambitions. In particular, the history of the Religious Right and the ascension of Jerry Falwell and the Moral Majority has been related in scores of books, and I won't try to retell it here. I'm interested instead in what came before the accession to power of the modern Religious Right. In particular, I started this book to understand the specific history that created the fundamentalist world in which I grew up. Who were my ancestors, including my grandfather? Why did they believe as they did? How did their religious ideas grow from the soil of their lives and condition their actions?

To find out, I researched as far back as I could go into my family's history, and then forward up to the death of my grandfather, John R. Rice, a fundamentalist leader whose career spanned the critical decades from the Scopes Monkey Trial in 1925 (at a time when fundamentalists were first attempting to forbid the teaching of evolution in public schools) to the national prominence of the Moral Majority in the 1980 election of President Ronald Reagan. I've done my best to place my family in the broader context of evangelical Christianity and Protestant fundamentalism in the history of the United States.

This book is not intended to be an exposé of fundamentalism or a polemic against fundamentalism. It is important to me to try my best to explore the truth about my family, our faith, and our history over the generations. So I have approached this task with humility and all the compassion I can muster. I am grateful to my fundamentalist family for instilling in me a profound love for others, high moral standards, and a deep commitment to justice.

Andrew Himes
January 31, 2011

Part I
Why We Care About Fundamentalism

Chapter 1
The Funeral of John R. Rice

"THE SWORD OF THE LORD...and of John R. Rice."— from the masthead of John R. Rice's newspaper, which began publication in 1935.

The morning of January 3, 1981 dawned gray and chill. I rode north along Interstate 65 from Birmingham toward the town of Murfreesboro, Tennessee. I was wearing a banged-up leather jacket and a pair of jeans. In a luggage box on the back of my Honda 400 motorcycle was an overnight bag with a toothbrush and a change of clothes—the only suit I owned, a cheap and unstylish Sears special with a clip-on tie and my only white dress shirt. My hair was shaggy, and my goatee and thick glasses made me look like a popeyed version of Vladimir Lenin. Every few miles I had to pull off the highway to wipe away the tears that streamed down my face so that I could see well enough to keep traveling. By the time I arrived at my grandparents' home in Murfreesboro, I had cried enough to fill a small bucket, but I was reasonably in control of myself.

Cars were pulled up on the gravel strip next to the side of the house, and the house itself was wall-to-wall with humanity—my own mom and dad and my brother and three sisters, all my aunts and uncles and cousins and old family friends and employees from my granddad's *Sword of the Lord* newspaper. People were rushing around, talking, laughing, crying, hugging, commiserating, singing, straightening each other's ties and dresses, and praying. The phone was ringing, and a stream of cars was driving up to the house and then driving away in the direction of the church.

The funeral was slated for early afternoon, and I had timed my arrival so as to avoid any serious conversations with anyone. I was not eager to discuss the length of my hair or the fact that I hadn't attended church anywhere for several years or explain why I wasn't turning out to be a Baptist preacher as everyone had expected me to. Despite my attempt to stay in the background amid all the hubbub, my grandmother tracked me down in a corner of her kitchen and gave me a big hug and a kiss.

"Andy," said Grandma, "I am so happy you're here! It's been such a long time since we've seen you. So I know you just got here, but I want you to be the lead pallbearer. You're the oldest grandson, and I know you're good at this sort of thing, so you get the other boys together and you'll be the ones at the end of the service to bring the casket down the aisle and then out the church door."

I started to speak but couldn't, and she looked at me with such love and said, "Don't worry, you'll do fine. You know he would be so proud of you."

If there was anything I was certain of in the world, it was that my granddad would not be proud of me. As a matter of fact, he'd expressed sharp disapproval of me for years, in a series of long, typewritten letters that I had kept but never answered. He and my grandmother—along with the rest of my large extended family—had prayed for me and pleaded with me and cajoled me, all to no avail. He had told my grandma and my mom years earlier that he hoped and prayed I would grow up to inherit his mantle as a preacher and fundamentalist leader. Instead of going off to Bob Jones University to prepare for the ministry, however, I had left home to attend the University of Wisconsin in Madison. There, I had immediately joined demonstrations against the war in Vietnam and in support of the civil rights movement, thus confirming all of Granddad's fears that Madison was an incubator of rebels and radicals. While my brother trained to be a missionary to Japan, I trained to be a proletarian revolutionary and overthrow the imperialist bourgeoisie. I had worked in the steel fabrication plants and foundries of Birmingham for several years, organizing strikes, passing out revolutionary literature, and building up my arrest record.

I ended up as much a Maoist failure as I had been a Christian failure. Souls were still unsaved, and the imperialist bourgeoisie was still in power. Before I graduated from high school, I had lost my faith in the fundamentalist God I had been trained to worship and serve. Now, at the age of 30, I had lost my faith in the secular gods of Karl Marx, Vladimir Lenin, and Mao Zedong. I had smashed into a brick wall that was both ideological and theological, and had no idea how to move forward. I was no longer part of the communist movement, and my life no longer had any meaning or direction. I was just beginning to understand that in moving from Christianity to Maoism I had merely traded one form of fundamentalism for another. I was so far removed from my family's reality that none of them knew much of anything about my views, actions, or past associations.

The parking lot of the Franklin Road Baptist Church was jam-packed, and over a thousand people filled the pews inside. Luminaries from across the fundamentalist world were gathered. All my aunts and uncles and my parents were seated in a semi-circle on the platform behind the pulpit. My uncle Sandy—Don Sandberg—sat at the piano playing a medley of gospel songs written by my granddad as I made my way up the aisle to the front pew where I was to sit with the other pallbearers, all of whom were my male cousins.

Uncle Sandy opened the long service by leading a large choir in singing Handel's Hallelujah Chorus. My dad and my five uncles provided eulogies, and a dozen other Baptist preachers offered up their heartfelt testimonies. The most celebrated speakers were Jack Hyles, pastor of the largest fundamentalist church in the world, located in Hammond, Indiana, and Jerry Falwell, leader of the Moral Majority, pastor of another large church in Lynchburg, Virginia, and founder of Liberty University. This being a fundamentalist service, of course, all the speakers were men, though my aunts and my mom together sang "Finally Home," and Aunt Joy read a poem titled "Someone Special is Coming Home," written by my Aunt Grace.

Falwell was at the apogee of his career. Only 18 months earlier he had founded the Moral Majority, a conservative political action group that endorsed Ronald Reagan before the contentious Republican convention and then claimed to have provided the winning margin for Reagan's election to the presidency in November 1980. Falwell would soon appear on the cover of *Time* magazine, hailed as the inspiration and founder of the Religious Right. His television programs, *Jerry Falwell Live* and the *Old Time Gospel Hour*, were broadcast to over 30 million American homes. In 1977, Falwell had told a rally of Miami voters, "so-called gay folks would just as soon kill you as look at you," and he would soon say that "AIDS is not just God's punishment for homosexuals. It is God's punishment for the society that tolerates homosexuals."[1] And he would warn: "If we do not act now, homosexuals will 'own' America! If you and I do not speak up now, this homosexual steamroller will literally crush all decent men, women, and children . . . and our nation will pay a terrible price!" He had expressed strong support for the "Christian" leaders of the apartheid regime in South Africa. He decried "women's lib" and instructed women to be subservient to their husbands.

When it came time for Falwell to speak at the funeral, he called John R. Rice's death the "passing of an era...He was God's man for the hour. I looked on him as the guardian of fundamentalist truth for this generation. More than any other person, he was the most trusted man in fundamentalism...He set the standard in the pulpit ministries of thousands of pastors and evangelists. So we pay tribute to one someone has called a 'titular leader of fundamentalism.' The mantle has fallen, not on one or two, but on thousands."[2]

At the end of the service, I led my younger cousins up to the front of the church where we lifted the coffin onto a cart and then formed lines on both sides to roll it down the center aisle and out the main doors to the waiting hearse. I got into a black limousine with my family and we rode 10 miles west on Franklin Road to the Bill Rice Ranch, a fundamentalist retreat center founded by my great uncle Bill. There, we interred the casket in a large marble sarcophagus at the top of the slope in our family cemetery. My cousins and I then stood for the next two hours as an honor guard while several hundred people came by in a long line to pay their respects, many of them weeping and pausing to pray or touch the cool gray stone. I wept also, as I stood by the grave, and I suppose I might have done something that could be thought of as prayer. It was a prayer for myself, in all of my sadness and confusion. I had been estranged from my granddad for years, though I had always thought of him as one of the kindest, funniest, and most honorable people I knew. I had raged against his support for racial injustice in the South and war in Vietnam. I thought his strictures against playing cards or going to movies or women cutting their hair and wearing pants were downright silly. But I also knew he was courageous, truthful and loving. He was the only granddad I had. So I wept because I knew how much I had lost when he died.

After the line had passed, we got back into the limousines to ride back to the fellowship hall at the church. The dining tables were set for eighty people or so—our large Rice clan together with close friends and speakers at the funeral. Name tags were at each of the places, instructing us where to sit.

An anonymous and well-intentioned schemer—probably one of my aunts—had thoughtfully placed my own name tag right next to Jerry Falwell's. Clearly, a plot was afoot to expose me—the only black sheep to appear in several generations of the family—to the tender conversational ministrations of the most famous fundamentalist in America. When my 85-year-old grandmother spotted me hesitating, she took me by the hand and led me over to Falwell, saying, "Andy, I want you to get to know one of my best friends! Dr. Falwell is one of the dearest, sweetest people you'll ever meet." And to Falwell, she said, "I want you to meet Andy, my oldest grandson and one of the most handsome and talented young men I know!"

Dr. Falwell and I sat down to eat tuna-noodle casserole made with canned tuna, mushroom soup and elbow macaroni, the whole concoction topped with a crust of potato chips and baked. We shared creamed green beans and orange Jell-O with chunks of fruit cocktail, and we washed down our store-bought pecan pie with Maxwell House Coffee from a giant silver urn as church ladies stood around waiting on us.

I had little to say to Falwell. For one thing, I was still fighting back the tears that have always come so easily to me—a trait I shared with my granddad. For another, I pretty much viewed Falwell as evil incarnate. Falwell, however, needed little help from me to maintain an abundant flow of words.

"Andy," he said, digging into his casserole, "I am so sorry for your loss. It was mine as well. I must tell you that John R. Rice was a father to me. I subscribed to *The Sword of the Lord* when I first became a pastor in Lynchburg, and I met him just a few years later. Your grandfather has been my mentor, my teacher, my friend, and my prayer partner."

I mumbled some words of gratitude, but couldn't think of much else to say. I certainly wasn't going to tell him anything about myself or my life, and he didn't ask me much after determining that I was married, lived in Birmingham, and was the father of a three-year-old daughter.

"Well, that's good, that's good," said Falwell. "I know that God is using you in a mighty way down there in Birmingham."

"I'm sure you're right," I replied, thinking of my abortive Maoist career, my lengthy FBI surveillance file, and my checkered employment history, which included stints as a foundry welder, a motorcycle salesman, a professional ideologue, and a taxi driver.

"Andy," said Falwell as he polished off his creamed green beans, "I spent all of last week out in California at Rancho del Cielo, where President Reagan lives. You know, they're already calling it the Western White House. We experienced such a sweet sense of fellowship and a deep gratitude for the work God is doing in the hearts of the American people."

Falwell fixed me with a gracious, friendly smile. "Andy," he said, "we can be satisfied that Jesus has a friend in Washington, DC. Ronald Reagan is a man after our own hearts. He's been saved and he knows it. He shares our values and believes the Bible just like we do. He wants to do the right thing for God if only he can get the help he needs from the rest of us. For the first time in a century we have a fundamentalist living at 1600 Pennsylvania Avenue."

I murmured something inoffensive, and asked Falwell another question to keep his conversational juices flowing, and then I turned all my attention to my fruit salad. Fundamentalism was a difficult and painful topic for me, to say the least, and I had no idea how to talk about it without getting into an unseemly and angry debate with Jerry Falwell, with all my family as witnesses.

Chapter 2
In Defense of Fundamentalism

> *"The sword of the Lord shall devour from the one end of*
> *the land even to the other end of the land: no flesh shall*
> *have peace."*—Jeremiah 12

I was a fundamentalist before I could walk, though I was at least four years old before I really could use the term. We attended church several times a week, and the preachers in those services were generally my dad, my granddad, one of my uncles, or some close family friend.

The women in my family never cut their hair and always wore skirts or dresses, never pants or shorts. The children in my family never said gee or golly for fear of using the name of the Lord in vain, even in a disguised form. We never attended movies at the local theater because we didn't want to support the "Hollywood cesspool." We made sure never to go dancing because we knew that dancing leads to sex before marriage and sex without marriage leads to depravity and Hell.

We never played card games with a deck of regular playing cards, which we understood had been invented by a crazy, evil Spanish prince named Charles, who designed the deck to portray God the Father who had sex with Mary the Mother who gave birth to an illegitimate Son named Jesus who was also the Jack of Spades.

We children called adult men "Sir" and adult women "Ma'am." We carried Bibles around to lots of places that normal people wouldn't be seen with them and we passed out Bible tracts on street corners and put leaflets for Vacation Bible School under the windshield wipers of thousands of cars.

A fundamentalist was set apart from "the world." We were definitely going to Heaven when we died, and those with different views on Heaven, Hell, God and Satan, sin and salvation were definitely going to

Hell, which was more than a shame because Hell involved eternal torment, literal flames, and wailing and gnashing of teeth.

Our job was to tell people about Jesus so they could avoid going to Hell. The only way to get saved was to ask Jesus into your heart. Just that one little sentence, spoken sincerely aloud or in your heart, and you were going to be okay forever, headed for Heaven. Most Catholics, however, were going to Hell because they were counting on the Pope or a confession to a priest or the benevolence of Mary or their own good works to save them rather than the blood of Jesus. Communists were going to Hell because they didn't believe in God at all. Many but not all Democrats were going to Hell, not because they were Democrats but because many of them didn't believe the Bible or understand the right way to get saved. Most liberals and modernists were going to Hell for the same reasons. Non-white people generally were going to Hell simply because they were more likely to live in remote, non-Christian places such as Africa or Asia or South America where they would not hear about Jesus dying for them on the cross and so they would be lost. Virtually everybody in Europe was going to Hell because there were very few genuine Christians in any European country. And it only stood to reason that almost everybody living behind the Iron Curtain in China, the Soviet Union, the Eastern Bloc, or Cuba was going to Hell.

From my limited and immature child's point of view, Heaven was therefore populated almost exclusively by white people who lived in the United States of America, along with the original disciples of Jesus, an uncalculated number of genuine Christians who had lived throughout the ages, and many but not all of those mentioned in *Foxe's Book of Martyrs*, which I first read at the age of eight when I found it on my parents' book shelf.

I had a front row seat on the division of the world between sheep and goats, and I soaked up thousands of sermons in regular weekly church services, revival meetings, and Bible camps. Although this book concentrates on the Rice side of my family, my dad Charles Himes was also a fundamentalist preacher, pastor, and evangelist for over 60 years. When I was a child, he preached in revival meetings, planted and shepherded small churches, and served on the staff of my grandfather's church in Wheaton, Illinois. Later, he served as full-time pastor of a string of small fundamentalist churches in the South and the Midwest.

When most of us think about Christian fundamentalism in America, we think about a particular strand of belief that is embodied in Protestant evangelical conservatism. We picture a set of people whom we think of as embodying or representing fundamentalist belief, including people such as James Dobson, Tim LaHaye, and Pat Robertson, or past fundamentalist luminaries such as Jerry Falwell, Bob Jones, and John R. Rice. Not all of these people have used the word "fundamentalist" to describe themselves, although several of them wore that title proudly.

When I was a child, the God I believed in was an old man, wise and powerful. He had complicated eyebrows, big ears, and eyelids that drooped alarmingly. God was very tall and he sometimes wore reading glasses. He had a deep voice that echoed when he spoke, and he was certain of his opinion on every conceivable topic. God wore a long white robe and sat on a golden throne from which flowed the river of life. He dwelt in a parallel universe far beyond the sky, in the center of a great city with twelve gates and golden streets lined with mansions where lived all the saints of Heaven. Perhaps coincidentally, God looked a lot like my granddad.

I thought of fundamentalists as a small group of people, led by my granddad and composed mainly of our family and people in our independent Baptist church and others who subscribed to *The Sword of the Lord* newspaper. My family then lived in Wheaton, Illinois, the heart of evangelical America, the home of Wheaton College and a town with more churches per capita than anywhere else in the country. As far as I knew, however, I was the only fundamentalist kid in my school. Most of the other kids attended evangelical or mainline Protestant churches in Wheaton, but they tended to think my family and I had a set of beliefs that were unusual and somewhat weird. For my part, I seriously believed that most of my supposedly Christian classmates were headed for Hell. I also assumed that someday I would be a fundamentalist preacher and inherit the mantle of my dad and my famous granddad.

I was steeped in the history and language of fundamentalism before I was 10 years old. In sermon after sermon, I heard my granddad preach about the heroes of fundamentalism—such evangelists as Charles Finney, D. L. Moody, R. A. Torrey, and Billy Sunday, and leaders such as William Jennings Bryan. And I heard him wage an ongoing theological war against people the likes of Nels Ferre, Harry Emerson Fosdick, and Clarence Darrow, whom he called liberals, modernists, and infidels. I did not understand this well. I just assumed that anyone who agreed with Granddad was a good person on the side of God, and anyone he disparaged was no friend of mine and would likely go to Hell.

As a child, I was comfortable as a fundamentalist. I was sure I knew everything there was to know about the world that was important. The Bible was the literal word of God. God was a powerful and angry yet somehow loving Father who lived in a literal and physically real heaven, and who sent sinners to Hell to spend eternity with a literal and evil guy named Satan. The list of my possible sins was long and specific and reliably elucidated by my granddad, the most authoritative person in the universe. The only way to be a Christian was to get saved. Anyone who was not saved was going straight to Hell at the end of life. God hated sin and Jesus died to save lost sinners. Once I was saved I would always be saved and could never be lost no matter what I did or how I failed. All of these were certainties.

I am the son of a Baptist preacher, and the grandson and great grandson of Baptist preachers, and the brother of a Baptist missionary to Japan. I am the nephew of five Baptist preachers and the great nephew of two. I have 23 cousins and uncountable second cousins, many of whom grew up to be preachers or missionaries.

I lived in the middle of this big and entertaining family that appeared to harbor no doubts about who we were or what God wanted us to do. I loved them all and I loved being a part of that extended family. My aunts were all gorgeous, and my uncles were all funny and smart, and my cousins and siblings, generally speaking, were sweet, adventurous, decent human beings who were fun to play with. I loved going to church on Sunday mornings, and I loved going over to my grandparents' house after church for a big family dinner every Sunday afternoon, after which we played some non-sinful game such as Carroms, Monopoly, Rook, or Dominoes. Within my family, everything was easy. It was only when we interacted with others outside our circle that I noticed the complexity of the world.

I can identify several specific ways in which my training as a fundamentalist bore good and healthy fruit, though I'm aware that a statement like that may be greeted with some skepticism by those who have only witnessed the world of fundamentalism from the outside. As a fundamentalist, I learned that it was perfectly all right for me to have an idea or outlook different from most folks, and to struggle for what I believed in the face of determined opposition. I learned that it was acceptable to be passionate about my values, and to care deeply about the consequences of my actions. I learned to view myself as an imperfect human who needs help from outside myself. I learned that faith and community are essential to life.

All of this discussion of fundamentalism begs the question of what fundamentalism is. The reality is that most of us mean quite different things by this heavily loaded word. My own favorite definition was provided by historian George Marsden in his book, *Understanding Fundamentalism and Evangelicalism*:

> A fundamentalist is an evangelical who is angry about
> something...A more precise statement of the same point

is that an American fundamentalist is an evangelical who is militant in opposition to liberal theology in the churches or to changes in cultural values or mores, such as those associated with "secular humanism"… Fundamentalists are not just religious conservatives, they are conservatives who are willing to take a stand and to fight.[3]

This is a definition distorted by the public proclamations of certain fundamentalist leaders, of course, and I know many fundamentalists who are not "angry" people (including most of my relatives). But it is also a definition that makes sense to me. I am no longer consciously a fundamentalist, but my family and closest friends will happily tell you that I have a deeply ingrained or at least well-trained propensity to be pugnacious and overly certain of my own opinions (along with more attractive traits such as my love for silly wordplay and my glorious hair). And I spent much of the first part of my life as an angry and arrogant young man, qualities that subsided only after I relaxed by learning how to juggle, unicycle, and run long distances. Now in my 60s, I've calmed down a bit, but I still exhibit occasional outbreaks of self-righteousness.

Ironically, the word fundamentalist has gone out of favor among fundamentalists in the 21st century. Few people want to be called a fundamentalist these days, and some people whose politics and theology are most deeply fundamentalist are precisely the people who do not want to be called fundamentalists anymore. It's easy to confirm this. Just visit the website of any of the principal institutions of the fundamentalist movement in America, such as Bob Jones University or *The Sword of the Lord* newspaper. Search for the "fundamentalist" label anywhere on any of these websites. You'll find references to the use of the word fundamentalist from 10, 15 or 100 years in the past, but no contemporary usage.

John R. Rice's friend Jerry Falwell was the leading fundamentalist in America in the decades after Granddad's death in 1980, and in 1981 Falwell published a book titled *The Fundamentalist Phenomenon*, which proclaimed the political and moral triumph of the movement. Today, however, search the website of *Liberty Journal*, the online publication of Jerry Falwell's Liberty University, and you get the following result:

> Your search - **fundamentalist** - did not match any documents.
> No pages were found containing "**fundamentalist**".
>
> Suggestions:
> Make sure all words are spelled correctly.

Try different keywords.
Try more general keywords.

Mark Driscoll is the prominent pastor of Mars Hill Church in a neighborhood near my home in Seattle. I've attended Driscoll's church several times to listen to his preaching and get a clear sense of his theology, which is identical in almost every respect with older fundamentalists such as John R. Rice, although he adds a twist of Calvinism (his belief that some people are simply doomed to Hell and others are elected by God and destined for Heaven).

Driscoll does not claim to be a fundamentalist, and many who today willingly accept the label of fundamentalist would not claim him as their sectarian brother. Nonetheless, Driscoll is a fundamentalist in everything but name, and shares virtually all his doctrinal positions and attitudes with any other fundamentalist.

Driscoll is aware that fundamentalists have developed a bad reputation for being judgmental and self-righteous. He therefore claims not to be one. He defines fundamentalists simply as people who do not like smoking, drinking, and cussing, and then he offers a shallow critique of fundamentalism.

"Fundamentalism is really losing the war," Driscoll said in an interview with *Christianity Today*, "and I think it is in part responsible for the rise of what we know as the more liberal end of the emerging church. Because a lot of what is fueling the left end of the emerging church is fatigue with hardcore fundamentalism that throws rocks at culture. But culture is the house that people live in, and it just seems really mean to keep throwing rocks at somebody's house."[4]

Driscoll's attempt to avoid the label of fundamentalism by suggesting the movement is only about "culture"—disapproval of cigars, pop music, and Hollywood picture shows—is the shallowest possible definition of fundamentalism. However, it seems to attract many who are uncomfortable with the cultural straitjacket of fundamentalism but open to Driscoll's fundamentalist interpretation of God and the Bible.

The September 11, 2001, terrorist attack was a significant factor in the modern demise of "fundamentalism" as a term used by a sizable number of Christians to describe themselves. The story that politicians, newscasters, and commentators repeated a million times over in the years after that tragic September was that terrorists generally were Muslim fundamentalists responsible for assaulting the foundations of the American way of life. Hearing terrorism equated with fundamentalism a few times is enough to make you want to avoid the label of fundamentalism altogether.

The basic doctrines and assumptions of fundamentalism, nonetheless, have influenced American history for over two centuries, and fundamentalist politics and religion have dramatically shaped American foreign policy and social policy for decades. Christian fundamentalism in America has its roots in the history of the South after the end of the Civil War. The underlying attitudes and assumptions leading to modern fundamentalism grew and flourished amid the wreckage of the war and reconstruction and as a response to the trauma of that war. They were nourished by the end of slavery and by the soil of poverty and defeat. They took root especially in the deepest South and particularly in the state of Texas during the first three decades of the 20th century, as my grandfather was beginning his ministry.

For all Christians—fundamentalist, evangelical, mainline Protestant, or Catholic—understanding fundamentalism matters because Christians are losing the struggle to have any appreciable influence in the thoughts, hearts, and lives of most Americans. The political dominance of the Religious Right over the past three decades in America has had a profoundly negative effect on how Americans think about Christianity. A groundbreaking survey titled *Unchristian: What a New Generation Really Thinks About Christianity* was published in 2007 by the evangelical Christian Barna Group. Its authors, David Kinnaman and Gabe Lyons, report that large majorities of non-churchgoing Americans are openly hostile to Christians. 87 percent believe that Christians are too judgmental of others. 86 percent believe that Christians are hypocritical, saying one thing and doing another. 75 percent believe that Christians are too involved in politics. Over two-thirds believe that Christians are out of touch with reality, insensitive to others, boring, and not accepting of other faiths. 90 percent believe that Christians hate homosexuals.

Younger Christians especially are likely to see and share these perceptions. As one survey respondent said, "Christians have become political, judgmental, intolerant, weak, religious, angry, and without balance. Christianity has become a nice Sunday drive. Where is the living God, the Holy Spirit, an amazing Jesus, the love, the compassion, the holiness? This type of life, how I yearn for that."[5]

For many Americans throughout our history, a neighbor was someone who looked like you, perhaps someone who lived next door and went to church with you and did business with you. A neighbor might be someone who was related to you by ties of blood or class or political affiliation. It's easy to feel "compassion" for that sort of neighbor. It's easy to put yourself in the other person's shoes when that other person shares your economic interests or your notion of God.

In general, a fundamentalist outlook made a lot of sense in a world in which you needed to be certain where to stand in order to survive the next day and to defend the lives and welfare of your family. Fundamentalism was a rational, and emotional, response to a dangerous world where you needed to know who was a sheep and who was a goat, who was for you and who was against you, who might slip a blade between your ribs and who would love you back.

Likewise, fundamentalist religion has reflected the absolutism of fundamentalist politics. Historically, Christian fundamentalists in America focused on identifying and proclaiming the set of doctrines—beliefs—that have been held by orthodox Christians since about the fourth century. Fundamentalists then militantly defended those doctrines against perceived heretical threats from liberals and modernists in the early twentieth century.

But what happens to fundamentalism when its original enemies have been defeated or have disappeared and the debate of a century ago becomes irrelevant? How does fundamentalism remain relevant in a world of evidently breathtaking diversity—an array of different spiritual practices, philosophies, and explorations of the meaning of God and spirit—none of which can seemingly claim to be authoritative? What does fundamentalism evolve into when the children of fundamentalists turn out to be more interested in following Jesus and practicing Christian love than arguing over arcane points of doctrine?

Part II
Revolution, Slavery, and War

Chapter 3
The Roots of Fundamentalism

"Death waits for you. There is now a Mortal and Contagious Disease in many houses; the Sword of the Lord is Drawn, and young men fall down apace slain under it...God will ere long pour down the Cataracts of His Wrath upon a sinful Nation, which hath of late been found guilty before the Lord of Signal Apostasy, Debauchery, and above all of nefandrous Contempt of the Pure and Powerful Dispensation of the Gospel."— Increase Mather, sermon preached in Boston, Massachusetts in 1668 during an epidemic of smallpox[6]

Each summer of my childhood I attended a fundamentalist Bible camp at the Bill Rice Ranch 10 miles west of Murfreesboro, Tennessee. The Ranch was a sacred place for me: a tabernacle, bunkhouses, and dining hall set amongst rocky hills cloaked with pines and scrub brush, with broad green pastures surrounding the fishing pond. Each July I arrived with hundreds of other campers for a week of Bible study, entertaining sermons, and training in soul-winning, combined with ping pong, shuffleboard, horseback rides, and storytelling around a campfire. My great uncle, evangelist Bill Rice, had purchased an old camp built by the Civilian Conservation Corps in 1953, and then restored and improved it. Each year, walking or riding a horse through the wilderness of the ranch, I felt inspired and refreshed. Each evening, listening to the clicking and whirring of the cicadas in the trees, the crackle of the campfire, the low murmur of voices, I felt the presence of God all around us.

Two of the hills overlooking the campgrounds were known as Arrowhead Mountain and Altar Mountain. Early one morning in the summer of 1961, I met my older cousin Pete Rice with a troop of several campers at the horse barn. I mounted an elderly plodding Appaloosa named Ginger and joined the line of other campers on their horses. Pete led us through the woods along a trail that had once been part of the Natchez Trace, and then up the ridge to a clearing at the top of Arrowhead Mountain. "You see this stone structure here?" said Pete. "It's about twenty feet long and shaped like a huge arrow half buried in the ground. It was shaped by the Indians who lived here hundreds of years ago, and it's pointing straight at the top of Altar Mountain."

The trail wound down through the pines, across a meadow, and then up along a ridge to the crest of Altar Mountain, where we found a scattering of mysterious, orderly, stone structures. They were clearly quite old, covered with moss and lichen, and they reminded me of an illustration in a book of Bible stories that depicted the altar on which Abraham had nearly sacrificed his son Isaac before God stayed his hand: circular in shape, three or four feet tall, built of flat rocks carefully fitted together like a three-dimensional puzzle. I could see perhaps 15 of the altars from where I sat atop Ginger.

"We've found about fifty of these altogether," said Pete. "An anthropologist came down from Knoxville to do a survey, and he says they've been here for hundreds of years. They were part of some kind of religious ceremony, but we don't know anything about it."

The early morning sun filtered through the pines as we sat silently contemplating the work of these ancient Indians, and I had a sudden flash of insight: *God was here! God came here many times, and the Indians spoke with God just like Abraham did!* The landscape was sacred for the Cherokee who lived here, just as it was for me. God was in the rocks and trees, in the hills and meadows, for the Cherokee, just as for me. The presence of God was all around us on the crest of the hill.

Although I did not make the connection at the time, I can now imagine my ancestor John Rice Sr. having a similar feeling when he first saw the hills of eastern Tennessee 200 years before me. He and his contemporaries considered the land uninhabited, though it was only so because the Cherokee had been violently displaced not long before. He paused for a moment, perhaps, and closed his eyes, smelling the same crisp sweet smell of fresh pine needles that I did that day on Altar Mountain. He and his family had journeyed far to arrive in this new land, fleeing conflict and persecution, seeking a country in which they could make their home and worship their God. I imagine they saw their little farm and the surrounding hills as a sacred landscape, created and infused with the very spirit of God.

The emigration of the Rice clan to America in the 18th century, along with hundreds of thousands of other Scots-Irish, was the result of a series of clashes that dated back to the late 1500s in the British Isles. A quick examination of these conflicts helps explain where modern American fundamentalism came from. At the end of the 16th century, two distinct struggles took place as Britain was in the throes of creating a modern state founded on the new democratic ideals of the Enlightenment. Both conflicts appeared to be religious disputes arising out of the Protestant Reformation. However, they gave birth to two movements in which 20th century fundamentalism germinated: the Presbyterianism of the Scots-Irish who settled the American South beginning in the 17th century, and the Puritanism of the religious refugees who settled New England beginning in the same century.

In the last decade of the 16th century, Queen Elizabeth of England engaged in a hard and bloody struggle to subdue the Catholics of Ireland and force them to submit to the authority of the British crown. The war pitted the army of Elizabeth against an array of Gaelic Irish chieftains led by Hugh O'Neill, the second Earl of Tyrone. After nine long years of continual violent conflict and many thousands of deaths, the English army used a combination of invasion, military victories, and a scorched earth policy to provoke famine and hardship for the Irish population and undermine support for O'Neill. The end of the war came in March of 1603, just a week following the death of Elizabeth. The new king of a unified Great Britain was James I, who confronted multiple problems on his accession to the throne. He decided that the solutions to two of those problems were happily related.

First, James wanted to dampen or extinguish the flames of Irish independence as permanently as possible. The idea that occurred to him was to evict all the Catholics from six counties of Ulster in Northern Ireland and to replace them with a sustainably large population of Protestants who would be loyal to the British crown. This project was known as the Plantation of Ulster, and it began in 1609, a few years after the war's end.

James' second problem was a troublesome group of dirt-poor, hardscrabble farmers and fighters in the borderlands and lowlands along the Scottish, English, and Welsh borders. They led a marginal existence, were famous for their cattle-rustling and raiding, and were considered to be pugnacious, contentious, and easily inflamed. They were known as the "Border Reivers"[*] or "Borderers" because they had played the

---

[*] The word *reive* is an early English word for "to rob," from the Scots Inglis verb *reifen* from the Old English *rēafian*, and thus related to the archaic

invaluable role of a buffer between the Scottish and English warring parties during 300 years of intermittent fighting.

James attempted to solve both of his problems by exporting a large number of these cantankerous Borderers to Ireland, providing them with land grants and planting them in Ulster in large enough communities to be sustainable and defensible. The immigrants were fairly diverse in their origins. Many of them were of Scottish heritage, but others were Welsh or English and had little or no Scottish ancestry. The arrival of the Borderers was coincident with the beginning of the "Troubles" that plagued Ireland into the 21st century.

The Borderers were militantly Protestant, espousing an especially dogmatic and anti-Catholic version of Calvinist Presbyterianism. They believed that every word of the Bible was literally true, and that anyone who disagreed with them on any speck of Biblical doctrine was headed straight for Hell, including the Irish Catholics with whom they had been at war for centuries, and the denizens of the Church of England whom they despised for slavish service to the British state and monarch. They were people of strong convictions, easily angered, and valued for their fighting prowess. They cherished their individual freedoms: their freedom from taxes, freedom from the interference of the state in their lives, freedom to practice their religion just as they pleased. They were a ferocious people of an egalitarian spirit, and did not easily accept the yoke of any king, governor, or politician.

They didn't get along with the native Irish, either. The next century was replete with complicated conflicts that would sputter for a time and then flare up into armed dispute with their Catholic neighbors to the south or rebellion against a British monarch who failed to appreciate their political demands or their Calvinist theology. Life continued to be marginal, brutish, and oppressive, and their sojourn in Ulster was not a happy one. They struggled with famine, wars, and religious persecution. The first large scale immigration of Scots-Irish to America was a group that arrived in Boston from County Londonderry in 1718, and then moved to New Hampshire, where they founded the town of Londonderry. They were followed by hundreds of thousands of other Scots-Irish over the next several decades. Many of them first settled in Pennsylvania, and then, finding all the eastern lands in the colonies either occupied or too expensive, they traveled south into Virginia and the Carolinas, and to the interior frontier lands, to the foothills of

---

Standard English verb *reave* ("to plunder," "to rob"). Merriam Webster Dictionary. The word appeared in William Faulkner's novel by that name, and was used in the science fiction TV series *Firefly* to refer to a pack of absolutely evil and very scary space pirate-murderers.

Appalachia—an area geographically very similar to their original homes in the borderlands between England and Scotland. By the beginning of the Revolutionary War, the Scots-Irish probably constituted about a quarter of the colonial American population, and on at least one occasion King George III referred to the war in North America as 'that Presbyterian revolt." Over the next several decades the Scots-Irish spread farther west and to the lowlands of the deeper South[7], and by the mid-19th century, they provided the dominant culture of the American South.

In *Outliers*, Malcolm Gladwell tells the story of the long history of murderous feuding in Harlan County, West Virginia during the 19th century, a culture that demanded an immediate and violent response to any perceived threat to the honor or welfare of the family. Gladwell asks,

> So why was Appalachia the way it was? It was because of where the original inhabitants of the region came from. The so-called American backcountry states—from the Pennsylvania border south and west through Virginia and West Virginia, Kentucky and Tennessee, North Carolina and South Carolina, and the northern end of Alabama and Georgia—were settled overwhelmingly by immigrants from one of the world's most ferocious cultures of honor. They were 'Scots-Irish'—that is, from the lowlands of Scotland, the northern counties of England, and Ulster in Northern Ireland.[8]

To this list of states must be added the state of Texas, which was settled by later generations of Scots-Irish who migrated from various other Southern states before, during, and after the Civil War. My Texas family, along with our neighbors and co-religionists, shared this heritage of strife and insecurity, of violent conflict and continual struggle for survival, and of the deep trauma of war passed down to the children of each generation.[*]

---

[*] Two psychologists at the University of Michigan named Dov Cohen and Richard Nisbett conducted an interesting experiment in the early 1990s to reveal how the Scots-Irish culture of honor might have lasting consequences on generations of Southerners long after the original settlers arrived in Appalachia and points south. They recruited two groups of young men—Southerners and those from northern parts of the United States—and set up experiments to insult them and then observe the results. In one experiment, the subject was walking along a hallway when a man blocked his way, jostled his shoulder, and said "Asshole" to him. In the experiments generally, the Southerners tended to immediately become angry and ready to fight, aggressively defending their

In the North it was a different story. The first immigrant Puritans arrived in New England in the early decades of the 17th century. Significantly, these Puritans were fleeing religious persecution in their native England, and they were known as "nonconformists" because they refused to maintain membership in the Church of England. The sect of Puritans who became known as Pilgrims had irreconcilable differences with the Church of England, which they believed still had far too much in common with the Catholic Church. They opposed priestly robes and prayer books, the practice of making the sign of the cross, the observance of Christmas, and other evidences of formalism. They organized their worship independently of the liturgy of the central state church and without its approval. This was problematic for them because meeting in a congregation outside the authority of the Church of England was a crime punishable by death.

Understandably, the Pilgrims arrived in Massachusetts with a passionate belief in their natural freedom to create a direct relationship with God, unmolested by any hierarchy of priests or any state bureaucracy. They had an active and aggressive religious life and disdained what they saw as the insincerity, empty eloquence, and hypocrisy of other Christians. They also arrived with their own strong intolerance of any religious belief other than their own. They exiled dissenters from their churches and communities, reserved all political power to the Puritan saints and excluded any non-church members from the right to vote.

Over the next few generations, the religious fervor of the original Scots-Irish and Pilgrim settlers subsided, and Calvinistic theology took a back seat to the hard work and dissipations of frontier life. Despite the persistence of influential Christian sects, many of the descendants of these two sets of early immigrants did not attend church or have any formal ties to any religious body. Colonial America was by and large a secular society.

Beginning in 1726, however, an extraordinary movement known as the Great Awakening began. It spread widely through the colonies and lasted until 1754 when it was interrupted by the French and Indian War, followed by the Revolutionary War. The Great Awakening was a vast revival that engaged millions of people North and South across the evangelical spectrum, including both the descendants of the Puritans in the North and those from the Scots-Irish migration in the South. The Awakening created intense religious activity, led to profound feelings of

---

territory or themselves. By contrast, Northerners tended to laugh off the insult, view it calmly, or consider it a joke.

spiritual rebirth, and spawned new churches as well as new secular and political movements. Its emphasis was on a direct, personal relationship with God, unmediated by priest or preacher, ritual or ceremony, and it sought to create a deep sense of spiritual guilt and a consciousness of the need for redemption.

The most famous revivalist was an eloquent Massachusetts Congregationalist named Jonathan Edwards. In 1733 Edwards began to preach a series of extraordinary sermons to his Northampton congregation. His sermons launched an ongoing religious revival that engulfed the town and brought virtually all business to a halt for six months while the townspeople gave in to amazing transports of extreme emotion—terror at the thought of languishing in Hell for eternity, and joy at the thought of escaping Hell to live in the presence of God. Hundreds of thousands across the colonies were inspired by the movement to profess their religious conversions and to join and start churches. One of Edwards's co-revivalists was newly arrived British Methodist preacher George Whitefield, who preached to several thousand people every day for months as he traveled all the way from New England to South Carolina on horseback.

In 1741 Edwards preached a sermon titled "Sinners in the Hands of an Angry God," which may have been the most terrifying hellfire-and-brimstone sermon ever delivered:

> Natural men are held in the hand of God, over the pit of Hell; they have deserved the fiery pit, and are already sentenced to it; and God is dreadfully provoked... the devil is waiting for them, Hell is gaping for them, the flames gather and flash about them, and would fain lay hold on them, and swallow them up; the fire pent up in their own hearts is struggling to break out: and they have no interest in any Mediator, there are no means within reach that can be any security to them.

It was said that throughout one of Edwards's sermons you could hear people weeping and wailing and gnashing their teeth, leaping up and down, and crying for joy. All this emotional untidiness created much friction between Edwards and the staid and conservative elders of the Congregationalist church. Nonetheless, the revival spread, and had lasting and unforeseen consequences.

In an important sense this Great Awakening was the concluding chapter of the Protestant Reformation that had begun two centuries earlier as an effort to reform the Catholic Church from within. Western

European Catholics such as Martin Luther, Ulrich Zwingli, and John Calvin attacked what they saw as the false doctrines and corruption rife in the church—exemplified by the teaching and selling of indulgences, and simony, and the buying and selling of clerical offices. Before long, however, the reformers were assaulting a myriad of church practices and doctrines and proclaiming a radically democratic revolution against the hierarchy and institutional power of the church. The result was the exodus of the reformers from the Catholic Church, and the founding of numerous Protestant denominations and sects such as the Scots-Irish Presbyterians and the English Puritans.

The Great Awakening, then, was the last and most extreme salvo of rebellion against bureaucracy, liturgical formalism, and the interposition of the Catholic Church between sinners and God. The movement appeared to be purely a revolution in *religious* democracy, with no political implications. Edwards, Whitefield and other revivalists emphasized that all are equal in the sight of God. God is no respecter of persons, they insisted. Men or women, rich or poor, slave or free, young or old, all are personally responsible, all are culpable, and all are doomed to Hell without a conscious, personal and intentional conversion to Christianity.

This religious notion, however, did have profound political implications. It helped prepare Americans for a democratic American revolution a few decades later that opened the door to a belief in the fundamental equality of all humans, of whatever class, race, sex, or age—a revolution whose founding document proclaimed all men to be created equal. For Americans, democracy would mean the freedom of individuals to live as and where they pleased, to work, to participate in the affairs of their government, and to worship as they chose.

Religious liberty continued to be an important rallying cry for the American Revolution. Many newly minted Americans had sailed west fleeing religious persecution and hoping for a peaceful haven for their practice of faith, yet they had found that in some colonies the religious problems of Europe were replicated in the New World.

In the colony of Virginia, for example, the Anglican Church was the official state church, just as in England. But Virginia was also home to a fair number of Baptists, a movement that was a significant outgrowth of the Great Awakening. Baptist belief was strongly focused on the importance of separating church and state, removing the power of the state to approve or endorse any particular religious expression.

In Virginia alone from 1760 to 1778, "there were at least 153 serious instances of persecution involving seventy-eight Baptists—including fifty-six jailings of forty-five different Baptist preachers…Most of the persecution was clustered in exactly the part of Virginia that gave us Madison, Mason, Washington, and Jefferson."[9] Baptist preachers were beaten while trying to deliver sermons, jailed for months on end, and tormented in a variety of ways.

Historian Lewis Peyton Little told of an Anglican minister who walked onto a stage where a Baptist preacher was sermonizing, stuck his riding crop into the man's mouth, and helped drag the man off to be beaten bloody by the sheriff. A mob interrupted David Barrow's service to force his head into water and mud until he nearly drowned. Little recorded numerous other instances of violence against Baptists: "dragged from his house," "meeting broken up by mob," "pulled down and hauled about by hair, hand, etc.," "tried to suffocate him with smoke," "shot with a shotgun," "jerked off stage—head beaten against ground."[10]

The struggle for religious freedom in America before and after the Revolution was long and arduous, and American Baptists proved to be the most radical and ardent opponents of government promotion of any religious practice. James Madison wrote: "The religion then of every man must be left to the conviction and conscience of every man; and it is the right of every man to exercise it as these may dictate. This right is in its nature an inalienable right."[11]

In 1785, Baptist preacher Jeremiah Walker drew up a petition averring that Christianity historically flourishes in the absence of support by a government: "The blessed author of the Christian religion not only maintained and supported his gospel in the world for several hundred years, without the aid of civil power but against all the powers of the earth, the excellent purity of its precepts and the unblamable behavior of its ministers made its way through all opposition."

The Baptist General Association in Orange County, Virginia protested that any notion that government should promote religion was "founded neither in Scripture, on reason, on sound policy; but is repugnant to each of them." In 1789, after significant struggle and debate, the Congress agreed on the words of the First Amendment to the Constitution: "Congress shall make no laws respecting an establishment of religion, or prohibiting the free exercise thereof." More ardently than any other group, Baptists were the driving force behind the constitutional principle of the separation of church and state.

Although the Baptists had gained some ground, many Scots-Irish still adhered to the muscular, independent Presbyterianism they had brought over from the old country. One of these was John Rice Sr. After 1778, while war between England and the rebellious American colonies still raged, Rice moved with his family to a little valley known in later years as House Wright Hollow, along the southern side of Clinch Mountain, a 150-mile-long ridge of the Appalachian Mountains in eastern Tennessee. Rice, an illiterate Scots-Irish farmer of Welsh[*] extraction, was my grandsire of six generations before my arrival, and is the earliest Rice ancestor about whom I know anything.

The family arrived after a long journey from Virginia by foot and horse-wagon along the Wilderness Road, which was more of a packed earth track through the dense forests than an actual road. It probably took the family some time to identify the optimal spot for their cabin and the acres they would clear to begin farming; the place they settled on was close by an unnamed stream that flowed into Possum Creek, buried in untracked woods and dales over 10 miles away from the tiny village of Rogersville.

When John and his neighbors first moved into the valleys "over the mountain," they doubtless hoped to avoid the danger to themselves and their families represented by the troubles between the colonies and Great Britain. John himself had at least 12 children to raise and protect. For the Scots-Irish of the foothills and valleys of western Virginia and eastern Tennessee as well as the western reaches of Carolina, the mighty struggles along the eastern Atlantic coast must have seemed far away. Their rough homes and small farms, their tiny and scattered villages posed no military threat to the British, and there were no strategic objectives or population centers to attract the British to send an army over the mountains.

What finally attracted the attention of the British behemoth was a relatively small yet pesky tactical threat. The Scots-Irish emerged from their hills and hollows from time to time and engaged the British troops in hit-and-run guerrilla warfare. They attacked in groups as small as 20 and usually no larger than 100, and then quickly faded back into the fens, forests, and hollows from which they had so devastatingly appeared. The American militia proved profoundly irritating to the British and kept a sizable number of redcoats and Loyalist militia chasing around Virginia and the Carolinas swatting mosquitoes.

By the summer of 1780, the British General Lord Cornwallis had been largely successful in his classical positional warfare against the Revolutionary army; however, he hadn't been able to deliver the final blow that could crush the Southern militias and enable him to devote full

---

[*] I am making an assumption here from the available evidence that our family name Rice was of Welsh origin, originally spelled "Rhys." Virtually all the immigrants to this part of Appalachia were Scots-Irish, and this group of immigrants included people who were originally English, Welsh, Scottish, and even some actual Irish.

attention to a final defeat of the organized American army led by George Washington in the north. The American forces had suffered a series of significant defeats in the Southern colonies, and did not seem to pose a strategic challenge to the British military. Nonetheless, the American militias were annoying. The farmers and frontier folk who lived in the mountains especially did not seem to understand when they had been beaten.

British major Patrick Ferguson, leading an army composed mainly of British Loyalist uniformed militia, sent a message to the American "rebels" that if they did not cease their opposition to the Crown, he would "march his army over the mountains, hang the leaders and lay waste their country with fire and sword." Ferguson's edict did not sit well with members of the American militias from Georgia, Virginia, and Carolina.

Many of the previously uninvolved Scots-Irish settlers of Appalachia were insulted, enraged, and spurred to action. On Tuesday morning, September 26, 1780, John Rice Sr. joined over 1,100 fellow citizen soldiers, who became known as the Overmountain men, to muster at Sycamore Shoals, located in what is now northeastern Tennessee, 35 miles in a bee-line and about 50 miles by road from the Rice farm. They each carried a knapsack, a hunting knife, and a long Deckard rifle, as well as skillets and blankets. Their buckskin shoulder pouches held cracked corn and jerky and crusts of bread. Many of them wore blue linen hunting shirts with tassels and fringes, and those with horses dressed them in fancy red and yellow decorations.

One of the commanding officers in John Rice's militia was Colonel Isaac Shelby, whose grandson, 82 years later, would be Confederate General Jo Shelby, the commanding cavalry officer for James Porter Rice, grandson of my forebear John Rice, Sr.

That September morning a Presbyterian minister named Samuel Doak, the first Presbyterian minister in the territory soon to be called Tennessee and later founder of many churches and schools on the frontier, preached a sermon to the assembled militia in a powerful and eloquent voice that stirred all who heard it. Known in later years as the "Sword of the Lord" sermon, it was delivered in language that recalled the words of the Old Testament prophets:

> Almighty and gracious God! Save us from the cruel hand of the savage, and of the Tyrant. Save the unprotected homes while fathers and husbands and sons are far away fighting for freedom and helping the oppressed. Thou, who promised to protect the Sparrow

in its flight, keep ceaseless watch, by day and by night, over our loved ones. The helpless women and little children, we commit to Thy care. Thou wilt not leave them or forsake them in times of loneliness and anxiety and terror. O God of Battle, Arise in thy might. Avenge the slaughter of thy people. Confound those who plot for our destruction. Crown this mighty effort with victory, and smite those who would exalt themselves against Liberty and Justice and Truth. Help us as good soldiers to wield the sword of the Lord and Gideon.[12]

Reverend Doak paused, raised his arms and shouted again, "Let that be your battle cry. The sword of the Lord and of Gideon!" On the final note of Doak's prayer, the Overmountain men shouted back "The sword of the Lord and of Gideon," brandished their rifles, let out a full-throated war cry, and marched out of their encampment in pursuit of the British. They quickly crossed the high mountains eastward, dropped down into the Carolina Piedmont hills, and twelve days later caught the British atop King's Mountain in South Carolina. Within a single hour, the American militia tore apart the Loyalist army. British Major Ferguson donned a checked duster-shirt in a vain attempt to hide his uniform, but he was mowed down by a volley from at least a dozen Americans. As the Americans flooded the British position, many of Ferguson's men cried for quarter, but the Overmountain men were in no mood to accept their surrender and the slaughter went on until the dead lay in great heaps. The Americans ended the battle by taking over 700 prisoners. Over 225 of the British and Tory troops were dead and 185 wounded, while American losses were 28 dead and 60 wounded.

The extraordinary defeat at King's Mountain led to a string of British retreats and disasters. Just over a year later General Washington's army decisively defeated a larger British force under Cornwallis, and the war was effectively over. Thomas Jefferson later referred to King's Mountain as "…that turn of the tide of success."

The militant, dogmatic, and literalistic Presbyterianism of the Scots-Irish served the cause of the Overmountain men well. People who lived such a poverty-stricken and marginal existence could ill afford the least uncertainty about whose side God was on. The Scots-Irish had learned over centuries of struggle the dark yet comforting habit of combining religion with warfare, sanctity with self-righteousness, fierceness and independence with theological certainty. The Presbyterians of the hill country were not tempted to show compassion and understanding for their enemies; they were more inclined to Joshua and Gideon than to

Solomon and Jesus. They believed strongly in using the sword to protect the ploughshare, and would not willingly lie down with the British lion.

Reverend Doak was by no means alone in his religious militancy and his warlike religion. Throughout the war against the British, American clergymen called down the wrath of the Almighty against their secular opponents. The Reverend Judah Champion went so far as to provide God with specific instruction for the strategic deployment of divine powers: "Oh Lord, we view with terror and dismay the approach of the enemies of Thy Holy religion. Wilt Thou send a storm and tempest and scatter them to the uttermost parts of the earth. But, peradventure, should any escape Thy vengeance, collect them together again, O Lord, and let Thy lightning play upon them in the hollow of Thy hand."[13]

It was thus clearly established early in the history of the country that God had a very particular point of view with regard to the American project. God was the sponsor of the fledgling American republic, and could be relied on to defend and protect the farmers, tradesmen, and merchants who assembled under the military banners of the new country. Patriots could discern a general and intimate relationship between God and the politics of armed combat, even as they proposed and supported a strict separation between the institutions of church and state in their new Constitution.

To the disquiet and umbrage of British patriots, who considered themselves "Christians," the American revolutionaries tended to view the established Church of England as an enemy of God and ally of the Devil. The rights recognized in the Constitution and approved by God included the right for citizens to worship as they chose, free from the dictates of their government or their neighbors. Those who opposed the will of God were clearly the enemies of God. The children of the English Puritans in the North and the children of the Scots-Irish Presbyterians in the South found common ground in the struggle to create a new democratic republic and oppose a monarchy that was working at cross-purposes to the evident will of God. The roots of 20th century American fundamentalism can be discerned in the confluence of these two streams of immigration, culture, and history. A unique American expression of evangelical Christianity emerged—profoundly democratic, anti-royalist and anti-clerical, militant and missional, convinced that God was naturally on the side of Americans. Any who disagreed might be suspected of being on some side other than God's.

The two decades after the Revolutionary War were quiet ones from the standpoint of American religious history. The country was focused on the work of creating a new political life and a new social and commercial history, and much of the energy of the people was focused on trade, construction and farming. Pioneers, many of them veterans of the war, pushed to the west across the Appalachians and into the wilds of Ohio, Kentucky, and Tennessee. The hills of eastern Tennessee rapidly filled up with the wave of Scots-Irish immigrants moving further west from their original stopping places in colonies such as Maryland, Virginia, and the Carolinas.

In late 1789, the state of North Carolina ceded its western lands to the United States. By the summer of 1790 Congress had organized those lands into a new territory that would become the state of Tennessee in 1796. As a bonus payment for his service as a soldier during the Revolutionary War, John Rice Sr. was able to file for a veteran's land grant. For the first time the Rice family could become the legal owners of the land they had squatted on years before. The family remained in Tennessee for the next three decades.

In the early 1800s, a second wave of revivalism hit Great Britain and the United States. This new national religious experience was also profoundly evangelical, and came to be known as the Second Great Awakening. It wasn't so much a separate movement as it was a continuation of the First Great Awakening, which had been interrupted by the French and Indian War from 1754-1763 and then by the political ferment and armed conflict of the American Revolution. A typical focus of the mass revival was a camp meeting involving many thousands of penitents that took place over several days of almost nonstop preaching, praying, and singing. The crowds were large enough that several different evangelists could preach simultaneously in different parts of the campground.

The first of these camp meetings took place at Creedence Clearwater Revival Church in Kentucky in the summer of 1800, and it was followed by many larger revival meetings up and down the east coast and throughout the Appalachian region. The movement then spread to draw massive crowds to hear flamboyant and emotional preachers call for mass repentance in packed auditoriums and open fields in larger cities.

This new movement emphasized the renewal of a Christian's sense of personal salvation. As in the earlier Awakening, these evangelicals focused on two core beliefs. First, they insisted on the freedom of every individual to commune directly with God and to make personal and individual decisions that determined where they would spend eternity. Second, they claimed that all had an individual responsibility for sinful behavior, and were answerable to God for their sins.

However, they also demanded a larger understanding of the role of Christian faith in the world. Those compelled by the need for revival believed they were required to address the suffering and injustice they saw around them, and to bring their public life into harmony with their personal relationship with God. Revivals drew millions of converts into the churches. But they also inspired thousands of people to launch social movements aimed at creating equality between men and women, ending slavery, eradicating the scourge of alcoholism, reforming the inhuman conditions of prisons, and caring for the handicapped and mentally ill.

Especially in Appalachian east Tennessee, where there were few slaves and few slave owners, the evangelical revivals of the Awakening movement cradled the abolition movement. The Scots-Irish farmers who had flocked to defeat the British because of their devotion to the freedom of the individual saw a powerful connection between the egalitarianism of the revival, in which it was made plain that "all are equal in the sight of God," and the moral argument of the abolitionists.

A principal leader of the revival movement in east Tennessee was Samuel Doak, the Presbyterian minister who had delivered his famous "Sword of the Lord" sermon in 1780 sending the Tennessee militia off to defeat the British. As the fires of revival flared up in the 1800s, Doak converted to abolitionism, freed all his slaves, and then traveled the countryside preaching that any true Christian would condemn and work to end the institution of slavery. Doak and other early abolitionists planted a host of Presbyterian churches and "log cabin colleges" that taught a strong antislavery doctrine. They laid the basis for eastern Tennessee to become the first true locus of the abolition movement in America.[14] *The Emancipator*, the first newspaper in America devoted entirely to ending slavery, was published in Jonesborough, Tennessee in 1820, in the same year Dangerfield Rice moved his family from nearby Bedford County out west to Missouri in order to take advantage of new opportunities for owning slaves.[15]

It's important to note here that the Protestant traditions in America— the Puritanism imported to New England by English immigrants and the Presbyterianism of the Scots-Irish who settled the South—did not lead naturally to either abolitionism or to a defense of slavery. They shared revolutionary roots in the British religious wars of the 17th century. Both embraced a radical egalitarianism that saw all human beings as equals in the sight of God, and that would inspire movements for social and economic justice and worker rights, and against such evils as slavery and discrimination, child labor, the oppression of women, and the denial of democratic rights to various groups. The same radical egalitarianism, however, could just as naturally lead to the belief that any white person, made in the image of God, should have an equal right to own any black person, who was naturally less than human. The theological conclusions one came to seemed to be a function of where one lived and what one's economy depended upon.

The Second Great Awakening, even more than the First, focused on the emotional and spiritual experience of salvation. To be truly saved, an individual had to have an intense, direct, and personal experience of profound guilt and "conviction" of sin, and then accept the death of Jesus as atonement for the sin and a way for sinners to escape the eternal punishment of Hell. Although all the Protestant denominations grew during this time of revivalism—including Congregationalists and Presbyterians—it was the Baptist and Methodist denominations in particular, with their emphasis on personal salvation, that underwent an extraordinary explosion of growth and influence. Thousands of Baptist and Methodist missionaries and circuit riding preachers traveled the country holding revival meetings and planting churches and religious schools. Though Methodists remained a tiny sect at the end of the Revolutionary War, by the middle of the 19th century they were the largest religious group in the country, and by 1868 General U.S. Grant could refer, only half-jokingly, to the three great parties in the United States: "The Republican, the Democratic, and the Methodist Church."

As the Protestant denominations—Presbyterian, Methodist, Baptist and others—were carried into the slave states of the South, into the Carolinas, Georgia, Florida, Alabama, Mississippi, Louisiana, Arkansas and Texas, their churches, pastors, and congregants were dipped in the culture and economy of the South, and increasingly found it necessary to defend and justify the practice of human bondage. As the same denominations moved west into the border states of Tennessee and Missouri, they displayed a profound ambivalence to slavery. When Presbyterians moved to the Missouri River Valley with its wide hemp plantations dependent on slave labor, they discovered that their Presbyterianism could justify slavery. But when they moved to another part of the state, away from the rich black bottomlands of the slave economy, they found that their Presbyterianism was opposed to slavery.

The revival movement was responsible for a tremendous spread of Christianity among slaves in the South. Slaves came in their thousands to camp meetings organized mainly by Baptists and Methodists, where they listened to the same sermons, succumbed to the same transports of emotion, and pledged themselves to the same spiritual renewal as white revivalists. At times white slave owners were known to undergo conversion at a revival meeting and then decide to free their slaves.

More commonly, though, the new black Baptists or Methodists found that their fellow white Christians expected the same unequal relationship between black and white outside the church to prevail inside the church as well. As early as 1774 the first black Baptist Church was founded outside of Augusta, Georgia, and in 1787 a group of black Methodists broke away from the white Methodists to found the African Methodist Episcopal (A. M. E.) Church.[16] The evangelicalism of the whites was dramatically different from the evangelicalism of the blacks. For many white Baptists and Methodists in the South, salvation was a matter of an individual sinner coming to a deeply felt and personal sense of guilt, and then seeking a personal salvation and personal regeneration as a Christian. Slave-owning Christians were careful to separate their faith from any implications regarding the justice or righteousness of owning slaves. By contrast, black evangelicalism was based on a theology of liberation from the beginning. Slaves took heart not only from the Old Testament story of the Israelites escaping slavery in Egypt to find freedom in the Promised Land, but also from the radically egalitarian teachings of Jesus in the New Testament. The Kingdom of Heaven, for black Baptists and Methodists, was a place where the practice of human bondage had doubtless been ended forever.[*]

The new evangelical movement in the early 19th century was strongly focused on social justice and social equality. The famous English preacher Charles Spurgeon saw some of his sermons burned in America due to his censure of slavery before the Civil War, calling it "a soul-destroying sin," "the foulest blot" which "may have to be washed out in blood." Spurgeon was also deeply concerned with social justice more generally, with the poverty, misery, and oppression of the lower classes in England. He was the founder of the Stockwell Orphanage, a leading institutional effort to address the needs of children, now known as Spurgeon's Child Care, one of the largest international Christian children's charities.

Charles G. Finney, known as "America's foremost revivalist," was a major leader of the Second Great Awakening. Finney was a fiery, entertaining, and spontaneous preacher, and was widely influential among millions of Americans. In addition, however, Finney was deeply concerned with social justice. He was an abolitionist leader who frequently denounced slavery from his pulpit and denied communion to slaveholders. He was president of Oberlin, the first college in America to

---

[*] By the middle of the 19th Century there were thousands of black Baptist and Methodist churches throughout the slave-owning South, and evangelicalism was established as the foundation of slave religion.

educate black and white men and women in the same classrooms. Through his influence over several decades in public life, Finney helped lay the basis for the Civil War to be a crusade to end slavery, and not just a clash between two different economic systems. For many, at the heart of evangelicalism was a demand for deep integration between one's private religion and public morality.

Chapter 4
The Missouri Slave Rush

> *"Thus saith the Lord, Choose thee either three years'*
> *famine; or three months to be destroyed before thy foes,*
> *while that the sword of thine enemies overtaketh thee; or*
> *else three days the sword of the Lord, even the*
> *pestilence, in the land, and the angel of the Lord*
> *destroying throughout all the coasts of Israel."*—
> Chronicles 21:12

On a sweltering August afternoon in the Year of Our Lord 1999, in a place called Stanley Valley on the verge of the Great Smoky Mountains, 40 or so people, ranging in age from seven to eighty-two, wandered chaotically across a field searching for ancient gravestones. The sun was hot in the sky, and the weeds grew high in the field, obscuring carved stones that bore names such as Miller and Johnson, Looney, Peters, and Rice. The leader of our expedition was my Aunt Libby, then 72 years old, who had conducted the research that led us to this spot in the rolling green hills of eastern Tennessee.

Prompted by a committee of aunts, we all wore our trademark red Rice Family kerchiefs about our necks. We were a gathering of the extant descendants of Will Rice, and before him of James Porter Rice, and Dangerfield Rice, and of John Rice Sr., the poor farmer and Revolutionary War veteran who had eked out a hardscrabble existence in these hills. To get to those fields we had earlier driven down House Wright Hollow and up Derrick Road, and if we had known to do so we might have gotten out of our convoy of cars and walked down and into an unnamed hollow to visit the original site of the Rice family home next to the unnamed stream that flowed into Possum Creek.

Every few minutes I heard a cry of delight or curiosity from one of the searching cousins, avid aunts, adventurous uncles, eager sons and daughters, brothers and sisters, moms and dads, and we would all crowd around a gravestone, kneeling together on the packed earth, brushing aside the long grass and weeds to read a name and an epitaph carved deep into the stone almost two hundred years ago and then weathered away into near invisibility by almost two centuries of wind and rain, sun and shadow, frost and searing heat.

My own Baptist preacher father, Charles Himes, at the age of 79, was deep in the mysterious realm of the Alzheimer's disease that would kill him three years later. He was unclear about who he was or where he was, and yet good natured about it all, and willing to go along, for the most part, with whatever people told him reality was. He wandered among the gravestones with us, wearing his comedic red kerchief about his skinny neck, his meager frame bent over like a question mark. I watched him pick up a rock and look at it, carefully. He muttered a word or two in quiet conversation with the rock and then carefully put it down on top of a gravestone that had tilted too far to hold it. The rock fell off onto the ground, and he looked at it reprovingly, and then wandered off across the hillside. I doubt that he knew what we were doing.

"Oh, look," yelled Aunt Libby, "Here's the grave of Margaret Looney!" Margaret, she explained, was a daughter of the neighboring Looney family which had been headed by its farmer patriarch Michael Looney, a fellow soldier with John Rice Sr. Michael had emigrated from the Isle of Man in the Irish Sea to settle in Bouteroit County, Virginia before the Revolutionary War, and when he finished fighting the British he moved his family to this valley to take up his war veteran's land grant in 1780.

Margaret grew up to marry John Rice Sr.'s son Dangerfield. Weeds now choked her gravesite. The stone was cracked and tilted. Its carved inscription was legible only to one who sought it with care and patience. With a start, I realized that Margaret Looney was the childhood sweetheart and first wife of my own great-great-great-grandfather.

The logic of evangelical Protestants in the 18th century led to an inescapable conclusion: If God was indeed no respecter of persons, and if all were equal in the sight of God—men and women, young and old, rich and poor, white and colored—then Christians had no business owning slaves or benefitting from their labor and suffering, and slavery itself was a crime against God.

The leading anti-slavery activist in Britain was William Wilberforce, a member of Parliament from Yorkshire. He underwent a conversion to evangelical Christianity in 1785 and then developed a lifelong passion for social justice. Taking up the cause of abolition, he spent the next 26 years of his life spearheading the campaign to prevent British citizens from conveying or trading slaves, which ended with the passage of the Slave Trade Act of 1807. The movement Wilberforce championed and led was ultimately successful in passing the Slavery Abolition Act of 1833. Thus, Britain abjured the "peculiar institution" a generation before Abraham Lincoln signed the Emancipation Proclamation.

Slavery proved to be a much more complicated issue for American evangelicals both North and South, who discovered that their religious attitudes and interpretations were colored by their economic interests. This pattern was played out in the history of the Rice family, whose evangelical theology underwent a transformation as they moved within two generations from being small yeoman farmers to landed proprietors whose wealth depended upon the system of chattel slavery.

John Rice's son Dangerfield had been born in 1775. At the age of 21, young Dangerfield married Margaret Looney, the young woman whose gravestone I had seen in Stanley Valley. Margaret died in 1804, followed by John in 1811. John was gracious enough to leave a will providing the magnificent sum of $3.33 to each of his twelve living children. John signed his will with an "x," followed by the words "his mark." I mention this not because it is particularly germane to my story but because I think it is remarkable, and says something about John's poverty and illiteracy as well as his demand for a precise equality among his children in the ordering of his affairs.

In 1812, Dangerfield with his new wife Nancy Brown Rice surveyed his limited prospects and did not like what he saw. The land around him lay thickly settled by poor farmers, each with a few hundred acres often left as a legacy to be divided among several sons, so the average size and fertility of farms was diminishing. Dangerfield might scratch out a living in eastern Tennessee, but he could never become a man of means there. Instead, the family moved west to Bedford County in middle Tennessee where Dangerfield bought another small farm.

Dangerfield apparently was a restless soul, not yet convinced he had arrived at the place where he could make his fortune. In 1820 he sold his Bedford County farm, pulled up stakes, and moved the whole kit, sons and daughters, horses, wagons, cats, and dogs, several hundred miles west to Missouri.

Why Missouri? In those days, before the discovery of gold in California, Missouri was widely believed to be the place for quick riches. In 1820, people from all over the slaveholding South were rushing to Missouri to seek their fortunes. There, with a little good fortune and substantial help from the government and from powerful and wealthy interests across the slaveowning South, an ambitious and adventurous man might put himself in the way of more money than he could ever spend.

The successful migration of Scots-Irish farmers such as the Rice clan was contingent upon two additional mass migrations underway in America during the 18th and 19th centuries—those of native Americans and enslaved blacks. First, the native people who inhabited the eastern lands where the Scots-Irish first settled were driven by war, murder, disease and diplomacy to abandon their homes and move west. This forced immigration had been going on since the mid-1700s, and would continue well into the 1840s, aided by the Indian Removal Act of 1830, signed into law by President Andrew Jackson. The strongest supporters of the Removal Act were from the South in states where many pioneers lived who were eager to lay their hands and plows on the territory of the "Five Civilized Tribes"—the Cherokee, Chickasaw, Choctaw, Creek, and Seminole, considered civilized by whites because they had adopted the Christian religion and many of the customs of the European settlers. They were educated and literate, lived in towns, and were thought to be good neighbors.

In 1831, the Choctaw were forced to remove from their homes in the Deep South. Of 15,000 who began the trip, over 2,500 Choctaws died along the way in a bitter tragedy that soon became known as the "Trail of Tears." Later, in 1838, 15,000 Cherokee were forced to relocate from the Cherokee reservation in South Carolina, and 4,000 of those died of exposure, disease, and starvation along the trail. The Cherokee Trail of Tears went north and west through McMinnville, Tennessee, and then Murfreesboro, and Nashville, through Missouri all the way to Fort Gibson in Indian Territory, now known as Oklahoma.

Much of this was yet to come when Missouri was admitted to the Union as a slave state in 1820 as part of an historic compromise between pro-slavery and anti-slavery factions in Congress. The government had driven the Sacs, Fox, Osage, and other Indian tribes from the state, penning them up on reservations in Oklahoma and points west, and was selling fertile Missouri River bottomland for two dollars an acre. Missouri's statehood triggered what could be dubbed the "Missouri Slave Rush," a migration of Southern whites to become slave owners. Within months, thousands of Southerners flooded there to take advantage of an immense opportunity. The soil in northwest Missouri was ideal for growing hemp, a prime cash crop of the antebellum South along with cotton. To get rich, all a man like Dangerfield Rice had to do was show up with capital, be ready to do some hard work, buy as much land as he could afford, and borrow more money to buy a few slaves. Thus, the first unofficial "trail of tears" was that of enslaved blacks, who were sold and transported from the South and Southeast to new plantations in Missouri's northwest corner where a relatively narrow strip of bottomland along the banks of the Missouri River proved suitable for a slave-powered agricultural economy focused on the production of hemp.

In 1821, close on the day when Missouri became a state that guaranteed legal slavery, Dangerfield Rice moved his family from Tennessee out to Johnson County, Missouri to the new little community of Hazel Hill. Along with them they carried their religious faith, a strongly Calvinist Presbyterianism, with a wrathful, judgmental God who would send the vast majority of humans into the eternal flames of Hell. Curiously, the Rice family left behind them the ferocious anti-slavery sentiments of their neighbors and co-religionists in the east Tennessee mountains. They now had a powerful economic reason for believing that God approved of chattel slavery.

On the day of their arrival on Hazel Hill my family's history and fortunes—and my own heritage—were first indissolubly linked with the enslavement of human beings. There Dangerfield bought his first slaves and began building a hemp plantation, the foundation of the family's wealth and success. Just a few years later, in 1827, he died a prominent citizen and prosperous landowner, leaving his second wife Nancy and 11 growing children.

Chapter 5
The "Peculiar Institution"

> *"And say to the land of Israel, Thus saith the Lord;*
> *Behold, I am against thee, and will draw forth my sword*
> *out of his sheath, and will cut off from thee the righteous*
> *and the wicked."*—Ezekiel 21:5

When I was 14, in the summer of 1964, I lived with my family in Millington, Tennessee, just north of Memphis. My public high school was restricted to white students, the little Baptist church that my dad pastored was segregated, and the sign over the men's room down at the local filling station said "For Whites Only." I was a passionate supporter of Barry Goldwater for the Republican presidential nomination. I put a Goldwater bumper sticker on my bike and rode it all over Millington delivering leaflets to homes and apartments, and then in July I watched the convention on television as Goldwater accepted the nomination.

In late August, the Democrats held their convention in Atlantic City, New Jersey, and I sat on the couch in our living room watching every minute of the drama on our little black-and-white TV. A lone black woman testified before the Credentials Committee. Her name was Fannie Lou Hamer, and she was a sharecropper from Sunflower County, Mississippi. She stared down those white men until they hushed up and turned toward her and quieted so they could hear what she had the nerve to say.

Hamer told of being arrested for trying to register to vote, and what happened when they carried her to jail. She said, "They left my cell and it wasn't too long before they came back. He said, 'You are from Ruleville all right,' and he used a curse word. And he said, 'We are going to make you wish you was dead.' I was carried out of that cell into another cell where they had two Negro prisoners. The State Highway Patrolmen ordered the first Negro to take the blackjack...I laid on my face and the first Negro began to beat. I was beat by the first Negro until he was exhausted. I was holding my hands behind me at that time on my left side, because I suffered from polio when I was six years old...The second Negro began to beat and I began to work my feet, and the State Highway Patrolman ordered the first Negro who had beat me to sit on my feet—to keep me from working my feet. I began to scream and one white man got up and began to beat me in my head and tell me to hush. One white man—my dress had worked up high—he walked over and pulled my dress—I pulled my dress down and he pulled my dress back up."

Hamer paused and looked up at the Committee members. She said, "All of this is on account of us wanting to register, to become first-class citizens, and...I question America. Is this America, the land of the free and the home of the brave, where we have to sleep with our telephones off of the hooks because our lives be threatened daily, because we want to live as decent human beings, in America?"

I was mesmerized by Hamer's story, and amazed by her presence and personality. I had growing questions about the all-white society in which I lived, but I hadn't yet concluded that it had systemic problems. Black people for me were largely an abstraction, a faceless category of other human beings who lived in a parallel universe. I knew as little about the lives of black people in my home town of Millington as I did about the people of China, Lapland, Argentina, or Tanzania. Hamer forced me to consider black people as human beings who could bleed, suffer, aspire, struggle, and rejoice. She inspired me to begin a process of listening, reading, and learning about black people that would change my life.

Five years later, I met Fannie Lou Hamer when she came to speak in Madison, Wisconsin where I was a college student. The two of us had dinner in the cafeteria, and then I introduced her to a small crowd in the Student Union building, and she talked about growing up in Ruleville, just 130 miles south of where I had lived in Millington.

"My grandparents was slaves," she said, "but in Sunflower County today we are still slaves. We have had no justice. We have had no rights that they must respect. We have had no way to live. But I will tell you this. I am sick and tired of being sick and tired. And we will have our freedom."

During the three decades before the Civil War, the Rice family thrived as slave owners. By 1860 they were wealthier than all but a handful of others in Johnson County, Missouri. The number of white people in Johnson County had grown to over 900 by 1860, but the slave population exploded to almost 6,400. By the outbreak of the Civil War in 1861, the Rice clan owned ninety-five slaves, raising livestock, hemp, tobacco and wheat on over 1,400 acres of fertile fields that stretched for miles along the Missouri River Valley. The 1860 census records the value of land encompassed by the Rice plantations at Hazel Hill as $9,600, or the equivalent, adjusted for inflation, of perhaps three million to five million dollars today. The slaves who worked that land were worth far more—over $30,000, or the equivalent in today's currency of between 10 million and 30 million dollars.

The human relations veiled by these statistics were tragic. Black slaves in Missouri were viewed and treated as beneath the level of human beings. Both custom and law forbade any white to do business with a slave without the prior consent of the owner. Any slave caught carrying a gun received thirty-nine lashes and forfeited the gun. Any slave engaged in rioting or illegal meetings or who made a speech encouraging sedition was subject to whipping. One Missouri law required that any Negro "who should commit or attempt to commit assault upon white women should be mutilated," while another law held that any white man who raped a slave woman was merely guilty of trespassing against the woman's master and owner. Any slave who offered resistance or opposition to any white person, or who disrupted a church service by "noise, riotous or disorderly conduct" was to be given thirty-nine lashes. An 1847 Missouri law specifically prohibited the education of Negros, and provided a five hundred dollar fine and up to six months in jail for anyone teaching a Negro how to read or write.

All of these laws supported the plantation economy and the political system that made possible the Rice family's fortunes. Did Nancy Rice treat her house slaves with kindness, charity, and compassion or with brutality, disdain and avariciousness? Did her son James think of himself as a loving father of primitive African humans entrusted to his care by a merciful God? Did he wield the whip against any slave of his who disrupted a church service, listening to the thwack, thwack, thwack sound made by the lash and watching the bloody back of the malefactor to make sure he would still be fit to work in the hemp fields the next day? Did James agree with the St. Louis jury of white citizens in the famous 1848 Dred Scott case that black slaves had "no rights that white men are compelled to respect"?

James Porter Rice inherited the mantle of the Rice family patriarchy when his father Dangerfield died in 1827. James had been born in Bedford County, Tennessee in 1816, and was only four years old when his family moved to western Missouri. He then grew up on the family plantation, and was formed along with that enterprise in the slave economy of the Missouri River Valley. He was conscious of the hard work and struggle required to build a growing plantation. He was aware of the family's increasing material wealth and comfort, and he knew that the success of such a farm depended on the careful use and cultivation of its material assets, including chattel slaves, black men and women who in most cases were separated by no more than a generation or two from their ancestral African homes.

In the year 1841 James turned 25 and married Sarah Whitsett, who then gave birth to two sons. The first, James Madison, was called "Matt" to distinguish him from his father, and the second was nicknamed "Daney" after his grandfather Dangerfield. Their mother Sarah died soon after Daney's birth, leaving James as a young widower with the care of his two boys.

James was a religious man, a professed Christian, and a member of one of the founding families of the little Presbyterian Church established in 1853 at Hazel Hill. At this point in the family history, at least, James saw no contradiction between his family's historic Presbyterian faith and his ownership of slaves.

One of Rice's neighbors, a man named Oliver Anderson, owned a factory in nearby Waverly where some of the hemp from the Rice plantations was probably processed into rope. In a public debate on slavery, Anderson went on record saying: "Slavery is a scriptural institution, and you and your Abolitionist friends are infidels. You are unwilling that God shall be a judge of what is proper and right, and desire yourself to determine what is proper, and that too, in direct opposition to God's revealed law as given to the Hebrews. Hence you say you want an Antislavery Bible and an Antislavery God."[17] It is probable that Rice shared Anderson's point of view, just as he shared the benefits Anderson gained from owning slaves.

Over the forty-two years that the Rice family lived in Missouri during the 19th century, the family evolved from poor dirt farmers to be the owners of many slaves and several contiguous plantations laid out on broad flat plains and green fields south of the wide river. They could leverage vast wealth embodied in human beings whom they owned as one might own a horse or a hat. They had powerful connections with the political elite of Missouri and beyond—a cousin of the family was the four-term governor of Georgia throughout the Civil War.

James Porter Rice and the members of his family doubtless heard many sermons in the Hazel Hill Presbyterian Church about man's sinful nature, about the evil embedded in the human heart, about how we are all justifiably subject to the eternal flames of Hell for our wickedness, how the stench of our sin rises to offend the nostrils of the living God.

Slavery itself, however, did not appear in that litany of sins. The slaveholders of Missouri commonly described how happy and grateful the slaves were to be slaves, how fortunate the slaves were to be taken care of with such loving kindness by their indulgent and compassionate masters. The story was told even by those who found the institution itself degrading, such as General George R. Smith of Sedalia, who recounted years after the Civil War:

> The masters were usually humane and there was often real affection between master and slave—very often great kindliness. There were merciful services, from each to the other: there was laughter, song, and happiness in the negro quarters... The old negroes had their comfortable quarters, where each family would sit by their own great sparkling log fires... They sang their plantation songs, grew hilarious over their corn shuckings and did the bidding of their gracious master. Their doctor's bills were paid; their clothing bought, or woven by themselves in their cabins, and made by their mistress; their sick nursed; and their dead laid away—all without thought from themselves.[18]

Who were the Rice slaves? No details about them have come down through the Rice family's oral or written history. By the census of 1870, all the Rices related to James Porter Rice had been gone from Missouri for seven years, and the census records only a single black family named Rice living near Hazel Hill: George Rice, then 35 years old, and his wife Lucinda Rice, 22 years old. It's possible, though not certain, that these two, George and Lucinda, had been owned by the Rice family.

In the first years after the Revolutionary War, Baptist evangelicals in the South as well as throughout the country were deeply opposed to slavery. They believed that all were equal in the sight of God, criticized the categories of race and class, and embraced the cause of freedom for African Americans. As a result, the ranks of black Baptists and the numbers of black Baptist congregations grew rapidly in the South, while the number of white Baptists increased much more slowly.

The advance of the Baptists nationally was triggered and supported by the revivals of the Second Great Awakening. Throughout the first few decades of the 19th century, thousands of new churches, schools, and associations were being established. Although the national Baptist association claimed neutrality on the issue of slavery, most Baptist leaders were personally sympathetic to the abolitionists. The Baptist teaching that all are equal in the sight of God seemed to run right up against the notion that any human being had a right to own another. By the middle of the century, however, sharp differences were manifest between Baptists in the slave-owning regions of the South and those from the North. White Baptist preachers in the South increasingly soft-peddled their opposition to slavery, and then began to actively justify slavery, claiming that it was approved and supported by the Bible. Moreover, many Southern preachers claimed that they had the God-given right to be both ministers of the gospel and slave owners.

The final split between Southern and Northern Baptists came in 1844 when Alabama Baptists requested that the American Baptist Home Mission Society choose a slaveholder to be a missionary for the society. The decision by the governors of the society to turn down the request triggered a Southern rebellion. In May of 1845, more than 200 Baptist leaders met in the First Baptist Church of Augusta, Georgia to organize the Southern Baptist Convention. The issue was purely about the morality of slavery, but the Southerners couched their rebellion in theological terms. God, they said, explicitly sanctioned slavery in multiple places in the Bible, and they were only following the word and will of God by owning slaves.

The Rice family at Hazel Hill, though Presbyterian, were probably in agreement with the Southern Baptists on the issue of slavery—despite the fact that the national Presbyterian assembly had condemned slavery before 1800. It was this issue that finally split the South and the country, both politically and theologically. Slavery was nowhere more controversial than in the states of Missouri and neighboring Kansas.

Congress passed the Kansas-Nebraska Act in 1854 with the aim of creating a temporary compromise between the slave-owning states of the South and the abolitionists of the North. The act repealed the Missouri Compromise of 1820, which had opened Missouri to a slave-owning economy and issued an invitation for settlers such as Dangerfield Rice to move to Missouri from eastern Tennessee and the slave-owning states deeper South. The act opened the territories of Kansas and Nebraska to white settlement, but declared that the new settlers would decide for themselves whether to allow slavery, in the name of "popular sovereignty." Its author, Democratic Senator Stephen Douglas, hoped it would ease tensions by allowing the expansion of slavery in the South while protecting its abolition in the North. He could not have been more mistaken.

The new Republican Party was formed to denounce the act and stop the expansion of slavery, and the abolitionists began to clean their rifles and grease their wagon wheels. Beginning in the summer of 1854, a flood of abolitionists arrived in the Kansas Territory in order to vote against Kansas becoming a slave state. Many of them settled in and around Lawrence, Kansas, which became known to the slave-owning Southerners who had previously immigrated to Missouri as the "Yankee Town." That fall, thousands of Missouri Southerners also crossed their western border to swing the vote for the first Congressional delegate from Kansas, thus stoking the fires of the conflict.

The following summer and fall of 1855, thousands more of the abolitionists arrived in Kansas to counteract the slave owners, and many of them passed through Missouri in order to reach Kansas. One of the migrants was a man named John Brown, a man with a powerful sense of moral outrage against injustice. Photographs of Brown show him with a long beard, medium-length hair combed straight back from a high forehead, and an intense and slightly deranged expression in a pair of piercing dark eyes.

Brown headed for Kansas because he felt called by God himself to take action, by any means necessary, to end the evil system of slavery. He was a fierce man with simple moral categories and an absolute belief in the literal truth of every passage in the Bible; in many ways he would have felt at home in the fundamentalist movement in late-20th century America.

Waverly was one of the Missouri River towns Brown passed through with his family. A major commercial center for the area, Waverly boasted a collection of frame houses, storefronts, and warehouses. It had the largest hemp warehouse and marketplace for miles around, a hemp rope factory, and a river landing where flat-bottomed steam boats jostled each other to load the coils of hemp to be transported down river, where they were destined for tying together bales of cotton on the plantations of the deeper South.

According to local legend in Missouri[19], on a crisp autumn day in the fall of 1855, an odd, roving group of travelers, known as "movers" by the people of the town, stopped for several days in Waverly to take care of a sick child. The movers kept to themselves and were reportedly cold and suspicious toward everyone in the town except for its black residents.

The child died, but no one knew it until John Brown, the leader of the party, a wild-looking old man with a stern glare, came into town from their encampment to buy a burial plot for the child. After a brief and private funeral, John Brown's movers left town. On their way west toward Kansas, they traveled along the Sante Fe Trail through fields of hemp and wheat where slaves toiled and green pastures where cattle grazed.

I imagine that Brown might have confronted James Rice along that road, perhaps near the school at the top of a ridge covered with hazel bushes. If they had met, the morning might have been crisp and sunny, one of those sharp autumn days that followed the bitterly cold nights described by John Brown in letters home to his wife during that fateful trip.

Brown and Rice would have glared at each other, I am sure—two Calvinists locked in mortal combat, Brown from his Puritanical moral absolutism and Rice with his Presbyterian and Scots-Irish fierceness, each of them using his God to justify himself and condemn his opponent.

Brown would have hurled the argument of religion in Rice's face, curling his lips and wrinkling his nose with distaste at being in the presence of a hated slaveholder. He would have narrowed his eyes and thrust his bearded chin forward as he said something along the lines of: "The stench of your sin offends the Almighty, and if it is deemed necessary that I should forfeit my life for the furtherance of the ends of justice, and mingle my blood further with the blood of my children and with the blood of millions in this slave country whose rights are disregarded by wicked, cruel, and unjust enactments—I will submit."[20]

I imagine Rice spitting into the dust at his feet and regarding Brown with contempt, as he replied: "You say that you do the will of God by seeking to foment disobedience and rebellion and to steal my property, but I tell you that God himself ordained that some should be slaves and others should be masters, and you will bring his holy wrath down upon your head if you persist in this abolitionist heresy!"[*]

Brown would have looked with silent contempt on the slave owner, as the movers moved on, the wagons loaded with men, women and children, their beds creaking and wheels rattling as they carried their cargo toward an uncertain future.

In fact, Brown and his family arrived in Kansas in the fall of 1855 to set up his homestead on Osawatomie Creek, 87 miles southwest of Hazel Hill, Missouri. Within weeks, the first shots were fired in a brutal guerrilla war so violent and destructive that it became known as "Bleeding Kansas." Along with Brown, most of the new settlers in Kansas were abolitionists, and the pro-slavery forces in Missouri realized

---

[*] Although I don't have a record of the views of James Porter Rice on slavery, this imagined quote is consistent with the views expressed by many other Southern slave owners, many of whom were deeply religious evangelical Christians.

that they had a serious fight on their hands to keep the new state on the side of the slaveholding south in the national conflict over slavery.

In November of 1855 a proslavery "bushwhacker" killed an abolitionist settler, and both sides mobilized for action. Hundreds of Kansas settlers mustered in the streets of Lawrence, guns brandished as politicians and soldiers gave angry speeches, and cannon were trundled in from arsenals as far away as Liberty, Lexington, and Jefferson City, Missouri. A patchwork army of over 1500 Missourians trekked across the border toward Lawrence. Among their leaders was 25-year-old Jo Orville Shelby, a neighbor of James Porter Rice. Shelby owned a plantation and hemp factory in Waverly, and his factory probably processed at least some of the raw hemp produced by the Rice plantations. A newspaper reporter coined the name "Border Ruffians" for this pro-slavery guerilla army that tried forcibly to pull Kansas into the camp of the slaveholders. The name was especially resonant, considering the history of these Missouri Scots-Irish whose ancestors had been called "Border Reivers," living as they did by raiding and rustling in the border regions between Scotland and England and Wales.

Repeatedly over the next few years, Shelby led gangs of his fellow "Ruffians" and Waverly neighbors on missions across the border into Kansas to vote illegally in Kansas elections, or to retaliate against abolitionist homesteaders for some slight or damage, or to terrorize the citizens of Lawrence or some other anti-slavery town.

On the other side were the abolitionist settlers—known by their popular designation of "jayhawkers"—who committed their share of raids and depredations against the Missouri interlopers in Kansas. Over a period of a year, over 200 people died in street corner murders, night-time raids, and pitched battles. At one point in 1856, an army of Ruffians occupied and sacked Lawrence, Kansas, burning over 20 of its buildings, destroying the offices of the antislavery newspaper with cannon fire, and carting off wagonloads of booty.

Among the jayhawkers was John Brown's small guerrilla army, who committed many crimes of their own. On one occasion, Brown, accompanied by four of his sons, one son-in-law, and two other abolitionists, visited the small community of Pottawatomie, Kansas. There, they kidnapped five pro-slavery settlers from their cabins, gave them a rump trial in the woods, and hacked them to death with broadswords.

U.S. President Franklin Pierce appointed a succession of territorial governors, who failed one after another in their attempts to bring the chaotic political situation under control. The violence at last abated somewhat by the winter of 1857, though the conflict simmered until it finally ignited into full-scale civil war in 1861 after the election of Lincoln and the Republicans.

According to local Missouri legend, John Brown returned to Waverly in 1857 or 1858 to dig up the body of the young mover girl who had died there—said to be his grandchild—and transport her to a Kansas grave so she would not lie in the soil of a slave state. What is known for certain is that in 1859 Brown moved his crusade east, organizing an armed band of abolitionists to occupy the Federal armory at Harpers Ferry, Virginia as part of a plot to inspire an uprising of armed slaves throughout the South. He was captured and his plot foiled by Federal soldiers under the command of Robert E. Lee, later the commanding General of the Army of the Confederacy.

American abolitionists and their allies across Europe hailed Brown as a hero and launched a tempestuous campaign to prevent his execution. French poet and human rights activist Victor Hugo agitated for Brown's pardon and release, and published a letter that was met with both acclaim and opposition on both sides of the Atlantic. In it, Hugo said:

> Politically speaking, the murder of John Brown would be an uncorrectable sin. It would create in the Union a latent fissure that would in the long run dislocate it. Brown's agony might perhaps consolidate slavery in Virginia, but it would certainly shake the whole American democracy. You save your shame, but you kill your glory. Morally speaking, it seems a part of the human light would put itself out, that the very notion of justice and injustice would hide itself in darkness, on that day where one would see the assassination of Emancipation by Liberty itself...Let America know and ponder on this: there is something more frightening than Cain killing Abel, and that is Washington killing Spartacus.[21]

Brown was found guilty of treason, insurrection, and murder, and hanged four months later on the gallows in Harpers Ferry. Brown's death galvanized the North into support for the abolitionist cause. The bitter struggle that followed was almost inevitable.

Chapter 6
The Civil War as a Theological Struggle

On the Fourth of July, 1955 I stood on the corner in front of my house on College Avenue in Wheaton, Illinois and watched a parade. The sun was shining brightly, a band was playing a lively marching tune somewhere up the street, and all around me people were clapping and cheering. I was five years old, and I held tightly to my daddy's hand. The mingled smells of roasted peanuts and firecracker smoke wafted around me. A parade float rolled by, followed by a long, shiny, black convertible. The driver of the car wore a striped shirt, bowler hat, and a handlebar mustache with ends that twirled out to a few inches on either side of his face.

In the back seat of the car, nestled between two girls in blue and orange cheerleading outfits waving their pompoms, sat a tiny, ancient man wearing a black visor cap festooned with gold braid. His cheeks were sunken, his eyes bright and bird-like. He nodded at the crowd with a grave and slightly dazed expression.

My dad picked me up so I could see better. "That," he said, "is Albert Woolson, the last living veteran of the Union Army in the Civil War."

The little old man raised his arm and waved at me as his car moved down the street, and I waved back at him.

"So, Dad," I said thoughtfully, "Isn't he too old to be in a war? Don't you have to be younger?"

"The Civil War was a long time ago, son. Mr. Woolson was a young boy at the time. He was a drummer boy in an army band."

I was a polite and respectful boy, so I didn't let on what I was thinking, which was that my otherwise reliable dad must believe I was foolish to swallow such an unlikely tale as this—that a miniscule and wrinkled person such as Mr. Woolson might have ever been young enough to be called a boy.

I developed an intense fascination with the Civil War as a child, and spent hours poring over a book of photographs by Matthew Brady that showed groups of solemn men with much facial hair regarding the camera with suspicion, indifference, or fascination; the bodies of dead soldiers lying scattered across battlefields in an attitude of startlement or incomprehension; army nurses tending to soldiers who had just emerged from operations to amputate their limbs and who lay on their cots with a clear expectation of imminent death.

My brother Johnny and I shared ownership of a set of plastic, blue or gray soldiers with molded horses and wagons and a metal, spring-loaded cannon that fired wooden matchsticks—the only reliable way to kill a plastic soldier. We spent hours creating forts with Lincoln Logs behind which our soldiers could shelter, and arguing whether a specific matchstick had actually killed a specific soldier or merely wounded him. In these battles, I was always the general of the Union side because I had been born in Illinois, while John was always the Confederate general because he had been born in Oklahoma. I had little grasp of the profound emotional consequences of that war, or of how the trauma of the war might continue to work within me, generations after the conflict had ended.

The Civil War was a theological crisis as much as it was an economic or political crisis. Although harboring conflicting notions of God and the devil, Heaven and Hell, justice, righteousness, eternity, and the nature of humankind, all parties to the war grew up within the theological confines of American evangelicalism. Historian Perry Miller called attention to the "unity amid diversity which sustained the majority of American Protestants" before the war, and which also "makes the Civil War the more poignant, for it was fought, not by Puritans against Cavaliers nor by republicans against royalists, but among the rank and file, all children of the Revival."[22]

The Second Great Awakening that had roused America in the early decades of the 19th century had transformed both the churches as religious institutions and the shape of political discourse in America. In his book, *The Civil War as a Theological Crisis*, Mark Noll points out that

> It was religion, narrowly considered, that drove an unprecedented ecclesiastical expansion—from about 700 Methodist churches in 1790 to nearly 20,000 in 1860; from fewer than 900 Baptist churches to more than 12,000; from no Cambellite or Restorationist or

Disciples churches to over 2,000; from about 700 Presbyterian churches to well over 6,000. In the helter-skelter of the new nation's experience, messages from the churches made sense. Preeminently from evangelical churches…came persuasive accounts of God, the human condition, and the means for finding reconciliation with God and neighbor.[23]

The nation's politics were embedded in a characteristically American and evangelical view of theology—a view that assumed the Bible to be the source of all truth and divine wisdom, that God took a direct and personal interest in the political struggles of Americans, that God's plan was to punish the wicked and elevate the righteous. Noll summed up that "the story of theology in the Civil War was a story of how a deeply entrenched intellectual synthesis divided against itself, even as its proponents were reassuring combatants on either side that each enjoyed a unique standing before God and each exercised a unique role as the true bearer of the nation's Christian civilization."[24]

Southerners viewed the war in strongly religious terms. The battle flag of the Confederacy was an adaptation of St. Andrew's Cross, the emblem of the patron saint of Scotland, the ancestral home of many of the Scots-Irish. Slavery, most Southerners believed, was an institution appointed and approved by God, and they believed, ironically, that they were fighting for their God-given and constitutionally guaranteed freedom to live their lives as they chose; the freedom of black slaves to live as they chose failed to enter into their moral equation.

In September of 1861, an Episcopal minister from Maryland named Edward Stearns had preached a sermon in opposition to the war that he believed was devouring his country. The title of his sermon was "The Sword of the Lord," and for his text he took a passage from Jeremiah 47:6:

O thou sword of the Lord, how long will it be ere thou be quiet? Put up thyself into thy scabbard, rest, and be still. How can it be quiet, seeing the Lord hath given it a charge against Ashkelon, and against the sea shore? There hath he appointed it.[25]

Reverend Stearns railed against the politicians and clergy of the North, whom he called Pharisees and hypocrites for wanting to fight a war to end slavery in the name of freedom, while oppressing the South and denying Southerners their constitutionally guaranteed right to own slaves. He accused Northern abolitionists of the sin of "busybodiness" against their Southern brethren, and concluded that God had unleashed his sword against both the North and the South in order to punish all for their sins against each other and against God himself.

Given the Protestant doctrine of *sola scriptura*—it is only necessary to read the Bible to find God's manifest truth—Southern preachers and theologians had an easy time justifying slavery. All one needed to do was to read the Bible with an open mind and a dose of common sense, according to them, to see that they were right. Any Bible student could easily find a dozen passages of scripture that seemed to justify slavery explicitly. God had cursed the descendants of Ham, son of Noah, with slavery because Ham had sinned against Noah after the Flood. Most any Southerner could relate the inference that Ham's descendants had gone to live in Africa: "And God said, Cursed be Canaan; a servant of servant shall he be unto his brethren. And he said, blessed be the Lord God of Shem; and Canaan shall be his servant. God shall enlarge Japheth, and he shall dwell in the tents of Shem; and Canaan shall be his servant."[26]

Furthermore, the ancient Hebrews were instructed in Leviticus 25 thusly: "However, you may purchase male or female slaves from among the foreigners who live among you. You may also purchase the children of such resident foreigners, including those who have been born in your land. You may treat them as your property, passing them on to your children as a permanent inheritance. You may treat your slaves like this, but the people of Israel, your relatives, must never be treated this way." It was not hard to find Bible passages that seemed to view slaves as less than human, or at least unworthy of protection as human beings, such as in Exodus 21: "When a man strikes his male or female slave with a rod so hard that the slave dies under his hand, he shall be punished. If, however, the slave survives for a day or two, he is not to be punished, since the slave is his own property."

In the New Testament, opponents of slavery could find ample support for ending slavery in the teachings of Paul and the egalitarian culture of the early church. For example, Paul wrote a letter to Philemon, whose slave Onesimus had fled to Paul for protection. In response, Paul sends Onesimus back, asking Philemon to accept him, "that you might receive him forever, no longer as a slave but more than a slave—a beloved brother, especially to me but how much more to you, both in the flesh and in the Lord."[27] However, Jesus never explicitly condemned slaveholding, and the apostle Paul explicitly taught that even Christian masters had no obligation to emancipate their slaves when the slaves converted to Christianity. In fact, Paul apparently suggested how the master-slave relationship might be regulated, but never that it should be ended. He wrote to the early church at Colossae: "Servants, obey in all things your masters; not with eye-service, as men-pleasers, but in singleness of heart, fearing God;…Masters, give unto your servants that which is just and equal, knowing that ye also have a Master in Heaven."[28]

The Protestant churches of the South—Southern Baptist, Methodist, Presbyterian, and Episcopal—loudly trumpeted the morality of slavery along with the righteousness of the Southern cause. They called the judgment of God down upon the Union armies for flaunting his will, and sent over 200 missionary chaplains into the ranks to evangelize the soldiers. As one Confederate chaplain summed up, they were there to help the men enter combat readily, fight fearlessly, and willingly surrender their souls to God with the certainty that they were fighting in the army of God.[29]

The abolitionist argument that slavery was contrary to the Bible was much less straightforward. Some argued that the system of slavery approved by the Bible was different from Southern slavery in the United States—Biblical slavery was much less cruel, really more like a modern relationship between any employer and employee. But the strongest appeal of the abolitionist was to the "spirit" of the Bible and the implications of the Christian message of love. Jonathan Blanchard, the future president of Wheaton College, referred in 1845 to "the broad principle of common equity and common sense" he found in scripture, to "the general principles of the Bible" and "the whole scope of the Bible," where he claimed that "the principles of the Bible are justice and righteousness." He claimed that "Abolitionists take their stand upon the New Testament doctrine of the natural equity of man, the one-bloodism of human kind; and upon those great principles of human rights, drawn from the New Testament, and announced in the American Declaration of Independence, declaring that all men have natural and inalienable rights to person, property and the pursuit of happiness."[30]

Such an argument was both innovative and theologically dangerous, because it clearly undermined the doctrine of *sola scriptura* and the literal reading of the Bible that was part of the revivalist tradition. Henry Ward Beecher, the minister and brother of Harriet Beecher Stowe, went even further in his fast day sermon on January 4, 1861. He acknowledged it was possible to find individual verses in the Bible that appeared to support the Southerners' view of slavery, but the Christian message was quite contrary to slavery:

> "I came to open the prison-doors," said Christ; and that
> is the text on which men justify shutting them and

locking them. "I came to loose those that are bound;" and that is the text out of which men spin cords to bind men, women, and children. "I came to carry light to them that are in darkness and deliverance to the oppressed;" and that is the Book from out of which they argue, with amazing ingenuity, all the infernal meshes and snares by which to keep men in bondage. It is pitiful.[31]

Martha Reamey married James Porter Rice in 1854 in Warrensburg, Missouri, the county seat eight miles from his home. In August, 1859 she gave birth at Hazel Hill to her third child, a baby boy. James and Martha named the child Will, and he was cared for by Martha, his older sister Nancy, and probably by one or more of the slave women owned by the family. The baby attended his first church service at the little Presbyterian church near Hazel Hill. He was my great-grandfather and John R. Rice's father.

Will Rice's older half-brother was 14-year-old Matt Rice, his father's right hand man around the plantation. Matt was the older brother Will would always look up to.

Will was born in a slim moment of respite from the savage border war between the slave owners of Missouri and abolitionists such as Brown who had flocked to Kansas in the 1850s. Before Will was two years old, Abraham Lincoln was elected president and the slave states of the South seceded from the Union, launching the Civil War. The war would be murderous and merciless beyond the capacity of any American to imagine in 1861, and both sides used their religion and their notion of God and his justice to define and defend their parts in the mayhem.

In November of 1861, Julia Ward Howe penned fresh words to a pre-war gospel tune. The "Battle Hymn of the Republic" became a standard sung by Union soldiers in the line of march and on hundreds of battlefields:

> Mine eyes have seen the glory
> of the coming of the Lord:
> He is trampling out the vintage
> where the grapes of wrath are stored;
> He hath loosed the fateful lightning
> of His terrible swift sword:
> His truth is marching on.

Howe's lyrics were a response to a Confederate anthem titled "God Save the South," written by Marylander George H. Miles following the outbreak of hostilities earlier in the year:

> God save the South, her altars and firesides,
> God save the South, now that the war is nigh,
> Now that we arm to die, chanting our battle cry,
> Freedom or death![32]

Generations of white Southerners have since then been taught to believe that the South seceded for such noble reasons as "freedom," or the defense of the Constitution, or to protect its democratic rights, or to resist oppression by Yankee imperialists. (I confess that I was one of these.) However, few Southern political or religious leaders at the time were under any such illusion. At the war's opening shots, lest any of his compatriots miss the point, President Jefferson Davis of the Confederacy defended the Southern secession that led to the bloodbath of the Civil War: "[Slavery] was established by decree of Almighty God...it is sanctioned in the Bible, in both Testaments, from Genesis to Revelation...it has existed in all ages, has been found among the people of the highest civilization, and in nations of the highest proficiency in the arts."

A Georgia cousin of James Porter Rice was Joe Brown, grandson of Dangerfield Rice and governor of Georgia from 1857 to 1865, a period encompassing the Civil War (and events in Margaret Mitchell's novel *Gone with the Wind*). On the eve of the Civil War, Joe Brown wrote a long "Open Letter to the People of Georgia," which clearly explained the basic argument for Georgia to secede from the Union:

> Mr. Lincoln is...the representative of a fanatical abolition sentiment—the mere instrument of a great triumphant political party, the principles of which are deadly hostile to the institution of Slavery and openly at war with the fundamental doctrines of the Constitution of the United States. The rights of the South and the institution of slavery are...in imminent danger from the triumph of the fanatical abolition sentiment which brought him into power as the candidate of the Northern section of the Union which has constantly denied our right to hold our slaves as property. Mr. Lincoln's election as the President will be the total abolition of slavery and the utter ruin of the South in less than

twenty-five years. If we submit now, we satisfy the
Northern people that come what may, we will never
resist.... the abolition of slavery which will visit
upon...non-slaveholders and poor white laborers in the
South the scene of the most misery and ruin.

Secession may have been foremost in the minds of Brown's fellow
Georgians, but in the early months of the war, Brown's Missouri
relatives in the James Rice family were overtaken by a tragedy closer to
home when Will's mother, James Rice's second wife Martha, died. Rice
was immediately concerned to find a mother to care of his four youngest
children, especially two-year-old Will. Within several months of his
wife's death, James married a new bride, Permelia Ann Atkinson, at the
small Presbyterian chapel at Hazel Hill. As it happened, the wedding
took place just before James was to be pulled away from his family by
the inexorable compulsion of the war.

James Rice knew his state was facing a larger and public
catastrophe. A majority of Missourians had voted to remain in the Union,
yet a minority of white Missouri citizens were avidly in favor of the
Confederacy. As a border state, Missouri was like to be the scene of
desperate fighting, and it was almost inevitable that James Rice would be
drawn into the war himself.

Although Missouri had been a slave state since it was admitted to the
Union in 1820, a majority of its white citizens were opposed to secession
and had no strong economic or political stake in the preservation of
slavery. The most enthusiastic partisans of the Confederacy were those
who lived in the plantation economy of the Missouri River Valley and
the counties south of the river, plus the western counties closest to the
border where the tumult of "Bleeding Kansas" had erupted. And
Lafayette County, just north of the Rice plantations around Hazel Hill,
was home to some of the most passionate Confederate sympathizers.

Early in the first year of the war, the Union beat back a Confederate
attempt at invading Missouri and established relatively firm military
control of the state. In response, Jo Orville Shelby, the Waverly hemp
manufacturer, formed a cavalry company of the secessionist Missouri
State Guard. He was elected its captain, and then led the company south
to join Confederate General Sterling Price, who intended to break the
Union Army's control of the state. Shelby was already experienced in the
art of war; he had led several sizable contingents of Border Ruffians
against the Kansas abolitionists over the previous half decade. He was
no ignorant bushwhacker, however. He had graduated from Transylvania

College, built a substantial rope-making business, and owned a patent on his own process for crushing hemp fibers to aid in making rope.

The Confederate forces fought their way north into Missouri from Arkansas, and at Wilson's Creek in the southwest corner of the state, Price's army—with Shelby's cavalry playing a conspicuous role in their first major battle—broke the Union Army under General Nathanial Lyon in a large and bloody affair. Price's army then followed up their victory by heading north for the heart of Missouri's slave economy concentrated along the Missouri River.

In St. Louis, a panicked Union General John Fremont, who had been the Republican candidate for president in 1856, reacted by declaring martial law across Missouri early in September, 1861. Anyone bearing arms without the authority of the Union Army was to be court-martialed and shot. All slaves would be freed immediately if they belonged to masters disloyal to the Union.

Fremont's emancipation proclamation in Missouri—predating Lincoln's presidential proclamation in 1863 freeing slaves across the Confederacy—was meant to put rebel activities in the state into a lockbox. Instead, it inflamed passions dramatically. The abolitionist press of the North congratulated Fremont on his courage, while Southern partisans howled their outrage. Jeff Thompson, a guerilla leader in the swamps of southeast Missouri, issued his own counter-proclamation in which he threatened that for every man executed by Fremont's forces he would "hang, draw, and quarter a minion of said Abraham Lincoln."[33]

In September of 1861 the Southern army of Price and Shelby reached the wealthy little town of Lexington, 27 miles from Hazel Hill. After a bitter and bloody eight day siege, the Union garrison of the town surrendered. Price's soldiers plundered the town and then his columns began a leisurely retreat back south toward Arkansas to rest and replenish their troops over the coming winter. After General Price's retreat, Missouri rested in Union hands although its safety seemed marginal at best. No one knew when an even larger Confederate Army would invade the state again.

The violence of the rhetoric on both sides set the stage for the ferocity with which the war was fought in the state. Over the next three and a half years, Missouri saw some of the most savage and continuous warfare in the history of the United States. Much of the conflict was between small bands of mounted guerrillas from both sides who destroyed or looted any civilian or military property that might be deemed useful to the other side. The guerrillas sometimes tortured and killed their captives, burned homes and farms indiscriminately, and used the cover of war to excuse crimes of robbery, murder, and plunder. By the end of the war in the spring of 1865, Missouri had witnessed over 1,000 battles and skirmishes, more than a third of the conflicts recorded throughout the entire Civil War.

For civilians such as the Rice family and their neighbors, the war was always right down the road, if not in the front yard. The protective presence of a Union detachment occupying the Johnson County courthouse in Warrensburg, less than 10 miles away from the Rice plantations, provided both security and danger. Stories were passed down the generations of our family about Yankee soldiers who marauded through the family barnyard taking plantation chickens as prisoners of war and executing rebel fowls on the spot to be consigned to the dinner pots of Northern troops.

But the greatest danger to the Rice family, to the Rice plantation, and to their slaveholding neighbors in Johnson County was not from the Union troops who occupied the town and the state. It was from the multiple roving gangs of guerrillas, especially the Kansas jayhawkers who fought on the side of the Yankee troops.

One of the most prominent of the jayhawkers was Doc Jennison from Lawrence, Kansas, who organized the Seventh Kansas Volunteer Cavalry Regiment. It operated as a large scale, organized raiding party from Kansas into Missouri throughout much of the war, looting property and burning the homes of Confederate sympathizers. Jennison called his regiment "self-sustaining." This meant that whenever they invaded one of the Missouri counties such as Johnson or Lafayette that were home to the slave owners, they invariably brought back booty that outweighed the supplies they used on the journey, including horses and wagons, jewelry, furniture, silverware, money, and stores of food and other supplies. Viewed as spoils of war by the jayhawkers, few of these items found their way to a Federal commissary to support the Union Army. Along with the booty, many of the slaves on Missouri plantations headed happily with the jayhawkers for Kansas and their new freedom.[34]

Danger also came from Missouri-based bushwhackers, who claimed to fight on the side of the Confederates and who enjoyed overwhelming support from the civilians living in the slave-owning counties along the Missouri River and on the western border with Kansas. Many families had husbands or sons riding with them, and they sheltered and fed them, spied for them, and smuggled ammunition to them. Presumably the Rice clan felt the same way as almost all their neighbors and joined with their neighbors in providing practical support to the guerillas. One of the most notorious bushwhackers was William Quantrill, a man with a long history going back to the "Bleeding Kansas" conflict before the Civil War. He called himself a colonel, though he fought without any commission from the Confederacy. His raiders had a well-earned reputation for looting farms and terrorizing civilians sympathetic to either side, and for torturing and executing any prisoners they took.

Johnson County where the Rice family lived, along with several other counties on the western end of the state, quickly became a free-fire zone in which any and all were viewed as combatants or sympathizers of the Union or Confederate armies, of the anti-slavery jayhawkers or pro-slavery bushwhackers. Although nominally occupied by the Union for most of the war, Johnson County was crossed time and again, by Confederate and Union armies, by guerrilla fighters under no particular authority, and by bands of criminals, murderers and thieves.

On the afternoon of March 26, 1862, Quantrill and a band of over 200 Confederate guerrillas abruptly appeared out of the woods to attack a force of 60 Union troops from the Seventh Missouri Cavalry stationed inside a thick wooden stockade surrounding the brick courthouse in Warrensburg, Johnson County. Quantrill's attack failed to dislodge the Union troops in their courthouse fortress that afternoon, and a second attack failed in the morning before the raiders gave up and fled back west to Jackson County.[35]

Attacks such as this led to Union Army countermeasures, seeking to undercut civilian support of the raiders in Johnson County. By summer, further raids by Quantrill and other raiders battling the Union occupiers, combined with plundering and burning expeditions by the pro-Union jayhawkers, pushed the countryside surrounding the Rice plantation into a spiral of violence, destruction, and despair.

For Confederate sympathizers in Missouri, the die was cast on July 22, 1862, when Union Brigadier General John M. Schofield issued an order requiring "every able-bodied man capable of bearing arms and subject to military duty...to repair without delay to the nearest military post and report for duty." In early August Schofield followed with General Order No. 24, requiring anyone who sympathized with the Confederacy to be enrolled and to surrender their arms or face prison.

43-year-old James Porter Rice and his son, 17-year-old Matt Rice, were the two males in the Rice family in the age range affected by the orders. They had limited options and little time to consider or maneuver. They could do the unthinkable and enroll in the Union Army. Or they could go to prison. Or they could evade prison by joining the nearest Confederate Army unit. Their choice became even clearer a few days later.

The Rice family owned more slaves than most other families in the vicinity of Warrensburg, and on August 13, 1862, the family fortunes suffered a severe blow. During the early part of the war, work had continued on the Pacific Railroad, west from St. Louis toward Kansas City, and by the summer of 1862 the railroad had been built to within four miles of Warrensburg. When the news got around that a detachment of Union troops was scheduled to withdraw from the town via the railroad, a large crowd of slaves gathered from all around the Warrensburg area, asking the soldiers to be taken along. Sheriff Charles Cunningham gathered an armed posse of six men and rode out to capture the slaves and return them to their owners. At first the Union commander seemed ready to let Cunningham take the slaves, but he faced an uprising from his troops, who were apparently ardent abolitionists. Cunningham later complained, "I undertook to catch one of them when a large number of [Union Army] guns were drawn on me and the Negroes released, with threats made on my life as well as that of my men with me."[36]

It is probable that some of the slaves owned by the Rice family were among those who escaped to freedom that August, and were then able to join the Union Army and then fight against their former masters. An escaped slave named Jerry Rice from the vicinity of the Rice plantations, whose owner was named William Rice—quite probably the brother of James Porter Rice—was listed as a volunteer for the United States Colored Troops for Missouri. Another volunteer Negro soldier named Scott Thomas reported that he had been owned by John Rice, probably also a son of Dangerfield Rice, brother of James Porter Rice, and uncle of my great-grandfather Will Rice.

A few days later, Confederate Colonel Jo Shelby rode north through Warrensburg leading several hundred cavalrymen on a recruiting expedition for the Confederacy. His timing could not have been more perfect. Shelby, an old neighbor, acquaintance, and business connection of the Rices and others of the slave-owning aristocracy in western Missouri, was on his way 20 miles north to his home in Waverly, the Missouri River port where he planned to muster a new Confederate regiment. Shelby settled down for a leisurely four-day visit with his wife at their pleasant riverside home as hundreds of volunteers streamed in from around the countryside.

James and Matt Rice gathered their belongings, cleaned their guns, saddled their horses, and said goodbye to James' mother Nancy, his wife Permelia, his younger sons Dangerfield, George, and Will, and his daughter Nancy. An unknown number of other family, close friends, and neighbors—mainly women, children and old folks —remained. Then James and Matt headed 24 miles up the road to join up with Shelby on the banks of the Missouri River. At a rally on the steps of the Christian Church in Waverly, Shelby recruited a thousand new soldiers into his ranks and led them south to join General Sterling Price's army.

With him rode James Porter Rice, newly elected captain of Company E of the new 10th Missouri Cavalry. Many of the soldiers in Company E were neighbors, relatives, and friends from Johnson County. Private Matt Rice rode with his father.

A year later, in August of 1863, much of western Missouri and eastern Kansas was in a state of even worse anarchy and terror as a result of the guerrillas and the battling armies. In an effort to bring the chaos under control, Union General Thomas Ewing issued General Order No. 10, which ordered the arrest of anyone giving aid and comfort to the enemy, which mainly meant the arrest of women and children related to the guerrillas.

In retaliation, on August 21, 1863, Quantrill organized a raid by 450 guerillas on the pro-Union town of Lawrence, Kansas. In four hours, Quantrill's guerrillas ravaged the town, burning many of the buildings, looting most stores and banks, and executing almost 200 men and boys in cold blood. In Quantrill's words, they were ordered to kill "anyone big enough to carry a gun."

Ewing's response was to issue the even more draconian Order No. 11, in which he essentially ordered a swath of Missouri counties along the Kansas border to be cleared for military operations. All civilians were to be evicted by the Union Army and every field, house, barn, and storeroom in the counties was to be burned, with the exception of a more densely populated area around Kansas City plus four small towns south of it.* Ewing's plan was to drain the sea of popular and tactical support in which the guerillas swam, and even though he ordered his soldiers to refrain from looting, they often stole or destroyed animals and other property as they drove everyone in the affected areas away from their homes. Within weeks, nothing but charred chimneys and blackened fields marked thousands of acres that had been fertile farmland.[37] Lying adjacent to Jackson and Cass counties, which were named in the order, was Johnson County, which experienced similar destruction though it wasn't explicitly named.

Order No. 11 gave rise to outrage and despair in the Rice family and in slave-owning families all through the Kansas border region and along the Missouri River in western and central Missouri. In the chaos and confusion of the order's aftermath, the Rice family's ninety-five slaves either escaped or were freed by Yankee troops. Their home and other property on Hazel Hill was destroyed or stolen and their lives were

---

* Ewing's Order No. 11 was similar to the policy of the U.S. Army in Vietnam a century later, which ordered Vietnamese civilians to leave their homes and assemble in "strategic hamlets" under the "protection" of the military.

threatened. Meanwhile, their men were missing, away south of the Missouri River with the army of Sterling Price or in some independent unit of Confederate cavalry or guerrilla warriors. After four decades in Missouri, first toiling for financial security, then arriving at a position of almost unimaginable wealth and privilege, and then struggling to survive an intense and violent conflict, the Rice family found itself homeless and almost penniless, together with other refugees who were fleeing in every direction to escape the devastation.

Johnson County, together with the other western border counties affected by Order No. 11, looked as though it had been ravaged by a prairie fire. Buildings lay in ruins, blackened chimneys rising from piles of ash and debris. The misery of the refugees was unbounded. An observer said, "the people are crazy with fear and terror with which their lives are filled…weeping and wailing like children." When their homes were gone, the refugees were crowded into "dilapidated outhouses" or in tents or huts "constructed from the boughs of trees…They are huddled together in the little villages at which posts have been established, and are suffering from the want of food and the other necessities of life."[38]

Several months later, a Union chaplain, Reverend Francis Springer, wrote that "Refugees from secession come into camp nearly every day…chiefly women and children…The wagons are usually loaded with bedclothes, wearing apparel, provisions, a few cooking utensils and other such articles of family convenience as they could pack on or tie to the wagon. For want of houses, they either live in their wagons or in tents made by spreading a few quilts over a pole resting at each end or on forked stakes planted in the ground…Unwashed, half-clad & shoeless boys and girls are all in pitiable abundance."[39]

Springer's harrowing descriptions might easily have applied to the Rice family when, in late 1863, they loaded everything they could save or carry onto two oxcarts and fled south toward the relative safety of Texas along an old road known as the Shawnee Trail. Most of the refugees who headed for Texas came from the slave-owning regions of Missouri and were strongly sympathetic to the Confederacy. Texas was largely untouched by the war and became a sanctuary for many others fleeing the fighting in less fortunate parts of the South. The Shawnee Trail had been used for several years before the war to drive cattle north from Texas to Sedalia and St. Joseph for shipment elsewhere by rail, and was in many places quite wide though still bone-jarringly rough. According to Rice family lore passed down through several generations, their oxcarts were part of an endless river of refugees, many of them neighbors from Johnson County. The wagons traveled with agonizing slowness, eking out a few miles a day over the trail. In the absence of the men, 12-year-old Nancy Rice drove one of the oxcarts most of the way. At the time of the journey, her little brother Will Rice was four years old.

They traveled for almost two months along the Shawnee Trail headed for Texas through war-wasted Missouri and the uninhabited stretches of Oklahoma wilderness as the train jolted along the ruts toward a dangerous and uncertain future. They were accompanied by hundreds of their Missouri neighbors in a wagon train that stretched as far as Will could see.

As they neared the Red River, young Will sat in the wagon's box next to Nancy. Ordinarily Nancy would be holding the reins, but on this dangerous stretch of road it was their stepmother Permelia who sat up front and drove the oxen. Will, Nancy, and the rest of the children and womenfolk in the family had left most of their possessions behind in the smoking ruin of their home back in Missouri or in piles of abandoned furniture and housewares along the way. Their most precious possessions now were each other, plus a few trunks and boxes of clothes, tools, utensils, and stores of food.

The Red River was swollen with rain at this time of year, no longer fordable as it had been under the sun's furnace in July and August. At the sloping edge of the river on the Oklahoma side, each wagon was carefully loaded onto a large raft and then ferried across the fast-moving river. This point was known as Red Rock Crossing, and on the south side of the river the road climbed precipitously along a steep, rocky bluff.

After the Rice family crossed, the animals drew the wagon up the narrow, rutted track, jolting Will and Nancy from side to side. Permelia, sitting on the narrow wooden driver's seat, strained to hold the oxen close to the rock wall away from the river. Inches away from the outside wagon wheel the bluff dropped away almost vertically into the river below.

"We're in Texas, Will!" said Nancy. "We've come all this way and we're all done traveling!" Will was too terrified to reply. He kept his eyes shut and huddled against his sister and tried to hear his daddy's voice in his head from the last time he'd seen him, saying, "It'll be all right, Will. You just hold on and I'll be right along."

When the Rice wagons had almost reached the top of the bluff, Will heard a huge commotion behind them on the trail. Women shouted, oxen bellowed, and Will heard the sound of crashing and creaking as one of the wagons behind them fell and exploded into the river below. A child screamed in the ruckus, and Permelia whipped the oxen into a trot up the few remaining feet to the level Texas plain. From there they could see the wreckage of a neighbor's wagon drifting down the flood, the oxen sinking under the weight of their yoke, the upturned face of a child, a wooden box popping to the surface, someone's bright red shirt floating away. And then silence. Will began to sob as Permelia took him into her arms.[*]

The Rice family entered Texas in 1863 somewhere near present-day Texarkana and followed the Red River to Fannin County. They settled in the little community of Savoy to wait for the hoped-for victory of the Confederacy, after which they planned to return home to Missouri and pick up the pieces of their lives.

While the rest of the family fled south, James Rice and his son Matt remained behind with Colonel Jo Shelby's Missouri cavalry. In the immediate wake of Ewing's order, Shelby and his 800 men rode north out of Arkadelphia, Arkansas and into Missouri on what was to be the longest cavalry raid of the war. The raid was successful in the face of the occupation of Missouri by over 40,000 Union troops. From September 22 to November 3, 1863, Shelby's brigade rode over 1,500 miles in a wide arc around the state, inflicting hundreds of casualties on the Union Army and burning or carrying off property and supplies worth two million dollars. "Shelby's Great Ride," as it became known after the war, was impressive as a military maneuver, and it succeeded in frightening a number of Union generals and politicians when it hit the front pages of Northern newspapers. In the end, however, Shelby's adventure only emphasized that the Union was able to maintain its overall control of Missouri, and that any rebel incursion was a temporary annoyance.

At some point during the next several months, James Porter Rice disappeared from the rolls of the 10th Missouri Cavalry. Family legend has it that Rice was captured by a unit of the Union Army. According to the story passed down through generations of the Rice family, the Union commander told Rice that by his rules of engagement, Rice was a criminal seditionist, and therefore subject to being shot on sight. The Union officer offered to let Rice save his life by forswearing the Confederacy and pledging his loyalty to the Union. "I'll be damned if I'll do so, sir!" Rice was said to reply. "If I had one drop of Yankee blood, I would open my veins and drain every last drop of my blood to make sure I have no Yankee blood left in me!"

In response, the Yankee supposedly laughed and told Rice he would be freed if he would give his parole promising to stop fighting. James Rice thought about it overnight, signed his parole in the morning, and

---

[*] I've done my best to imagine this scene. The story has come down through several generations of my family, though I obviously don't know the exact dialogue and details.

probably headed back toward Johnson County to wait out the war and keep his eye on the family property.

His son Matt, meanwhile, fought on as a private of Company E of the 10th Cavalry in General Jo Shelby's Iron Brigade, but with a new captain to replace his father. The following September of 1864, the Confederate Army of 12,000 soldiers under Sterling Price once again invaded Missouri from Arkansas. This was the final campaign of the war west of the Mississippi River. Price marched north toward St. Louis and then west toward Kansas City, fighting scores of small engagements with units of the Union Army and destroying millions of dollars' worth of property along the way. But his army was exhausted and ill-equipped, and began to melt away under the unrelenting pursuit of the Union Army. After a disastrous defeat at the town of Westport south of Kansas City, the army retreated south, splintering as it went, and ended its war by escaping westward through Indian Territory before returning to southern Arkansas. By the end of Price's last raid, his army of 12,000 had shrunk to 6,000, and was rapidly dissolving. Price's defeat contributed to Lincoln's re-election to the presidency in November of 1864.

Matt Rice was wounded on October 25 at the Battle of Mine Creek as Price's exhausted army was fleeing south, and his service as a private in the Iron Brigade probably then came to an end. His commanding officer General Jo Shelby, however, was not a man to give up the fight. He had begun fighting for the cause of the Confederacy—including his personal right to own slaves and the collective rights of slave owners in Missouri and across the South—years before the secession, as a captain of the Border Ruffians who fought to keep Kansas out of the hands of the "damned abolitionists." As commander of the Missouri Cavalry of the Confederate Army in the west, he had fought a hundred battles and traveled thousands of miles.

After every other Confederate military unit had surrendered across the South in April and May of 1865, Shelby attempted to gather the remaining divisions and brigades of Price's Confederate Army in a last-ditch attempt to carry on. When his fellow commanders decided instead to surrender, Shelby issued a furious proclamation to his troops and had it printed up on a broadside to be passed out in the army's encampment:

> Soldiers! You have been betrayed! The generals whom you trusted have refused to lead you. Let us begin the battle again by a Revolution. Lift up the flag that has been cast down and dishonored. Unsheathe the sword that it may remain unsullied and victorious! If you desire

it, I will lead; if you demand it, I will follow. We are the Army and the Cause. To talk of surrender is to be a traitor. Let us seize the traitors and attack the enemy. Forward for the South and Liberty![40]

After a final failed attempt to reconstitute the Confederate Army, Jo Shelby led almost 1,000 of his remaining troops on their last ride, south through Texas to the banks of the Rio Grande, where they sank their battle flag in the river before crossing over into Mexico. In doing so, Shelby and his men invented the myth of the "Lost Cause," a noble yet quixotic struggle for high and romantic ideals that could go on forever because Shelby's Iron Brigade had never surrendered

Indeed, Shelby's Lost Cause soon became a palatable explanation for the situation. The tens of thousands of former slave owners and Confederate partisans who had trekked from Missouri to Texas in the fall of 1863 found themselves in dire straits at the end of the war. Unlike the vast majority of war refugees who had returned to their homes in other states, those from Missouri remained as permanent residents of Texas after the war. In Missouri, they had fought their own neighbors and relations in the most bitter and violent chapter of the Civil War to preserve the institution of slavery and the privileges of the slavocracy, and had been defeated and exiled. They could return only if they accepted the shame of their defeat in terms dictated by their conquerors. Remaining in Texas allowed them to maintain the illusion that they had fought for some great cause of freedom from the tyranny and oppression of the North, rather than to protect the institution of slavery, which had now lost some of its former pretense at morality and divine sanction.

After the war, James Porter Rice was able to find and rejoin his family in north Texas, along with his son Matt. The trail of Johnson County refugees had been wide and easy to follow. There in Texas they stayed in company with the other refugees from Missouri. The influx of Civil War refugees had significance for the future evolution of Texas culture and politics in the decades after the war. The descendants of the refugees would be among the most embittered, and hardcore in their opposition to the post-war rule of the Union Army and the Reconstruction policies of the national government.

For the Rice family and for the many other Missouri refugees in Texas, as for General Shelby, the battle continued to rage long past 1865 in new forms that echoed the ferocity and violence of the Civil War. It was as though the spirit of the war had seeped into their very marrow. It suffused their dreams, conditioned their actions, warped their relationships, and redefined their notions of what it took to survive in a bleak and bitter world.

Chapter 7
The Aftermath of the War

> *"Ye have feared the sword; and I will bring a sword upon you, saith the Lord God. And I will bring you out of the midst thereof, and deliver you into the hands of strangers, and will execute judgments among you. Ye shall fall by the sword; I will judge you in the border of Israel; and ye shall know that I am the Lord."*—Ezekiel 11:9

In the fall of 1960, when I was 10 years old, I reached way into a corner of the third shelf on the bookcase in our living room. I pulled out a tattered 64-page paperback with a torn red and blue cover emblazoned with the title *Texas History Movies*. Once again, I turned to the most dog-eared pages of all, a series of cartoons depicting the battle of San Jacinto. The year was 1836, and the Texans had died to their last defender at the Alamo, and Mexican President Santa Anna then ordered 330 Texan prisoners executed at Goliad.

Now the Texans are thirsting for revenge. The first cartoon shows Santa Anna sleeping in his tent as his guard says "Ho hum" and swats at the flies buzzing about his general's head. Then the Texans attack. "Caramba!" says a Mexican soldier as a bullet goes through his head. The brave Texans holler their battle cry of "Remember the Alamo!" and "Remember Goliad!" as they stick their bayonets through the bodies of several surprised and silly-looking Mexican soldiers, whose hats fly off their heads. Other Mexicans plead for mercy, claiming "Me no Alamo!" and "Me no Goliad!" At last, Santa Anna is captured while crawling around in the grass pretending to be a common soldier, and is ratted on by his own troops. The Mexicans have suffered 1500 casualties, while the smarter and braver Texans, who were obviously better shots as well, lose only six dead and twenty-four wounded. Texas is now its own free and democratic republic.

By the age of 10, I had read this booklet a couple of dozen times, but I was not the young person responsible for its unseemly condition. That culprit was my mother, who had owned it since 1936, and had probably read it at least 100 times as a child. *Texas History Movies* was a book of entertaining cartoon stories of early Texas, beginning with early explorations and settlements by the Spanish, the immigration of whites from the United States to Texas and their wars against the Indians and rebellions against the Mexican Government, the short-lived Republic of Texas, annexation by the U.S., and finally the Civil War. It was funny, irreverent, entrancing, and entertaining. It succeeded at popularizing a carefully crafted yet racially-corrupted self-image for Texans.

The cartoons were first published in a Dallas newspaper in the late 1920s, and then the paperback was published courtesy of the Magnolia Petroleum Company. For the next several decades every Texas student in the sixth or seventh grade was given a free copy. *Texas History Movies* proved to be amazingly popular, and shaped the collective understanding and historical outlook of generations of young Texans. In the cartoons, Texans were generally brave, well-intentioned, resourceful, honest, undisciplined soldiers but excellent shots, and lovers of freedom and democracy. By contrast, Mexicans were swarthy, craven critters with big black mustaches who spoke broken English and betrayed each other at every opportunity. Indians were shiftless, deceitful, childlike, violent pagans who also spoke broken English. When black people appeared, they had large lips, pop-eyes, and a vast love of watermelon. The only mention of the Civil War claimed merely that most Texans wanted to secede and fight for their freedom. No mention was made of slavery as a cause of the war.

Despite the fact that I was born in the land of the Yankees and had never been to Texas, I strongly identified with my Texas heritage. I vowed that when I grew up I would find a way to move back to that glorious state where my mom, all of her sisters, and my grandparents had been born. I might even get up to Fannin County, named after James Fannin, the heroic Texan revolutionist executed along with his compatriots by Santa Anna at Goliad, as depicted in a cartoon in *Texas History Movies.*

In 1860, Savoy was a tiny village of a few hundred residents in Fannin County, Texas, just five miles south of the Red River. Fannin was one of four adjoining northeastern counties known as Corners Country. Fewer than 10,000 people lived in the county, and the major occupation was growing corn, beans, potatoes, onions, pumpkins, cotton, and squash. Most of the inhabitants were independent yeoman farmers who worked by themselves or with one or two slaves. A small number of cotton plantations dotted the county, and these were worked by larger numbers of slaves. The people were divided between those who supported the Union or the Confederacy, with a likely majority leaning toward the Union.

State Senator Robert Taylor from Fannin County was a strong Union man and an ally of Governor Sam Houston, a founding Texas statesman and former President of the Republic of Texas before statehood. Houston was a slaveholder and opponent of abolitionism; nonetheless he was ejected from office at the beginning of the war when he refused to sign an oath of loyalty to the Confederacy. He said, "I love Texas too well to bring civil strife and bloodshed upon her. To avert this calamity, I shall make no endeavor to maintain my authority as Chief Executive of this State, except by the peaceful exercise of my functions." Houston correctly predicted the coming disaster. Most of the South would be turned into a vast wasteland by a bloody and useless war of attrition, he said, and in the end slavery would be abolished.

When Texans voted on secession in 1860, 90 percent of the white residents of the Red River counties owned no slaves. The voters of Fannin County followed Houston in opposing secession by a vote of 656 to 471, and similar majorities supported the Union in several neighboring counties as well. As the war began, a few companies of soldiers were organized to leave Texas and head north to join the Union armies, and underground movements began in several of the counties to remove themselves from Texas and join the Union. In response, the Confederate Army invaded the Red River counties to quash any move to secede from the secessionists.

In 1862, the town of Gainesville, county seat of nearby Cooke County where John R. Rice and his wife Lloys Cooke Rice were later born, was the site of one of the most heinous crimes of the Civil War. Confederate soldiers under the command of Colonel James G. Bourland, one of the largest slaveholders in the county, arrived in Gainesville with several hundred soldiers to round up almost 200 men and boys they suspected of intending to evade the Confederate draft. The soldiers were more of a mob out to eliminate anyone who might conceivably be sympathetic to the Union than anything resembling a disciplined military unit.

After a mock trial on October 1 at which no legal evidence was presented, the soldiers hanged seven Gainesville residents. The Confederate mob then lost its patience with quasi-legal procedures and simply lynched another 14 suspected Unionists. The next week, the soldiers held more trials, lynched 19 more men, and shot two who tried to escape. A total of 42 were killed initially, and over the next few weeks several dozen more Texans were lynched by Confederate soldiers on suspicion that they might be loyal to the Union. The event became known as the Great Hanging at Gainesville.[41] Across the state of Texas, Democratic newspapers applauded the mass lynching. The legislature reimbursed the troops for their expenses, and Governor Francis Lubbock praised their actions. Newspapers across the South congratulated Texas for eliminating "traitors" to the Southern cause, and northern newspapers ran editorials condemning "Rebel barbarism."

Since early in the 20th century, the grounds of the county courthouse in Gainesville have featured a towering statue of a Confederate soldier facing northward in a heroic pose. The statue was erected by the United Daughters of the Confederacy as a memorial to the brave soldiers who defended Texas from Yankee oppression and invasion.

On the base of the monument is inscribed the following poetic legend:

> God holds the scales of justice;
> He will measure praise and blame;
> And the South will stand the verdict,
> And will stand it without shame.
>
> Oh, home of tears, but let her bear
> This blazoned to the end of time;
> No nation rose so white and fair,
> None fell so free of crime.

The statue stands as an embodiment of the Lost Cause, romantic homage to wounded Confederates and their noble sacrifice. The words, however, are ironic, given the true history of Gainesville.

Along with the rest of Texas, Fannin County was little touched by the physical destruction of the war. However, the war affected the county deeply, and the area saw much violence between those with opposite sympathies. The vast and inaccessible thickets at the center of the Corners were used as winter quarters and hideouts for large gangs of Confederate guerillas and deserters. Quantrill's Raiders, infamous for massacring almost 200 civilians when they sacked and burned Lawrence, Kansas, camped in Fannin County during the winter before resuming their raids in Missouri and Kansas. By 1863, tens of thousands of refugees from the slave-owning regions of Missouri were streaming south across the Red River. At the end of the war, the population had grown by half, and most of the new arrivals, such as the Rice family, were deeply traumatized and embittered ex-Confederates. Many were the families of former slave owners and Confederate soldiers.

Will Rice was six years old in 1865. His earliest memories were in all likelihood of fleeing the Rice plantation at the age of four and heading south in an oxcart toward Texas as a refugee from the war. As a toddler, he had doubtless experienced hunger, witnessed murder, and feared death. His family had lost everything, and now had to start over in a new place with few resources. His father James and older brother Matt had lived through three years of extraordinary violence and had participated in scores of battles. Both of them may have suffered from an ailment first diagnosed during the Civil War as "soldier's heart," a term signifying that a soldier, haunted by his wartime experiences, could be subject to the most intense spiritual and psychological distress, nightmares, violence, depression, and suicidal and homicidal rages. In the Great War it would be called shellshock, in World War II it would be known as combat fatigue, and in Vietnam it would be diagnosed as post-traumatic stress disorder, but it all came down to the same thing: the terrible violence of war lived on in the souls of veterans long after the war itself ended. Did James and Matt Rice wake from nightmares of blood and fire and grief? If so, they were still required to go on with their lives, to work and support their families in a despairing and difficult time.

The state of Texas in particular was primed to be an incubator of bitter reaction. While it suffered great losses during the war, along with the rest of the Confederacy, Texas was never invaded and never witnessed large scale battles or invasions by Union armies. By the end of the war, much of the South was a smoking ruin, with a devastated economy, ruined crops, and a generation of its youth sick, wounded, or moldering in graves—while Texas was largely untouched. Because of its proximity to Mexico and ports on the Gulf, and in comparison with the other Southern states, Texas businesses and their trade thrived. As a result, while the rest of the Confederacy suffered greatly as a result of losing the war, many Texans were never really forced to acknowledge the depth of the disaster. It would be in some ways easier in Texas than elsewhere to maintain the romantic illusion of the Lost Cause. Texas had never been truly defeated, people said, and if ever the South should rise again it would be led by Texas.

In November of 1865, Major General William Strong toured Northeast Texas as the Inspector General of the Freedman's Bureau, an agency set up to help the former slaves make the transition to a new way of life. He wrote that he was shocked and amazed at the "most intense hatred" displayed by the former secessionists toward the freedmen, toward the Union Army, and toward white Unionists. These Southerners had never acknowledged the consequences of their rebellion, and had never seen the death and dying that accompanied the bloody fighting in Virginia or Tennessee or Mississippi, or the carnage that wracked Missouri, or the flames and misery that followed Sherman's march through Georgia. As a result, said Strong, they intended to resist Reconstruction with all their might, and would reinstitute slavery if they could.

Will Rice lived with the trauma of war on daily display in his home as he was growing up, and must have inherited some of that terror and bitterness. As a child he probably shared the terrible resentment of many white Southerners toward the newly freed slaves, the Yankees who had freed them, and the wrenching changes spawned by the war. Together with the other Missouri refugees, his family probably approved of and supported the efforts of the Klan and other ex-Confederate guerillas to intimidate, murder, or drive away the freedmen and Unionists of Fannin County.

The Rice family had fled Johnson County, Missouri, one of the most blood-drenched and burned-over counties in the United States during the war, and they had arrived in Fannin County, which quickly became the center of the most murderous area of the defeated South. From 1865 to 1871, a confusing welter of ex-Confederate guerrillas, bandits, deserters, and assorted criminals fought a second Civil War against committed Unionists, freed slaves, and Union Army troops.

Lt. Colonel George Armstrong Custer was commander of a region that included northeast Texas, and as early as mid-1865 he reported that organized guerilla bands were operating throughout the region and had no fear of Union troops who were trying to establish law and order. He wrote that "the raiders ambushed patrols and robbed wagon trains, whiles sheriffs and judges loyal to the Southern ideal protected the gang members." Custer added that "many men in the public-at-large also protected the raiders, perhaps because such men claimed that they represented the Lost Cause."[42]

Many of the guerrilla raiders rode under the banner of the Ku Klux Klan, a paramilitary organization founded by ex-Confederate officers in Pulaski, Tennessee in 1865. Others in Texas called themselves Ku Klux Rangers, or the Knights of the White Camellia, or the White Caps. The Klan launched a reign of terror in the states of the former Confederacy with a panoply of lynching, beatings, jailings, intimidation, and threats against the newly freed black slaves and Unionists. Many Klan members wore white robes and covered their faces with white masks when they rode on midnight parades and silent rides designed to induce terror in their targets, who included blacks, Yankee "carpetbaggers," and Southern "scalawags" who worked with the federal government and Northern educational and aid societies to improve the condition of the former slaves.

Early in 1866, the white majority of Texas dominated a state constitutional convention that reversed all the verdicts of the war by passing the "Black Codes," returning black people to a state of virtual slavery worse than their bondage before the war. Black people were given no civil rights other than their token freedom under the Thirteenth Amendment. They could not vote, hold office, or serve on juries. They were required to work on contract for whites who had complete control over both the workers and their family members. Employers were given the legal right to fine their employees and beat them for infractions.

In short, the system of slavery was cruelly re-designed, in Texas as in other Southern states, to fit the new post-war realities. One of the new faces of slavery was the innovative scheme of "convict labor" introduced by James Porter Rice's cousin, and my own distant relative, ex-governor Joe Brown of Georgia. Companies that leased convicts from a state prison system had no financial motivation to protect any investment in the health or welfare of the convict, unlike slave owners who needed to keep their slaves alive and productive. So companies such as Joe Brown's Raccoon Mountain Coal Mine often simply worked their convicts to death and then ordered replacements from the prison system. In order to ensure a steady supply of captive labor, black men were imprisoned for many years on slim pretext, and then provided as low-cost labor.

Between 1865 and 1871 thousands of freedmen and Unionists were murdered across Texas by ex-Confederate raiders and terrorists, many of whom wore Klan robes. The killers gave a variety of simple reasons for why they killed black people, including "did not remove hat," "wouldn't give up his whiskey flask," "wanted to thin out the niggers a little," and "wanted to see a damned nigger kick."[43] One guerilla from Fannin County claimed that he killed an average of three ex-slaves per day for several months. His numbers were questioned but the basic fact that he had murdered was not.

As mayhem erupted all around them in Fannin County, the Rice family was struggling to survive. Between one and two hundred people lived in their tiny settlement of Savoy, about 15 miles away from the county seat in Bonham where the nearest sheriff could be found. The farm families in Savoy operated mainly in a barter economy. Most of them were subsistence farmers, and the first effort of a refugee family when they arrived in 1863 would have been dig an acre or two for their garden—one of the first set of crops they had raised without the help of their slaves. Planting corn, tomatoes, squash, and other vegetables that flourished in the rich black bottomland of Fannin County was essential for a family's survival. They would probably wait a year or two to plant an acre of the cotton that was the most important cash crop in the county.

Five miles north of Savoy was the Red River, and there Matt Rice lived for a time on an old wooden riverboat, recovering from the wound he had received in 1864 at the Battle of Mine Creek, probably working a bit and saving what he could. Rent for the boat was doubtless cheap, and Matt was a young man who had plans for his life. In 1868, Matt, now 23, moved down to Savoy and onto a patch of land next door to the Rice family home where his father James lived with his stepmother Permelia and their children, including Will.[44] Matt married a 16-year-old girl named Sophronia that year, and shortly they had a baby girl named Sarah. The baby was nine years younger than her uncle and neighbor Will Rice, and like him would grow up surrounded by violence and trauma.

One of the most deadly encounters during this time took place south of Corners Country in Brazos County. In the middle of July, 1868, a group of armed whites paraded under the name of the Klan through Freedman's Town, threatening blacks who tried to organize politically for upcoming elections. The freedmen drove them out, but the Klan members returned to kill an estimated 25 men, including George Brooks, a Methodist minister who had formed a local chapter of the Union League, an association of Union sympathizers. [45]

By the fall of 1868, Texas authorities had issued indictments for 5,000 murders, but had executed just one man—a former slave. Thousands of additional killings went unreported because freedmen and Unionists were afraid for their lives. In Fannin County alone there may have been over 1,000 murders, and one of the guerilla leaders, a former Confederate soldier and deserter named Bob Lee, claimed that he personally had killed 42 freedmen and Unionists. When Union troops from the Sixth Cavalry swept into Corners Country in 1868 in an effort to control the violence, they had to fight a series of pitched battles with guerilla bands that could muster as many as 500 riders led by Bob Lee, Benjamin Bickerstaff and other chieftains.

Ultimately, the Klan and others who fought to reinstate de facto slavery and wrest control of Texas from the Unionists were largely successful. The Union Army stepped in to enforce laws governing elections and voting, and for a brief period in 1868 the strategy seemed to be working. In the Fannin County election for the legislature that year, several hundred new black voters turned out at the polls, and the Republican candidate was elected by a landslide. The Klan and the Fannin County Democratic club stepped up their efforts to intimidate the newly freed slaves, and by the next year turnout dropped by 418 voters, mostly black, and the Democratic candidate won a narrow victory. Statewide that year, a Republican governor and legislature took office with the help of a minority of white voters and overwhelming support from blacks. However, by 1871, the year that Will Rice turned 12 years old, the Democrats were back in power and busily dismantling the fragile and temporary gains made by the former slaves.

The mythical story of Texas during Reconstruction told by many white Texans, the story bequeathed to Will Rice as a child, and to Will's son John, and even to me in the 1950s, was summed up by an editorial in the *Democratic Statesman* in the fall of 1873. The real problems of the people of Texas, said the newspaper, were created by the Republicans who dominated the 1870-71 legislature, a body made up of "reckless Northern carpet-baggers, dirty Southern scalawags, and poor ignorant negroes, who were the mere tools of others, and all together commenced a system of extravagance, appropriation, and pillage, previously unknown."

The reality was far different from the rhetoric attached to the myth. In fact, blacks were a tiny minority in both houses of the state legislature—only two blacks sat in the Senate and they constituted 10 percent of the House membership. The concerns of the black legislators were to protect the civil rights of blacks and to initiate a state-supported educational system, understandably enough. Otherwise, the vast majority of the Republican members of the legislature and all the Democrats were native white Texans; there were no "carpetbaggers" from the Northern states in the House, and only two in the Senate. The programs of Republican Governor Davis included: establishing civil order and stability in the state; investing in roads and railroads to spur economic growth, building institutions for the deaf, the blind, and the mentally ill; and promoting public education. All of Davis' social programs were overturned when the Democrats retook power, black voting was severely restricted, and the antebellum social order was largely reestablished.

The myth was important, though. It connected Texans to the Lost Cause. It framed their opposition to the Republicans and to the North as noble, courageous, and in service to democracy and the Constitution. It justified a further century of segregation and discrimination, a broad-based denial of human rights and opportunity for millions of black people.

Powerful white politicians attempted to tar the reputation of the Texas Republican administration with accusations of malfeasance, corruption and deceit. Governor Davis and the legislature had approved a substantial increase in spending to build school buildings across the state and furnish the students with slate boards on which to write. The Democrats charged that the purpose of the expenditure was to make school administrators wealthy and build a political machine to subjugate Texans. Investigations proved the rumors false, but they were repeated as the truth for decades afterward.

Extreme violence by the Klan and other ex-Confederate organizations against the freedmen and Unionists in Walker and Hill Counties led the governor to declare martial law; the Democrats then charged that Davis had violated the state constitution by suspending the writ of *habeas corpus* and by trying citizens before military tribunals. No evidence existed of the governor actually abusing his power, but Democratic newspapers used the language of a political apocalypse to assault the governor. The *Democratic Statesman* criticized the taxing policies of the Davis administration, and then announced, "We are fully impressed with the conviction that constitutional government in this State is in danger of utter extermination, and that the cause of human rights and civil liberty were never in greater peril."

Combined with aggressive assaults on the Republicans during the 1871 campaign, Democratic clubs and groups of Klansmen aimed violence at black communities across the state in order to scare those voters away from the polls. In Bastrop County in May, masked men destroyed a black church being used as a school, whipped one of the teachers, and then burned a schoolhouse. The attackers told witnesses they were hunting for "negro school teachers, mean negroes, and radicals." Local police arrested the men, but a local grand jury refused to bring indictments.[46]

In 1871 the campaign of lies, terror, and intimidation of black voters was a success. Black voters in Texas simply disappeared from the polls, and the Democrats swept the elections for Congress. Within two years the Democrats in Texas had an unbreakable lock on the legislature and all statewide offices, and most of the gains in the areas of civil rights, social justice, education, and tax reform had been turned back.

By 1873, the Klan had largely disbanded in Fannin County, in Corners Country, and across the state of Texas. Its services were no longer needed.

When the Rice family relocated to Texas during the war, they left their Presbyterianism behind; eventually, Will Rice experienced a conversion and joined a Baptist church. The first Baptist missionaries had reached Texas in 1812 in company with the first white American settlers who crossed the Red River. By 1848, there still were only 950 Baptists in the state, 250 of them black slaves. Baptists were a somewhat radical sect in those days. They believed that blacks and whites were all the children of God, equal in the sight and judgment of God, and equally deserving of salvation, so Baptist missionaries were sent out to both the slaves and to the whites. Many of the early white missionaries were deeply opposed to slavery, and believed that Christianizing the slaves was the first step toward abolishing slavery. They saw their work as uplifting both the soul and the body. Their religion was naturally egalitarian, and black and white Baptists attended the same churches together, with slaves and slave owners sitting in different benches or on opposite sides of the aisle. More than any other denomination, the Baptists were firm advocates of the separation of church and state; they insisted on strict equality between different religious sects. Their tireless missionary efforts bore fruit, and by 1860 a solid majority of white and black Texan churchgoers were Baptists, a smaller number were Methodists, and smaller numbers were represented in other sects.

The biographer of Rufus Burleson, one of the first Baptist preachers in Texas and long-time president of Baylor University, wrote, "The depressed and languishing condition of the country during the years immediately succeeding the War Between the States, was a supreme crisis in the history of every interest in Texas. During that bloody period services in hundreds of churches were suspended and never resumed. The doors to innumerable schoolhouses were closed and never reopened. Plans for thousands of religious, educational, and industrial enterprises were formulated that never materialized. Church edifices and school buildings decayed and finally fell into ruin."[47]

In Fannin County, where the Rice family settled, residents had been holding camp meeting revivals since 1840, but the first church, Rehobeth Chapel, wasn't built until 1850. By the mid-60s there were still only three other churches in the county, two of them Baptist and one Methodist.[48] Over the two decades before the war, as the cotton plantations grew in scope and the slave system was firmly implanted in the state, white Baptists gradually changed their theology to accord with the economic interests of the slaveholders. By 1860 white Baptists in Texas were claiming that God had ordained slavery as the natural ordering of human affairs, and it was the job of white Christians to lead their black brothers and sisters toward God through the civilizing influence of the church.

Immediately after the war, blacks separated from white churches to start their own thriving churches. Tens of thousands of freedmen joined the new black Baptist churches, which quickly became the most important centers of community life in black townships and rural villages. Whites accused these churches of being spawning grounds for social and political discontent, which they undoubtedly were. Black resistance to the Klan's violence and the attempts by white politicians to deprive blacks of civil rights and access to education was centered in the black churches. Individual white Baptists were ambivalent toward black Baptists. Many were suspicious of the danger they thought the blacks posed to white interests, and many still viewed the blacks as little better than jungle animals who were aping their betters. However, many white Baptists, although they had supported or fought for the Confederacy, seemed to genuinely desire the education and uplifting of blacks.

By 1887 there were approximately 180,000 white Baptists in Texas and over 70,000 black Baptists with their own separate institutions—colleges and secondary schools and churches—in every corner of the state.

Rufus Burleson, the white president of Baylor University who headed the Baptist Committee on Colored Population, said in 1889, "To the statesman, the race problem, or the destiny of the colored people, increases daily in importance. But to the Christian the salvation of these people involves a responsibility of transcendent importance. We rejoice that the glorious work of evangelizing and educating these people is advancing rapidly."

Black Baptists were doubtless happy to have help, but the former slaves were suspicious of white motives and used their churches to build their own community leadership and strongly shared spirituality, and to consolidate their freedom. From the beginning, black churches had both a religious mission and a mission of social justice. Black progress in 19th century Texas depended on the black church, just as the civil rights movement of the 1950s and 60s would germinate and blossom in black churches.

By 1877, the Rice family had moved a few miles from Savoy to the Fannin County seat of Bonham. Will Rice was 18 years old when he came down with a wasting disease that almost killed him. He coughed chronically, spit up blood, and suffered pain in his chest. He couldn't sleep at night, endured endless fevers, and lost energy to do more than lie in bed for weeks. The doctor provided a diagnosis of galloping consumption, a disease known today as tuberculosis. In the absence of modern antibiotic medicines, Will somehow survived and began working his way back toward health. The doctor advised him to sleep out of doors and try to breathe clean dry air, so when he was able, Will said goodbye to his family and traveled a few counties farther west to find work on a cattle ranch.

Within a few years, Will returned to Gainesville in Cooke County, about 10 miles from the Red River and within easy distance of Bonham. By his 25th year, Will Rice had settled down to marry his sweetheart, Katie Pittman, and they soon had a boy and a girl, Jesse and Jimmie. Will made a living for his little family by doing some work for area ranchers and by trading horses, for which he seemed to have a real knack.

In 1889, five years after their marriage, Katie was pregnant with their third child. One day Will was out working and Katie was at home alone. She spotted some Indians riding toward the house, and knew they must have crossed the Red River into Texas from Indian Territory in Oklahoma. Assuming they meant to harm her, she panicked and tried to escape out a back window of the house. In her fall, both she and her unborn child were killed.

Will was left with his grief and with two young children to take care of. He moved himself and his children in to live with his brother George and sister-in-law Gertrude in Decatur. A few months later, Gertrude urged Will to attend a few services of a revival meeting in the First Baptist Church of Gainesville. He had always been a wheeler-dealer, looking out for opportunities to make money any way he could, including horse trading, and he was starting to feel guilty about some of his methods. Will attended the revival, and one evening during the service the evangelist said, "All horse traders are crooked and they'll go to Hell if they don't repent!"

Gertrude was indignant and in tears because of what the preacher had said, and felt bad because she had urged Will to go to the revival meeting, only to have him be insulted there. Will, however, looked at his sister-in-law and said, "I'm sorry, but it's true. Every horse trader is a crook."

In the middle of the night, in the depths of guilt and despair, Will asked Jesus to save him and finally found peace. Early the next morning the janitor found Will Rice sitting on the front steps of the First Baptist Church waiting for the sunrise service so he could tell the world about his conversion.

Will soon felt called by God to become a preacher. He spent a year at Baylor University Academy in Waco, Texas, a Baptist school where he got his first real education of any kind. Sometime during that year he met a young school teacher named Sarah Laprade, known as Sallie or

Sadie, from the little Cooke County village of Callisburg and developed
something more than a mere acquaintance with her. Both of the young
people were "visiting" various friends, but neither was truly in a serious
courtship.

In the fall of 1891 he asked his sister to take care of his children, and
he headed off to Louisville, Kentucky to study at the Southern Baptist
Theological Seminary. While there, Will corresponded with Sadie. In
October she found a way to gently express both her affectionate ambition
to be his "best girl," and the Christian faith she shared with him—a
thoughtful way to remind him that she would be a good wife for a
Baptist preacher!

> You don't know how glad I was, to hear from you, and
> to hear that you was well pleased with your school. I do
> hope that a course through the Seminary will be a great
> benefit to you. Oh! I see someone coming in a buggie!
> ...Mr. Rice, I have just returned from a singing in
> Callisburg. Mrs. Evans showed me where, she said, your
> best girl friend lived in town. I believe she said it was
> Miss Lewis. I know you will not mind telling me if it is
> so; I know I am too inquisitive, but please don't think
> too hard of me, I thought if she was your "best girl," you
> would not mind telling me, as you and I have promised
> to be friends. Mr. Rice, I do pray you may be studious,
> and that you may do all the good that you can, in our
> Blessed Master's cause. How good it is to have a blessed
> Savior who will forgive all our sins if we will only ask
> him. When you are pondering over your studies in the
> school room think of one down here in Texas who is
> thinking of you every day. I remain as ever your friend,
> Sallie Laprade.[49]

During the 1880s, Will's father James Porter Rice and other family
members had moved to Parker County, Texas. In 1892 while Will was
off at seminary, James Porter Rice died at the age of 76 and was buried
in the Greenwood City Cemetery in Weatherford.

In 1893, after a year at seminary, Will moved back to Cooke County,
Texas to be with his children. He started work again as a farmer, served
as pastor of a little church in the Vilot Community outside of
Gainesville, and married Sadie, who bore five children over the next
eight years. The second of those children was John R. Rice, a boy with a

cherubic face who appeared in an early photo with an earnest expression and sizable ears.

In 1901, Sadie's youngest baby, Porter, died. After a year's bout with tuberculosis Sadie herself died, leaving behind an emotionally devastated and poverty-stricken family with several children, including John, who was only six at the time. John and his brothers and sisters were playing with a little red wagon and some dolls in the ravine near the farmhouse of their Uncle Tom and Aunt Nannie, near Red River in Cooke County, Texas, when Cousin Georgia came to tell the children to hurry to the house. There they found their father Will and the rest of the family gathered around Sadie's bed. Fifteen-year-old Jesse, child of Will's first marriage, was sobbing into his crossed arms, and six-year-old John, Uncle Tom and his wife Nannie with their three children were there.

The only one not weeping was Sadie, who turned to her cousin Georgia and said, "Georgia, sing and play for me?" Georgia asked, "What should I sing, Aunt Sadie?" and Sadie answered, "Sing "How Firm a Foundation." Cousin Georgia went to the small pump organ in the corner and sang with a voice choked by a mixture of the desolation of her loss and of her own hope of Heaven:

> How firm a foundation,
> Ye saints of the Lord,
> Is laid for your faith
> In His excellent Word.

Sadie's long, black, braided hair framed her head on the pillow. She clapped her hands during the singing and said, "Praise the Lord!" Then she lifted up her hands and looked toward Heaven, smiling, seeing already the golden streets, seeing already her baby Porter in the arms of Jesus and reaching out to them, going to meet them.

Half a century later, in one of John R. Rice's sermons, he told the story of her death:

> I remember the November day when we lay her body
> away. My father knelt beside the open grave. There was
> no white muslin to hide the raw dirt of the grave—like a
> wound in the earth. No fake, manmade carpet of grass
> was thrown over the clods. My father put one arm
> around his two little orphan girls and one around his two
> little boys, and watched as they lowered the precious
> body in its dark casket into the bosom of Mother Earth.

> The rain beat down upon us, and a friendly neighbor held an umbrella over our heads.[50]

In that paragraph is the core of the grief that remained with John R. Rice throughout his life, and that fueled his passion to win souls to Jesus. It was an impulse toward redemption, sacrifice, and love, and what he thought of as Heaven itself, in the most literal sense.

The death of Sadie Rice deeply marked the whole family. Her eldest son John grew up with the intense sadness and loneliness of a boy who had the love and care of his mother for too short a time and who needed it all the more. As he reported many times in his sermons, his own longing and love for her was a vital factor in his compassion for lost sinners, his drive to spread the Gospel around the world, his desire to win millions to Jesus, and his capacity to understand the sadness and suffering of others. An old photograph of Sadie with four of the children shows a serious, good-looking woman whose features are remarkably well reflected in the face of her son John. After Sadie's death, Will must have been reminded of his second wife every time he looked at young John.

Chapter 8
Searching for God in a New Century

> *"The Lord will punish the world by fire and by his*
> *sword. He will judge the earth, and many will be killed*
> *by him. Those who 'consecrate' and 'purify' themselves*
> *in a sacred garden with its idol in the center—feasting*
> *on pork and rats and other detestable meats—will come*
> *to a terrible end, says the Lord."*—Isaiah 66:16-17

In January of 1966 I turned 16 and began a slide into rage and despair that lasted for several years. Everything turned topsy-turvy for me. I rapidly lost my faith in the God I saw worshipped in the fundamentalist community I had grown up in. I had seen white people who claimed to be good "Christians" walk out of our little Baptist church in Millington, Tennessee rather than sit in the same building with a black man on a Sunday morning. I had seen white children in my segregated Tennessee school, most of whom came from families claiming to be "Christian," violently attacking two little black children who tried to integrate the school. I had seen self-professed "Christians" expressing contempt for the very idea of alleviating poverty in America. I had heard so-called "Christian" military and political leaders proposing that the U.S. bomb the dikes and dams along the Red River delta in Vietnam in order to "defeat Communism," thus potentially killing hundreds of thousands of Vietnamese people. I began asking myself, what sort of religion would justify such arrogance and criminality?

I started having arguments with various people in my church about these terrible things that they believed "God" was in favor of. Soon I began to believe that this "God" couldn't exist at all. I couldn't imagine that a God who was essentially good and loving might possibly be in favor of racial segregation, mass murder, and social injustice.

A book I read compulsively was one sent to me by my grandmother Lloys Rice for my birthday in 1966. The title was *In His Steps: What Would Jesus Do?* Her letter to me, written in her quavery longhand with a No. 2 pencil, said, "Andy, I want you to have this book because I think you will think highly of it. Your granddad read this book when he was a teenager just as you are now. He loved it and found it inspiring. The story in this book is one of the reasons he became a preacher. After you read it I hope you will tell me what you think of it! Your loving grandmother."

In His Steps: What Would Jesus Do?, by Charles Sheldon, was published in 1896. It was a novel that began with a stranger arriving at the door of a church in the fictional town of Raymond, looking for help. He was a shabby tramp with a faded hat, poor and homeless, hungry and unemployed. He had lost his job, his wife had died gasping for breath in a filthy tenement, and he himself was fatally ill. He had looked for help, or even for a kind word, all over this small town full of people who called themselves Christians, and had found none. So he came to church on Sunday morning and issued a challenge to the Christians there:

> It seems to me there's an awful lot of trouble in the world that somehow wouldn't exist if all the people who sing such songs [about following Jesus] went and lived them out. I suppose I don't understand. But what would Jesus do? Is that what you mean by following His steps? It seems to me sometimes as if the people in the big churches had good clothes and nice houses to live in, and money to spend for luxuries, and could go away on summer vacations and all that, while the people outside the churches, thousands of them, I mean, die in tenements, and walk the streets for jobs, and never have a piano or a picture in the house, and grow up in misery and drunkenness and sin.[51]

Within a week, the stranger had died, leaving his small daughter in the care of the congregation, and leaving the pastor of the church, Reverend Henry Maxwell, to voice the most existentially critical question that confronts any true Christian: "What would Jesus do?" Reverend Maxwell looked out at the congregation of the First Church of Raymond that Sunday and said:

> The appearance and words of this stranger in the church last Sunday made a very powerful impression on me. I

am not able to conceal from you or myself the fact that what he said, followed as it has been by his death in my house, has compelled me to ask as I never asked before: 'What does following Jesus mean?' I am not in a position yet to utter any condemnation of this people or, to a certain extent, of myself, either in our Christ-like relations to this man or the numbers that he represents in the world. But all that does not prevent me from feeling that much that the man said was so vitally true that we must face it in an attempt to answer it or else stand condemned as Christian disciples.[52]

If there were a true religion, I thought to myself when I read the book my grandmother gave me, it would have this question at the heart of it. If there were a true community of believers, this is how they would express their faith. But for me in 1966 the contradiction between the doctrines and the deeds of some people who claimed to be the only "true" Christians was too apparent and painful to sustain my belief in any God whatsoever. I crashed out into the wilderness of unbelief.

According to my grandmother, the young John R. Rice read Sheldon's book with a passion equal to mine, but with different results. This, John thought in 1915 when he read Sheldon's book, was a question that could guide his whole life. He wanted to be a true Christian, following the true Christ and living as Jesus himself would have lived.

He wasn't alone in his desire. The few decades leading up to the entry of the U.S. into the Great War saw a Third Great Awakening, another huge wave of spiritual revival that called on Americans to bring their Christian beliefs to life. This new movement was marked by a massive expansion of Christian churches and missions, by swelling membership rolls in the major Protestant denominations—especially the Methodists and the Baptists—and a radically diverse set of theological ideas and movements. Increasing numbers of Christians were concerned not just with the ultimate and eternal destination of human souls but with the quality of human life on earth. Evangelical thinkers and leaders noticed the profound social problems of a rapidly growing population in the throes of transformation. Masses of immigrants from a score of European countries were flooding into the United States, fleeing poverty, anti-Semitic pogroms, religious intolerance, or violent conflict. By the early 1900s, several thousand immigrants per day were being processed through the immigration station on Ellis Island in New York Harbor, and at the height of the boom in 1907 over a million people flooded through its cavernous brick processing hall. And as the country became transformed into a world-class industrial power in the decades between the Civil War in the U.S. and the Great War in Europe, millions of people moved from the countryside to the cities to take jobs in mills and factories.

The revolutionary changes in the economy were accompanied by vast dislocations and deep social problems of poverty, racial injustice, and poor living conditions. Millions of families were crowded into filthy and decrepit housing or faced homelessness and starvation.

In the face of such suffering, Christians such as Reverend Maxwell proclaimed the Social Gospel. Preachers of the Social Gospel launched movements to end the practice of child labor, enforce compulsory elementary education, protect women against exploitation in factories, and prohibit alcohol. Advocates of the Social Gospel emphasized the importance of discipleship—learning from and living the example of Jesus, his compassion and care for the poor and the dispossessed, the love that infused his life and ministry.

As the Presbyterians said in a denominational resolution, "The great ends of the church are the proclamation of the gospel for the salvation of humankind; the shelter, nurture, and spiritual fellowship of the children of God; the maintenance of divine worship; the preservation of truth; the promotion of social righteousness; and the exhibition of the Kingdom of Heaven to the world."[53]

This understanding of the "Kingdom of Heaven" was quite down-to-earth, actually. It was no pie-in-the-sky promise of golden streets and expensive celestial real estate. Instead, it was rooted in a practical concern for justice on earth, and it implied that Christians were accountable to God for behaving with compassion and motivated to offer loving service to their fellow humans.

It was also entirely within the mainstream of 19th century evangelical Christian thinking. Evangelicals believed that in the sight of God all were equally sinners in need of salvation, all equally redeemed by the death and resurrection of Jesus, all in need of divine grace. The evangelical belief in the "universal priesthood of believers" implied that among Christians there was no hierarchy, no justifiable distinction among people of different races, different classes, or different sexes, and there could be no interposition of a priest of the church between believers and their God. The Protestant reformation, in the eyes of many evangelicals, implied a social and political revolution as well.

For more than 100 years, indeed, dating back to the 1700s, evangelical Christians had cultivated a tradition of working to bring about the Kingdom of God on earth and of confronting social injustice.

John Wesley, the founder of Methodism and the most eloquent and influential evangelical preacher of the 18th century, fought to shorten the work day and remove abuses and oppression in factories and mines, supported the self-organization of workers into unions, created orphanages, and supported laws to protect children and women and end poverty. Wesley was the most prominent and passionate opponent of slavery in his time, declaring to slave merchants: "You are the spring that puts all the rest in motion—captains, slave owners, kidnappers, murderers…Thy brother's blood crieth unto thee…Thy hands, thy bed, thy furniture, thy house, thy lands are at present stained with blood…whether you are a Christian or not, show yourself a man; be not more savage than a lion or a bear."[54] It was the work of all true Christians, Wesley urged, to act as instruments of God for the suppression of slavery.

Although Wesley was not a pacifist, he was deeply opposed to war, which he said was "a horrid reproach to the Christian name, yea, to the name of man, to all reason and humanity…When war breaks out, God is forgotten…So long as this monster stalks uncontrolled, where is reason, virtue, humanity? They are utterly excluded."[55]

Influenced by Wesley and the revival movement, Englishman William Wilberforce led the successful movement to abolish slavery throughout the British Empire. Fellow Englishman Charles Spurgeon was a fierce opponent of social injustice, especially slavery, and joined other evangelicals in crusades to eliminate poverty, hunger, and homelessness, especially for children. In the U.S., Charles G. Finney was a key leader of the abolition movement for decades in the 19th century. This concern for social justice reverberated down through the decades, giving birth to the Prohibition movement that began to gather steam in the years before the Great War. The unrestricted use of alcohol was often at the root of sins both individual and collective. The uncontrolled consumption of whiskey, wine, and beer led to addiction, to family violence, and to irresponsible or criminal behavior, and these led to poverty, to prison, and to the poorhouse.

The evangelical tradition itself arose from the 18th century movement that came to be known as the Enlightenment. The philosophers, religious leaders, and political thinkers of the Enlightenment had declared freedom and democracy to be the principle values of human society, and reason to be the source of all authority. The Enlightenment promoted a vigorous public life, an emphasis on rational discourse as the path to truth, and an embrace of the scientific method. Leaders such as Benjamin Franklin, James Madison, and Thomas Jefferson considered the ideas of the Enlightenment to be the very foundation of the new American republic, and documents such as the Declaration of Independence to be the height of Enlightenment thinking.

In the first sentence of Immanuel Kant's essay *What is Enlightenment?*, published in 1784 just three years before the adoption of the U.S. Constitution, the German philosopher defined enlightenment as "man's emergence from his self-incurred immaturity." Enlightenment, Kant suggested, required the courage to think for ourselves, to use God-given powers of reason, intellect, and wisdom to understand our world and chart our actions. Kant attacked the view that any religious synod or presbytery should be able to "commit itself by oath to a certain unalterable set of doctrines," because such a contract would prevent "all further enlightenment of mankind forever." For humankind to gain wisdom and maturity, human individuals must be free to use their powers of reason to question and critique any religious doctrine.

The heart of enlightenment was, Kant said, the ability to question religious orthodoxy. From this application of human reason grew the ability to create democratic governments, to develop our understanding of the natural world, and to place increasing human knowledge at the service of human progress.

Though most Enlightenment philosophers rejected rigid or dogmatic religious thinking, they did not reject religion—and neither did Kant. As Dorinda Outram points out, "One way out was Deism, with its total hostility to revelation. Another was to reject the attempt to make Christianity 'reasonable', and return to a view of religion which emphasized faith, trust in revelation, and personal witness to religious experience."[56]

A majority of colonial Americans were either Protestants or unaffiliated with any church. However, many of the leaders of the American Revolution and signers of its Constitution such as Thomas Jefferson and Benjamin Franklin were Deists, along with James Madison, John Adams, and possibly Thomas Paine, Ethan Allen, and Alexander Hamilton. Most Deists believed in a supreme being who had created the universe along with the natural laws that governed it, but who then took a relatively hands-off approach to human affairs. The supreme being of the Deists could be apprehended by practical investigation and the use of reason to understand natural laws. Religious faith was not needed, nor were miracles, divine inspiration, or personal revelations of God's spirit.

The alternative to Deism was a more profoundly personal religious experience such as that offered by the revivalism of the Great Awakenings. The explosion of churches and membership in the new

Methodist and Baptist sects was directly connected with the personal freedom and personal responsibility demanded by the Age of Enlightenment. The evangelicals were both religious revolutionaries and political revolutionaries. They were in "enthusiastic" rebellion against the stultifying formalism of the Church of England, demanding a direct relationship with God unmediated by the hierarchy of the established church. And, along with the Deists, the evangelicals demanded an absolute right to freedom of religion and conscience as enshrined in the First Amendment to the U.S. Constitution.

While the Enlightenment supported a profound expansion of human freedom, it also led paradoxically to the theological certainty that would be required by Christian fundamentalism. Evangelicals held up historic Christian beliefs as the sole standard of orthodoxy, and they saw the Bible itself as an Enlightenment text and the source of authority for Christians. The Bible was to be understood as the inspired word of God. Read the Bible, they said, and apply your God-given faculties of prayerful inquiry and reason. In the pages of the Bible you would learn all you might learn about the nature of God, the depravity of man, the atoning death and resurrection of Jesus, and the coming end of the world. In the Bible you would learn about God's plans to transform the world, about God's love for the poor and oppressed, about God's righteousness and justice. However, the evangelicals of the Enlightenment believed that salvation was both social and individual. Salvation was required both for sinful human individuals and sin-wracked human society. And salvation depended upon a direct, personal experience of God, a direct revelation of the divine in human lives and human history.

Thus, a powerful contradiction lay at the very heart of evangelical Protestantism. The young John R. Rice opened himself to that tension when he read Charles Sheldon's book *In His Steps: What Would Jesus Do?*

On the one hand, Christians were called to a standard of personal holiness and concern for the salvation of individual souls. Sheldon challenged Christians to "live in a simple, plain manner, without needless luxury...preach fearlessly to the hypocrites in the church no matter what their social importance or wealth...engage in business for the purpose of glorifying God and not making money...save souls from the infernal sulphur of the lowest hell."

On the other hand, Christians were called to rescue society itself from the earthly hells of poverty, degradation, misery, disease, and desperation. Sheldon urged Christians to "give their talents to the poor and wretched of the city...show in some practical form sympathy and love for the common people as well as for the well to do, educated, refined people…identify with the great causes of humanity…love and rescue the poor, the degraded, the abandoned."

In the century after Sheldon's book was published, however, many evangelical Christians would find themselves pulled toward one of two alternatives: Did following Jesus require a joint focus on both individual salvation and on serving the poor, on social righteousness and social justice? Or did following Jesus mean limiting one's concern to the salvation of individual souls? An impending struggle over Christian doctrine would lead fundamentalists toward abandoning social justice and instead concentrating on saving souls.

Part III
Launching the Fundamentalist Movement

Chapter 9
Damned and Saved in Dundee

"I saw (in a vision) a hand in Heaven with a sword, upon which was written, 'The sword of the Lord will descend on the Earth swiftly and soon!' and over the hand was written, 'True and just are the judgments of the Lord.'"—Girolamo Savonarola of Florence, Italy in a sermon predicting the end of the world and the downfall of the ruling Medici family before his death by hanging for heresy in 1498

At the age of five, I walked down the middle aisle in the Calvary Baptist Church in Wheaton, Illinois to get saved. My granddad was preaching that Sunday night, and I was very clear about what I needed to get saved from and how to do it. I was a poor lost sinner. I had committed a number of serious crimes in my short life, including at least one occasion of lying to my mother about whether I had taken a Saturday night bath, multiple times when I had been mean to my baby brother Johnny, one instance of stealing a Mars bar from the popcorn store on Front Street, and many, many instances of running around hollering outside the church after Sunday evening services when I had been instructed to be quiet and dignified. I clearly deserved to writhe in the flames of Hell forever. So I was ready for my dad to lead me to the Lord.

We knelt at the altar, and with Dad's help I prayed: "Dear Jesus, I know I am a poor lost sinner. I know that you died on the cross for me. So please come into my heart and take away my sins so I can go to be with you in Heaven. Amen. And thank you, Jesus."

That was it! Salvation was the simplest possible thing! Jesus was in my heart, and I had nothing more to fear from anyone or anything! I went home that night with a feeling of complete joy and perfect peace about the world. I was saved, and nothing could take salvation away from me.

My most important possession as a child was that feeling of utter security in my world. God and his love for me was everywhere: outside our kitchen in the lilac bush with its sweet purple blossoms; spinning in the rubber tires of my bicycle; in the touch of my mother's hands as she shampooed my hair every Saturday night before Sunday morning church; even in the basement of our ancient house within the hellish orange flames behind the door of our coal-fired furnace. Jesus walked with me, invisibly, as I trundled my red Western Flyer wagon all over our neighborhood in Wheaton to deliver copies of the *Chicago Daily News* to my customers. I knew that nothing and no one could truly hurt me, and that God truly loved me. Whenever I was afraid or feeling the oppressive weight of the darkness outside of the protective circle of love in which I lived, I recited the Twenty-Third Psalm: "Yea, though I walk through the valley of the shadow of death, I will fear no evil: for thou art with me; thy rod and thy staff they comfort me…Surely goodness and mercy shall follow me all the days of my life: and I will dwell in the house of the Lord forever."

The world was not as secure for my great grandfather Will Rice and his children after the loss of his wife Sadie. Will Rice was forty-two years old when Sadie died. He had now lost two wives to illness, and faced the prospect of raising the five remaining children alone while struggling to keep the farm outside Gainesville going. According to family photographs, Will was a handsome man, well-built, maybe six feet tall. He had a ready grin but not a lot of discipline. After Sadie's death, Will went from one project or deal-making attempt to the next. He had set out to be a preacher and he preached on occasion, as Sadie had doubtless wanted him to, although not with the deep and abiding passion she would have preferred. His son John later said, "My father would get so interested in making money that he would give up the ministry. When this happened, God made sure that he lost everything he had; then he would go back to preaching."[57]

Despite his inconstancy as a preacher, Will Rice was keenly interested in "the things of the Lord." After Sadie died he sometimes filled in the pulpit at one of the nearby Baptist churches. Whenever a traveling evangelist came through town to hold revival services in a church or in a tent on the big open field on the outskirts of Gainesville, the evangelist was invariably invited out to the Rice farm for a chicken dinner with cornbread and greens. Dinner was followed by hours of discussion and debate about God and the Bible, with its stories and doctrines, heroes and villains—a discussion preceded by and capped with long collective prayers, divine pleading, political gossip, and always a humorous story or two.

Young John grew up hearing those sermons and dinner table conversations and was as educated theologically as any young Texan might have been. The first book read to him was probably the Bible. The first public speech he heard may have been a sermon on the inescapable human choice between a Heaven in which saints walked down golden streets and a Hell in which smoke-wreathed sinners screamed in eternal agony. The first song he may have learned was a revival hymn beseeching him to repent of his sins: "Just as I am, and waiting not to rid my soul of one dark blot. To Thee whose blood can cleanse each spot, O Lamb of God, I come, I come."

Early in life John developed an acute understanding of his own sinful nature and the doom toward which he was headed, and he was receptive to the adjurations of various preachers toward the salvation of his soul. When he was nine, John attended a service at the First Baptist Church of Gainesville, where Pastor A.B. Ingram preached on the parable of the prodigal son—a passage of scripture used for almost two millennia to awaken a horror of riotous behavior, dissolute living, and sinful depravity, as well as a corresponding desire for repentance and forgiveness.

Although John hadn't had time yet in his young life to sink into such a gutter as the prodigal son had, he was a sensitive child and could easily imagine descending to such depths, and knew he deserved Hell as much. At the end of Pastor Ingram's sermon, John went forward to ask Jesus for salvation and seek assurance that his sins were forgiven. The pastor asked John to sit off to the side while he counseled the adults who had come, and John went home without being able to talk to anyone about his terrible feelings of guilt and his longing to be saved.

When John later asked to be baptized and join the church, his father dismissed him with a few words: "When you are old enough to really repent of your sins and be regenerated, then will be time enough to join the church." The subject was dropped, clearly not to be raised again soon.

John was left to stew. Was he really saved after all? Had he really been too young to be saved? Would he really escape Hell if he were to die in his sins? The boy endured agonies of self-doubt and tremors of fear that he might never see his mother in Heaven with Jesus, that he might die in his sins before his father deemed him old enough to be truly repentant and truly saved. He had no friend or family member to whom he could turn for loving counsel or assurance that he might escape an eternity in Hell. In later years, John remembered: "I sat stricken and silent before my father. I did not know what all those big words meant— repentance and regeneration and more. I simply knew my father did not think I was saved! Well, I thought my father was the wisest man in the world and a preacher, besides; and if he thought I was not saved, I supposed I was not…I wish I could tell you all the sadness and disappointment of the next three years."[58]

From a purely practical point of view, Will Rice couldn't afford to remain a single parent for long. He had five children to care for, feed, and clothe while he scraped to earn a living in any way he could. When he wasn't preaching, he farmed and ranched sporadically, traded livestock and land and anything else he thought he could make a profit on. He seemed to have boundless energy, unlimited ideas, big plans, and a certain charming foolhardiness. On several occasions he got involved in business deals and speculations in which he either made a lot of money or lost a lot of money. He invariably ended up poor and returned to farming and preaching. Life was desperately hard for the family. Will often found his finances short and resources strained. He was forced to give up his oldest daughter Jimmie, from his first marriage, to be raised by his sister's family.

In 1905, Will moved his family 120 miles south to join his older brother on the newly acquired 6,000 acre Rice Ranch four miles outside the town of Dundee, with a population of about 300. There they lived in a plain little box house out in the country. Soon the 46-year-old Will married again, this time to Dolous Bellah, the daughter of a nearby rancher. Dolous was two decades younger than Will. She was a handsome young woman and an excellent horseback rider who knew almost as much about farming as Will did. The two made a good match as friends and companions, but Dolous had little interest in being a replacement mother for John and the other children. She lacked domestic inclinations, and often left food and dishes on the table from an earlier meal, simply brushing leftover food and mouse droppings off the table when she served the next meal.

With Will and Dolous focusing their attention on the farm and each other, there wasn't much love left over for young John or his siblings. He found himself left alone much of the time and expected to work like an adult on his assigned chores. He started early in the morning and kept busy till late in the day. He fed and watered chickens and cows, horses and mules. He hoed and planted and weeded in the vegetable garden, painted the barn, cleaned out the earthen pond where they stored water, and hauled water to the cistern at the house. He got help hooking up the six-mule team to the long grain drill, but then the nine-year-old was expected to drive the mules by himself for miles across the flat Texas prairie under the torrid sun dropping seed-grain into the furrows.

In December of 1905, just after John's 10th birthday, Will hitched the horses to the wagon and loaded his family into it—Dolous, and John's brother George and sisters Gertrude and Ruth—and headed off down the dirt road for a Christmas trip to visit family members 118 miles away in Weatherford. All except John made the trip. As the oldest boy, John was assigned to stay behind, feeding and caring for the animals. Christmastime, for several days each year, became for John the most sad and lonely time of the year, with no presents and little human company. *

For several years after John had walked the aisle to be saved at the Baptist church in Gainesville, he continued to be tormented by doubts about his own salvation. He told the story in a sermon years later:

> My mother had gone to Heaven and I was a motherless boy... I got no assurance about salvation. Again and again I prayed for God to save me. Once I asked a godly preacher to pray for me and he asked me to pray for myself. So that night when I got home from the little church, I went out into the horse's stall, knelt down and asked God to save me. Then I prepared for bed and knelt by the bed as I usually did for a good-night prayer and asked God to forgive my sins and save me. I felt no change. I did not have any glorious experience. I did not see any light shining round about me. I did not hear the

---

* When I first heard this story from two of my aunts and my mother—young John left by himself for several days each Christmas—I found it beyond belief, even though they all confirmed they had heard it from their father or mother several decades ago. I could barely imagine what the experience must have been like for the little boy who became my grandfather. The story is more believable now that I understand the harsh conditions of their lives, the extreme poverty of the family, and how the children were trained and expected to pitch in and work like adults as early in their lives as possible—picking cotton, hoeing the garden, or feeding the chickens. The family lived continually on the knife's edge of survival. One of the reasons so many babies were born into this and other families during that time was that so many children were expected to die. Will Rice may have believed he was helping his son to grow up and accept the responsibilities of a man; staying home with the stock at Christmastime was an opportunity for young John to shine. The emotional and psychological cost in loneliness, insecurity, and depression must have been high for John. And it was compounded by his fear of death and Hell—an unsaved boy confronting the terrors of solitude and unknown dangers in a little house under the arc of the great Texas skies.

flutter of angels' wings. No electricity came in at my head or went out at my fingers and toes! So I sadly went to bed with no assurance of salvation. Then I thought, Well, I had better settle this thing for good some way or other. So I got out of bed and prayed again [but still received no peace].[59]

John at last was deemed old enough to join the little Dundee Baptist Church and was asked to give his "experience" of becoming a Christian. He could only say, "I had thought about the matter a great deal, and I did not want to be a Methodist, so I had decided to be a Baptist!"

It was after the 12-year-old boy was baptized that he found a measure of security by reading a verse quoting Jesus in the book of John: "He that hears my word and believes on him that sent me hath everlasting life, and shall not come into condemnation but is passed from death into life." From that day, John had no more nightmares of being tormented forever in the flames of Hell when he died, and no more doubts that he would see his mother again in Heaven. He was saved and sure of it, and found a great peace.

Years later he said, "From that day to this I have never doubted for a moment that I am God's child. I know one thing beyond any doubt: when I trusted Jesus, depended on him to forgive me, he did! The word of God says so and that makes it so. On these promises I have hung the eternal welfare of my soul, and how sure, how unchanging is that blessed foundation for my faith!"

Chapter 10
Billy Sunday and the Premillennialists

"I've drawn the sword in the defense of God, home, wife, children and native land and I will never sheath it until the undertaker pumps me full of embalming fluid, and if my wife is still alive I think I shall call her to my bedside, and say, 'Nell, when I'm dead, you send for the butcher and skin me and have my hide tanned and made into drum heads and hire men to go up and down the line and beat those drums and say, 'My husband Billy Sunday still lives and gives the whiskey gang a run for its money.'"—Billy Sunday sermon opening a 1910 revival in Bellingham, Washington

The summer after I turned 12, C. B. "Red" Smith came to the Bill Rice Ranch and brought along Apostle the Premillennialist Horse. On the first night of the camp meeting in the open-air tabernacle at the Ranch, Brother Smith himself stepped up to the pulpit and led the singing for the first gospel song. He was a tall man with curly brown hair, a pink, whiskerless face, and laugh wrinkles around his eyes. He tilted back his head on the high notes and pointed his chin down at the floor on the low notes, and held back nothing.

"When we ALLLLL get to heaven," sang Brother Smith, "what a DAY of rejoicing that will BE! When we ALLLLL see Jesus, we'll SING and SHOUT the victorEEEEE!"

Sitting in the second row, I was fascinated by the way his throat quivered with vibrato when he held the long note at the end of each verse. I admired his glossy black cowboy boots with the fancy, rainbow-colored needlework, his pure white shirt with the embroidered loops on both pockets and silver buttons all up and down the front and on both sleeves, and his black string tie with silver tips dangling halfway down his chest

"We've got a guest speaker in the house tonight," said Brother Smith with a big grin that showed off a gold-capped tooth. "He's a good friend of mine, and he's come all the way from Jonesboro, Arkansas."

Brother Smith walked down the stairs at the corner of the platform and disappeared out the open side of the tabernacle into the parking lot. Heads craned to see where he was going, and a murmuring passed through the assembled young people. I could look out and just see the purplish mercury light down by the road alongside the tabernacle. A few moments passed, and Brother Smith walked back in leading a horse to the front of the tabernacle. The horse's large, wise blue eye rolled at me as he went past, his hooves clattering loudly on the concrete floor. Brother Smith led him up onto the platform next to the pulpit, and just as he got to the top of the stairs he nickered loudly, as if to announce his presence. I stood up and leaned over the pew so I could see. The horse stomped a forefoot on the platform and snorted loudly.

Apostle was grayish-white, with a long white tail and pointy ears that twitched back and forth. His eyes rolled around looking at Brother Smith and out across the congregation. He wore a bright red saddle blanket with a white cross on each side, and a gray canvas diaper on his rear, and his mane was combed and braided with silver ribbons.

"Please allow me to introduce Apostle the Premillennialist Horse," said Brother Smith with a twinkle in his eye. "Apostle, say hello to all the folks out here."

Apostle whinnied and rolled his eyeballs.

"All right now, Apostle," said Brother Smith, "what's our chapter and verse for tonight?"

Apostle tossed his head, then picked up his right forefoot and stomped deliberately, four times in a row. It sounded like someone chopping down a tree with an ax.

"Yes, sir," said Brother Smith.

Apostle shook his head, cocked his ears as if considering, then began stomping his foot again, with Brother Smith counting right along with him: "One, two, three...fourteen, fifteen, sixteen! Amen! So that's Thessalonians chapter four, verse sixteen, is it Apostle?

The horse nodded and nickered. Brother Smith ruffled the pages in his worn Bible, and read, "For the Lord himself shall descend from heaven with a shout, with the voice of the archangel and with the trump of God, and the dead in Christ shall rise first. Then we which are alive and remain shall be caught up together with them in the clouds to meet the Lord in the air. And so shall we ever be with the Lord!"

"Yes, sir," said Brother Smith. "So tonight, young people, we'll preach on the Second Coming of Jesus. I'll take Apostle to his trailer, and I'll be right back." Brother Smith and Apostle clomped down the stairs and back out through the side of the tabernacle and into the parking lot.

My great-uncle Bill Rice stepped up to the pulpit, waved to the woman seated at the piano, and launched into a spirited rendition of an old revival favorite: "Give me that old-time religion, give me that old-time religion, give me that old-time religion, it's good enough for me!"

The most famous evangelist of the early 20th century was the passionate and eloquent William Ashley "Billy" Sunday, a poor Iowa farm boy who made good playing professional baseball for the Chicago White Stockings. Billy Sunday was only an average hitter for the National League Champions and later for the Philadelphia Phillies, but he was a flamboyant player, popular with the fans. He dove for stunning catches in the outfield, ran the bases faster than almost anyone, and was quick with a memorable quote for the legions of sportswriters who crowded around him after a stellar performance. Sunday committed more than his share of errors on the field, but he consistently ranked among the top base stealers in the league.

When he quit major league baseball and emerged as an evangelist in the early 1890s, the news hit the front pages of newspapers across the country. Sunday spent a number of years learning the ropes and honing his pulpit skills and then launched his evangelistic career in 1897. He bought a big tent and began touring the country, speaking in revivals that lasted weeks and led to hundreds and then thousands of conversions. By 1908, Sunday had left his tent behind and was preaching to large and enthusiastic crowds in custom-built temporary tabernacles seating many thousands, and the next dozen years saw Sunday preaching in major cities across the country.

One of the first breakout Billy Sunday revivals with huge and sustained crowds was in Bellingham, Washington. It was there that the term "trail hitters" was first used to describe people who were "hitting the sawdust trail," walking the aisles at Sunday's invitation to indicate their public repentance and newfound Christianity. The term had a double meaning. The dirt floors of Sunday's hurriedly fabricated temporary tabernacles were covered with sawdust to hold down the dust and noise and keep the building clean and smelling sweet. A second meaning derived from the logging industry, for which Bellingham was a shipping center, where the massive logs from the old growth forests of the Cascades were trucked to be sent by boat to lumber mills all along the west coast.

When lumberjacks entered a forbidding primeval forest to mark a new territory for cutting, they sometimes took along a bag of sawdust, which they scattered along the unmarked forest floor to lay a trail they could use to retrace their steps to the sunlight. Billy's wife Nell, his business manager and partner in ministry, said: "In that country, that sawdust trail represents coming from what would have been a lost condition, from a dark, uninteresting and unsatisfactory place to back home, to light and comfort, and friends and family...As people started to go forward and take Billy's hand and accept the Lord Jesus Christ as their Savior, some man spoke aloud in the meeting and said, 'Oh, they're hitting the sawdust trail.'" The metaphor implied that lost sinners were moving from darkness to the light; from the shadows of the primeval forest toward the warmth and welcome of home.

Billy Sunday's crowds were massive by the standards of any age, and he made a great deal of money through his preaching. In 1915, when he preached in Philadelphia, over forty thousand people answered his invitation to walk the aisle for Jesus, and the Sunday campaign collected over $50,000 in offerings ($1 million in 2010 dollars). In Boston in 1917 he saw 64,000 people saved and the campaign collected $55,000. By the time Sunday reached New York City in 1917, he was among the most well-known and influential Americans of the age. When his private Pullman car pulled into Grand Central Terminal, he was greeted by a cheering, jubilant mob of over 5,000, and he was hosted and fêted by all the most powerful and influential people in the City. Over the 10 weeks of the crusade, Sunday preached to between one million and two million people, and over 98,000 hit the sawdust trail after one of his hundreds of sermons. When the Sundays left town the coffers of the campaign bulged with over $120,000 in "freewill offerings" ($2.4 million in 2010 dollars), and all the money was donated to support American soldiers fighting in World War I.

Sunday was charismatic, charming and pugnacious, funny and dramatic. In memorable sermons, he said, "Listen, I'm against sin. I'll kick it as long as I've got a foot, I'll fight it as long as I've got a fist, I'll butt it as long as I've got a head, and I'll bite it as long as I've got a tooth. And when I'm old, fistless, footless and toothless, I'll gum it till I go home to glory and it goes home to perdition."

In an era before mass media such as radio or television, and without the aid of loud speaking equipment, Billy Sunday preached in person to over 100 million people. However, as Sunday became more and more successful, and ever wealthier and more influential, he focused less and less on the calling of Christians to seek justice on earth, and more and more on the fate of individual souls in the eternity after death. He became convinced that his only mission was to recruit more and more sinners to "walk the sawdust trail and get right with God." It wasn't the quality of their lives on earth that mattered, but the location of their souls in Heaven or Hell after death.

Despite their internal disputes over various religious doctrines, 19th century Protestant Christians across the theological spectrum had generally believed in both social redemption and individual salvation. They were opposed to poverty and injustice, in favor of various programs for social progress, and sometimes quite radical in their advocacy of racial and sexual equality and peace among nations. The spirit of Christ, most believed, called upon Christians to "seek the Kingdom of Heaven" by striving for justice and embodying God's love through their lives and actions on earth.

Ironically, however, though Billy Sunday had grown up in poverty and expressed compassion for the poor, he decided that the "social gospel" of Charles Sheldon's book *In His Steps* wasn't for him. He was convinced that human beings were naturally so sinful and depraved that no amount of social improvement could fix what he thought was the fundamental problem. "Nothing short of absolute regeneration would ever stop and heal the awful ravages of sin," said Sunday. "To attempt reform in the black depths of the great city would be as useless as trying to purify the ocean by pouring into it a few gallons of spring water." The only solution he recognized was for people to repent of their sins and "get right with God."[60]

This distinction drawn by Sunday was critical. Ever since St. Augustine systematized the doctrine in the fourth century, *amillennialism* had been the prevailing view of Christian scholars, traditions, and theologians. The term amillennialism referred to the church's rejection of the belief that Jesus Christ would have a 1000-year physical reign on earth. Amillennialism held that the thousand years referred to in Revelation 20 was a symbolic number, and the "millennium" mentioned was a symbolic period in which Christians should work to realize the Kingdom of God on earth, striving for justice, loving one's neighbor, serving the poor, and generally embodying the love of Christ. Amillennialism was a principal doctrine of the Catholic Church throughout history, and was the dominant view of the Protestant Reformation as well, defended by Martin Luther and John Calvin among many others, and it continues to be the view of most mainline American Protestants in the 21st century.

Beginning in the 18th and 19th centuries, however, many American evangelicals were persuaded by the doctrine of *postmillennialism*, which posits that Christ's return to earth will take place only after the Millennium, a golden age of peace and prosperity in which Christian principles will prevail. Postmillennialism is inherently optimistic, believing that good will triumph over evil, and that the expanding Kingdom of God will defeat Satan's forces. Christians are required to be reformers, remaking society in the image of God's love and righteousness. Throughout the 19th century, evangelicals used the doctrine of postmillennialism to justify social activism to end slavery, expand human rights, seek equality for women, establish public schools, and reduce the exploitation and abuse of laborers.

However, an opposing movement sprang up in the early 19th century. In the 1830s, British preacher John Nelson Darby concocted a new set of doctrines that became known as premillennialism. This literal interpretation of selected passages in Revelations insisted that Jesus would return to earth before the millennium of his reign on earth and transport Christians out of the world before its descent into horrible global suffering and massive bloodshed. In the first century AD, Christians had believed Jesus would return to soon to establish his earthly kingdom, but the church had given up that belief when Jesus's return was delayed beyond their expectations. Darby taught that according to the Bible the history of the world since creation could be divided into seven different eras, or "dispensations," and his system became known as dispensationalism. The sixth dispensation would be signaled by the "Rapture," in which all the Christians alive and dead would be taken instantaneously to Heaven, followed by "seven years of tribulation" on earth and ending with the "apocalyptic" battle of Armageddon, a climactic struggle to destroy an evil person known as the Antichrist and institute the seventh dispensation—the millennial reign of Christ on earth.

Darby's account relied on carefully selecting certain dark, complicated, and heavily metaphorical passages from the Book of Revelations, ignoring the historical context in which they were written, and stitching them together to create a distorted theological portrait. Revelations was written in the first century A.D., and the word *apocalypse* meant "unveiling" or "exposing." Revelations was part of a powerful tradition of apocalyptic literature responding to the imperial domination and oppression of Christians by the Roman Empire. Darby, however, claimed that Revelations was to be read as a factual prediction of future events. His theory of "dispensationalism" cloaked itself in the language of 19th century scientific investigation, but it was profoundly opposed to the progressive spirit of 19th century evangelicalism.

Darby's followers assumed that any attempt to reform society according to Christian principles was both fruitless and heretical. They believed the Kingdom of Heaven to be a literal place where God reigned on a literal golden throne and where Christians went to live for eternity after death. They began in other ways to elevate the text (or 'worship the text' according to Darby's critics) of the Bible as no previous generation of Christians had found sensible or necessary.

Premillennialists were fearful that new tools of cultural and textual analysis being applied to the Bible would result in heretical departures from orthodoxy. In response, they took an increasingly extreme position that the Bible was *inerrant* in its original form. The Bible was an absolutely reliable source of truth, containing no mistakes, no internal contradictions, no flaws or blemishes. The people who wrote the Bible were directly inspired by God, and the meaning of any passage in the Bible was unambiguous and crystalline; any attempt to interpret the Bible was misguided because it spoke clearly for itself. The most aggressive expression of this new literalism became known as plenary or verbal inspiration, which meant that every word in the Bible was chosen directly under the guidance of God— every word came from God, and not just the meaning, messages, or ideas behind the words.

Darby's theory of dispensationalism (and premillennialism) was enshrined in the *Scofield Reference Bible*, first published in 1909, just as Billy Sunday was reaching the height of his career. During the 1910s the *Scofield* had a profound influence on a generation of conservative evangelicals, and became a founding document of the fundamentalist movement after the war.

Increasingly for premillennialists such as Billy Sunday, "Biblical inerrancy" came to mean the same thing as "Biblical literalism." If the Bible said that sinners would be "cast into a furnace of fire where there shall be wailing and gnashing of teeth,"[61] then Christians must believe that it would be unchristian to believe that Jesus was speaking in metaphor in this instance; the fire must be literal fire, it must be very hot, and it must provide literal and unending torment for the vast majority of humans who did not claim to be Christians. The Bible could only be read metaphorically when the context offered no other option. For example, in John 6, when Jesus said, "I am the living bread which came down from heaven. If anyone eats of this bread, he will live forever;" he clearly was not claiming literally to be a loaf of bread.

For philosopher John Stuart Mill, writing a generation earlier on the importance of individual freedom and the power of human reason to transform the world, this literalist reading of the Bible—and the premillennialist notion of God—was horrifying and evil. In his *Autobiography*, Mill remembered his father saying that:

> All ages and nations have represented their gods as wicked, in a constantly increasing progression, that mankind have gone on adding trait after trait till they reached the most perfect conception of wickedness which the human mind can devise, and have called this God, and prostrated themselves before it. This *ne plus ultra* of wickedness he considered to be embodied in what is commonly presented to mankind as the creed of Christianity. Think (he used to say) of a being who would make a hell—who would create the human race with the infallible foreknowledge, and therefore with the intention—that the great majority of them were to be consigned to horrible and everlasting torment. The time, I believe, is drawing near when this dreadful conception of an object of worship will no longer be identified with Christianity.[62]

John Stuart Mill was disappointed in his expectation of the impending demise of premillennialism. Far from disappearing, premillennialism and its "wicked" notion of God—in the conception of John R. Rice, God both as a loving Father and as a "dirty bully"[63]— furnished the essence of fundamentalist theology in the 20th century. In recent times it was enshrined in millions of copies of books published as part of the *Left Behind* series by Tim Lahaye and his co-authors, and informed the feverish imaginings of fundamentalist Pat Robertson when he proposed that the deaths of 250,000 earthquake victims in Haiti in the winter of 2010 were God's punishment for a presumed "pact with the Devil" by Haitians in the 19th century.

For premillennialists, human history was a cesspool of sin and depravity, disobedience to God, corruption and heresy. The second coming of Jesus was imminent. The critical task for Christians was to try to save as many souls as possible from the flames of Hell. Among evangelicals, premillennialists and postmillennialists fought a fierce battle to define the nature of God. Was God an angry God who condemned his own creation and was willing to see the vast majority of humanity suffer the torments of the damned for all eternity? Or was God a God of love and mercy who dreamed of a world ruled by compassion and justice?

For many premillennialists, God was both an angry God and a God of love, a God intolerant of sin and eager to forgive. They believed Christians should be concerned both with social reform on earth and the fate of one's soul in the afterlife. For the most extreme premillennialists, however, no other problem on earth truly mattered compared to saving souls from a literal and eternal hell—not poverty, injustice, hunger, inequality, ignorance, disease, slavery, or war. None of these weighed as much in the scales of eternity as the welfare of the soul and its relationship to God. Those who proclaimed the Kingdom of Heaven on earth were infidels and heretics at best, and agents of the Devil at worst.

In this debate over the nature of the Millennium—a golden age of peace and prosperity in which Christian principles will prevail, or a literal reign of Christ following seven years of horrible global suffering and massive bloodshed—lay the seeds of a Great Schism, the divide between fundamentalist and mainline churches that would dominate Protestant America in the 20th century.

Chapter 11
"The Fundamentals"

> *"The word of God is the sword of the spirit. The word of God is the seed the Spirit sows and quickens....It is when the Spirit Himself uses His own sword that it manifests its real temper, keenness and power."*—Reuben A. Torrey, *How to Obtain Fullness of Power*, 1897[64]

On a Tuesday morning in the fall of 1961, I boarded a bus on the street in front of Oliver Wendell Holmes Elementary School with my 24 classmates in the sixth grade and our teacher, Mr. Heaton. I was wearing my favorite green shirt, a clean pair of blue jeans, and a pair of black high-top sneakers, and I was carrying a small brown paper bag that contained an apple and a baloney sandwich—Peter Wheat bread slathered with mayonnaise. On this field trip, we were headed some thirty miles up Roosevelt Road to Chicago, where we would tour the universe with the assistance of Adler Planetarium.

We settled into our seats in the Sky Theater and leaned back as the lights dimmed all around the rim of the circular room. A clarinet began to play softly as sprinkles of illumination began to appear here and there on the domed roof until the room had darkened completely and our eyes had adjusted. The illusion was remarkable. Spread out above us was a crystalline night sky that fairly hummed with thousands of pinpricks of starlight. We oohed and nudged each other and chattered, recollecting what we had learned about stars and constellations in our class, recognizing the Big Dipper, searching for Polaris.

A deep voice came over the loudspeaker system as the clarinet faded. "Today we'll take a space flight through the universe," the man said. "We'll visit planets and stars, constellations and galaxies. We'll ride a moonbeam to an asteroid, and skim the rings of Saturn before launching ourselves into interstellar space."

"How do we measure distances in space?" the man asked. "Our measuring stick is light, which always travels at exactly the same speed! In one second, a beam of light could travel seven times around the earth. In eight minutes, the light of the sun travels to our planet Earth. The next nearest star to Earth is named Alpha Centauri, and its light took over four years to travel to Earth, where you can see it as this little point of starlight." One of the stars in the sky suddenly became much brighter and pulsed a few times before fading to its original lack of prominence.

"Our Milky Way galaxy is 100,000 light years across, with tens of millions of stars. But the universe is far larger and older than we can imagine, with literally billions of stars, many of them millions of light years away. The closest galaxy to ours is Andromeda." Another speck of light brightened and pulsed. "The light from Andromeda has been traveling to your eyes for over 2.7 million years."

I tapped Mr. Heaton on the shoulder, and he turned in his seat. "Yes, Andy?"

"But that's crazy," I whispered. "Everybody knows that God created the heavens and the earth just 6,000 years ago. The Bible says so!" Mr. Heaton's mouth opened and he looked at me queerly, and then he turned back to the presentation without responding.

I was right, of course. My dad's *Scofield Reference Bible* included a chronology of Biblical events created by Anglican Archbishop James Ussher in 1650. By carefully comparing Biblical texts, Ussher constructed a timeline that assigned very precise dates to specific Biblical events. For example, he concluded that the first day of Creation commenced at the nightfall before Sunday, October 23, 4004 BCE. There was simply no way for Andromeda's light to have traveled all that distance in just 6,000 years. Obviously, God had created the stars, the light, and the Earth in the same moment.

What I did not know at the age of eleven was that Bishop Ussher published his chronology in the midst of a scientific revolution in the 16th and 17th centuries, when new ideas in human anatomy, chemistry, physics, astronomy, biology, and other disciplines led the way to a rupture with older ideas and laid the foundations of modern science.

In response, for the first time in the history of the Christian church, Ussher and his fellow theologians developed the notion that the Bible itself must be a source for scientific knowledge about human history and the natural world, and that the Bible must be read for the literal, factually based truths it contained. The historic boundary between religion and science was smashed at one blow. Ussher's assumption set up an historic clash between a religion that assumed a questionable authority in matters of science, and a scientific community that increasingly regarded religious knowledge and faith with suspicion or outright hostility.

Erasmus in the sixteenth century and Spinoza in the seventeenth had used textual analysis of the Bible to draw conclusions about the meaning of Biblical passages. Rationalist and Enlightenment thinkers such as Benjamin Franklin, Thomas Jefferson, John Locke, and Adam Smith in the eighteenth century had proposed than no area should be off-limits to observation and analysis.

At first, the scientific method of empirical observation and summing up natural laws was directed at the natural world of plants and animals, planets and stars. But inevitably some people began using these new tools to look at human society, human history, and human creations. If scientific methods could be used to understand cell reproduction, chemical interactions, and the weather, then why not the evolution of human cultures, human intellectual development, and systems of human belief and behavior?

Many Bible scholars and theologians began to wonder whether they might be able to use some of the new tools of research and analysis to explain the Bible as a set of historical documents written and assembled over a millennium by flesh-and-blood human beings. This effort was known as "higher criticism," and some of the leading practitioners were German theologians. Most of these people and their American counterparts believed the Bible had been inspired by God, but that God had used fallible human beings, living in historical times, to convey universal spiritual truths. Along with more conservative theologians, they believed that in order to understand the Bible it helped to understand the conditions in which the Bible was written and what passages of the Bible meant in their historical context. However, the "higher critics" went further to investigate the sources of a Biblical text, and compared them to other texts written at about the same time, in order to determine who wrote the text and when. For example, higher critics considered how the four gospels relate to each other, and found discrepancies and contradictions that called into question various traditional beliefs about their authorship. They concluded that parts of some books of the Bible were added by other writers than the original authors, or for reasons other than simply accurately reporting events. There was nothing innately foreign or "German" about this kind of criticism. Indeed, it was historically suited to American culture, with its insistence on practicality, on investigation, on pragmatic solutions to complicated problems.

For most people today, such "higher criticism" sounds like a simple idea, and unobjectionable. But it led to much controversy among American Christians in the 19th century. People fell into all sorts of contentious arguments about various doctrines that had been enshrined as dogma for hundreds of years, and now were open to new interpretations. The conservatives responded by demanding that the Bible's "inerrancy" must be an article of faith, and identified these new interpretations as "modernism." They attacked the conclusions of higher criticism as a departure from historical Christian orthodox beliefs.

The roots of cultural modernism lay especially in the mid-19th century work of naturalist Charles Darwin and political scientist Karl Marx.

In his theory of evolution, Darwin explained how all species of life descended and adapted over millions of years from common ancestors through a process he called natural selection. Darwin's discovery provided a unifying explanation for the life sciences of biology, chemistry, and physics and a variety of multidisciplinary fields, as well as for the diversity of life on earth. Darwin was raised in the Church of England and throughout his life claimed there was no contradiction between a belief in God and his evolutionary theory. In 1879 he wrote that he had never been an atheist and thought it "absurd to doubt that a man might be an ardent theist and an evolutionist," but acknowledged that he considered himself an agnostic.

Charles Darwin was not the first scientist to suggest that living species of plants and animals evolved from earlier species. In 1800, French naturalist Jean-Baptiste Lamarck had proposed that characteristics acquired during the lifetime of an organism could be transmitted to its children. For example, a giraffe might continually reach for leaves higher and higher on a tree, thus marginally stretching out its neck throughout its life, and then its offspring might inherit the trait of a longer neck than its ancestors. This Lamarckian theory of evolution assumed that complex life-forms evolved from simpler species, and that each possessed a certain "vital force" that drove its development. Throughout the 19th century most conservative Christians saw nothing to oppose in Lamarck's theory of evolution, because they believed it to be entirely consistent with the Bible's account of creation. Charles Darwin's theory of evolution by natural selection was a different story. It posited a world in which species naturally evolved in response to their environment without the need for any special guidance from a supreme being. Random changes occurred in the characteristics of an organism, and these changes made the next generation more or less fit to survive in the competition among species and individuals.

Many conservative Christians believed God to be an all-powerful divine monarch who personally observed or guided every microscopic transaction or transition in the lives of his creatures on the earth. For these Christians, Darwin was the ultimate heretic, his research and conclusions blasphemy. Darwin's work, they believed, called God's very existence into question, degraded the divine inspiration of the Bible, and undermined their literal reading of the Bible's account of creation. For more liberal Christians, modern scientific theories like Darwin's revealed only the richness, beauty, and complexity of God's creation. They believed the rigid certainties of the past needed to be challenged. The new tools of scientific investigation and analysis should deepen one's sense of awe at the mystery that is creation rather than undermine our sense of the sacred.

In either case, Darwin's theory of natural selection didn't matter much for Christian theologians in the 19th century. When Darwin's *Origin of Species* was published in 1859, virtually all biological scientists were Lamarckians, but within a few decades they agreed almost universally with Darwin's thesis, despite the fact that little was known of the core biomolecular processes at the heart of organic evolution. They were won over to Darwin's conclusions because his observations were careful and detailed, and his arguments were eloquent. Rigorous scientific proof of Darwin's theories would be delayed until the early 20th century. In the meantime, conservative Christians could agree with Lamarckian evolution while quietly despising Darwin.

Karl Marx, meanwhile, had helped lay the foundations of cultural modernism by revealing the hidden contradictions within capitalism that gave rise to violent and irreconcilable clashes between capitalists and workers. Capitalism, said Marx, rather than offering a golden path toward universal prosperity, harbored the seeds of its own demise. Far from being freed by the mechanism of the capitalist market, workers were turned into wage-slaves, powerless to control society or their own individual destinies. Marx held that the system of capitalism would inevitably become more and more corrupt and moribund, less and less capable of meeting the needs of human society, until it finally brought about its own destruction and could be replaced by a system of socialism. At last, human society could be aligned with modern science; true freedom and democracy would be available for the vast majority of humans, while the former ruling class of capitalists would be suppressed. For Marx, the rationalism of the Enlightenment was the ideology of the bourgeoisie, and for the bourgeoisie a "rational" society was dominated by the new capitalists who acted in their own rational self-interest to maximize their profit and grow their wealth. The capitalist system would be supplanted through political revolution by a system Marx called "scientific socialism." Cultural modernism was the harbinger of Marx's communist vision.

By the early 20th century, a new way of thinking had begun to grow in a number of spheres that old assumptions, systems, and philosophies had to be thrown over altogether—not just revised or altered to accommodate recent scientific research or discoveries. Cultural modernism, it was seen, would have revolutionary implications in many areas of human knowledge and practice. Steam-powered industrialism was transforming human relations, bringing material abundance for capitalist bankers, moguls and barons and exploitation for working people. Instant means of communication such as the telegraph were challenging the very notion of time. Visual artists such as the French Impressionists suggested that human beings don't view objects, but rather see only the light reflected from objects. Psychologists such as Sigmund Freud claimed that human behavior was driven by primal urges deep beneath the surface of our consciousness. Architects created new forms such as the Eiffel Tower that reinvented the shape of cities and challenged ideas of how tall the laws of God would allow buildings to be.

Protestant Christianity was not sheltered from these winds of change. The Reformation itself was a 17th century revolution in theology that had produced the formal doctrine *sola scriptura*, the belief that the Bible is the singular authority for Christians, and was verbally inspired by God, is the word of God, and is available to anyone without the necessary interposition of a priest or pope between the believer and sacred truth.

The Westminster Confession of Faith had said as early as 1646: "All things in Scripture are not alike plain in themselves, nor alike clear unto all; yet those things which are necessary to be known, believed, and observed, for salvation, are so clearly propounded and opened in some place of Scripture or other, that not only the learned, but the unlearned, in a due use of the ordinary means, may attain unto a sufficient understanding of them."

However, before the end of the 18th century, few Christian theologians had claimed that the Bible as a whole was without internal contradictions, or textual or factual errors. Such a position would have been thought absurd, for the texts comprising the Old and New Testament canons were written over several hundred years, and then debated, in some cases edited, and finally assembled by groups of priests, monks, scholars, and theologians over a long period from many individual fragments of texts.

The oldest extant texts of both the Old and New Testaments were Greek manuscripts dating from the fourth century, but the canons developed over time, and there was no complete canon dating back to the time of the apostles. The final list of canonical books was still being sharply disputed in the 16th century during the Reformation, and to this day, Protestants, Catholics, and Orthodox theologians disagree about the list.

Most of the manuscripts that formed the basis of the Bible we have today date from the Middle Ages, and almost none of these were fully identical. The content of the most current Bible translations available at the beginning of the 20th century, including the popular King James Version, subsumed the content of over 16,000 ancient manuscripts in Greek, Latin and various other languages, which differed from each other in tens of thousands of details. It was inevitable that in all of the collating, translating, editing, and copying that took place over the centuries, a certain number of human errors would creep into the Biblical text—though the vast majority of these errors were insignificant scribal errors that were self-evident and easily discounted.

During the 19th century, however, Christians across the theological spectrum, along with Americans generally, came more and more to believe that religious ideas needed to be filtered through the lens of scientific and historical accuracy. "Facts" established with the aid of objective investigation, through scientific analysis, and by the employment of human reason were paramount. Modernists and conservatives viewed "science" in very different ways, but they were responding to the same essential problem. When the new historical critiques were applied to the Bible, and if Bible statements were taken literally, significant anomalies became apparent. The same event was sometimes recounted twice in the Old Testament, and in contradictory versions. The four gospels contradicted each other in major ways. The Pauline epistles seemed to conflict with the teachings of Jesus. Old Testament prophecies did not seem to forecast the arrival of Jesus after all. Jesus seemed to be predicting his imminent return, and his disciples clearly expected the establishment of the Kingdom of Heaven within a short time of his death. Moreover, the natural sciences raised large questions. Geological discoveries seemed to indicate the earth was much older than Biblical chronology indicated. Darwin's theory of evolution offered a naturalistic explanation for how life could arise and adapt itself to a changing environment. Supernatural explanations for Bible events seemed to be called into question.

Religious modernists responded to these anomalies and new information by broadening their standards for interpreting the Bible. The revelation of God through the Bible was progressive, they believed. The Bible itself was written by divinely inspired humans who lived in specific historical periods and who wrote within the limitations of their culture, knowledge, and assumptions. To understand the Bible, it was necessary to understand the language, history, and spiritual identity of the people of God who had written it. Moreover, dogma evolves over time, conditioned by historical and cultural circumstances.

Conservative theologians on the other hand, responded by narrowing their standards for interpreting the Bible. God's revelation was both static and universal, they believed. It had been delivered once and for all time to a group of men who were essentially scribes—not exactly taking dictation from God, but certainly not creating anything outside of God's direct prompting. The Bible contained a complete system describing different eras, or dispensations, through which God was working his will. Any inconsistencies were only apparent, and could be readily dismissed if we understood how various Bible stories or prophecies were referring to different times, places, and dispensations.

As previously mentioned, increasingly in the late 19th century conservatives began to use the term "inerrant" to describe Biblical texts. The Bible, they said, was authored and delivered by God with the aid of humans, and was therefore perfect and complete in every respect, just as God was perfect. The entire text of the Bible constituted the "facts" that were the basis of investigation for any theologian who wanted to be scientific in his analysis. As Arthur T. Pierson said at a conservative Bible conference in 1895, "I like Biblical theology that does not start with the superficial Aristotelian method of reason, that does not begin with an hypothesis, and then warp the facts and the philosophy to fit the crook of our dogma, but a Baconian system, which first gathers the teachings of the word of God, and then seeks to deduce some general law upon which the facts can be arranged."[65]

The German theologians who engaged in "higher criticism" would have agreed with Pierson about the importance of reading and studying the actual text of the Bible, without preconceptions and with any motive to prove a pre-existing theory. However, they also believed that true understanding of Bible required a study of the culture, language, and human civilization in which the Bible was produced, including other documents that had been created in the Middle East by non-Biblical authors.

From the point of view of Christian fundamentalists, the avalanche of modernism—and secularism—was deeply threatening. It called into question all the moral and ethical certainties of the past. Religious modernism, they feared, might lead to a repudiation of historic Christian orthodoxy. It might involve a denial of what they viewed as fundamental Bible doctrines. Religious modernists, it was assumed, might be led to doubt the deity of Christ, the virgin birth, the depravity of sinful humans, and the death and resurrection of Jesus. A modernist outlook might lead to contempt for the Bible, and the end of true Christianity.

The controversy between modernists and conservatives became increasingly bitter over the last years of the 19th century and into the first two decades of the 20th. More and more, Protestant Christians began to feel that they were being forced to take sides in what was rapidly becoming an historic split. American Protestantism—along with what had been a broadly held Evangelical consensus—began to divide between two great mega-denominations.

On one side were Christians who were more liberal in their outlook and more willing to accept new ideas that had emerged from "higher criticism" and study of the Bible as an historical text. They also tended to be more politically progressive, more attuned to the "social gospel," and more intent on the message of social justice they discerned in the teachings and life of Jesus.

On the other side was a growing chorus of conservative voices expressing dismay at these new ideas of the mainliners. The conservatives claimed to represent the historic Christian faith, in opposition to the modernists, who they believed were betraying and abandoning orthodox Christian beliefs. They were more focused on individual sin and the need for individual redemption and salvation. They were more prone to emphasize the importance of saving individual souls from a literal and fiery hell than the need to transform human societies on earth. They tended to identify the "Kingdom of Heaven" more as a literal city with golden streets beyond the sky than as a social revolution on earth.

Actually, both religious conservatives and religious modernists were reacting to the advance of science and the arrival of the modern era by introducing new concepts into Christianity. Although previous generations of Christians had believed the Bible to be inspired by God, few orthodox theologians had felt it necessary to insist on the absolute, reductive, factual flawlessness of the Bible. It was commonly understood that the Bible contained mystery, metaphor, and multiple meanings embedded in the text, and that the "leading" of God was required to grasp the complex yet simple truth of God's word. The arrival of modern science and its evident success in explaining the natural world had created a conundrum for Christians. Scientists argued that human knowledge was infinitely expandable, requiring only that humans use their God-given capacities to explore, observe, compare, propose, test, and verify hypotheses. For both conservatives and modernists, the text of the Bible was available as material for a scientific exploration and analysis. Everybody agreed on this, but different factions used "science" as an aid to support opposite conclusions.

Many progressive evangelical Christians, upholding the principle of *sola scriptura*, believed that the Bible contained the word of God. However, they said, any passage had to be read carefully to understand how it applied to a specific human community at a moment of historical time, and whether it could be applied universally. The Bible was rich with stories and parables, miracles and metaphors, and any passage might be laden with deep meanings that must be teased out with the aid of prayer, study, contemplation, and dialogue. They also realized that the Bible contained factual errors as well as contradictions between writers who lived in different times and were expressing their own evolving understanding of God and the world.

However, a group of conservative Protestants decided that Christianity was in danger from a variety of encroaching heresies: higher criticism, liberal theology, modernism, Catholicism, socialism, atheism, spiritualism, evolutionism, and a variety of other movements and sects. They decided to unite Christians around a core, or "fundamental" set of beliefs that every orthodox Christian ought to be able to agree on. They saw this as an effort to promote harmony and unity among true Christians, while drawing a clear line of demarcation between themselves and the modernists.

With funding from Lyman Stewart, a wealthy businessman and the founder of Union Oil, between 1910 and 1915 the Bible Institute of Los Angeles (BIOLA) published a set of 12 booklets with essays by 64 different authors, titled *The Fundamentals; A Testimony to the Truth*. The books summed up several principles as core beliefs of Christianity, and among these principles were five recognized as especially important by fundamentalists: the inerrancy of the Bible, the Virgin Birth and deity of Jesus, the belief that Jesus died to redeem mankind's sin, the physical resurrection of Jesus, and the literal truth of the miraculous elements in the Bible. (Some especially conservative people replaced this last "fundamental" with an affirmation of the premillennial return of Jesus to earth.) It is notable that these five doctrines were chosen because conservative Christians believed them to be under attack by modernists—and not because they included every "fundamental" doctrine. For example, the idea that salvation could be achieved through faith and faith alone (otherwise known as the doctrine of justification by faith) was the historical fault line distinguishing Protestants from Catholics at the beginning of the Reformation. (Catholics believed that salvation depended, in part, on the good works performed during a lifetime.) However, the doctrine of justification by faith was not included in the list of "five fundamentals" because conservatives did not feel threatened by the modernists on this point.

The movement that began to grow out of the publication of *The Fundamentals* wasn't only a negative reaction to modernism and religious progressives. It was also driven by a positive desire to establish a great plane of agreement on which Christians could gather to defend what they viewed as the historic Christian faith, and from which they could carry the good news of salvation out to the masses.

Chapter 12
Race and Fundamentalism in the South

In 1963 when I was 13, my dad was pastor of the Southside Baptist Church in Millington, Tennessee. Many in our congregation were employed at or lived on the nearby Memphis Naval Air Station. Our little church was a plain brick building with white trim set amid acres of soybeans, cotton and Johnson grass 10 miles east of the broad brown waters of the Mississippi River. Outside our little church the "race question" was exploding across the South. Civil rights activists marched, rallied, and conducted sit-ins at lunch counters and department stores and bus stations. Klan members retaliated with a church bombing in Birmingham that killed four little girls. Mississippi civil rights leader Medgar Evers was shot in the back by a shadowy assassin just 50 miles south of my front door.

On a transcendently beautiful Sunday morning in October, a black sailor from the Navy base walked in the front door of our church with three white sailor friends and occupied a wooden pew in the center of the sanctuary. My dad glanced at them but continued preaching his sermon. Our lead deacon, a chief petty officer named Mel Hogan, also in his Navy dress uniform, conferred with his fellow deacons and then strode up onto the platform for a public and urgent, yet whispered conversation. My dad shook his head a few times, and continued preaching. Deacon Hogan hopped off the platform to gather his troops, and then he and his family, and all the other deacons and *their* families, marched out of our church building rather than spend a minute in the company of a black man on a Sunday morning. My dad did not want to stop the service for a confrontation with the sailor. However, after the service my dad informed the young man that he could not attend our church, but should find a Negro church where he would be more welcome.

Within months, the deacons fired my dad. Soon he had a new job as pastor of a little Baptist church in Wisconsin. I was stunned, and my faith shaken to its very roots. If our church was the body of Christ, was Christianity a religion of petty hypocrites? Or were those deacons merely misguided Christians who believed, incredibly, that Jesus did not want them to associate with Negroes? Did God hate black people? Or was he offended by the hateful behavior of Mel Hogan and his fellow deacons? Why did my granddad preach that God was opposed to integration? How could it be that Martin Luther King Jr., a fellow Baptist preacher, was a modernist and socialist, not a true Christian? Why did no one in my church or family speak out against the Alabama church bombings or the murders of activists? Why did I know almost nothing about the lives of my black neighbors, a majority of the population in Shelby County, Tennessee? These were troublesome questions, but I didn't know how to bring them up. No one in my family or church seemed to want to talk about them either. So they festered, and began to eat away at my faith.

I had come face to face with a core issue for white Southern conservatives: race.

Southern conservative theologians were largely isolated from the national debate between modernists and conservatives, and few of them enjoyed a national reputation. The Civil War had been a triumph of Northern theology as well as Northern arms and industry. Southern Protestant ministers, churches, denominations, and seminaries had been tarred by their religious justification of slavery. The South had a general reputation for backwardness, and anti-intellectualism, and harboring religious ignoramuses. This an unfair generalization, but was not surprising given that the East Coast had been largely settled a century or two before much of the South. Most southerners were only a generation or two removed from their parents' or grandparents' original migration to the frontier. By comparison to the North, a higher proportion of southerners were farmers, and most had little access to education. Southerners struggled to survive and had sparse exposure to culture. Southern theologians were left without any real voice in a serious national discussion.

A key issue for Southern conservatives was race, and always had been race. Southern conservatives were saddled with an historic dilemma, a conflict between their religious beliefs and the new legal reality of emancipation. Before the Civil War, the slave owners of Missouri and Texas and the rest of the South had defended their right to own human beings by claiming that God literally approved of slavery in multiple places in the Bible. Many white Southerners were locked into a theological justification for the oppression of black people, based on this literal reading of the Bible. If God approved of slavery in the 19th century, he undoubtedly endorsed Plessy v. Ferguson—the Supreme Court's landmark 1896 decision upholding the constitutionality of racial segregation in public accommodations (particularly railroads), under the doctrine of "separate but equal." Racial segregation was mandated by God, and racial integration would be a sin against God.

Northern conservative Christians were no more progressive in racial matters than their brethren south of the Mason-Dixon Line; however, they did not have the same need to justify the racial politics of the South. They could afford to bring a more relaxed understanding of Christian orthodoxy as it applied to black people, and were less inclined to justify their racial politics through literal interpretations of certain Scriptures. Thus, in differing beliefs about race and the Bible, seeds were planted for a future schism in the fundamentalist movement.

The South proved especially congenial to a rigid and defensive theology. The South saw itself as a region under fire, facing continuing imminent threats to its economy, its culture and political system, and the purity of its Christian faith. Beginning decades before the Civil War, white Southerners had been sensitive to attacks by Northern Christians on slavery and had used a self-serving reading of the Bible to defend the institution. Indeed, the Southern Baptist Convention had been born out of the South's need to defend slavery. The terrible trauma of the Civil War had emphasized and cemented the South's fears of destruction and domination by outsiders. The political and economic elites of the other Southern states—especially Missouri—fled to Texas to find refuge after the war. Texas therefore became the center of the most bitter resistance to Reconstruction. The state was home to the greatest amount of internecine violence after the war, especially in the northern Texas counties where Missouri refugees had settled.

Along with the Missouri refugees in Texas, the citizens of Georgia had seen some of the greatest destruction and trauma during the Civil War, and it was in Georgia that the consequences of that trauma first resurfaced in the form of the Ku Klux Klan.

On Confederate Memorial Day in 1913, a 14-year-old white girl named Mary Phagen was raped and strangled in the basement of a pencil factory in Atlanta, Georgia. Mary was a working class girl who supported a widowed mother and several sisters and brothers. She had gone to the factory to pick up her $1.20 paycheck and never returned home. At first a black watchman at the plant named Jimmy Conley was arrested when he was discovered with a bloodstained shirt and told a series of conflicting stories. Conley had a history of crime and drunken violence, and was accused of the killing by two witnesses. He in turn accused Leo Frank, the 29-year-old Jewish manager of the factory, who was soon arrested for the crime. [66]

The only evidence against Frank was slim and purely circumstantial. Frank's lawyers presented many witnesses providing Frank with comprehensive alibis for the entire time during which the murder might have taken place. Nonetheless, the case against Frank gave rise to an intense media circus starring hundreds of characters, including police, prosecutors, and politicians, competing and sensationalistic newspapers, an ever-changing cast of countervailing witnesses, and a thousand contradictory and lurid stories of sex, murder, money, and mayhem.

At the center of the controversy was Will Rice's second cousin, Georgia governor Joe Mackey Brown. Governor Brown was the son of the famous Joe Brown who had served his own four terms as Georgia governor throughout the Civil War, and he was the great-grandson of Dangerfield Rice, who was in turn the grandfather of Will Rice. Governor Brown played up the race issue for all it was worth and intervened to demand Frank's conviction. Atlanta newspapers published bizarre and fantastic stories about rape and sex orgies supposedly conducted by Frank at the factory. The *Georgian* published a completely fictional account of the factory: "Pictures of Salome dancers in scanty raiment and of chorus girls in different postures adorned the walls of the National Pencil Company plant."[67] The Atlanta police conducted a corrupt and incompetent investigation during which the news media generated thousands of false leads from sensationalistic coverage. Evidence was lost, created from nothing, or "accidentally" destroyed.

The entire focus of the trial was on race, and it revealed a virulent stream of anti-Semitism as ugly as white Southern attitudes toward blacks. As the Baptist pastor of the church where Mary Phagen attended said:

> My feelings, upon the arrest of the old Negro watchman, were to the effect that this one old Negro would be atonement for the life of this innocent girl. But, when on the next day, the police arrested a Jew, and a Yankee Jew at that, all of the inborn prejudice against Jews rose up in a feeling of satisfaction that here would be a victim worthy to pay for the crime.[68]

At the trial, Frank's defense lawyer argued that Conley, the watchman, was the murderer all along and had falsely accused Frank in order to escape the noose. "If Frank hadn't been a Jew," he said, "he would never have been prosecuted" and, "Conley is a plain, beastly, drunken, filthy, lying nigger with a spreading nose through which probably tons of cocaine has been sniffed."[69]

Outside on the street, the racist filth spread by Frank's own lawyer was mirrored by Governor Brown, who led a mob that threatened to lynch the judge, the defense attorney, or any member of the jury who might vote for acquittal. With the help of sensationalistic newspaper articles, vicious race-baiting sermons from many Atlanta pulpits, and a vitriolic campaign of leafleting and street-corner rallies, public opinion in Atlanta began to turn strongly against Leo Frank. Intimidated by the mob, the jury convicted Frank, to no one's surprise.

Almost immediately strong new evidence came to light that Conley was almost certainly the killer. Frank's appeals to the Georgia State Supreme Court as well as the U.S. Supreme Court failed. Referring to Governor Brown's mob, Justice Oliver Wendell Holmes stated in a minority opinion, "I very seriously doubt if the petitioner… has had due process of law…because of the trial taking place in the presence of a hostile demonstration and seemingly dangerous crowd, thought by the presiding judge to be ready for violence unless a verdict of guilty was rendered."[70]

Remarkably, Governor Brown and the white citizens of Atlanta eagerly forsook their opportunity to lynch a black man when they were presented with the opportunity to railroad a Jew. Brown evidently found Frank especially offensive, even when confronted with strong evidence of his innocence.

Brown's actions in the Frank case helped to inspire *Birth of a Nation,* a pioneering and technically innovative movie released in February of 1915 to great controversy. The film claimed to be the heroic story of the original Ku Klux Klan, which arose to protect the gentle and noble white Christian population of the post-war South from the ravages of sex-mad, murderous Negroes and the corrupt, villainous Yankees and Southern scalawags who were their accomplices. In the film, the renegade Negro Gus traps Flora Cameron, a young white woman, on a precipice in the forest; she then throws herself off the cliff in order to avoid being raped. Flora's story was inspired by the supposed experience of Mary Phagen.

The movie tapped into the myth of the Lost Cause, which had kept alive a perverted and historically inaccurate portrait of the Confederacy in the minds and hearts of three generations of Southerners. According to the myth, the Civil War had nothing to do with slavery, and everything to do with Northern oppression of the South. The Ku Klux Klan had nothing to do with re-enslaving blacks and everything to do with protecting whites from "the votes of ignorant Negroes" and the machinations of "unscrupulous Yankee carpetbaggers." A card shown between scenes in *Birth of a Nation* quoted President Woodrow Wilson: "The white men were roused by a mere instinct of self-preservation…until at last there had sprung into existence a great Ku Klux Klan, a veritable empire of the South, to protect the Southern country."

Joe Mackey Brown served two terms as Georgia governor through mid-1913. After the end of his term, however, he resurfaced in the Frank case. In 1915, Leo Frank applied for clemency to the new governor of Georgia, John Slaton, who pored over 10,000 pages of documents, including the new evidence that incriminated Conley, the black watchman. The most prominent speaker at the clemency hearing was ex-governor Brown, who issued an explicit threat to take the law into his own hands: "Now in all frankness," he said to Slaton, "if Your Excellency wishes to ensure lynch law in Georgia…you can strike this dangerous blow at our institutions…by retrying this case." Despite Brown's threat, Slaton proceeded to commute Frank's sentence to life in prison, and announced his conclusion that Frank's innocence would be soon established and he would be set free.

Immediately after the hearing, Joe Mackey Brown openly began to recruit and organize a lynch mob. He and other prominent Atlanta citizens, including judges, prosecutors, politicians, and bankers, convened a group calling itself the Knights of Mary Phagen, and publicly announced plans to kidnap Frank from the state prison farm and take him 150 miles away to Marietta, Georgia for his lynching. They recruited and interviewed 26 men who they thought had the necessary skills. Then on August 16, 1915, Joe Mackey Brown led his mob to the prison farm, took Frank at gunpoint, and hanged him outside of Marietta with a rope and table supplied by Marietta sheriff and co-conspirator William Frey.

The Knights of Mary Phagen climbed Stone Mountain one evening two months later, along with two elderly members of the original Reconstruction-era Klan, and there they burned a giant cross that could be seen from anywhere in the city of Atlanta. In the company of a Methodist Episcopal preacher named William Joseph Simmons, they announced the revival of the Ku Klux Klan, which they called a Christian organization. The Klan insisted that its purpose was to defend the virtue and morality of Southern white womanhood, to oppose the debasement of the white race, and to uphold the cross of Jesus. It echoed the older Klan of the years after the Civil War in its fear and hatred of blacks; in its use of terror, violence, and intimidation to achieve its objectives; and in its cynical use of Christianity to justify its criminal actions.

From Georgia, the new Klan began to spread rapidly across the nation and then develop strength even in key Northern and Western states such as Indiana and Oregon. The Klan's strength, however, would be in the South, and Texas would be the locus of some of the most successful organizing by the new Klan.

Not coincidentally, Texas would be the place where the modern fundamentalist movement in the U.S. would be most fully defined and nurtured during the 1920s and 1930s.

Chapter 13
Dundee to Decatur

Throughout my years of growing up, my dad's favorite occupation, aside from reading his Bible, was reading Western novels, most of them by Zane Grey. An entire shelf in our library was taken up by over 40 Zane Grey paperbacks. The novels presented a thoroughly idealized version of the Old West. Each book had a colorful cover illustration and featured a large cast of stock characters who generally included one or more cowboys, a clutch of cattle rustlers, intolerant Mormon elders and circuit-riding Methodist preachers, evil cattle barons, and noble gunslingers and their Indian sidekicks who didn't speak much but were really good trackers. The females were generally spirited young women who were nonetheless childlike and submissive in the presence of their fathers or husbands even as they transformed the men in their lives through their exercise of female virtue. Grey's writing was often sentimental, characterized by stiff language and stereotypical dialogue. But he knew how to tell a good yarn marked by explicit violence and vivid details.

Close by Zane Grey's books on the shelves were a few Westerns by the Texas novelist Ben Capps Jr., my mother's cousin. Capps was born in Dundee, Texas in 1922 to John R. Rice's sister Ruth, and it was my considered critical opinion as a child that Capps was a much better writer than Zane Grey.

Capps described a fictionalized Archer County in his novel *Sam Chance*, the story of a Confederate veteran who arrives in Texas to start his life over after the Civil War. The character was based partly on Capps' own great-grandfather, James Porter Rice:

> It was only after they had crossed the Red River at Colbert's Ferry, going south, that the new feeling about the land became definite in him. Through Arkansas into

Indian Territory they had followed fair roads over hills
and through valleys to old Fort Gibson, then had turned
down the Texas Road with a party driving three wagons.
The land had changed slowly, subtly...it was late
summer and the grass on the rolling prairie was golden
under a pitiless sun. Nowhere on the horizon could he
see blue distant mountains. The land seemed boundless.
The horizon did not express the limits of a valley;
instead they said that there was more beyond, that the
bare treeless land stretched away and away. He felt that
he was in a big land... In it was boundless potential, as
harsh as the heat waves that lay over the bare grass, as
grand as the human imagination wanted to make it.[71]

Dundee, Texas was right on the edge of the southern Great Plains.
When the Rice family moved there in 1905 it was still essentially a
frontier town. Only a few years had passed since the last Indian uprisings
were crushed by the U.S. Army; it had been just 15 years since the
Wichita Valley Railway had been built to allow farmers and ranchers in
northern Archer County to move their crops and herds easily to market;
it was only six years after railroad baron Ned Green brought the first
automobile to Texas, a two-cylinder St. Louis Gas Car surrey.[72]

The U.S. Census for Archer County, Texas for 1900 reported a
population of 2,508 living mainly on the 356 farms or ranches in the
county. Every recorded resident was white; there were no blacks or
Mexicans listed, and not one of the Apaches, Wichitas, Tawakonis,
Kichais, Caddoes, Comanches, and Kiowas who only a quarter century
earlier had camped and hunted in the area now known as Archer County.
The inhabitants reported mainly rural occupations such as farmer or farm
laborer, cattle drover, line rider, prairie dog killer, ranchman, and
stockman, along with jobs in the county's small towns, such as day
laborer, blacksmith, clerk, saloon keeper, and merchant, and one
physician.

Life and death were closely intertwined on the Texas prairie outside
of Dundee. The land was cheap to purchase but expensive to farm, arid
and inhospitable, blazing in the summertime and frigid past belief in
winter when the chill wind swept across the flat land with nothing to
alter its flow except for an occasional barn or farmhouse. Its inhabitants
sometimes cursed their poor judgment in choosing such a godforsaken
place to put down stakes. Such a life required spiritual sustenance and
physical endurance, and was aided by a measure of luck, a sense of
humor, and a powerful sense of divine providence. It also ended with

your soul forever resident in one of only two real and literal places: in Heaven or in Hell. Given such radical opposites, it was better to be certain about your destination and with a strong knowledge of God's mercy.

Eternity was just past the front gate, out by the barn, in the cane brake, out among the chaparral, the prickly pear cactuses and mesquite bushes hidden in the wind that blew across the grasslands and the fields of wheat and corn and cotton. The men in John R. Rice's family worked year round and sunup to sundown, grubbing the mesquite to clear the earth for planting, plowing a thousand acres behind the mule team, dropping seeds into the dirt, praying for rain, harvesting crops, running cattle, repairing fence lines, and then beginning all of it again. The women in the family worked just as hard and just as long, planting, weeding, and reaping in the vegetable garden, slopping hogs, nursing sick cows, preparing food, canning, cooking meals and washing dishes, making and mending clothes, gathering firewood, bearing and caring for children, mopping floors and mending socks.

The year after Will married his third wife Dolous, she was pregnant, and while the baby was still unborn they named him William H. Rice Jr. This baby quickened before its time, and died at birth. They buried him down in the old Dundee Cemetery a mile out of town, and Dolous wept and prayed and soon was pregnant again. This time the child lived, and they called him Joe.

Dolous became pregnant a third time; once more they named the baby William H. Rice Jr., hoping against hope. This one also was stillborn, and they buried the third infant next to its dead older brother. Dolous and Will tried yet again. At last, never giving up hope, Dolous in 1912 gave birth a fourth time to a baby who would live to adulthood, and whom they named, unsurprisingly, William H. Rice Jr. [*]

Will Rice's school-age children from his previous marriages, including John, got an uncertain and incomplete education in the little Rice Ranch Community School. There, some thirty students from nearby farms studied whatever classes the three teachers happened to know anything about—reading and writing, elementary arithmetic, some history and geography and bits of other subjects—until they had taken the available classes and dropped out in their early teens to work full-time on the family farm. Few in the community had even seen the inside of a high school; only one out of seven residents was listed in the census

---

[*] These three brothers—John and Joe and Bill—all grew up to be Baptist preachers, following the prayers of Sadie and Dolous and in the footsteps of their father Will. All three would be buried next to each other at the top of the rise in the family graveyard near Murfreesboro, Tennessee.

as having any formal schooling, and few of those had gone above the fifth grade.

Will Rice had been unusual in gaining the rough equivalent of a high school education and then in attending the Southern Baptist Seminary in Louisville. John, Ruth, and the other Rice children doubtless acquired literacy and a love of words and language from their father's example, and from reading their Bibles, as much as from their formal schooling.

As the oldest boy in the growing blended family, John R. Rice had heavy responsibilities. He was a ranch hand for his father from an early age, he was expected to help care for the younger children, and whatever education he got depended on his own initiative. Nonetheless, he took every class available in the Rice Ranch Community School. By his late teens he thought he might have the makings of a school teacher. At the age of 18 he passed an exam in Archer City for a Texas state teacher's certificate, and then taught grades one through eight in a little school 15 miles away from Dundee. The school was open for only four months, and his total annual salary was $220. He supplemented his income by working on the ranch for the rest of the year.

Increasingly, however, John felt trapped by his rural roots and his lack of education. He was beginning to sense a larger mission for his life, and the small world of Dundee and Archer County couldn't contain his sense of the possible. Who knew where he might go or what he might do in his life? He might be a politician or college professor, a preacher or a philosopher. He believed that God took a personal interest in him and must have a plan for his life, but he wondered what that plan might be. He was sure he had a mission and future beyond the confines of his small Texas home town, though he didn't know how to reach that future. He had little or no money and couldn't hope to get any sort of financial help from his father.

Will Rice wanted his children to go to college, but when they were old enough to think about it he had no help to give them. He was enmeshed in his own ongoing fiscal crises. When John's older sister Gertrude went off to Baylor University, Will wrote to her: "Dear Girl: I am sorry you did not have money for the dress you needed for college. I do not have much money but I would always borrow the $20 for you to have what you need for school. Please do not show this letter to anyone, and tear it up when you have read it for I am not a good speller..."

It was clear to John that he would have to struggle through somehow using only his own financial resources and relying on his faith in God. After two years of teaching in his little country grade school, he at last reached a personal crisis. He would leave Archer County forever if God would show him the way forward. On the cold clear night of January 13,

1916, 20-year-old John knelt under a bush in the chaparral out past the corral on his family's farm and committed everything he had to serving God. He recounted the story of that night decades later: "I told God that I would do anything He wanted me to do. I would preach the Gospel, or I would be a Gospel singer, or do anything else if He should clearly lead. I told Him that since this burden was on my heart it must be from Him, and I must ask Him to give me the means to go through College."

John came back to the house to pack his clothes in a little wooden trunk given him by his mother, asked his father to ship the trunk to him, then mounted his cow pony and rode off in the rain toward Decatur Baptist College, 120 miles away. In his pocket was his life savings of $9.35. He stopped by the Power State Bank in Archer City along the way, where he convinced the cashier to give him a six-month loan of $60 to help him pay tuition plus room and board at the school. When he arrived in Decatur he used his own brand of cheerful stubbornness to convince the college president to let him enter school in the middle of the year and give him a job milking the college cows. Before the end of the year his clothes were so worn and patched that he was afraid his pants would split if he leaned over or sat down too quickly.

John prayed for a solution to his threatened pantslessness, and a surprisingly timely check for $25 arrived in the mail from his uncle George Rice—more than enough to replenish his wardrobe.[73]

Early in the fall of 1916, Lloys McClure Cooke was delivered to the campus by her father, James Hezekiah Cooke, in his Maxwell car, enough of a rarity in those days to create a stir on their arrival. Just a week earlier, Lloys had been planning to attend the Texas Women's College at Denton to prepare to become a doctor. Then a traveling evangelist took Mr. Cooke aside and warned him that if she attended a state school she would "marry the wrong kind of man." Abruptly, without warning or consulting Lloys, Cooke changed his daughter's plans for her life, installed her and her luggage in the Maxwell, and drove off to enroll her at Decatur Baptist College a week after the fall semester had begun.

John R. Rice met Lloys at a literary society event that fall and almost immediately began a precipitous courtship. By the next year they were engaged.

Chapter 14
The Struggle Against Modernism

> *"See now that I, even I, am He, and there is no god with me: I kill, and I make alive; I wound, and I heal: neither is there any that can deliver out of my hand. For I lift up my hand to Heaven, and say, I live forever. If I whet my glittering sword, and mine hand take hold on judgment; I will render vengeance to mine enemies, and will reward them that hate me."*—Deuteronomy 32:39-41

In October of 1967, I stood in the sanctuary of an African Methodist Episcopal church on the west side of Racine, Wisconsin and found myself in the grip of a powerful contradiction. I was one of a handful of white people in that church, surrounded by hundreds of black people, swaying and holding hands, packed together, standing close, chanting, praying for freedom. We had marched through the streets of Racine together, holding hand-lettered signs that demanded justice, insisting on equality in Racine's housing industry and opportunity for all to live in a decent home.

That month in Racine at the age of 17, I had decided that God no longer existed. For me, the notion of a loving God who cared about the welfare of the least sparrow was incompatible with slavery and segregation, with poverty and murder, with genocide and the demons of the war in Vietnam. I tossed God onto the refuse heap of history. This was not easy for me. I walked along the deserted shore of Lake Michigan at midnight screaming at the sky. I spent hours staring at the animals in the Racine Zoo behind the rusting iron bars in their drab concrete cages. I woke in the early morning hours crying piteously, half-remembering the fragments of a dream in which lost souls were dying and God was among the missing.

From the pulpit, a black preacher with a bald dome and the build of a linebacker held both hands high over his head, and said in a booming voice, "There is a Lord above who said he would never forsake or fail us! There is a God in Heaven who hears the cry of the wretched and the dispossessed and the plea of the poor in spirit! Today we know what Paul meant when he said, 'When I am weak, then am I strong.'"

The sanctuary swelled with hallelujahs and amens, shouts and murmurs and fragments of songs. I found myself short of breath, wanting only to run from that place but hemmed in by the close-packed bodies around me.

"We come together on the streets of Racine in our weakness and infirmity," said the preacher. "We come because there is a thorn in our side, and it is the thorn of injustice! We come because when we are together in our weakness and infirmity we have the strength to confront evil and to overcome injustice! We come because the God who delivered the Hebrews from bondage in Egypt is here in sprit and in truth, and he will use these poor, frail vessels to do a mighty work!"

Unbidden now the voices of the multitude around me arose in a new song, or at least new to me, but recalling the rhythm and power of my granddad's revival songs: "We shall overcome, we shall overcome, we shall overcome some day. Deep in my heart, I do believe that we shall overcome some day." I found that I couldn't sing with them; my throat had closed and vision blurred as tears flowed freely down my face. But I gripped the hands of the people on either side of me and I hummed brokenly this new song.

Billy Sunday had been raised in an evangelical tradition focused on individual salvation, but his tradition was also attuned to social justice and racial progress. He had always been sensitive to the problems of poverty, and spent much of his ministry in service to the urban poor before his arrival on the national stage as a successful mass revivalist. Despite Sunday's eventual rejection of the Social Gospel, he demonstrated a concern for racial justice and racial reconciliation at the height of his career that was nothing short of breathtaking.

In the autumn of 1917 he conducted a giant citywide revival meeting in Atlanta, Georgia. Many people believed the recent history of the city and the revival of the Ku Klux Klan spelled the doom of any effort to bring blacks and whites together in any endeavor, Christian or secular. Sunday was warned that if he attempted to hold integrated services, he would be shut down by racial rioting, violent attacks on his tabernacle, and police connivance with his opponents. Nonetheless, Sunday announced to white political and religious leaders that he intended to reach out to and partner with both white and black communities. When he came to Atlanta, he met with black church leaders, preached in several black churches, and hosted black preachers in all of the revival meetings. He set aside one night for black attendance, and 16,000 black people packed the pews and aisles of the tabernacle. Sunday preached that Jesus called us to "cooperation between the races," and praised black leaders from various times in history.

A few days later he produced an extraordinary black choir to sing before an all-white congregation of over 12,000. The journal *Current Opinion* reported: "...a remarkable situation—an audience of Southern white people, a choir of Southern colored people and a Northern man standing in between. 'The very air,' Dr. Proctor says, 'was tense with excitement.' The choir consisted of a thousand voices under the direction of a skilled leader. Picked voices from colleges...Haunting melodies, the cry of the negro heart, resounded through the tabernacle. They were a revelation to the people of Atlanta.'" Remarkably, in the midst of the Great War, the most popular song sung that night was 'Ain't Goin' to Study War No More!'[74]

Billy Sunday's Atlanta revival may have been the apex of an era of big revival meetings with hellfire-and-brimstone preaching designed to shake people out of their moral torpor and get them reverted or converted and on their way to spreading the gospel and heading for Heaven. His ministry expressed a conservative theology—a black-and-white universe containing God and the Devil, human depravity and divine atonement, Heaven and Hell, sin and salvation, and a literal interpretation of scripture—that today we would clearly identify with fundamentalism. But Sunday's "fundamentalism" could be combined with relatively benign and progressive social and racial politics. The world was changing rapidly in ways that would make that combination less probable.

The Great War, within a generation to be known as the First World War, gave powerful impetus to the development of modernism, creating a schism that helped move fundamentalists away from the work of social justice.

Modernists saw the Great War as evidence that all the old certainties and traditional assumptions of the Enlightenment were breaking down in the face of a rapidly emerging modern and industrialized society. Cultural modernists were ready to question every axiom of the past— especially the idealistic Enlightenment assumption that human civilization was inherently good, and that humankind naturally advanced through history toward freedom, justice, peace, and material abundance. Those who emerged from the war with their senses intact, or who had been too young to be ground up in the machine of European militarism, tended to embrace an opposite set of conclusions. Every previous "truth" was to be held up to the harsh light of the war's savagery; every idea that had arisen from the previous Enlightenment optimism was to be examined pitilessly; all comfortable notions about the inherent goodness of governments or religious institutions or the capitalist system of trade and industry were to be challenged.

Religious modernists were also ready to believe that the work of religion was to reform and improve society. Shailer Mathews, a modernist Baptist professor of historical and comparative theology at the University of Chicago and dean of its Divinity School, accepted the scientific method as the most reliable path to truth. He believed all human understanding—including religious understanding and doctrines—was imperfect and required continual re-evaluation and development.

"What then is Modernism?" asked Mathews.

> A heresy? An infidelity? A denial of truth? A new religion? So its ecclesiastical opponents have called it. But it is none of these…It is the use of the methods of modern science to find, state and use the permanent and central values of inherited orthodoxy in meeting the needs of a modern world…Modernists endeavor to reach beliefs and their application in the same way that chemists or historians reach and apply their conclusions…The Dogmatist starts with doctrines, the Modernist with the religion that gave rise to doctrines. The Dogmatist relies on conformity through group authority; the Modernist, upon inductive method and action in accord with group loyalty.[75]

From the point of view of conservatives, however, modernism ultimately led to a rejection of God, to infidelism, perhaps even to perversion and atheism. From the point of view of fundamentalists, Christianity was pitted against the worship of science, logic, and technology. Modernism, believed the fundamentalists, was both morally and politically corrupt, and was especially dangerous in the era immediately following the war, when the evidence of moral decline and depravity seemed to appear on all sides. Conservative Christians were alarmed by all sorts of moral and technological innovations, from jazz to foul language; from skirts that crept ever farther above the ankle toward the knee and beyond to dances that became ever more lewd and bawdy;

and by Hollywood movies that dipped ever further into a moral cesspool of lust and adultery, mannish broads and drunken heroes, and the celebration of sinners and sinning.

In addition, the war delivered a great shock to the political sensibilities of conservative evangelicals. Before the war, a belief that the Bible was the inspired word of God was at the heart of the dominant public proclamation of religion in America. The set of beliefs espoused in *The Fundamentals* united a broad audience of millions of evangelicals in the North and the South, and Christians were generally restrained and diplomatic when they debated other Christians on theological matters.

But the war changed the landscape dramatically, as many conservative Christians began to see the face of the Antichrist in the war's massive slaughter. In their view, German rationalism gave rise to a religion of science, of progress and modernity, and then had seeded the development of German militarism itself. German rationalism had helped to birth the "higher criticism" of the Bible in the 19th century, and was doubtless responsible for the theory of evolution and other attempts to undermine America's faith in God. German rationalism was connected at its ideological roots with American liberalism and modernism, which had their roots in the rationalism of Northern science and technology. And German rationalism had inspired the German military machine. Premillennialist speakers and writers were fond of recounting stories of German war atrocities as evidence of the workings of the Antichrist in the last days before the Second Coming. Howard Kellogg, speaking at the Bible Institute of Los Angeles in the summer of 1918, charged that Germany's atrocious behavior was due in part to the modernist theology of its churches: "Loud are the cries against German Kultur...Let this now be identified with Evolution, and the truth begins to be told. [This philosophy was responsible for] a monster plotting world domination, the wreck of civilization and the destruction of Christianity itself."[76]

Moreover, conservative Christians were afraid that the destruction of the Great War had spawned a generation of youth supremely cynical about the existence of God and the life of the spirit generally. Their fears were not entirely without foundation. The war had seemed the triumph of science, technology, and a terribly fatal and bloodthirsty "logic" over the romantic, pastoral illusions of the past. Civilization itself was at stake. The Armistice that ended the war in November 1918 signaled the end of the secular struggle fought in the trenches of Europe with guns, tanks, and airplanes. The real war had only begun, however, and the stakes were in the view of some of its participants even higher than the merely physical struggle of the Great War in Europe. It was a struggle for the heart and soul of Christianity in America. It was a fight to claim and define God on behalf of an American democracy. Conservative Christians believed that God was an omnipotent and cosmic consciousness who was personally involved in human history. They believed that God had a plan for America, and that he expected Christians to follow a very specific set of secular doctrines in addition to the theological doctrines that defined fundamentalism.

Christians were invited to accept God's grace, and God's loving offer of forgiveness and redemption. However, Christians were also required to have a certain consciousness and set of beliefs about the heavenly and earthly spheres. On the one hand, Christians were to believe that Jesus was born of a virgin, that Heaven and Hell were real and literal places, that all humanity is judged and condemned as lost sinners, that Jesus died on the cross to save sinners from a fiery Hell, and that he was resurrected, abides in Heaven, and will return to take Christians home to Heaven while the rest of humanity suffers the torments of the damned. On the other hand, conservative Christians believed that the forces of Satan were active in the secular world and made use of such human tools as bartenders who served liquor, teachers who taught evolutionary science, and liberal theologians who swerved from fundamentalist orthodoxy in teaching naïve young Christians to lose their faith in the God of the fundamentalists.

Before the Great War, conservative Christians were part of a broad national evangelical coalition which had dominated American religious life for a century, and which included a wide range of political and theological beliefs. Fundamentalism did not exist as a separate movement. Conservative leadership was mainly located in the cities of the North, the Midwest, and the West. The publication of *The Fundamentals* from 1910 to 1915—the pamphlet series that first defined fundamentalist orthodoxy—had been sponsored by the Bible Institute of Los Angeles, and the writers of the pamphlets had overwhelmingly been theologians and pastors in Northern and Western churches and seminaries. The *Scofield Reference Bible*, a seminal work of fundamentalist and premillennial scholarship, had been annotated by Cyrus Scofield, a Midwesterner, and published by Oxford University Press in 1909. [*]

---

[*] Only later did it begin to be axiomatic that fundamentalism was a Southern phenomenon, after the Scopes Monkey Trial in 1925, and after the defeat of fundamentalists in their effort to control the Northern Protestant denominations. (More about this struggle in subsequent chapters.) However, most of the leaders of the early fundamentalist movement who lived in Northern cities were originally from the South, including William Bell Riley, A. C. Dixon, Curtis Lee Laws, John Roach Straton, and J. Gresham Machen.

Conservatives took part in the governance and leadership of virtually all the major Protestant denominations alongside modernists, they taught in the faculties of Christian colleges and seminaries side by side with modernists, and they served on mission boards with modernists. Conservatism itself was relatively diverse theologically and politically before the war. Conservatives expressed a range of contradictory views on a multitude of subjects from the war to the teaching of evolution in schools, and they were divided among postmillennialists and premillennialists.

In 1915, William Jennings Bryan, later to become the most celebrated spokesman for the anti-evolution cause, resigned from Woodrow Wilson's cabinet as secretary of state because he was opposed to the entrance of the United States into the Great War, and then spent the next two years barnstorming against it. Bryan offered only lukewarm support after the U.S. began sending troops into battle. Prominent conservative journals such as *The King's Business* opposed the war on premillennialist grounds: the world was doomed to slip further and further toward war, sin, and corruption until the Second Coming of Jesus, and therefore Christians should be focused only on saving lost souls. In 1917, the journal warned against the disastrous and demoralizing impact of war, arguing that Christians were required to "love our enemies, even if they were Germans."

On the other hand, Billy Sunday was an ardent militarist who castigated German soldiers as "that weazen-eyed, low-lived, bull-neck, low-down gang of cutthroats of the Kaiser;" the "dirty bunch that would stand aside and see a Turk outrage a woman;" a "great pack of wolfish Huns whose fangs drip with blood and gore;" and "that bunch of pretzel-chewing, sauerkraut spawn of blood-thirsty Huns." The choice for war was simple, said Sunday: "'Either you are loyal or you are not…You are either a patriot or a black-hearted traitor. There is no sitting on the fence at this time."[77]

Likewise, before the war conservative Christians disagreed about whether evolution contradicted the Bible's account of creation, and their disagreement was not thought to be critical to conservative beliefs. Princeton theologian B. B. Warfield contributed an essay for in the first volume of *The Fundamentals* that endorsed the idea of evolution guided by God. James Orr in his essay in *The Fundamentals* claimed that Darwinism had been debunked but that evolution was "coming to be recognized as but a new name for 'creation,'" and that "Here, again, the Bible and science are felt in harmony." Orr felt that it was unfortunate that Darwinism had come to be identified with evolution. Prominent evangelist, educator, and theologian R. A. Torrey, one of the principle editors of *The Fundamentals*, claimed before the war that a Christian could "believe thoroughly in the absolute infallibility of the Bible and still be an evolutionist of a certain type."[78] Even the *Scofield Reference Bible*, the very sourcebook for fundamentalist theology and dispensationalism, published in 1909, left the way open for evolutionary theory by suggesting in a note on the first chapter of Genesis that the six "days" of creation might not be literal days, but rather a "period of time, long or short, during which certain revealed purposes of God are to be accomplished."

The shock and trauma of the Great War, however, drew many conservatives into a consolidated fundamentalist movement with a unified platform. In 1918, it was no longer easy to find a conservative who didn't characterize the war as a struggle between the forces of God and Satan: good and morality and patriotic righteousness squared off against the forces of evil and the Antichrist. *The King's Business* led the charge to find theological unity between the war aims of the government and the obligations of Christians: "The Kaiser threw down the gage of battle—infidel Germany against the believing world—Kultur against Christianity—the Gospel of Hate against the Gospel of Love. Thus is Satan personified—'Myself and God'…Never did Crusader lift battle-ax in holier war against the Saracen than is waged by our soldiers of the cross against the Germans."[79]

The formal launch of fundamentalism as a movement took place at the World Conference on Christian Fundamentals in May of 1919, where 6,000 attendees met in Philadelphia. A key leader and convener of the conference was William Bell Riley from Minnesota, pastor of the First Baptist Church of Minneapolis. In 1891 Riley had launched *The Fundamentalist*, a journal of sermons, essays, and articles from conservative Protestants. In 1902, he founded Northwestern Bible and Missionary Training School to train future generations of fundamentalist leaders. (Riley served as president of Northwestern until 1948, when he died and was succeeded by young evangelist Billy Graham.)

Riley opened the 1919 gathering with a stirring speech that sought to capture an historic moment: "The future will look back to the World Conference on Christian Fundamentals…as an event of more historical moment than the nailing up, at Wittenburg, of Martin Luther's ninety-five theses. The hour has struck for the rise of a new Protestantism."

The tone of the conference was alarming, even apocalyptic. "The Great Apostasy has been spreading like a plague throughout Christendom," said the call to the conference. "Thousands of False Teachers, many of them occupying high ecclesiastical positions, are bringing in damnable heresies, even denying the Lord that bought them, and bring upon themselves swift destruction." The Bible has been "wounded in the house of its friends," cardinal doctrines have been "rejected as archaic and effete; false science has created many false apostles of Christ; indeed, they have been seeing that 'Satan himself is transformed into an angel of light.'"[80]

A. C. Dixon, co-editor with R. A. Torrey of *The Fundamentals*, raised a new issue at the conference with profound consequences for American political battles over the next century—or at least revived an old issue with a new urgency and in a new context. That issue was the teaching of evolution in the public schools of America. George Marsden summed up Dixon's breathtaking synthesis of fundamentalist doctrine and conservative politics in his book *Fundamentalism and American Culture*:

> Greek philosophers, descended from Cain, had first developed evolutionary theory between 700 and 300 BC. Darwin had added to this the idea of the "survival of the fittest," which Dixon described as giving "the strong and fit the scientific right to destroy the weak and the unfit." In Germany Nietzsche expanded this doctrine, and together with the German attacks on the Bible as the proper basis for civilization, this led inevitably to the German atrocities of World War I. By contrast, American civilization was founded on the Bible...democracy and freedom, and the principles of Abraham Lincoln. America had always stood with the weak and the oppressed against the oppressors*...Here Dixon, although a premillennialist, harked back to postmillennial visions of a democratic America leading the world to the triumph of righteousness. The agenda for the next evangelical crusade was an attack on the anti-democratic, "might is right," Bible-denying philosophy of evolution.[81]

As the movement gathered steam, the stakes were seen as ever higher. By 1920, David Kennedy, writing in the firebrand journal *The Presbyterian*, summed up the view that was beginning to be widely shared in the new movement—now explicitly called "fundamentalism" —when he proposed that Americans must counteract:

---

* In making this assertion, obviously, Dixon conveniently forgot much of American history as it affected blacks and native Americans.

...that German destructive criticism which has found its way into the religious and moral thought of our people as the conception and propaganda of the Reds have found their way with poisoning and overthrowing influence into their civil and industrial life. The Bible and the God of the Bible is our only hope. America is narrowed to a choice. She must restore the Bible to its historic place in the family, the day school, the college and university, the church and Sabbath-school, and thus through daily life and thought revive and build up her moral life and faith, or else she might collapse and fail the world in this crucial age.[82]

Kennedy and most other fundamentalists at the end of the war were focused on a struggle over questions of theology and Biblical doctrine. So at first the battle between fundamentalists and modernists took place almost entirely within the realm of the church—theologians arguing with other theologians. However, the single issue of evolution reflected all the crucial concerns of the new fundamentalist movement. Evolution, A. C. Dixon had said, concentrated "the conflict of the ages, darkness versus light, Cain versus Abel, autocracy versus civilized democracy."

The growing influence of Darwin's theory reflected and predicted, in the view of fundamentalists, the decline of moral standards, the growth of heretical doctrines in churches and seminaries, the barbaric atrocities the Germans had been accused of in the Great War, and the impending doom of civilization itself. Opposition to evolution would be a battle cry of the new movement.

The dean of the Southern fundamentalists was J. Frank Norris, the controversial and entertaining pastor of the First Baptist Church in Fort Worth, Texas, and the first evangelical preacher to start a widely heard radio ministry. Sometimes known as "The Texas Tornado" or "The Texas Cyclone" for his vicious and sometimes indiscriminant attacks on opponents, Norris was a charismatic preacher, an angry and eloquent speaker, and a man who courted outrage and conflict. He had a sizable ego, and his influence among fundamentalists was felt far beyond the borders of the state. It was impossible to have a mild opinion about J. Frank Norris. He reveled in being either adored or reviled. He expressed hatred for virtually anyone who failed to share his religion, race or ethnicity, and political leanings.

Norris was especially passionate about Prohibition, which was a symbol of struggle against the moral degeneracy threatening America.

As his biographer wrote, "He sprinkled his sermons with stories of people ruined by alcohol. He told of one man who had stayed sober for several months after Prohibition went into effect but who had succumbed once again to alcohol when the bootleggers got to him. In an analogy appealing to Texas racism, Norris charged that the bootlegger was just as bad as a black rapist who raped and murdered white women, and he reasoned that the bootleggers could only operate effectively in the absence of rigorous enforcement of Prohibition."[83]

Norris viewed the greatest threat to Prohibition as coming from the Catholics, whom he viewed with the greatest suspicion. From his pulpit and newspaper, as well as in dozens of radio broadcasts, he unleashed floods of vituperation on immigrant communities—from Germany, Italy, and Ireland, and other countries with large Catholic populations. These immigrants, he said, were the demon spawn of the Antichrist himself. "The Roman Catholic Church knows allegiance only to the Pope," he wrote. "They would behead every Protestant preacher and disembowel every Protestant mother. They would burn to ashes every Protestant church and dynamite every Protestant school. They would destroy the public schools and annihilate every one of our institutions." In accusing Roman Catholics of trying to take over public education, Norris said, "When the time comes that they seek to dominate and control the free institutions of this country, then it's high time that every man speak out as a true-blooded American citizen."[84] Norris claimed that Catholics could not possibly be real Americans because the Pope was the authority for Catholics in all spheres, in the voting booth as well as the confessional.

Although Norris allied himself with fundamentalists from the North such as James Gray from the Moody Bible Institute in Chicago, and William Bell Riley, founder of the World Christian Fundamentals Association, he also saw the battle against modernism as a continuation of the Lost Cause of the South, as a rebellion against the German rationalism and secularism that had already conquered the North, and as a stand against the Roman Catholic papist conspiracy that threatened the whole country. These immigrants, he said, were "low-browed foreigners." He stated: "Let others do as they may. As far as we are concerned, in Texas we stand for 100 per cent Americanism, for the Bible, for the home, and against every evil and against every foreign influence that seeks to corrupt and undermine our cherished and Christian institutions." [85]

No one understood better how to oppose modernism and the Papacy than Norris. He argued that Fort Worth should fire all Catholics from their jobs in city government, and claimed that the good Southern cities of El Paso and Birmingham had already done so: "The American people, the real white folks, the Protestant population rose up and put the Catholic machine out of business, and a Roman Catholic is not even allowed to clean spittoons in the Court House or City Hall in Birmingham."

As Norris biographer Barry Hankins said, "The battle lines were drawn along the Mason-Dixon Line, and Norris called Southerners to battle against northern infidelity." Norris wrote: "That everyone in the South will be compelled to take sides in the present war to a finish between Fundamentalist and Modernists of the Northern Convention goes without saying." Furthermore, Norris proposed sending missionaries from the "orthodox South to the modernist camp in the North."[86]

Fundamentalists like Norris were calling for a new struggle to preserve Southern values, Southern religion, Southern culture, and the Southern way of life. And this new battle against modernism was more critical and historically significant even than the Lost Cause of the 19th century, fought to defend the God-given rights of Southern white people to own black slaves. This new fight was for the heart and soul of America against the tide of racially degenerate immigrants who sought to dilute her Anglo-Saxon bloodlines and undermine her Christian identity with their Roman Catholic conspiracies.

As the struggle against modernism picked up steam, the nativism and anti-Catholicism of fundamentalists such as Norris assured leaders of the reconstituted Ku Klux Klan that their enterprise had been blessed by God. In the climate of fear whipped up by fundamentalist preachers and Southern politicians, the Klan rapidly spread after 1918 from Georgia to other states North and South, including Texas, four states to the west.

Chapter 15
Called to Preach

"It hath ever been by the sword of the Lord that I have vanquished mine enemies. During the time I am here I shall wield it with more power than ever, for I shall translate into the tongue of the people the Gospels written by the Evangelists." —Martin Luther, in Joseph Hocking's 1909 novel The Sword of the Lord [87]

My call to preach on a Sunday evening in 1957 was no glorious flash of light, no transcendent realization of God's will, no recapitulation of Paul's moment of religious *ecstasis* on the road to Damascus. At no discreet moment (for example, while excursioning for three days in the belly of a large fish) did I (like Jonah) repent of my intransigence and commit myself to spreading the good word of God's grace to the heathen. Instead, from my earliest days of toddlerhood, as soon as I verged on being a conscious human being and developed a memory and knew anything about God, I knew that I was destined to preach the gospel of Jesus Christ.

The evidence of my calling was all around me, in the faces of my dad, my granddad, and my several uncles and great uncle, all of whom were Baptist preachers. The call was emblazoned across the pages of *The Sword of the Lord* newspaper when it arrived in our home each week, and it was chiseled on my heart with the sharpest of tools whenever I considered the millions of humans for whose souls I would become accountable if I failed to become a soul-winner.

At the age of seven, I accompanied my dad to the Jesus Saves Rescue Mission down on Skid Row in Chicago to give my personal testimony to a gathering of bums in a holy place. I walked right up to the edge of the platform and looked out over the faces of the men. Most of them were unshaven, bleary-eyed, with aged, tired faces. A majority of them were white, with several colored faces thrown into the mix, and these colored faces I looked at with greatest care, for they seemed the most open and friendly, the most aware of me. I had something to say to these old men.

"Before I got saved," I said. "I was a sinner. Sometimes I didn't do what my mother told me to do. Once I stole a candy bar at the counter in the corner grocery store, and I never told anyone about it. And I knew I would go to Hell because I had a heart that was black and evil, and I was a sinner. Then one day my granddad said that Jesus had died on the cross for me and washed my sins away and I could get saved and I would go to Heaven if I ever died. And I did get saved, because I asked Jesus to come into my heart and take my sins away. So now I know I am going to Heaven when I die, no matter what. And you can too, if you love Jesus and ask him to come into your heart and wash it clean."

Later, in the mission basement eating a sacramental supper of Hungarian goulash and cornbread with our Skid Row congregation, I felt aglow with love for these sad, poor men. I knew that God had called me to that place on that night to serve them—and him.

In his early 20s, John R. Rice looked askance at the developing Klan movement and its claim to uphold the "Christian" heritage of the South. He was a generation removed from the trauma of fear and displacement that Will Rice experienced as a child in Missouri during the Civil War and afterwards as a war refugee in Texas. He wanted to live a life of service and purpose, and was focused on getting the education he would need.

In the spring of 1918 John R. Rice was drafted into the army just two days before he was ready to graduate from Decatur Baptist College. His army portrait shows a handsome young man looking straight into the camera and wearing a khaki uniform and a large, flat-brimmed campaign hat. He bears a remarkable resemblance to his famous older contemporary, cowboy story teller, comedian, and actor Will Rogers, complete with big ears and friendly smile. Rice immediately left campus to join the Seventh Division to begin training at Camp MacArthur, and Lloys sat next to his empty, flag-draped chair at the commencement exercises. He went through infantry training and was ready to be shipped off to France with his unit when he came down with a bad case of the mumps and had to remain behind. He then spent the last several months of the World War at the Camp dental infirmary working as a dental clerk and exchanging daily letters with Lloys. John found it hard being away for an extended period from the first person who had offered him unconditional love since his mother died. Over and over again in his letters to Lloys, he expressed his besottedness with her, his grave and deep passion, his profound need of her. Lloys returned his love in her letters, but she didn't quite match the ardor he expressed. Her love was a bit more genteel and reserved than his.

As soon as the war ended and John was able to leave the army, he enrolled at Baylor University, the premiere Southern Baptist institution, in Waco, Texas. Lloys joined him there and their terms overlapped, but he graduated a year before her. John then spent a year teaching at Wayland Baptist College in West Texas while Lloys completed her final year at Baylor. In October of 1920 he wrote, "My dearest dear, Mrs. Fife is playing the piano and I can hardly keep from singing. I wish you were here to play for me, oh, I do want that day to come! I am so lonesome and hungry for you and homesick. Please can't you come to see me? I am getting so impatient and lonely I can hardly keep from telling everybody about it. Mr. Fife told me today that married life was the only satisfactory life, and I believe it."

After teaching that autumn in Wayland, John was feeling impatient and ambitious. Increasingly, he was noticing the limits of his background and the choices available for someone who had never left Texas. He wanted a larger landscape of possibilities to choose from, and he wouldn't find those educational options in Waco, no matter how lonely he felt for Lloys. In the kind of abrupt and surprising move that can only be made by a young man in a hurry, John decided to move north to study for a master's degree in education at the University of Chicago.

Considering John R. Rice's subsequent career, his choice of schools was remarkable. The University of Chicago was founded in 1890 by the American Baptist Education Society with money from oil magnate John D. Rockefeller and department store prince Marshall Field. The dream of its first president, William Rainey Harper, was to combine a German-style graduate research university with an undergraduate liberal arts college to unite the study of all the sciences in one place. The school had rapidly evolved to embrace a philosophy of broad and nonsectarian humanistic education, and by 1921 the only remaining part of the institution labeling itself Baptist was the Divinity School. In the dispute between modernists and conservatives during and immediately after the Great War, the University of Chicago was the command post for aggressive theological assaults by modernists on the conservatives and premillennialists across town at Moody Bible Institute. The very fact that John decided to enroll at the University of Chicago was evidence that he was feeling a strong pull away from the rigid orthodoxy of the small churches in Texas where he had grown up, and the narrow cultural horizons of the Deep South. He was reaching for a larger understanding of his mission and his life, and he wanted to open himself to a broader range of religious ideas.

In the middle of the winter of 1921, John headed north on the train from Fort Worth and across the Red River, north through Oklahoma, paralleling the Texas Trail that had been followed south by his relatives and ancestors in 1863 in the wake of their disastrous losses in the Civil War. He traveled north through the Kansas prairie, so close to the Kansas-Missouri border that he could almost look east out the window of the train and across to Jackson County, where his family had owned plantations, and the human beings who worked thousands of acres devoted to the growing of hemp and the piling up of wealth beyond his own memory or imagination. He traveled north and east from Kansas City across the flat plains and rolling hills of Missouri, and he changed trains in St. Louis. He crossed the Mississippi River and rode through 300 miles of Illinois cornfields now fallow and shrouded in a blanket of white winter snow. His journey ended in the chilly metropolis of Chicago, where he alighted with his bag and went off to enroll at the university.

At the time of his arrival in Chicago, John still believed his calling was to become a teacher. He was sure his plan was to get Lloys to marry him that year and join him in Chicago. And he might go on to get a doctorate—the first in his family!—and set out to become an accomplished and famous professor at a prestigious university, probably not in Texas. Maybe even in a place where he could escape his small-town Texas roots forever. An historic conflict was shaping up, however, that would redirect the course of his life.

The fundamentalist campaign led by William Bell Riley and the World Christian Fundamentals Association had begun in 1919. The campaign first of all aimed at expelling liberals or modernists from Protestant denominational conferences and the colleges, universities, and seminaries associated with the denominations. Fundamentalist caucuses or informal committees emerged within most of the national church groups. Conservatives commenced agitation to roll back the modernist "tide of immorality and unbelief," as R. A. Torrey phrased it.[88] The fundamentalist pitch was simple: Historic Christianity was in danger of becoming distorted or diluted beyond recognition. It was the job of true Christians to expose the heretics who were posing as Christian leaders, "denying the Bible" and "following false doctrines." It was time to reclaim Christian institutions from the "infidels" who infested them.

Between 1920 and 1925, the newborn fundamentalist movement conducted an institutional campaign to take control of the major

Protestant denominations and purge modernists from seminaries, pulpits, and mission boards. At the same time, fundamentalists launched a public campaign to remove the teaching of evolution from every classroom in America.

William Bell Riley of the World Christian Fundamentals Association suggested that "an international Jewish-Bolshevik-Darwinist conspiracy to promote evolutionism in the classroom" was attempting to destroy the moral fiber of America's youth.[89] One of Riley's allies, an overheated preacher named T. T. Martin, asserted that German soldiers who allegedly killed Belgian and French children by giving them poisoned candy were angels compared to those who spread evolutionary ideas in schools.[90]

As the battle lines hardened, the attacks by the fundamentalists became more extreme and their language more violent. As the fundamentalists sharpened and codified their statements of belief, they discovered more and more ways in which they were at odds with the modernists. Soon, old friends were no longer speaking to each other, prominent pastors were being forced to resign from their churches because they were viewed as liberals or modernists, and fundamentalists were launching campaigns to take over denominations and seminaries that they believed had been captured by the "infidels."

To the delight of Riley and his allies in the fundamentalist movement, William Jennings Bryan took up the anti-evolution cause in the most public way possible beginning in 1920. Bryan was a political progressive and Democratic Party candidate for president of the United States in 1896, 1900, and 1908. He had campaigned against war and imperialism; against corruption, economic monopolies and trusts; against the wealthy oligarchs who ruled early 20th century America; and on behalf of the common people, the poor, the farmers and working people of America. He was a gifted orator who had burst into public consciousness in 1896 when, at the age of 36, he became the youngest presidential nominee in U.S. history with an extraordinary speech that would be known forever as the "Cross of Gold Speech." The crux of that speech was Bryan's charge that U.S. bankers had restricted the money supply by linking the value of money to the amount of gold held by the government, thus causing the depression of 1893. Bryan concluded by saying: "Having behind us the producing masses of this nation and the world, supported by the commercial interests, the laboring interests and the toilers everywhere, we will answer their demand for a gold standard by saying to them: You shall not press down upon the brow of labor this crown of thorns, you shall not crucify mankind upon a cross of gold." Bryan paused before the silent crowd and stretched out his arms for several seconds as though he were Jesus on the cross, and then the crowd went absolutely mad. The *New York Times* reported that "a wild, raging irresistible mob" rushed the stage.[91] Although Bryan lost the election, he was established as a significant national leader for the next three decades.

At the capstone of Bryan's political career, he served as secretary of state under Woodrow Wilson during the Great War. By the end of the war, along with many of his supporters, he was also passionately and publicly opposed to the instruction of evolution in schools. More than any other factor, his horror at the ravages of the war sparked his opposition to the teaching of evolution. In a 1920 speech to the World Brotherhood Congress, he charged that the theory of evolution was "the most paralyzing influence with which civilization has had to deal in the last century." Bryan said that Friedrich Nietzsche—a German philosopher of the 19th century—in carrying the theory of evolution to its logical conclusion, "promulgated a philosophy that condemned democracy...denounced Christianity...denied the existence of God, overturned all concepts of morality...and endeavored to substitute the worship of the superhuman for the worship of Jehovah."[92]

It was necessary to oppose the teaching of evolution in schools, Bryan said, because the teaching of evolution inevitably led to atheism, and when young people stopped believing in God they often became criminals, psychopaths, and communists. The foundation of civilization itself was at stake. If modernists and atheists claimed they were not teaching atheism, said Bryan, but "only a scientific interpretation of Christianity, we reply that nine-tenths of the Christians believe the orthodox interpretation of Christianity, and if they cannot teach the views of the majority in the schools, supported by taxation, then a few people cannot teach at public expense their scientific interpretation that attacks every vital principle of Christianity."

In alliance with the World Christian Fundamentals Association, the Defenders of the Christian Faith, and the Anti-Evolution League, Bryan barnstormed around the country denouncing evolutionary theory and leading fierce battles in several states to combat its teaching in the public schools.

Although Bryan recited in almost every speech a long list of academic degrees he appended to his name in order to support his attacks on the "scientific merit" of Darwin's theory, he never came up with a serious objection to evolution on the grounds of scientific evidence or analysis. He claimed that anyone with "common sense" and no particular education could see that no complex form of life could evolve from a simpler form. He claimed it was necessary to read only a single Bible verse, Genesis 1:24, where God said, "Let the earth bring forth the living creature after his kind," in order to be convinced that there never could and never would be any change in any species from one generation to the next.[93]

Despite his overblown claims to scientific expertise, Bryan understood that genuine scientific evidence was relatively unimportant to his argument. It was necessary to reject evolution because it posed a danger to religious faith, regardless of whether it was "true" in any factual or evidentiary sense. Especially in the wake of the recent Great War, with its history of mass slaughter aided by technology, Bryan believed that Christians had to stand up and fight against any slight attempt to move away from "traditional and orthodox" Christianity by reading any new or "modern" meaning into the text of the Bible. He claimed that propagandists for the German war machine had used the Darwinian phrase "survival of the fittest" to justify building their weapons of mass destruction, and feared that modern war-making had the capacity to destroy civilization itself. The phrase "survival of the fittest" was, of course, never used by Darwin in any of his writings, and Darwin would likely have been horrified by any such misapplication as Bryan suggested.

Bryan read the first chapter of Genesis as a precise and literal description of the specific and practical process by which God created the earth. In a speech titled "The Bible or Evolution,"[94] Bryan charged that evolution was "a scientific excuse for discarding God, and for discarding his Word, and for discarding Christ. That is the only thing there is, and it is a menace to the Christian civilization of the world; it is also a menace to society, and to civilization. That is why I am defending the Bible. It gives us that upon which the world must build, and there is no hope for the future if we give it up."

On May 4, 1921, the 26-year-old John R. Rice heard Bryan give a speech at a Chicago church. Bryan's speech was titled "The Bible and Its Enemies." He declared that Christians were called by God to stand firm in an historic defense of the Bible's authority against a variety of modern threats, from evolutionists who challenged a literal acceptance of the Bible's account of creation to religious leaders who questioned the virgin birth of Jesus or the inerrancy of the Bible as the literally inspired word of God. Bryan said, "Give the modernist three words, 'allegorical,' 'poetical,' and 'symbolically,' and he can suck the meaning out of every vital doctrine of the Christian Church and every passage in the Bible to which he objects."

In short, the Bible was under assault, America was being undermined by Satan, and God needed a new generation of domestic missionaries and spiritual warriors willing to devote their lives to defending Christianity from infidels and assailants, misinterpreters and modernists, cynics and religious miscreants and purveyors of perdition in all its forms. God required human partners, and if good Christians failed to defend the inerrancy and authority of scripture, then the witness of God's word would be destroyed, and the Christian nation of America could go to Hell.

For Rice, the key moment of Bryan's talk was his assertion that the theory of evolution was grounded in spiritual fallacy and opposition to a literal account of creation in Genesis. [95] As a 26-year-old in the big northern city of Chicago for the first time in his life, exploring new ideas and a vibrant intellectual atmosphere so different from his small-town Texas roots, Rice had been considering whether there might be some agreement between the science of evolution and the spirit of the Creation story. In short, he was evaluating theistic evolution, which he had begun to see as an interesting compromise between the claims of science and the fundamentals of the faith.

No, said Bryan. Either you were on God's side, or on the side of evolution and the Prince of Darkness. We all had to choose. John R. Rice went home that night deeply attracted by the starkness of the choice, and with growing doubts about the plans he had made for his life.

That spring, John had spent much time volunteering and worshipping at the Pacific Garden Mission in downtown Chicago, where Billy Sunday had been converted and where the congregation consisted of drunks, sinners, and bums, many of them homeless and jobless. He counseled and witnessed to men who were without hope or means, alone in the world and living in a gutter of poverty and self-hatred. He made himself useful singing gospel songs and serving food in the soup line, and he felt happier helping the bums and down-and-outers at the mission than sitting in faculty tea parties and graduate student soirees at the university.

One night he heard a preacher at the mission praising God for calling him to preach despite having only a fifth grade education. Rice, with his own brand new, yet barely used, college education, felt that with his own greater gifts and advantages, God had greater expectations of him.

And then came an evening that changed things for him:

> I remember the time when I knelt by a drunken bum...and showed him how to be saved. I saw the transformation in his face, the evidence of wonderful peace in his heart, and the change that took place in his life. And suddenly God gave me a glimpse of the eternal

value of a soul, and of the joy of winning souls for Jesus and Heaven. That night I lost my taste for the college classroom where I had been teaching. I lost my ambition and my dreams to be a great educator. I saw at a glance that this was the great labor, the labor with eternal rewards, the labor beside which no other toil or effort in the universe is comparable.[96]

In June of 1921, Rice preached his first sermon at the Pacific Garden Mission in Chicago. His text was from the book of Romans, a verse aimed at winning souls for Jesus: "For the wages of sin is death, but the gift of God is eternal life through Jesus Christ our Lord." Years later in an article in *The Sword of the Lord*, he reflected that he had never been called to do anything other than be a preacher. "I know now that before I was born I was destined to be a preacher of the gospel. I know that my mind and heart were colored and controlled very largely by the Lord in answer to my mother's devoted prayer. At the Pacific Garden Mission, my mother's prayers caught up with me, and I saw that I could never have any joy, peace, or really adequate occupation, except in winning souls."

After that first sermon, John returned to Texas and immediately plunged into the work he felt God had called him to. He was the song leader for older evangelists in several revivals that summer of 1921. He then conducted his own first revival as a preacher in a small church in Corinth, Texas, at which 23 souls were saved. In the fall John and Lloys borrowed $100 from family members to get married, and the newlyweds both enrolled at Southwestern Baptist on Seminary Hill in Fort Worth—the seminary that had been started by Baylor University. In October John was ordained a preacher at the Decatur First Baptist Church.

John had finally decided to commit himself fully to being a preacher, and Lloys was along for the ride, wherever it took them. John spent the next two years studying theology and preaching on street corners, in jails, and in small country churches outside of Fort Worth. He later recalled with some easy humor that Lloys made better grades in Hebrew than he did. The newly married couple stayed at Southwestern Seminary for two years until 1923, when Rice was offered his first job as assistant pastor of the First Baptist Church in Plainview, Texas. He was impatient to begin his life as a preacher full time. After they moved to Plainview, he started and edited his first newspaper, the *Plainview Baptist*, a small publication supported by local advertising. A year later, he was called to the pastorate of the First Baptist Church of Shamrock, a promotion to the pulpit of his own church. Once again, he started a newspaper, which he called the *Shamrock Baptist*. He opened his ministry with a successful revival and led the church with hard work and great enthusiasm. Within two years the church had grown from 200 to 460 members and was ready to move from its small wooden "tabernacle" into a new brick building. The little town was booming with the discovery of oil in the surrounding countryside. The streets of the town were paved for the first time, new people were arriving all the time, and the church was overflowing with new converts, meetings, programs, and committees.

Rice was dissatisfied, however. He was frustrated with the bureaucracy of the church and felt that he was called by God to become a full-time evangelist. It wasn't the leadership of a local church that he was called to. It wasn't being recognized as a community leader that he was called to. Instead, he was called to be a revivalist. He was burdened with a desire to spend every available waking moment working to bring lost sinners to Jesus and introduce them to the possibility of eternal salvation. He was driven by a desire to bring the Gospel of Jesus to the whole world, and he was propelled by something deeper and more powerful than anything he knew how to express.

Years later he wrote a book titled *The Soul-Winner's Fire*, in which he said:

> When I first began preaching, I remember how I wept from the beginning to the end of my sermons. I was embarrassed about it. This was wholly unlike the college debating, the commencement addresses and other public speaking to which I had been accustomed. The tears flowed down my cheeks almost continually and I was so broken up that sometimes I could scarcely talk. Then I grew ashamed of my tears and longed to speak more logically. As I recall, I asked the Lord to give me better control of myself as I preached. My tears soon vanished and I found I had only the dry husk of preaching left. Then I begged God to give me again the broken heart, the concern, even if that meant tears in public, and a trembling voice. I feel the same need today. We preachers ought to cry out like Jeremiah, "Oh that my head were waters, and mine eyes a fountain of tears, that I might weep day and night for the slain of the daughter of my people!"[97]

Rice would carry that burden for saving lost souls for the rest of his life, and it was driven by genuinely heartfelt compassion based on a powerful rationale: if sinners were going to burn in the literal flames of a materially real eternal fire unless they accepted the atoning sacrifice of Jesus on the cross, then any sensible, empathetic, and responsible person would devote all of his life to saving non-Christians from their God-ordained fate.

Chapter 16
Unfortunate Associations

In the fall of 1978, when I was 28, the Ku Klux Klan was undergoing one of its periodic revivals in the South. In May that year, Decatur, Alabama police had arrested a black man named Tommy Lee Hines. Tommy was a 25-year-old mentally disabled student in a day school for the retarded. He reportedly had mental capacity of a five-year-old, and was incapable of carrying on a conversation or even riding a bicycle by himself. Police charged Hines with the rapes of three white women. One of the accusing women weighed 200 pounds, while Tommy weighed 120.

The Klan held a rally that attracted a crowd of 5,000 in the spring demanding Hines' conviction and execution. At the rally, an 80-year-old Baptist preacher told a reporter, "God will have a special place for the Ku Klux Klan in Heaven." Another rally of 9,000 Klan supporters took place in September 1978 before a trial on the first rape charge. At trial, the purported rape victim testified she recognized Tommy, while also claiming her attacker had a plastic bag over his face. After three hours of deliberation, an all-white jury convicted Hines, and the judge sentenced him to three decades in prison.

In the wake of Hines' conviction, Don Black, the Grand Wizard of the reconstituted Knights of the Ku Klux Klan, announced a Klan march to the Birmingham City Hall, where they would promote the Klan's "pro-white and pro-Christian platform."

Black was a slick, young graduate of the University of Alabama in Tuscaloosa, complete with a three-piece suit, fluency in the English language, and well-polished teeth. This new Klan proclaimed that it was a modernized organization that advocated nonviolent protection for white people whose civil rights were endangered. The Klan for the first time accepted women as equal members and welcomed membership applications from Catholics, whom they had excoriated in the past.

The October morning of the march found Black and two dozen other Klansmen in their trademark white robes pinned up against the doors of the City Hall, protected by a ring of several score Birmingham police officers dressed in riot gear and wielding batons. Both the police and the Klansmen were surrounded by a very angry crowd of over 2,000 overwhelmingly black anti-Klan protesters who hollered insults at the Klansmen across their line of protective cops.

I was in the vanguard of the demonstrators, only a few feet away from Don Black. As a member of the Birmingham Coalition to Stop the Klan, I had worked feverishly to organize a response to the Klan march. I printed the anti-Klan leaflets on the printing press installed on my back porch, and I had spent the previous evening constructing a silly looking and highly flammable effigy of a Klansman dressed in a ceremonial bed sheet.

With my fellow demonstrators, I chanted slogans at the top of my lungs: "Death to the Klan! Down with the Klan! Cops and Klan work hand in hand!" The effigy was hung by its neck from the end of a broomstick that I waved vigorously in the air. Don Black and his Klansmen looked terrified and said nothing, cowering far back into the recessed doorway. At the height of the tumult, I lowered the effigy into the crowd behind me, where a black steelworker named Trane dowsed it with lighter fluid and fired it up with his Bic lighter. I raised my broomstick and the effigy flared, igniting cheers. Happiness was a combustible mixture of lighter fluid, Alabama sunlight, the gleeful rambunctiousness of the demonstrators, the breeze whipping around the corner of City Hall, and an intense aroma from the purple azaleas surrounding the plaza.

My delight was paired with rage. I identified the Klan with its violent oppression of black people in the South for a century and a half. But at a deeper level, I was incensed that the Klan could pretend to be a "pro-Christian" organization, despite the fact that I no longer thought of myself as a Christian. In a way I couldn't articulate, I felt that the Klan's claim to the mantle of Christianity was personally offensive and insulting to me as well as to my whole family.

Two more decades would pass before I discovered, almost by chance, that my own great-grandfather had been a Klansman.

By the fall of 1922, as John R. Rice ended the first year of his career as an evangelist, the Texas Klan had grown so rapidly that it had become the largest and most influential force in the state, with a grassroots membership of perhaps 150,000. The Klan decided to use its political muscle in an attempt to take over the reins of political power in Texas, and prepared a slate of candidates in most of the 254 counties in the state. For governor, the Klan supported Democrat Pat Neff; in the race for United States senate, the Klan nod went to Earle Bradford Mayfield. Another of Mayfield's supporters was fundamentalist leader J. Frank Norris, who urged all Protestant ministers to join his endorsement of Mayfield.

For a state senate seat in northeast Texas near the Red River, the Klan supported Will Rice,[98] an avid leader of the Klan from Cooke County. My great-grandfather Will was 61 years old when he joined the Klan in 1920. He was prominent in the north Texas counties that shared a border with Oklahoma along the Red River. Many of his neighbors were also descended from refugees who had arrived there after fleeing Missouri during the Civil War. He owned a farm outside Decatur where his family had raised cash crops for a generation. Unlike his prosperous Missouri ancestors, he had inherited a hardscrabble life, struggling to make a living in good years and barely making it in bad ones. He found diverse ways to support his family, and had seen money come and go in his life. He had traded horses for a living for several years, speculated in land and livestock, and sometimes preached in little Baptist churches around north Texas. He always found he could fall back on farming.

His earliest memories were connected with the trauma of the Civil War. He had seen his father and older brother James leave for the war, and had endured their absence. He had been uprooted from the place of his birth and had fled with his family to a new place in the distant south, where they arrived with few possessions. He had grown up in the region of Texas most cursed by violence, and where the wounds of the conflict between former slave owners and former abolitionists still festered. He had been raised in a family whose founding myth was rooted in a need to justify the ownership of other human beings.

Will Rice saw the Ku Klux Klan as an heroic embodiment of the Old South, as protectors of Christian beliefs and defenders of white womanhood, as soldiers who wielded a holy sword in service to the Lost Cause.

The fall election in 1922 was nearly a clean sweep for Klan-endorsed candidates. Neff, Mayfield, and Will Rice all won their races handily, along with enough probable Klan supporters to hold a majority of the seats in the state house, and enough Klan sympathizers in the senate to dominate the proceedings. Klansmen probably were a majority in the house of representatives of the 38th Texas Legislature, which met in January.

On the wall in the basement of the Texas state capital in Austin is a framed display of members of the 38th Senate. There in a little oval portrait you can find the face of Will Rice himself, looking stern, handsome, and heroic, a defender of civilization if ever there was one, representative in the august senate of the white folks of Decatur, Texas. Legally, at least, he also represented the black folks and a rare Indian or Mexican, although they were legally prevented from voting for or against him, and would not have considered him one of their own.

In addition to the state government, the Klan worked hard to establish influence in local areas, and by 1923 the Klan firmly controlled city governments in Dallas, Fort Worth, and Wichita Falls. In the minds of many Texans, the principle attraction of the Klan was its defense of Christian morality. The Klan presented itself as a contender for the historic Christian faith, a defender of Christian civilization, and an advocate for the good Christian people of the South and the country. Most Texas Klan supporters saw no contradiction between the politics of the Klan and the fundamentalist theology of the Baptist churches many of them attended on Sunday mornings. As Reverend I. E. Gates, pastor of the First Baptist Church in San Antonio, said in 1924, "Hubbard City, Texas, has given to the world three great geniuses—Hiram W. Evans, the imperial wizard of the Ku Klux Klan; Tris Speaker, of baseball fame; and J. Frank Norris, the greatest preacher of modern times."[99]

In the early 1920s, J. Frank Norris, the prominent pastor of the First Baptist Church in Fort Worth, Texas, launched a series of vitriolic personal attacks on his fellow preachers in the Southern Baptist Convention, which he considered a viper pit of modernism and liberalism and whose denominational programs he accused of being "dictatorial, unscriptural, a foolish waste of hard earned mission money." In 1922, he was censured by the Baptist General Convention of Texas for his unbrotherly viciousness, and began to think about leaving the ranks of the Southern Baptists, who were too liberal for him.

Norris was convinced that he alone could lead the fight on the side of God, and he was ruthless in defense of his personal brand of fundamentalism. In the mid-1920s, Norris launched open warfare against Roman Catholicism. He published a sermon in his newspaper *The Searchlight* in 1924 titled "The Purple, Scarlet-Robed Woman of Prophecy and History," in which he attempted to demonstrate that the Roman Catholic Church was the "Great Whore of Babylon" and would play a major part in the war of the Antichrist against Christians at the end of history. Then he preached about "The Menace of Roman Catholicism and Politics," suggesting that "Romanism" was against America, Christianity, and Prohibition. He accused Roman Catholics of planning a huge broadcasting scheme to turn the United States into a Catholic country.

Norris's politics fit well with the Klan because he had a holistic view of how race, religion, morality, and politics fit together. Commenting on an interracial marriage that took place at a church in New York, Norris said, "I can name to you a people south of the Mason-Dixon Line that if a Negro should take a white girl's hand in marriage that girl would be without a Negro husband before the sun arose the next morning." Furthermore, said Norris, he would gladly perform the funeral. [100]

The Klan's supreme reign over Texas politics lasted only a couple of years.[101] A horrific case came to light in which several Klansmen nearly beat to death a young white veteran of the Great War who had offended them. When this man went out for a Sunday drive with a widow woman of whom they disapproved, they ran him off the road, cracked his skull with a gun and covered his head with a sack, then drove him into the countryside. They tied him to a barbed wire fence and flogged him, then drove him to City Hall, where they chained him to a tree and drenched him with hot tar. A fearless young prosecutor named Dan Moody used this case to convict the Klansmen and to tarnish the Klan's reputation.[102]

In the next statewide election in the fall of 1924, J. Frank Norris did his best to prop up the Klan's political fortunes by endorsing Klan candidate and fellow Baptist Felix D. Robertson for governor. When Norris announced his support of Robertson, he claimed that every "black-bosomed celibate Roman Catholic from El Paso to Galveston is fighting him tooth and nail."

Norris's support failed to make any significant difference, however. Robertson was trounced in the governor's race along with the Klan candidate for lieutenant governor. Dan Moody ran for attorney general, and beat the Klan candidate by a two to one margin. The Klan's political dominance and fearsome reputation had been largely destroyed. The *New York Times* editorialized: "The smashing defeat suffered by the Klan in Texas ought to be a signal to start warfare against it all over the country." And the *Houston Chronicle* reported: "The open season for the Ku Klux Klan as a political force in Texas ended on August 23, 1924."

The Klan was down, but by no means out. Although its power in the Texas state government was severely limited, the organization continued to play an influential role in the state for years to come, and the Klan's views on a host of issues dear to its constituency continued to be highly popular among Texas voters, including the Klan's racial politics, its opposition to Catholics and immigrants, its support for continuing Prohibition, and its anti-evolution campaign. In the backlash against the Klan's politics, however, Will Rice was defeated for re-election. My great-granddad returned from the statehouse in Austin to the shade tree outside the courthouse in his home town, where he resumed telling jokes and stories, speculating on real estate, trading horses, and expressing his opinion about a myriad of current events.

Also in 1924, after one vicious attack too many on his fellow Baptists, J. Frank Norris was expelled by the Texas association of Southern Baptists. It was an expulsion he had intentionally provoked, and it allowed Norris to cast himself as a martyr in the struggle against liberalism and modernism and "denominationalism." He responded with ever more virulent attacks and by setting out to create an independent Baptist movement, led by his First Baptist Church in Fort Worth.

A prominent ally of Norris was Mordecai Ham, a Kentucky preacher and evangelist. Both men were born in 1877 and they shared much beyond their birth year and fundamentalist beliefs. Each of them displayed a charismatic stage presence, a flair for the dramatic, a colorful speaking style, and a demonstrated intolerance for anyone who might disagree with them about matters spiritual or political.

Mordecai Ham was descended from eight generations of Baptist preachers. At the age of 22 Ham had answered the call to be an evangelist and preached in revival meetings throughout Kentucky. Soon he was in demand for revival meetings throughout the South. In April, 1911, Ham held his first of many Texas revival meetings in a soul-winning extravaganza hosted by J. Frank Norris and the First Baptist Church.

Over the next few decades, Ham preached in hundreds of revival meetings and saw thousands of converts. With his balding dome and bushy white mustache, Ham resembled an insurance salesman or bank president more than a tent revivalist. But on a platform he became a passionate and riveting orator who connected strongly with Southern culture, fears, and hopes. Ham preached that the Anglo-Saxon, Scandinavian, Celtic, Germanic, and kindred peoples were the Lost Tribes of Israel, a theory he defended at the Seventh Annual Conference of the British Israel World Federation on October 4, 1926: "I know of no truth today that can so restore confidence as this Anglo Israel Truth, because in my country, in the southland of America, you find the old Anglo-Saxon Puritan blood in the ascendancy. We still believe this Book, in spite of all the attacks that are being made upon it."[103]

Ham had a comprehensive worldview that somehow combined his love for Jesus and desire to save lost souls with God's approval of white supremacy and hatred of alcohol and communism. For Ham, virtually every evil in the world was wrapped up in or inspired by the Russian revolution and the international Communist movement. He typically concluded his sermon against the teaching of evolution by warning that "the day is not distant when you will be in the grip of the Red Terror and your children will be taught free love by the damnable theory of evolution."

Ham's rhetorical bombast sometimes got him into trouble. A notable example was Ham's 1924 revival in Elizabeth City, New Jersey, when he attacked Jews for plotting the downfall of Western civilization. Jewish philanthropist Julius Rosenwald, president of Chicago-based Sears, Roebuck, was well known for spending millions to support the education of African-Americans across the South. Without a shred of evidence, Ham accused Rosenwald of operating houses of prostitution in Chicago featuring white slavery and interracial perversion.

The editor of the local newspaper published evidence that Ham's attack amounted to nothing more than lies and racist propaganda, and denounced him as a demagogue "gifted in the art of making people hate." [104] Ham was forced to end his revival campaign prematurely and leave the state for some time until the stink of his public disgrace dispersed. The incident proved to be a permanent stain on Ham's reputation. *

Ham was not the only well-known evangelist to damage the reputation of revivalists in the minds of many Americans. Billy Sunday's career had skyrocketed from 1909 on, and by the end of the Great War he had reached the zenith of American public life: invitations to the White House, and close friendship with prominent and wealthy people from politicians and sports stars to investment bankers and society mavens. Incidentally, Sunday was also preaching to audiences of tens and hundreds of thousands in cities across the country, and seeing many in those audiences walk the sawdust trail to a Christian conversion.

However, Sunday was also raking in cash by the truckload, and was increasingly enamored of the lifestyle permitted by his success as a preacher. Early in his career he had never especially noticed the money that began to flow in to the coffers of his revival campaigns. He had clearly been driven to win lost souls for Jesus, and he had been true to his humble roots. But as his crowds and popular acclaim grew, Billy's attitude began to change, along with that of his wife Nell, who served as his business manager. After 1910, Nell Sunday became obsessive. She "suspected that people did not count the offerings correctly. She was also increasingly convinced that local expenses were not as high as people said. She kept a close eye on the money counters, demanded detailed accounts of expenses, and made sure that every penny in excess of

---

* Decades later, a recollection of the incident would raise questions about the theology and politics of Billy Graham, who was later saved under Ham's ministry.

expenses went to Billy and his team." Nell's obsession spread to Billy, who often criticized his audiences for their parsimony and said more than once, "Don't let me hear any coins fall into those buckets; I want to hear the rustle of paper."[105]

Increasingly, the Sundays' lifestyle shifted. They bought expensive cars, wore fancy clothes, traveled first class, and indulged their children with rich gifts. As Billy became a celebrity and began to hang out with investment bankers and national politicians, his press coverage changed. Billy's story as reported in the newspapers early in his career could be summed up this way: "A poor farm boy becomes a successful and acclaimed professional baseball player, and then gives it all up to serve Jesus and the poor." But at the height of Billy's career, even as he was preaching to enormous crowds in revival tabernacles across the land, critical reporters began to report a different story: "An honest preacher becomes corrupted with cash, develops an arrogant attitude, and transmogrifies into a fraud." As Sunday's biographer said, "Even as they challenged others to live by faith and pointed to Christ's teachings that disciples should not store up treasures on earth, the Sundays were stocking away investments by the tens of thousands each year between 1908 and 1920. Their own records show that they held sizable sums in savings, and they invested thousands upon thousands in second deeds of trust through several banks in Chicago and other parts of the Midwest."[106]

For years, news story followed news story, with little impact on Sunday's growing crowds and expanding influence. But by the latter half of the 1920s the stories were having an impact on Sunday's reputation. Americans were beginning to develop a profound resistance to the apparent hypocrisy of fundamentalist revivalists such as Sunday. Jeering editorials and satirical cartoons would take their toll and help shift how many Americans looked at evangelical Christians.

Chapter 17
The Scopes Monkey Trial

> *"Put on the whole armor of God that ye may be able to stand against the wiles of the devil. For we wrestle not against flesh and blood, but against principalities, against powers, against the rulers of the darkness of this world, against spiritual wickedness in high places. ...Stand therefore, having your loins girt about with truth, and having on the breastplate of righteousness; And your feet shod with the preparation of the gospel of peace; Above all, taking the shield of faith, wherewith ye shall be able to quench all the fiery darts of the wicked. And take the helmet of salvation, and the sword of the Spirit, which is the word of God."*—Ephesians 6:10-17

At the age of 10 I was already a grizzled two-year veteran of the Wheaton, Illinois newspaper wars. I delivered copies of the *Chicago Daily News* in 1960 every day of the year to over 70 customers along a circuitous three-mile route. My chariot of choice, purchased with my own hard-earned cash, was now a blue Western Flyer bike with balloon tires and a big shiny basket, an equipment upgrade from my original little red wagon

When I was a good three blocks away from home, I stopped to attach an ace of hearts to my rear wheel with a clothespin in order to make a noise wonderfully like a motorcycle engine when I got up to speed. I was careful to do so out of my mom's sight, because I knew that even touching or looking at certain playing cards was an offense against the Holy Spirit. Spades, of course, were shaped like Satan's tail, and Jesus was symbolized by the Jack, presumed to be the illegitimate son of the King.

Between my stops, I joyfully sang a song of my own composition, inspired by my granddad's sermons in which he smote the liberals and modernists against whom we fundamentalists were engaged in a great battle to defend the Christian faith. As a child, I knew little of the labyrinthine theological disputes connected with our struggle against modernism. However, I had heard enough sermons to know that one man in particular—Harry Emerson Fosdick—was an apostate and infidel, worthy of my most profound contempt. And so I flipped my newspapers onto porches to my own anti-Fosdick lyrics, bellowed to the tune of the Battle Hymn of the Republic:

> Harry Emerson Fosdick got a brick dropped on his toes
> Hollered like the demon that did sit upon his nose
> The flames of hell surrounded him;
> he struck a tortured pose,
> As eternity began!
> Glory, glory, Harry Fosdick!
> Glory, glory, Harry Fosdick!
> Glory, glory, Harry Fosdick!
> The modernists are doomed!

For a time in the early 1920s, it was not clear whether the fundamentalists would succeed in claiming the mantle of mainstream Christian orthodoxy. The fundamentalists were certain of the righteousness of their cause. They were passionately opposed to the liberals and refused to compromise. In several of the major evangelical denominations the struggle began to play itself out, engendering increasing bitterness and resentment on the part of those who were targets of attempted purges.

Harry Emerson Fosdick was a prominent Baptist preacher who was serving as pastor of the First Presbyterian Church in New York. He was a well-educated and distinguished liberal and an eloquent and authoritative preacher, with striking dark eyes, a high forehead and a crown of bushy hair. The controversy broke into the public eye when Fosdick preached a Sunday morning sermon in May of 1922 titled "Shall the Fundamentalists Win?" Fosdick noted that:

> A great mass of new knowledge has come into man's possession: new knowledge about the physical universe, its origin, its forces, its laws; new knowledge about human history and in particular about the ways in which the ancient peoples used to think in matters of religion

and the methods by which they phrased and explained their spiritual experiences; and new knowledge, also, about other religions and the strangely similar ways in which men's faiths and religious practices have developed everywhere.[107]

Fosdick questioned a number of orthodox assumptions, and then suggested that the fundamentalists were guilty of arrogance and intolerance for demanding that everyone toe the fundamentalist line in all matters of doctrinal belief. He pleaded for "an intellectually hospitable, tolerant, liberty-loving church." He claimed that divine revelation, contrary to the assumptions of the fundamentalist, was progressive: "The thought of God moves out from Oriental kingship to compassionate fatherhood; treatment of unbelievers moves out from the use of force to the appeals of love; polygamy gives way to monogamy; slavery, never explicitly condemned before the New Testament closes, is nevertheless being undermined by ideas that in the end, like dynamite, will blast its foundations to pieces."

The appeal of modernists such as Fosdick to the principle of tolerance and religious freedom was especially dangerous to the position of the fundamentalists. Much of the attraction and power of evangelical Christianity had historically resided in its demand for freedom of conscience. The adoption of the First Amendment to the U.S. Constitution was driven by evangelicals—Baptists in particular—concerned about religious oppression and a history of brutal insistence on religious conformity by the British Crown, the established Church, and colonial governors. Fosdick's critique of the fundamentalists painted them as allies of their own historically worst enemies.

Fosdick's sermon lit a firestorm of protest and controversy within both the Presbyterian Church in the U. S. A. and in the Northern Baptist Convention. His supporters published and circulated it to virtually every Protestant pastor in the country, and his detractors called for his immediate firing from his Presbyterian pastorate on charges of heresy. The story hit the front pages of most U.S. newspapers, and editorials ran in scores of other publications either denouncing or praising him.

Although the split affected almost every Protestant denomination, it was most bitter among the Presbyterians and the Northern Baptists because supporters of each side of the argument were numerically strong in those denominations. By contrast, more liberal Northern denominations were relatively unaffected, and the Southern Baptist Convention escaped the controversy almost unscathed. Baptists in the South were deeply conservative and almost naturally fundamentalist in both doctrine and outlook. A relatively small number of Southern fundamentalists—most prominently J. Frank Norris—would ultimately find it necessary to leave (or be kicked out of) the Southern Baptist Convention.

Side by side with the doctrinal battles waged within the denominations, fundamentalists such as William Bell Riley, William Jennings Bryan, Billy Sunday, and J. Frank Norris were campaigning furiously against the teaching of evolution in schools. From 1920 through 1925, they experienced a cascade of successes. Bryan spoke in dozens of cities before enthusiastic and growing crowds, offering to debate any evolutionist bold enough to join him on a platform. Bryan was by then in his mid-60s; he had gained weight since his days as a young firebrand, and lost much of his hair, but he remained a fiery and eloquent speaker, and was a commanding presence on a stage. Just a year older than Bryan, but with a much more impressive shock of white hair, William Bell Riley staged lively debates in the West from Portland to Los Angeles with noted evolutionist Maynard Shipley of the Science League of America, a national association founded to protect freedom for teachers and resist attempts to connect church and state.

Historian Doug Linder recorded:

> By the beginning of 1923, Riley could report in a letter to William Jennings Bryan, "The whole country is seething on the evolution question." Riley debated science writer Maynard Shipley before large crowds up and down the West Coast. Bryan cheered his efforts, observing in a letter, "He seemed to have the audience overwhelmingly with him in Los Angeles, Oakland, and Portland. This is very encouraging; it shows that the ape-man hypothesis is not very strong outside the colleges and [modernist] pulpits..." In 1923, Riley in an article linked evolution to "anarchistic socialistic propaganda" and labeled those who would teach it "atheists." [108]

Kentucky Baptists conducted a statewide campaign to ban the teaching of evolution that came within a single vote of success in the House of Representatives. The World Christian Fundamentals Association launched campaigns in 15 other states, including Texas and Tennessee, both of which were deemed ripe for conversion. Bryan visited Texas several times in 1923 and 1924 as part of the anti-evolution crusade, and developed a close relationship with J. Frank Norris, appearing with Norris on various platforms and then preaching at Norris' First Baptist Church in Fort Worth in 1924.

However, both Riley and Bryan spent more of their time in Tennessee than any other state. Tennessee was considered to be the home of the fundamentalist movement. More than half of the state's citizens were Baptists, and leading newspapers were fervently anti-evolution. By the fall elections of 1924, evolution was a burning issue for the voters of Tennessee, and politicians from Memphis to Knoxville were appealing for votes based on their claimed "Christian" opposition to the supposedly "godless" theory of evolution. The issue got traction especially from rural voters whose children were being exposed to formal education for the first time. In 1920, the number of students enrolled in Tennessee high schools had reached 50,000, 10 times the enrollment of 1890. Suddenly, the unlettered parents of those students were being told by Bryan, a former presidential candidate whom most of them had voted for on three occasions, that the new Tennessee high schools were training their offspring to be atheists. This was not an outcome that Tennessee voters would easily put up with.

Early in 1925, the Tennessee legislature met to consider the Butler Act, a bill forbidding the teaching in public schools of "any theory that denies the story of the Divine Creation of man as taught in the Bible, and to teach instead that man has descended from a lower order of animals." The four principal leaders of the anti-evolution crusade—William Bell Riley, Billy Sunday, Frank Norris, and William Jennings Bryan—led a massive and successful grassroots campaign aimed at persuading uncommitted lawmakers to join the anti-evolution camp. In early March, Bryan gave a speech in Nashville titled "Is the Bible True?" His speech was printed and circulated to every member of the General Assembly. On March 13, 1925, the Tennessee lawmakers passed the Butler Act, and Bryan sent a telegram to Governor Austin Peay: "The Christian parents of the State owe you a debt of gratitude for saving their children from the poisonous influence of an unproven hypothesis."

The ACLU offered to pay for the legal defense of any Tennessee teacher who agreed to challenge the law. John Scopes, a 10th grade biology teacher and football coach in the little Tennessee town of Dayton, volunteered to be the guinea pig. Scopes was an ideal hero for advocates of the teaching of evolution: clean cut, slightly built, studious-looking with his round, horn-rimmed glasses, modest, assiduous in his attendance at the local Presbyterian church, and popular with his students. Scopes had taught for several years using *A Civic Biology*, a well-regarded textbook by George William Hunter, who noted that "in nature, the variations which best fitted a plant or animal for life in its environment were the ones which were handed down because those having variations which were not fitted for life in that particular environment would die." Darwin's theory thus explained how new species might "arise from very slight variations, continuing during long periods of years." In early May, Scopes was arrested by the local sheriff, and a copy of Hunter's textbook was taken to be used as evidence in his trial.

By happenstance, William Jennings Bryan was at the time speaking at the national convention of the World Christian Fundamentals Association in Memphis, hosted by William Bell Riley and sharing the platform with J. Frank Norris. A few days after Scopes' arrest and the end of the convention, Riley sent a telegram to Bryan inviting him to represent the interests of the WCFA as an associate prosecutor at Scopes' trial in Dayton. Bryan accepted the invitation with alacrity.

Bryan's involvement quickly drew an offer from Clarence Darrow, the most famous defense attorney in the country, to represent Scopes. The presence of both Bryan and Darrow ensured that the trial would dominate national news, including prominent coverage on the front page of the *New York Times*.

Over 100 newspaper reporters converged on Dayton during the trial, and for the first time in history a Chicago radio station broadcast on-the-spot coverage of what became known as "The Monkey Trial." Every afternoon, a small plane landed in a local field to pick up movie film from that day's legal jousting. The trial was an intense media circus, perhaps the first such trial of the 20th century, setting a high American standard for buffoonery, profundity, silliness, melodrama, bombast, and long-lasting historic impact that trials of the Chicago Seven or OJ Simpson scarcely matched in later decades.

On the second day of the trial, Clarence Darrow stood behind a table next to Scopes to open the case for the defense. Darrow was then 68 years old, and combined a folksy manner with a pugnacious face. His body conveyed aggressiveness honed in hundreds of courtrooms over 47 years of law practice. He outlined the defense of John Scopes by describing him as a defender of democratic rights, freedom of speech and individual conscience:

> If today you can take a thing like evolution and make it a crime to teach it in the public school, tomorrow you can make it a crime to teach it in the private schools, and the next year you can make it a crime to teach it to the hustings or in the church. At the next session you may ban books and the newspapers. Soon you may set

Catholic against Protestant and Protestant against Protestant, and try to foist your own religion upon the minds of men. If you can do one you can do the other. Ignorance and fanaticism is ever busy and needs feeding. Always it is feeding and gloating for more. Today it is the public school teachers, tomorrow the private. The next day the preachers and the lectures, the magazines, the books, the newspapers. After awhile, your honor, it is the setting of man against man and creed against creed until with flying banners and beating drums we are marching backward to the glorious ages of the sixteenth century when bigots lighted fagots to burn the men who dared to bring any intelligence and enlightenment and culture to the human mind.[109]

Bryan first took the stage on the fifth day of the trial to give a bombastic speech urging that the defense not be allowed to offer several prominent scientists to provide expert testimony on the validity of Darwin's theory. For an hour, he castigated Darwin for his "absurdities," arguing that his scientific theory threatened morality and civilization itself. He waved around a copy of *A Civic Biology*, labeled it "nonsense," and accused Hunter of lumping humans into a category of "thirty-four hundred and ninety-nine other mammals—including elephants!" He concluded by pitting his personal religious beliefs squarely against any possible scientific conclusions that might contradict them: "The Bible is not going to be driven out of this court by experts." Although Bryan received respectful applause, he left many in the audience scratching their heads at his denial that humans were mammals, and unsure what to make of his rambling dissertation.

Darrow's associate attorney Dudley Malone then stood to argue for the admission of expert testimony on the basis of both his own Christian faith and his passionate regard for the truth. Bryan, said Malone, "is not the only one who believes in God…The children of this generation are pretty wise. If we teach them the truth as best we understand it, they might make a better world of this than we have been able to make of it….For God's sake, let the children have their minds kept open."

Malone concluded with a passionate plea:

There is never a duel with the truth. The truth always wins and we are not afraid of it. The truth is no coward. The truth does not need the law. The truth does not need the force of government. The truth does not need Mr.

Bryan. The truth is imperishable, eternal and immortal and needs no human agency to support it. We are ready to tell the truth as we understand it and we do not fear all the truth that they can present as facts. We feel we stand with progress. We feel we stand with science. We feel we stand with intelligence. We feel we stand with fundamental freedom in America…We ask Your Honor to admit the evidence as a matter of correct law, as a matter of sound procedure and as a matter of justice to the defense in this case.[110]

Malone's response drew raucous and sustained applause from the courtroom's several hundred onlookers, who were probably demonstrating their appreciation for the power of his oratory more than their agreement with his point of view.

The most dramatic episode of the trial took place when Darrow summoned Bryan to the stand as an expert witness on the Bible. To the surprise of everyone, Bryan agreed happily to Darrow's questioning. The judge moved this direct confrontation between the two famous lawyers outside to the courthouse lawn. There they faced off between two great maple trees before an audience of several thousand spectators. Bryan, sweltering in the 100-degree heat and continually fanning himself with a large palm-leaf fan, melted in the heat of Darrow's interrogation. He became agitated and confused at times. At first Bryan contended that "everything in the Bible should be accepted as it is given there." Then, however, he admitted that the "six days" of creation mentioned in Genesis might not literally be six 24-hour periods, thus making it clear that his "literal" reading of the Bible lacked a certain consistency.

In the nation's newspapers, Bryan, fundamentalists generally, and the entire population of Dayton, Tennessee were held up as laughingstocks and rubes. Yankee journalist H. L. Mencken called Dayton's inhabitants yokels, Neanderthals, morons, and fanatics in his daily trial reports. He called Bryan's speeches "theologic bilge," but termed defense lawyer Clarence Darrow eloquent and magnificent. Mencken conflated Christianity with the narrow and backward brand of Christian fundamentalism that had led to the passage of a law making the teaching of evolution a crime punishable by law.

"This is a strictly Christian community," said Mencken, "and such is its notion of fairness, justice and due process of law… Its people are simply unable to imagine a man who rejects the literal authority of the Bible. The most they can conjure up, straining until they are red in the face, is a man who is in error about the meaning of this or that text. Thus one accused of heresy among them is like one accused of boiling his grandmother to make soap in Maryland."

Bryan himself was mocked by Mencken as an old buzzard who,

> …having failed to raise the mob against its rulers, now prepares to raise it against its teachers. He can never be the peasants' President, but there is still a chance to be the peasants' Pope. He leads a new crusade, his bald head glistening, his face streaming with sweat, his chest heaving beneath his rumpled alpaca coat. One somehow pities him, despite his so palpable imbecilities. It is a tragedy, indeed, to begin life as a hero and to end it as a buffoon. But let no one, laughing at him, underestimate the magic that lies in his black, malignant eye, his frayed but still eloquent voice. He can shake and inflame these poor ignoramuses as no other man among us can shake and inflame them, and he is desperately eager to order the charge.[111]

The trial ended the only way it could have, with a conviction of Scopes, who was fined $100. The trial jury had been instructed to find Scopes guilty based only on the evidence of whether he had taught that humans evolved from a lower order of animals. The verdict was obvious. Scopes had clearly broken the law in Dayton, Tennessee.

Although Bryan and the prosecution had won the trial in purely legal terms, the trial was nonetheless a devastating public relations defeat for fundamentalists, now treated by the American press with scorn and derision. The image of fundamentalists was a caricature of rural idiocy and anti-intellectualism, delivered with a Southern drawl.

A few days after the trial's conclusion, Bryan died in Dayton, Tennessee while taking a Sunday afternoon nap. His physician announced that "Bryan died of diabetes mellitus, the immediate cause being the fatigue incident to the heat and his extraordinary exertions due to the Scopes trial." His death seemed to be emblematic of the blow dealt to the image of fundamentalists.

The practical result of the trial was ambiguous. Scope's conviction was overturned by the Tennessee Supreme Court on a technicality, which prevented Darrow from appealing the conviction to the U.S. Supreme Court and setting a broad precedent against laws such as the one in Tennessee. The anti-evolution movement suffered a series of legislative defeats over the next few years. Though the Tennessee law would remain on the books until 1967, when the legislature repealed it after a teacher complained that it restricted his right to free speech, out of the 15 states considering the enacting of anti-evolution laws in 1925 only two additional states—Arkansas and Mississippi—did so.

Despite the failure of the campaign to enact anti-evolution laws, the movement found a way to successfully remove the teaching of evolution from classrooms that did not depend on the cooperation of lawmakers. Instead, fundamentalist tacticians focused on influencing the content of the textbooks themselves. In the year after the Scopes trial, the Louisiana state superintendent of education demanded that the publisher of the textbook used in the Dayton trial as well as the most popular biology textbook in the country—Hunter's *A Civic Biology*—remove the only six pages that explained the Darwinian theory of evolution. Sure enough, in the 1927 edition all references to evolution were revised or removed, and the word *evolution* was invariably changed to *development*.

Other textbook publishers followed suit, and for at least the next three decades, most American teenagers would find no introduction or even marginal reference to the theory of evolution in their high school biology textbooks. The subject of evolution only re-entered the public school curricula after 1957 when the Soviet Union launched its Sputnik satellite into space. By John F. Kennedy's election to the presidency, a new generation of American parents had been terrified into believing that their country was losing its vaunted lead in science and technology, and it was no longer dangerous for textbook publishers to explain the scientific foundation of Darwin's theory. The danger began to return, tentatively, only in the 1990s as a rejuvenated fundamentalist movement began again to campaign for textbooks scrubbed of what fundamentalists perceived as Darwinian bias.

Though they may have won the battle against teaching evolution in the public schools, fundamentalists decisively lost the battle for control of the major national Protestant denominations such as Northern Baptists and the Presbyterian Church in the U. S. A. between 1925 and 1930. A significant reason for their failure to control the seminary faculties, conventions, and mission boards was that they overreached themselves. They attempted to narrowly define the acceptable bounds of Christian doctrine, hoping to force out any who disagreed with them and establish a new and rigid standard for evangelical orthodoxy. Instead, they discovered to their surprise that fundamentalists were a small minority in denominations that were growing steadily more liberal. As a result, the fundamentalists gave the impression of being intolerant, arrogant, and anti-democratic. As they lost their battle for control, the Northern fundamentalists either resigned themselves to being powerless minorities in the large mainline denominations or withdrew to create their own, separate, much smaller denominations, pure in doctrine and untainted by association with modernists.

In the South, the most extreme fundamentalists also lost the struggle to expel modernists from the large Southern Baptist Convention, but the struggle was much less significant because there were far fewer contenders on the liberal side of the equation. J. Frank Norris may have been dismissed as an infuriating if entertaining lunatic by his more staid Southern Baptist brethren, but the theological and political positions he took were highly popular and well-represented within the Convention. After 1925, American fundamentalism shifted dramatically toward becoming an overwhelmingly Southern phenomenon. Although relatively small networks of fundamentalists persisted in the North— such as the General Association of Regular Baptist Churches—national leadership mainly passed to Southerners. The bulk of fundamentalist church membership was in the South—including within the Southern Baptist Convention. The most prominent and influential fundamentalist colleges and universities were in the South.

Over the next several years many in the fundamentalist movement in America embarked on a sorrowful and indignant, half-century-long retreat from public life. The retreat was marked by an extreme form of separatism, preached and promoted by prominent fundamentalist leaders. Fundamentalist Christians, they said, alone represented historic orthodox Christianity, and should in no way be allied or partnered with people who claimed to be Christians but disagreed about doctrines deemed to be "fundamental." Liberals and modernists were "infidels," "unbelievers," "Bible-deniers," "heretics." It was a sin against God for a fundamentalist Christian to associate in any religious sphere with any liberal or modernist. So if a Protestant denomination had modernists teaching in a seminary or modernists leading churches or mission boards, then fundamentalists should leave the denomination. Good fundamentalists should never pray with modernists, never preach with modernists, never consort or cavort or collaborate with modernists.

Within a few years after the death of William Jennings Bryan, the view among fundamentalists had become more consolidated. Separatism meant a more complete separation. It meant separating from potential political allies with unorthodox or modernistic or secular views on any other topic. It meant withdrawing from political life, concentrating on protecting the orthodoxy claimed by the fundamentalist community and converting lost souls to Christianity. Revivalism was linked to both soul-winning and doctrinal purity.

Chapter 18
A Soul-Winner's Fire

By the time I entered fifth grade, I had wholeheartedly embraced my destiny and worked conscientiously to spread the Word and win souls to Christ. Every day on my paper route, I took along a small stack of pink, rectangular Bible tracts written by my granddad and titled *What Must I Do to Be Saved*, and passed them out to people I met on the street.

One afternoon I rang the doorbell of a big brick house owned by Mr. Edman, a distinguished-looking, balding gentleman who lived across the street from the campus of Wheaton College, to collect the $4.50 he owed me for one month's delivery of his newspaper.

"Mr. Edman," I said earnestly. "I'd like to give you a tract that tells you all about Jesus."

"Thank you, Andy!" he said.

"Mr. Edman," I said, "do you mind if I ask you a question?"

"Why, sure, Andy," he said. "Please do."

"Mr. Edman, do you know for sure, if you died tonight, would you go to Heaven or Hell?"

"Andy," he said smiling, "I certainly do. If I died tonight, I'd go to Heaven because I've got Jesus in my heart. And I'm so glad you asked me that question!"

Mr. Edman paid me for his newspaper, tipped me an extra dollar, and waved goodbye. Later, Mrs. Edman called my mother to report on my evangelical activities and express appreciation that I had been concerned for the spiritual welfare of the Edman household.

Dr. V. Raymond Edman was the president of Wheaton College and a founder of the National Association of Evangelicals.

John R. Rice began his full-time career as a revival evangelist in 1926, shortly after the Scopes trial and in the midst of the Great Schism of the fundamentalist movement from mainline Protestantism. At first glance, his timing couldn't have been worse. In the wake of the Great War, the American public had lost their stomach for revivals and revivalists, civic reform campaigns, cleaning up the bootleggers, and personal salvation. Before the war, famous evangelists such as Billy Sunday had been able to pack tens of thousands of people into giant auditoriums for citywide revival campaigns. Now Sunday was reduced to speaking in little churches in small towns to insignificant congregations. After the Scopes trial, many Americans saw evangelists as buffoons and fundamentalists as fools.

Riding the anti-evangelical wave of American opinion in 1927, novelist Sinclair Lewis published *Elmer Gantry*, the story of a football-playing, high-living, womanizing reprobate who "converts" to Christianity and develops a successful career as an evangelist. Gantry is a consummate hypocrite and fraud. He steals, lies, drinks, and cheats, all the while preaching against sin.

The novel was profane, hilarious, flamboyant, and farcical, a runaway hit. It was the top fiction bestseller of 1927 and garnered enormous press attention. The book was banned in Boston and other places; Lewis was denounced from thousands of pulpits across the U.S. and threatened with physical harm by a variety of kooks and evangelical extremists.

Lewis claimed that he modeled the Gantry character on a number of ministers he met and interviewed in Kansas. However, Gantry's portrayal seems clearly influenced by the career of the famous Billy Sunday, a sports hero with a knack for colorful language, a passion for the almighty dollar, and panoply of embarrassing family scandals. In an indignant response to the obvious reference, Sunday called Lewis "Satan's cohort."[112] In an earlier day, Sunday's attack might have had some kick to it. But Billy Sunday, who had been a "prizefighter in the ring with sin" for decades, was an old, worn out, punch-drunk boxer past his prime. In 1927, he continued preaching through a strenuous round of revival meetings, but to far smaller crowds and with comparatively miserable results. Increasingly, Sunday drew disdain and derision from a public that had once idolized him.

Billy Sunday's career offered both a positive example and cautionary lesson for young evangelist John R. Rice. On one hand, Sunday was a powerful preacher with a gift for colorful, attention getting oratory. He had conducted mass, citywide "union" revival campaigns sponsored by multiple churches across denominational lines that offered a model for Rice to emulate and promote. On the other hand, Sunday had damaged his reputation and lost much of his effectiveness because of his unfortunate attraction to money. By contrast, John R. Rice would never suffer the slightest harm to his reputation because of greed or money problems. Instead, from the beginning of his career he carefully nurtured a reputation for honesty, frugality, and financial transparency.

In the mid-1920s, it would have been natural to expect Rice to conduct his entire career as a revivalist within the Southern Baptist Convention (SBC). He had been raised, saved and baptized in a Southern Baptist church, and his own father was a Southern Baptist preacher. He had attended three different Southern Baptist schools—Decatur Bible College, Baylor University, and Southwestern Baptist Theological Seminary—and taught at one—Wayland Baptist College. He preached in revival meetings for Southern Baptist churches and was a member of Seminary Hill, one of the most prominent Baptist Churches in Texas. Moreover, the SBC was a stronghold of doctrinal conservatives and a natural theological home for John R. Rice. As he said in a letter from Chicago to his future wife Lloys Cooke in March 1921, "I feel as never before that the salvation of the world lies heavily upon Southern Baptists."[113]

Already, however, Rice was concerned about Southern Baptist leaders who he felt were insufficiently militant in their support of the fundamentalist cause. For example, he wrote a letter in 1925 to Frank S. Groner, the General Secretary of the Baptist General Convention of Texas, suggesting that Southern Baptists were afraid to support fundamentalists such as William Bell Riley because they might become less popular among the Baptist rank and file, and accusing Groner of being more concerned about keeping peace inside the denomination than about maintaining doctrinal purity. [114]

It was difficult to find explicit examples of liberalism or modernism inside the SBC. A handful of Texas Baptists believed in "theistic evolution," though not in Darwinism, and a good many more were critical of the aggression, anger, and self-righteousness they saw some fundamentalists such as Norris display. But the vast majority of Southern Baptists in Texas were firmly in the camp of fundamentalists on all the big questions of Christian doctrine. The major weakness of the SBC and of the Texas Baptist Conference, from Rice's point of view, was a certain weakness in exposing and opposing modernism at all costs. The leaders of the Texas Baptist Conference were a bit more interested in dialogue than confrontation, and marginally more tolerant of diverse interpretations on minor doctrines.

For the young John R. Rice, however, being a Christian required an aggressive spirit of militancy on all fronts: fight against the teaching of evolution in schools, fight to expose and purge any hint of modernism in

Protestant denominations, and fight to win lost souls for Jesus through revivalism.

Increasingly, as Rice began preaching regularly in revival meetings around Texas, he moved into an ever closer relationship with J. Frank Norris, on whom Rice had modeled his own criticism of the Southern Baptists since 1920. Norris began to serve as his mentor and sponsor. The partnership was natural for Rice. The two men shared a passion for attacking modernism. Both wanted to uproot the weeds of liberal theology wherever they poked up in the garden of their own Southern Baptist Convention. Norris was always on the lookout for younger men who would support his leadership of the fundamentalist movement in the South.

In 1926, Norris' life became a little too interesting for comfort. He had been attacking Catholics employed in city government in Fort Worth on the basis of his belief that their actions were controlled by the Pope rather than the citizens of the city. Finally, Norris went a little too far, and accused the Catholic mayor of Fort Worth of unsubstantiated crimes of corruption and low morality. A friend of the mayor's named Dexter Chipps visited Norris in his office and argued with him. Norris pulled a gun out of his desk and fired three shots, killing Chipps.

Norris was catapulted into national notoriety when he was indicted for murder. On Sunday, August 2, 1926, when his First Baptist Church of Fort Worth took up a collection to pay his legal expenses, members of the congregation put over $16,000 into a galvanized tub at the front of the church.

When Norris was finally tried for murder the following January, the jury acquitted him based on Norris's claim that Chipps had threatened his life and he was only defending himself. The controversy about Norris's killing of Chipps only spread his fame, provoked and encouraged his supporters, and enhanced his popularity. Perversely, Norris's bizarre behavior and his vicious attacks on his opponents helped him to become one of the most powerful religious leaders in the South, and among the most prominent fundamentalists in the country.

Norris' prominence provided ammunition for those who sought to portray the movement as the province of crackpots, racists, and reactionaries. Ever fewer conservative Christians wanted to call themselves fundamentalists, regardless of how much they might agree with the movement's theology or its politics. Walter Lippman, a reporter, critic, and philosopher, expressed deep sympathy with the attack on religious modernism by fundamentalist leaders such as J. Gresham Machen. Nonetheless, Lippman was distressed by the symbolically important behavior of fundamentalists: "In actual practice, this movement has become entangled with all sorts of bizarre and barbarous agitations, with the Ku Klux Klan, with fanatical Prohibition, with the 'anti-evolution laws,' and with much persecution and intolerance. This is in itself significant. For it shows that the central truth, which the fundamentalists have grasped, no longer appeals to the best brains and the good sense of a modern community, and that the movement is largely recruited from the isolated, the inexperienced, and the uneducated."[115]

Precisely at the time when conservatives such as Lippman were dismissing fundamentalism, Rice's own career as a fundamentalist leader began to blossom. Norris offered him a platform that introduced him to an ever larger audience. Rice began a weekly radio program on Norris' radio station, KFQB. Norris began to heavily endorse and promote Rice on his own program and through the pages of his newspaper, *The Fundamentalist*. He called Rice "a great preacher of the gospel of Christ," and invited him to preach more and more frequently at his First Baptist Church of Fort Worth, one of the largest churches in Texas.

On Sunday, February 19, 1928, Rice preached four sermons at the First Baptist Church titled "Can God Save a Bootlegger?," "Can God Save an Infidel?," "How Young Can God Save a Child?," and "Why I Am a Big F Fundamentalist." In the fourth sermon, Rice proudly proclaimed that despite the image problem the word "fundamentalist" had in the press, "I am a Fundamentalist. I believe that Christ is the Son of God, was born of a virgin, was buried and rose the third day according to the scriptures, and that He is coming again. So I don't mind spelling it with a capital F."[116]

Rice argued that being a good fundamentalist required an aggressive and principled struggle on behalf of the Bible and its teachings, including attacks on those with whom he had doctrinal disputes: "In my case Fundamentalism means more than believing in the Bible. It means, if necessary, being ostracized for it, it means, if necessary, speaking against men I love and who love me, for it. It means, if necessary, offending and grieving people and institutions that have meant a great deal in my life."[117]

The "people and institutions" Rice was speaking about were Texas Baptist leaders and Texas Baptist seminaries. By associating himself with Norris, preaching on Norris's radio station, and filling Norris's pulpit, Rice had irretrievably alienated himself from the Texas Baptist establishment that had so often been Norris's target.

The critical breaking point came just a month after Rice preached his sermon on Big F Fundamentalism. On March 17, 1928, a delegation of Southern Baptist leaders came to visit Rice and discuss his partnership with Norris. They included the pastor of the Seminary Hill Baptist

Church where Rice was a member and two professors from Southwestern Seminary, which he had attended. They asked him to sever his relationship with Norris, find a different radio station for his weekly program, and stop preaching from the pulpit at Norris' church.

Rice not only refused their demands, but responded by following Norris out of the Southern Baptist Convention.

In 1928, Norris became strongly focused on that year's presidential campaign. Democrat Al Smith was pitted against Republican Herbert Hoover. Despite the ties of white Texans such as Norris and Rice to the Republican Party, the Democrats had historically been the party of white Southerners since before the Civil War. Al Smith was too much for Texans or fundamentalists generally to swallow. As a Catholic, Smith was a representative of an alien religion, and could not be truly considered a Christian. As a Northerner, Smith was suspect for his views on racial issues and drew support from such foreign-born Americans as Italians, Irish, and Germans. As an opponent of Prohibition, Smith was clearly doing the work of the Devil.

Norris vowed to do everything in his power to get Texans and Southerners generally to vote for a Republican for the first time since the party's founding before the Civil War. He sought help from other fundamentalist preachers such as his young friend John R. Rice and his old friend Mordecai Ham, and he was joined by Bob Jones Sr., who took time out from nurturing his fledgling eponymous college to campaign for Hoover. Norris spoke at dozens of rallies in the summer and fall of 1928 against Smith. At various rallies, Norris was joined by Rice or Ham. At one rally during that summer of 1928, Mordecai Ham said: "If you vote for Al Smith, you're voting against Christ and you will all be damned." At another rally, Norris said, "What a conglomeration, Tammany Hall, Roman Catholicism, bootleggers, carpetbag politicians, and negroes. What will the white people of Texas do?"

The 1928 presidential election was the first in which large numbers of white southerners were drawn to a Republican nominee, and speeches by Norris, Jones, Rice, and Ham foreshadowed the breakup of the solid Democratic South four decades later. The most prominent fundamentalist leaders at rallies across the South promoted the fear that black people would be encouraged by Northern Democrats to "get out of line" and seek to change the status quo.

In October at an Alabama rally, Norris said: "Al Smith believes in social equality. He approves of miscegenation, the intermarriage of negroes with whites. He associates with negroes. He stoops to social equality to get negro votes. He ran for the New York Assembly on the same ticket with negroes. He has negro members of his legislature. He has taken the negro away from the Republican Party. He has made the negro believe that he will be welcome in the White House when he is elected. If he is elected, it will be because the negro and the foreign-born vote enables him to carry the east while the South remains solid."[118]

In an ironic twist, the Ku Klux Klan also supported the Republican candidate because the Klan's focus had shifted. The target of the original Klan that surfaced in Texas and throughout the South after the Civil War had been the newly freed black people. However, the reconstituted Klan of the 1920s was far more worried about the threat to America from Catholics and various non-Anglo-Saxon immigrants. Although Norris was not a Klan member himself, he often spoke positively about the Klan, and in May of 1928 he published an anti-Smith article in the *Fundamentalist* by the imperial wizard of the Klan, Hiram Wesley Evans.[119]

By the late 1920s, with the help of Norris, my granddad was becoming well-known as a revivalist in Texas, though he was seldom invited into any of the more reputable or established Baptist churches that were members of the Southern Baptist Convention. John R. Rice bought a big tent about 60 by 80 feet in size. He would go into some town in the heart of Texas, rent a field on the outskirts of town or set up his big tent in the public square, recruit a singer, rent or borrow a piano, and stay for 10 or 12 weeks. He knew how to speak the common tongue of the working people, ranchers and farmers, factory workers and shopkeepers. He was a natural storyteller and by turns could be hilarious, terrifying, and powerfully persuasive.

One of his first revival campaigns outside of Fort Worth was in Decatur in Wise County, where he had gone to junior college and where his father lived. He brought his big revival tent to that small town, and one of Rice's biographers says that "Will Rice hitched his Chevrolet car on to a block and tackle to help his son raise the big 800-pound center poles. They built the seats with volunteer labor and got out handbills to announce the meeting. He stayed there preaching nightly 10 weeks; the little county seat town was deeply stirred, there were hundreds of remarkable conversions, and a new church organized."[120] At the beginning of the Decatur revival Rice had no intention of starting a new church. He quickly discovered that all the existing Baptist churches in the County shunned him for his opposition to the Baptist establishment in Texas, although their members flocked to his services. He preached one hellfire-and-brimstone sermon after another every night for over three months. Hundreds were saved in Wise County, and very quickly more people were attending Rice's revival meetings than any of the churches. He needed to begin baptizing his masses of converts, but found that none of the churches would allow him to use their buildings for the purpose. So Rice had a temporary baptistery built in the tent, and a deacons' committee was formed to raise money, buy a piece of ground, and build a large, permanent tabernacle on South State Street.

Rice served as the first pastor of the church, and within a few months the fledgling congregation hired its first permanent pastor at a salary of $200 a month as my granddad moved on. The Decatur revival set a pattern for the establishment of many more fundamentalist churches in Texas. Rice put up his big tent to conduct a revival for a month or two or three in some small or middle-sized Texas town, got the church going with a few hundred members, named it "Fundamental Baptist Church," and then turned it over to a permanent pastor. These churches were clearly opposed to the Southern Baptist Convention and acted as satellites of the First Baptist Church led by Norris.

Just as John R. Rice's career began to take off, his father Will died of "heart trouble" in 1930 at the age of 71 at his home in Decatur. Widowed three times, he had settled into a gentle retirement, still preaching from time to time, honored for his short yet "distinguished career" in the legislature. He was buried next to his wife Dolous in the hard-packed earth of Oaklawn Cemetery on the prairie northeast of Decatur.

Will Rice had grown up in the stew of post-war Texas. He inherited all the complexity of Southern white culture, with its class consciousness and its religious defense of slavery, but none of the financial security that had gone along with being part of the aristocracy before the war. He embraced the South's focus on race, its acceptance of violence as a method of keeping black people in their place, its religiosity and romanticism. He also embodied its striving toward faith, righteousness, and salvation. Deep in his childhood, in the midst of war, terror, hunger, and poverty, with the antebellum peace of slave-owning Missouri in pieces all around him, Will Rice had mixed the bitter potion of racism with his religious faith. To the end of his life, he was never able to reach beyond adherence to this heritage of the Lost Cause.

Will Rice's son John would always be troubled by his father's membership in the Klan. He came to believe that secret societies such as the Klan and the Masonic Lodge were contrary to the will of God, and that good Christians would not join such groups. His criticism of the Klan was not related to its racial politics. Instead, he opposed the Klan as a secret order that engaged in violence. In a polemic against lodges and secret orders published in 1943, Rice wrote:

> There are many known cases where the Ku Klux Klan
> resorted to violence and some proven cases of
> assassination. While the Ku Klux Klan is now in general
> disrepute, it is only fair to remember that members of
> other secret societies took part in the work of the Klan.
> This was the case of my father who was both a Mason
> and an Odd Fellow and joined the Klan. My father told
> me of cases of violence by lodge action, which he
> justified. The spirit of vengeance is inseparably
> connected with the horrible oaths and penalties of the
> secret orders.[121]

Despite John R. Rice's dislike of the Klan, he was the son of his father, a Southerner born and bred. He had grown up in a culture bathed in the ideology, politics, and religion of race. He had been taught as a child that God ordained the subordination of some races and the superiority of other races. He was born in Gainesville, Cooke County, Texas, only three decades after the end of the Civil War, and he had been raised 110 miles west of Gainesville in Dundee, Archer County, a place where only white people lived. He had never attended school with a person of color, other than, perhaps, when he briefly attended graduate school at the University of Chicago. He had attended only segregated churches with white congregations, and there is no evidence that any black person ever heard him preach in a revival meeting or at one of the churches he pastored during the first two decades of his career.

His home state of Texas, beginning in the first decade of the 20th century, instituted a poll tax to prevent black people from voting. The Democratic Party excluded black voters with a white-only primary, and the Texas Republican Party, which Rice adopted as his own during the 1920s, had progressively restricted the participation of blacks. Racial lynching had been commonplace in Texas since the Civil War, and Texas stood third after Mississippi and Georgia in the number of such mob acts. The number of lynching incidents diminished in the late 1800s and then increased again with the application of Jim Crow laws and the rise of the Klan after the Great War. In 1922, during the Texas Senate term of professed Klansman Will Rice, the number of lynch mobs peaked at 13 mobs claiming 15 victims.

The town of Sherman near the Red River in north Texas was the scene of one of the most violent racial incidents, the Sherman Riot, at the beginning of the Great Depression. In May of 1930, a black man named George Hughes was accused of raping a white woman, arrested, and held in the Grayson County Courthouse. A mob of 5,000 angry whites surrounded the building and assaulted various contingents of firemen, Texas Rangers, and national guardsmen who had been assigned to protect the courthouse, the trial, and Hughes. After driving off the guardsmen, the mob broke into the vault where Hughes was being held, threw his body out onto the yard, and set fire to the courthouse:

> Hughes's body was...then dragged behind a car to the front of a drugstore in the black business section, where it was hanged from a tree. The store furnishings were used to fuel a fire under the hanging corpse. The mob also burned down the drugstore and other businesses in the area and prevented firemen from saving the burning buildings. By daybreak of May 10, most of the town's black businesses, as well as a residence, lay in ashes.[122]

One year later, John R. Rice was invited by some locals to conduct a revival in Sherman. In June of 1931, the Sherman city council permitted him to set up his revival tent in the very center of town, on the vacant spot where the courthouse had stood before it had been burned down during the riot and lynching of George Hughes.

Although Southern Baptist pastors in Sherman ordered their congregants not to attend, many hundreds showed up anyway to hear Rice preach on "adultery and lust and on drinking." Rice went further, saying, "I have exposed the doctors and druggists who prescribe and sell whiskey, calling their names." When a local Baptist pastor named J. A. Ellis held a "mixed bathing party" for the Baptist Young People's Union, Rice denounced him by name from the pulpit.[123]

Doubtless, some of those who took part in the Sherman Riot attended his revival services—and the subjects Rice did not mention were as significant as his sermon topics. He did not preach on the murder of George Hughes, which took place within a few yards of where his plywood pulpit stood. He did not justify Hughes's death, but neither did he condemn it. He did not support mob violence, but neither did he preach against the burning down of the courthouse and all the black businesses in town. He did not preach against the sin of attacking and driving out virtually all the black people in a town of 16,000, nor did he acknowledge or defend it. None of these, apparently, were sins worth mentioning.

Instead, he preached, with wrath and righteousness, against the sin of "mixed bathing."

The revival tent on the courthouse square of Sherman was full almost every night for 13 weeks. The white crowds came from other

Baptist churches around town, and white sinners flocked weeping and singing down the aisle between the ranks of temporary wooden benches. By the middle of August, the Fundamentalist Baptist Church had been formed, and by August the church had almost 300 members, 89 of them newly baptized.[124]

Nothing in John R. Rice's life or career suggests that he would ever condone or support the racist mob violence that had been on display in Sherman in 1930. But his failure to criticize the Sherman Riot or to call for racial reconciliation or repentance for racial crimes can be attributed to some basic assumptions he must have made.

First, if Rice had preached to his all-white Texas audience in 1930 against racial injustice or oppression he would have been castigated as a modernist, a radical socialist, or a social gospel do-gooder, and lost all his influence in the fundamentalist movement, most or all of his friends, and maybe even his life. And secondly, he would have been taking his eye off the only objective that mattered to him. As he said several years later in his book *The Soul-Winner's Fire*:

> Three principal thoughts seem especially urgent to me: first, that every Christian ought to win souls; second, that we ought to have a holy passion, a tearful and compelling earnestness, and apostolic fervor of soul in this holy business; and third, that we must have a divine enablement, the power of the Holy Spirit, fire from Heaven, to work miracles in the saving of souls.[125]

The focus on social and racial justice that strongly marked John Wesley, William Wilberforce, Charles G. Finney, Jonathan Blanchard, Charles Spurgeon, and other evangelical leaders in the 18th and 19th centuries was absent from the millions of words and scores of books John R. Rice penned during his lifetime. The fundamentalists, in their struggle against the modernists, had identified the "Social Gospel" and the concern for social justice expressed in Charles Sheldon's seminal work asking "What would Jesus do?" as a hallmark of heresy. Rice and other fundamentalists viewed the "Social Gospel" as tantamount to believing in salvation through "works" rather than faith. Salvation, they averred, was the result of God's unearned grace rather than anything humans might do for themselves. They charged the modernists with imagining salvation might be achieved by working to improve society.

Fundamentalists would continue to work for the moral regeneration and reclamation of individuals through their support of homes for orphans and unwed mothers, through missions to alcoholics or the homeless or the destitute, and to provide for the least fortunate. However, they would henceforth be missing from broad movements for social justice, against racial discrimination, for peace, in support of equal rights and opportunities for women, in defense of the rights of children, or to eliminate systemic poverty.

Fundamentalists had begun to identify a concern for social justice as tantamount to ignoring the Great Commandment, which was largely reduced to winning souls. By the time of John R. Rice's Sherman, Texas revival in 1930, the acrimonious dispute in the 1920s between modernists and fundamentalists in American Protestantism had borne bitter fruit.

Part IV
Revive Us Again:
Fundamentalism in Mid-Century

Chapter 19
The Sword of the Lord...and of John R. Rice

"So Gideon, and the hundred men that were with him, came unto the outside of the camp in the beginning of the middle watch; and they had but newly set the watch: and they blew the trumpets, and brake the pitchers that were in their hands. And the three companies blew the trumpets, and brake the pitchers, and held the lamps in their left hands, and the trumpets in their right hands to blow withal: and they cried, The Sword of the Lord, and of Gideon. And they stood every man in his place round about the camp: and all the host ran, and cried, and fled."—Judges 7:19

The Sword of the Lord production offices in Wheaton, Illinois were in a converted brick warehouse on West Wesley Street in the center of town. It was 1960, and on Fridays I finished my newspaper route and rode my bike downtown to turn in the quarters and dollar bills I'd collected from my *Chicago Daily News* customers and then ride away with my profits. I often stopped to buy a sherbet cone at the White Castle, and then parked my bike a block away in front of the *Sword* offices and went in to visit. Up the front steps of the warehouse and through the aging wooden front door, I entered a ceaseless buzz of activity.

Men and women were walking around and conferring with each other, shuffling papers and clattering away on black Remington typewriters, and talking on black Bakelite rotary-dial telephones. The smell of sawdust permeated the air, and from the basement came the muffled bass beat of the giant printing press used to churn out over 100,000 copies of the newspaper every week.

Rows of desks marched across a wide-open, worn-plank floor, shoved so closely together you had to turn sideways to fit through when someone was coming the other way. A dozen folks in the editorial department were in another building a block away, but here on the main floor of the warehouse was the newspaper's central nervous system: its production, circulation, and marketing staff of over 50 people. They also provided support for the conferences, campaigns, and revival meetings created or sponsored by the *Sword*.

In the center of the office was a bright red pop machine that held icy bottles of Coke, and a water jug with little round white paper cone cups. In the very back of the floor was one of the only offices with a door that could be shut, and from there my granddad, John R. Rice, ran the show. Often when I visited, Granddad was dictating one article, book chapter, or sermon after another to an unending stream of secretaries. His dictation machine in the 1940s and 50s used spools of wire to hold his words, and each spool was preserved in a little paper packet labeled with a title.

I sometimes asked Mr. Thomas, the janitor, if I could hang around and sweep the floor, just so I could feel a part of this great mission we were all on. With every push of my broom, I was helping to save lost souls. With every staccato click of a typewriter key, we were getting the gospel out to a dying world. With every throb of the printing press from the basement, we were preparing for the day, soon to come, when Jesus would return to Earth and call us to account: What had we done to get people ready to go to Heaven?

In the eyes of many Americans, Christian fundamentalism had been delivered a fatal blow by the Scopes trial. Fundamentalists were widely thought to be ignorant country bumpkins, in revolt against the modern world and its industry and "practicality," out of touch with scientific reality. Nationally, mainstream Protestantism reigned supreme as the definition of American-style Christianity and as the arbiter of the orthodox. In the South, the role of the white Christian establishment was mainly played by the Southern Baptist Convention, with its many thousands of member churches and millions of individual members.

With the Tennessee debacle of William Jennings Bryan, fundamentalism was down temporarily, but not defeated. And by 1930 the Great Depression had refocused the attention of many Southerners, especially poor and working class whites, on the simple messages preached by fundamentalist evangelists and pastors. In the depths of economic catastrophe, the world seemed like a dangerously complicated place, but it was easy to understand certain fundamentals: The wages of sin are death, Hell is hot, Jesus saves, and Heaven is a reward for the redeemed.

Moreover, the social, cultural, and technological innovations of the 20th century had brought heightened dangers. The Great War was only the first of the century's dramatic illustrations that civilization was sliding toward an abyss. Americans were tempted and corrupted by the post-Prohibition availability of alcohol, by Hollywood picture shows, by lewd language, immodest clothing styles, immoral dances dripping with sexual innuendo, wild new hair styles, and suggestive popular music. In this new, modern industrial age of evil and evildoers, true Christians must be warriors for the truth, and continually on guard against those who would "compromise" fundamental Christian beliefs or even ally in any way with those who might accept compromise. Christians were at war with the forces of evil, and at stake were millions of souls doomed to Hell. No departure from separatism could be tolerated—not even from the leaders of the largest and most conservative body of Baptists in the world. What began as a rebellion against "liberals" and "compromisers" inside Southern Baptist Convention (SBC) churches, SBC denominational programs, and SBC seminaries, quickly snowballed into a full-blown exodus from the SBC.

In July of 1932, John R. Rice went to Dallas, where he announced his plans to conduct the greatest revival Dallas had ever seen, and then to found a new church which he hoped would grow into "one of the largest congregations in the world, a lighthouse of gospel teaching and preaching that will shine, God willing, around the world." One day on his radio program on KFQB, he announced that he had paid the first week's rent of $5 on a vacant lot, and on a certain morning he would begin building bleachers with the help of anyone who showed up. The church was formally organized a few weeks later and within three months had a congregation of over 400 people.

This was not a church community comprised of wealthy people. The neighborhood where the first rough gospel tabernacle was built was a poor one, and more than half of the church members were unemployed or on relief. The church in Dallas grew and prospered, even as Rice continued conducting revival meetings in other towns and cities in Texas and then across the South and in Northern cities as well.

Rice stayed in Dallas for eight years as pastor of the Fundamentalist Baptist Church. During those years the church grew dramatically as over 7,000 people answered an invitation to be saved after hearing a sermon by John R. Rice. The young preacher proved to be a sensationalist who could draw in the crowds with dramatic sermon titles such as "Wild Oats in Dallas—How Dallas People Sow Them and How They Are Reaped"; "Company for Supper—and Not a Bite in the House"; "Filling Stations on the Highway to Hell"; "The Man Who Went to Heaven Without Baptism, Without Joining a Church, Without a Mourner's Bench, Without Even Living a Good Life."

With bodies packing the church pews, John R. Rice displayed a dramatic, emotional, and personable pulpit style. He was an old-fashioned, pulpit-pounding, sin-condemning, story-telling, hymn-singing evangelist. In an era before television dramas and sitcoms, he was the best entertainment available in Dallas.

Rice continued to work closely with J. Frank Norris, preaching on Norris' radio station, speaking at his Bible conferences, and collaborating with him in building a network of fundamentalist churches inspired by Norris' work. Norris praised Rice effusively: "We have heard Brother Rice on many occasions, but there was a depth and height and richness and power in his teaching we have never seen or heard by him before... He is a cultured, spirit-filled evangelist; now building a great church in the city of Dallas; erecting a temple at this time that will seat several thousand; defender of the faith and builder for Christ."

In a private letter to a friend in November of 1932, Norris wrote:

> Every day brings news of the rapid growth of these independent Fundamentalist Baptist Churches. A thousand preachers with the machine are ready to break over and in the words of General Winfield Scott at the battle of Vera Cruz, "A little more grapeshot and the field is ours." John R. Rice is sweeping Dallas, already reaching the 400 mark and [the church is] only a little more than 2 months old. John is going to go over there with a big tent on the north side of the Trinity as soon as winter breaks and one of the keenest young men in our ranks will take his church in Oak Cliff. I think you are right. John Rice is the greatest Bible teacher among us.[126]

By the end of 1932, Rice's fame had spread beyond Texas and the South, all the way up to Wheaton, Illinois, a small town 30 miles or so to the west of Chicago. Wheaton was home to Wheaton College, already by that time renowned as the most preeminent orthodox conservative Christian school in the U.S. and highly regarded by fundamentalists both for its theology and its high academic standards. Rice's success as a revivalist and his uncompromising opposition to what he viewed as the

Southern Baptist Convention's slide toward modernism earned him an invitation to speak in chapel services at Wheaton College. His sermon topic was "separation"—the supposed Biblical injunction for Christians to be separate from the non-Christian world.

Increasingly, along with Bob Jones Sr., John R. Rice was evolving into one of the leading thinkers and fundamentalist spokesmen on the doctrine of separatism. For fundamentalists such as Jones and Rice, Christians were to be separate not only from worldly culture and behavior—that is, against drinking, smoking, dancing, cussing, card-playing, and movie-going—but also separate from any taint of association with Christians with whom they had "fundamental" doctrinal disagreements. If another Christian disagreed with any of the fundamental doctrines of the faith, he was an infidel and heretic and no true Christian. A fundamentalist must avoid any association with such modernists and infidels in order not to pollute the preaching of the gospel with questionable or Satan-inspired theology.

In 1934, Rice founded his third weekly newspaper, *The Sword of the Lord*. He printed the first copy of his newspaper as a personal, religious, and militant call to arms against all forms of liberalism, modernism, and ecumenicalism. The masthead read *"THE SWORD OF THE LORD,"* followed by the tag line *"...and of John R. Rice."*

The name of the publication was taken from the Old Testament tale of Gideon, who was advised by God to select a tiny army of only 300 Israelite soldiers to battle a horde of "the Midianites and the Amalekites and all the children of the east who lay along in the valley like grasshoppers for multitude; and their camels were without number, as the sand by the sea side for multitude." Gideon instructed his army to surround the camp of their enemies in the darkness of the night, each soldier equipped with a trumpet, a torch, and a pitcher to hide the flame of the torch. "When I blow with a trumpet," said Gideon, "I and all that are with me, then blow ye the trumpets also on every side of all the camp, and say, 'The sword of the Lord, and of Gideon.'" The result was mass panic and mutual slaughter on the part of the Midianites and the Amalekites, and complete victory by Gideon and his troops.

Printed below the name of the newspaper was the horizontal image of a flaming sword—not the ancient type used by Gideon, not a modern cavalry saber from the 19th or 20th centuries, but a broadsword such as those used during the Middle Ages in battle against Moslem hordes by Crusader armies. *The Sword of the Lord* had a provocative and colorful style, with sermon titles such as "The Curse of God on Beer-Drinking and Beer-Selling Dallas!"; "Whiskey—The Devil in Liquid Form";

"Courtship and the Dangers of Petting"; and "What is Wrong with the Movies?"

The Sword began as a four-page weekly newsletter for the Fundamentalist Baptist Church, distributed door-to-door in nearby Dallas neighborhoods, but its circulation quickly grew, as did the fame of its editor.

In September of 1934, evangelist Mordecai Ham brought his revival crusade to Charlotte, North Carolina. Ham's team combined with local sponsors to construct a ramshackle pine tabernacle on the edge of town, on Pecan Avenue next to the Cole Manufacturing Company. The tabernacle was large enough accommodate 5,000 saints and sinners, and the floor was covered with sawdust from a nearby pulp mill. Mordecai Ham preached every morning and every night except Mondays for several weeks, and the revival grew in size and impact so that by November it was still going strong.

One night a 16-year-old boy named Billy Graham decided to see what was happening out at the tabernacle. He was stunned by what he saw. Every available seat was filled. Gospel music swelled out into the dark night beyond the pine walls, and Ham's oratory soared and plunged as he called for sinners to repent in order to be spared the wrath of a just God. Ham pleaded and condemned, wept and prayed, shouted and threatened. The auditorium exploded with the drama of sinners repenting, souls being saved, and hundreds of Graham's fellow townspeople crowding down the sawdust trail to kneel at a makeshift altar and dedicate their lives to God. It was a theatrical tableau for the skinny teenager, full of powerful emotional tension and dramatic resolution, and it proved irresistible.

Graham returned to witness the revival drama for several nights in a row as his feelings of guilt and self-condemnation grew. Finally one night he walked down the aisle to give his life to God. "When my decision for Christ was made," Billy Graham later said, "I walked slowly down and knelt in prayer. I opened my heart and knew for the first time the sweetness and joy of God, of truly being born again."[127]

By the time Graham graduated from high school two years later, he was convinced that God had called him to preach. He attended Bob Jones College (later Bob Jones University) in Cleveland, Tennessee for a year, but he was oppressed by the strict campus rules and the conformity enforced by the school. When he met with Bob Jones Sr. to resign from the school, Dr. Bob urged him to stay and warned him that he was throwing his life away: "At best, all you could amount to would be a poor country Baptist preacher somewhere out in the sticks.... You have a voice that pulls. God can use that voice of yours. He can use it mightily."[128] Graham chose to ignore Jones's advice and headed south to spend the next couple of years at Florida Bible College.

The Great War—with almost 16 million deaths and a continent devastated—had been deeply traumatic for the United States, despite its late entry and relatively low casualties. The United Kingdom of Great Britain and Ireland, for example, suffered almost 2.5 million casualties, while the United States suffered only a third of a million casualties with double the UK's population.[129] Germany, despite its defeat in the war, had seemed to be especially dangerous. Germany was the home of theologians who invented the "higher criticism" that seemed to question divine inspiration of the Bible in the 19th century. Germany was the home of Friedrich Nietzsche, who had famously opined that "God is dead" by way of calling for a deeper moral foundation than what he believed was provided by Christian values. Germany was the home of German rationalism, German science, and German industrialism, all of which made Southern fundamentalists more than a little squeamish.

Fundamentalists celebrated Germany's defeat for theological as well as political reasons. Nonetheless, they were horrified by the massive slaughter that had attended the war. As a result, the fundamentalist response to the rise of Hitler and the approach of a second world war was complicated and contradictory.

A deep strain of anti-Semitism ran through the teachings and sermons of many fundamentalist leaders such as Ham and William Bell Riley. In a 1934 article "The Blood of the Jew vs. the Blood of Jesus," Riley, founder of the World Christian Fundamentals Association, argued that a Jewish cabal had as its ultimate goal "the establishment of a single government headed by 'the king despot of Zion,' whose place and power will be made secure by a reign of terror that will put to the most torturous death any and every opponent; the plan being to exalt a few of Jewish blood to honor and untold opulence, and retain them there at the expense of the world's millions."[130]

Riley claimed in his 1934 book *Protocols and Communism* that Jewish Communists in the U.S. wanted to "filch the land of all its gold, take over its capital and its farms, and possess themselves of all its factories, arts and industries." He further suggested that "today in our land many of the biggest trusts, banks, and manufacturing interests are controlled by Jews; tobacco, cotton, and sugar they handle in overwhelming proportions."

Riley applauded the way that God had helped Hitler to snatch "Germany from the very jaws of atheistic communism." He deplored

Hitler's critics who began "tearing their hair...the moment that a Jew-Communist in Germany had his store closed." And he agreed with Hitler that the Jews had earned the hatred of many against them: "Jewry, from the day that she crucified Jesus Christ until the present time, has given many occasions for her own rejection... Hear Hitler, who speaks from firsthand knowledge: 'the Jew is the cause and beneficiary of our slavery. The Jew has caused our misery, and today he lives on our troubles. That is the reason that as nationalists, we are enemies of the Jew. He has ruined our race, rotted our morals, corrupted our traditions, and broken our power.'"[131]

But many conservative Americans had suspicions and reservations about Adolf Hitler as he began his rise to power. The Fifth Baptist World Congress held in Berlin in 1934 included over 40 Baptist denominations—including the Southern Baptist Convention but not the independent fundamentalist Baptists represented by Jones, Norris, and Rice. The congress denounced "racialism" as a "violation of the law of God, the Heavenly Father, all racial animosity and every form of unfair discrimination towards the Jews, towards colored people, or towards subject races in any part of the world."[132]

However, many of the Baptists in attendance were impressed with Hitler's conservative politics and crusades for "social morality." After his return to the U.S. from Berlin, Boston's John Bradbury said: "It was a great relief to be in a country where salacious sex literature cannot be sold, where putrid motion pictures and gangster films cannot be shown. The new Germany has burned great masses of corrupting books and magazines along with its bonfires of Jewish and communistic libraries." And the Fifth Baptist World Congress itself pronounced that "Chancellor Hitler gives to the temperance movement the prestige of his personal example since he neither uses intoxicants nor smokes."[133]

M. E. Dodd, president of the Southern Baptist Convention, expressed his belief that Hitler's moves against German Jews were unfortunately necessary because they had used their strengths "for self-aggrandizement to the injury of the German people," and he charged that "since the war some 200,000 Jews from Russia and other Eastern places had come to Germany. Most of these were Communist agitators against the government."

J. Frank Norris, in this regard typical of most fundamentalists and conservatives, went through a dramatic evolution in his views of Hitler, from early support to profound hostility later on. In 1937, for example, Norris wrote in his newspaper *The Fundamentalist* that Germany had improved since the Great War. Earlier he had witnessed despair; however, now "as you move around among the people they are happy, they are not in fear." He claimed there was no unemployment and that even a Jewish store owner told him business was good. "Keep your eye on that forty-seven-year-old bachelor," said Norris after attending a Nazi demonstration. "He is a teetotaler, a vegetarian, drinks nothing but milk. He is a veritable dynamo. He is Napoleonic in his personality and influence over the masses."[134] In the same year, however, Norris had already begun to condemn Hitler for his persecution of the Jews, and by Pearl Harbor Norris viewed Hitler as a potential Antichrist, harbinger of the end of history and evidence of the near-term Second Coming of Christ.[135]

Increasingly, John R. Rice's success brought him into conflict with the ego and ambitions of J. Frank Norris. The conflict began as a private spat over minor issues, but it quickly evolved into public warfare between the two fundamentalist leaders. At the heart of the conflict were not any matters of religion, faith, or belief. Rice operated independently and did not seek permission from Norris to build his church or to begin a ministry of evangelism that stretched far beyond the borders of Texas. The core issue appeared to be that Norris resented anyone who rivaled him for the affection of the Christian masses. The two men traded objections and criticisms in the pages of their newspapers at first. Then, Norris undertook what Rice saw as a dishonest and underhanded betrayal.

Rice arranged to hold a citywide revival campaign sponsored by the Fundamentalist Baptist Association in Binghamton, New York. The revival would begin in January of 1936, and would represent Rice's first such major revival crusade in any Northern city—a breakthrough onto the national stage of revivalism. On the eve of the revival, Rice received a telegram from the sponsoring committee canceling the meeting. Certain unnamed "friends" had accused him of various heretical practices well-known among Pentecostal Christians—Holy Rollers— such as snake handling, faith healing, and glossalalia, or speaking in tongues. These were far outside the realm of behavior acceptable in a fundamentalist preacher.

Rice immediately sent a letter testifying to his fundamentalist orthodoxy and announcing that he would be coming anyway. He packed his wife, his secretary, and his (then only) five daughters in the family car and set out for Binghamton with just enough cash to buy gas for a one way trip. When he arrived in upstate New York, he found that the committee had decided to go ahead and sponsor the meeting after all.

The revival in Binghamton turned out to be a great success, with all the evangelical churches involved and many thousands of people attending services for over a month.

Soon, Rice discovered that the source of the various lies and slanders designed to disrupt or prevent the Binghamton revival was none other than J. Frank Norris. The friendship and alliance between the two men was over. In a letter published in *The Fundamentalist*, Norris said: "In the tremendous glorious sweep of fundamentalism among Baptists, I consider this cult [of John R. Rice] the most dangerous enemy of the truth, far more dangerous than out-and-out rationalistic modernism—all this crowd that believes in the 'anointing with oil,' and that the Bible miracles are for the present day."

In reply, Rice changed the masthead of *The Sword of the Lord* so that it read: "An independent, religious weekly, standing for the verbal inspiration of the Bible, the Deity of Christ, His blood atonement, salvation by faith, New Testament soul-winning and the Pre-Millennial return of Christ. Opposes Sin, Modernism, and Denominational Overlordship."

The "overlordship" he was referring to was by Norris—not the Southern Baptist Convention—and to make the point clear, in an article inside the paper he asked, "Shall one man, with his paper, radio, Bible school and paid helpers rule the fundamentalist movement?" Rice's answer was clearly no.

Despite the rift between Norris and Rice in 1936, John R. Rice advised his friends to love and pray for Dr. Norris: "He is a great man, has won many thousands of souls, and has stood for the fundamentals of the Faith in a way that has greatly honored God."[*]

---

[*] My granddad, I am convinced, at the least felt uncomfortable around Norris's comparatively extreme and blatant racism. Rice never was quoted in any sermon or speech as approving of the Klan, and he did not share some of Norris's extreme beliefs about "negroes, Catholics, and foreigners" generally. My granddad's close friendship and association with Norris, for me, is one of the most troubling periods of his life. I have a hard time reconciling Norris's reputation—his spitefulness and arrogance, his hatred of others, his violent attacks on anyone who disagreed with him—with the fact that he was Granddad's close advisor and mentor. Norris helped to launch John R. Rice's career as a prominent and influential fundamentalist leader, but their friendship could only last so long. In the end, Norris appeared to be much more concerned about his own ego and reputation than about "saving souls" or building the fundamentalist movement, and he felt threatened by Rice's growing influence and popularity among grassroots fundamentalists. It is striking to me that my granddad did not attack and expose Norris for his extreme racism, for Norris's mean and self-righteous assaults on fellow Christians, for his idiotic attacks on

Rice's Fundamentalist Baptist Church in Dallas prospered, becoming one of the largest such churches in the country. The name Fundamentalist Baptist Church, however, was synonymous in Texas with the name of J. Frank Norris, and such churches were generally known as "Norrisite" churches, signifying that Norris was essentially the moderator of an independent denomination in competition with the Southern Baptist Convention. In the wake of his split with Norris, Rice changed the name of his Dallas church to "Galilean Baptist Church."

The number of subscribers for *The Sword of the Lord* multiplied. Rice saw himself as a general in the army of God, an enemy of Satan and his works, a leader and defender of the fundamentals of the true faith, and a prophet of the good, the pure, and the righteous.

Throughout the next two decades, he conducted revival campaigns in cities across the South and North, and became a close friend and ally of other leading fundamentalists such as Bob Jones Sr., Lee Roberson, and Harry Ironside. He often took along his wife Lloys and their six daughters to his revival meetings. There they served as his supporting staff and as part of the program of revival music. Lloys sat at a book table in the back of the revival tabernacle, tent or auditorium, selling subscriptions to the *Sword* and copies of his many books and pamphlets. Their daughters sang in a close harmony sextet about winning souls to Jesus, many of their songs written by their father, to the accompaniment of an inexpensive gold-and-white Hohner accordion played by one of the girls.

His personal tools included a powerful speaking voice; an encyclopedic knowledge of the Bible; a complete assurance that he correctly understood the will and Word of God; a narrow, literal and precise interpretation of the Bible; a disdain for and dismissal of any who disagreed with him on what he considered fundamental doctrines; and a talent for aggressive self-promotion in the service of God. His tactics were to hold revival meetings in towns and cities across the country; to use the new medium of radio in aggressive and creative ways; to found fundamentalist churches; to encourage and promote fundamentalist preachers; and to train thousands of fundamentalist Sunday school teachers, fundamentalist pastors, fundamentalist ministers, and fundamentalist deacons.

Catholics and Jews, or for his many provocative and public lies. Instead, Rice made good use of Norris' endorsement and resources, and then split from him only when conflict with Norris became unavoidable.

Along with many other Americans, John R. Rice had supported the involvement of the U.S. in the Great War as his patriotic duty, apparently without questioning the morality or justice of that war. Also in common with many Americans, Rice witnessed the war's savage bloodletting, its matter-of-fact killing of millions of soldiers and civilians, with a kind of unbelieving horror. The relative remoteness of most Americans from the European battlefields may have made their shock greater. It was as though humanity had willingly entered a long, dark, bloody hallway leading to the appearance of the Antichrist on earth and the ultimate barbaric savagery and wholesale slaughter of Armageddon predicted in the pages of Revelation. Many Christians of all denominations and sects in the U.S. developed a profound distaste for war, along with a desire to withdraw from the rest of the world and protect America's life and livelihood in the cocoon of isolationism.

In the years before World War II, John R. Rice opposed U.S. involvement in what he considered a "European war." In a series of articles in *The Sword of the Lord* in 1939 and 1940, Rice expressed strikingly antiwar and even pacifistic beliefs:

> War is a hateful and terrible business. Let no one encourage it; let all of us stay out of it if we can…The great mass of soldiers have been bloody, vengeful, wicked men. Generally war is mass murder, inspired by hate, fed by lies, directed by vain ambitions and desire for power or gain. Usually war destroys civilization, lowers morals, brings untold misery and leaves an aftermath of debt, poverty, hate, ruined bodies and damned souls. I advise every boy to stay out of the army and navy even in peacetime unless conscripted. If drafted by the army, I advise young men to seek noncombatant work. If conscience will not allow one to fight, then follow conscience and serve God at any cost.[136]

Even as Rice expressed his horror of war, however, he was laying the basis for shifting his position to support for a war he could define as just. He saw a strong relationship between the sinfulness of the Nazis and the sinfulness of some Americans, such as labor union saboteurs "who willingly commit themselves to murder, to sabotage—such men are not different in spirit and in heart than those who deliberately plunged Europe into war, or the Japanese who ravished China, or the Italians who massacred helpless Ethiopia."[137] By the time the Japanese attacked Pearl Harbor in 1941, Rice and his fellow fundamentalists were fully on board with the war aims of the United States and its allies. War in the abstract might be abominable, but when your own country's welfare and safety were at stake, war in the particular became inescapable, noble, and even righteous in the sight of God.

Chapter 20
Out of the Cradle: From Dallas to Wheaton

*"I saw the Lord standing upon the altar: and he said,
Smite the lintel of the door, that the posts may shake:
and cut them in the head, all of them; and I will slay the
last of them with the sword: he that fleeth of them shall
not flee away, and he that escapeth of them shall not be
delivered."*—Amos 9:1

Billy Graham was the skinniest kid Mary Lloys Rice had ever seen.

In 1940, Mary Lloys—my mom—plus her five sisters and my grandparents had moved a thousand miles north from Dallas and into their new home in Wheaton, Illinois on West Franklin Street, a big yellow frame house with white trim in a neighborhood shaded by massive maples and spreading elms. The dining room was big enough to welcome an oak table with plenty of leaves to accommodate all eight members of the Rice family plus two to four traveling preachers, missionaries, seminary students, or workers from *The Sword of the Lord* office.

The entryway of the house was spacious enough to house a piano that would be the focus of the family's unanimous and enthusiastic passion for music. All six daughters played piano and sang gospel songs at the drop of a hat, including while running to and from school or competing for the use of the bathroom as well as singing solos, duets, trios, or quartets at revivals and church services.

Billy Graham showed up one fall day in 1941 on the front porch of my grandparents' house, a year after the Rice family arrived from Dallas. Billy had a flatbed truck and a crew of students from nearby Wheaton College, and Granddad had hired him to move a baby grand piano into that entryway. The piano had a black enamel finish and a deliciously curvy shape with a mile-long ivory keyboard and a top that flipped up to reveal a latticework of shining steel strings and a plush row of 88 felt-covered hammers. Billy was wearing a sweater with elbow patches and some old cotton workpants. At the age of 23, he was a sophomore at Wheaton College and a recent transfer from the Florida Bible Institute.

My mom, 16 at the time, recalls that Billy had started his little moving company to earn his way through college. Many years later, she recounted how she met Billy as he helped muscle their new piano through the front door: "He was so skinny if he turned sideways he almost disappeared. Billy talked fast, and he moved even faster!"

By the late 1930s, John R. Rice was beginning to think about emigrating from the Texas plains to some location that might better support his big plans. Rice started his evangelistic career in Texas, and over a dozen years he had concentrated and built his ministry there and founded a number of churches. *The Sword of the Lord* itself had begun as a newsletter for Rice's church in Dallas, but had quickly grown and attracted a national readership. Before long, he created the Sword of the Lord Foundation as an evangelistic institute and publishing house with a mission and programs separate from the church. On more and more Sundays, Rice could be found preaching in some pulpit far from Dallas. In 1938 alone he traveled to churches in Oregon, Missouri, Iowa, Mississippi, California, and a dozen other states. He spoke at a Bible school in Oklahoma City, was awarded an honorary Doctor of Divinity degree by Los Angeles Baptist Theological Seminary, and hosted his own "Dallas Bible School." He considered 40 to 50 invitations per year to speak in revival meetings across the country. His calling wasn't to sit in Dallas taking care of his one church, marrying and burying his parishioners and providing pastoral counseling. Instead, John R. Rice felt called to be an evangelist, and he believed that the highest calling of a Christian was to be a soul-winner.

Consequently, in April 1940, John R. Rice moved his wife, his six daughters, and several employees of the Sword of the Lord Foundation to the small Midwest town of Wheaton, Illinois. Wheaton was a small, sleepy Midwestern town about 30 miles west of Chicago, with a population of fewer than 10,000. The move was a dramatic shift from the plains of Texas.

Wheaton College, with 1100 students in 1940, was one of a handful of colleges in the country with a strong fundamentalist and evangelical orientation. Its first president had been Jonathan Blanchard, a prominent abolitionist minister closely associated with Charles G. Finney and Oberlin College.

Blanchard came from a long line of New England Pilgrims and Puritans. His relatives had helped to found Brattleboro, Vermont, and Jonathan was born to the north of Brattleboro, in Rockingham, in 1811. Blanchard was raised as a Congregationalist, strong in his faith and evangelical in his outlook. While at Andover Theological Seminary, Blanchard organized an anti-slavery society, was reproved by the faculty for doing so, and left school to become a lecturer for the American Anti-Slavery Society. He then studied at Lane Seminary in Cincinnati as a student of the famous preacher Lyman Beecher, and became friends with Beecher's several children, who would grow up to be highly accomplished and well-known in their own right, including abolitionist Harriet Beecher Stowe, the author of *Uncle Tom's Cabin*.[138]

In the progressive vein of many 19th century evangelicals, Blanchard was a reformer who fought public battles to end slavery, create equality for women, and establish universal access to public education. Under his leadership, when Wheaton College first opened in 1860, the school was a stop on the Underground Railroad for fugitive slaves, and was the first school in Illinois with a college-level women's program and co-educational classrooms.[139]

Wheaton, with its strong history of educating women, offered the best choice for John R. Rice's six daughters to attend college. There they could all get a fine Christian education in the liberal arts, and as a bonus they might all meet and marry budding preachers-to-be, who could be found aplenty at Wheaton College.

As a Northern school, Wheaton's egalitarian theology was a sharp break from the racially-tinged fundamentalism of the South. Although Rice identified himself as a fundamentalist, he sought a national platform for his focus on revival and soul-winning. He saw himself as a leader who could help white Southerners move past their fixation on race, which he believed was detrimental to their mission as Christians. The move to Wheaton was an explicit rejection of the cultural narrowness of Texas, and a definitive separation from the racial and political extremism of men such as J. Frank Norris. Finally, it placed him near the population center of the country, where it would be easy to find rail transportation to almost anywhere he might conduct revival meetings, and from where he hoped to achieve prominence and national influence.

Having left his pastorate in Dallas behind, Rice focused on his work as editor of *The Sword of the Lord*. He saw himself as a national movement builder. More than just a preacher, pastor, or evangelist, he would be the creator and cultivator of a growing network of fundamentalists united around a common program and common doctrines. With his newspaper, he set out to mentor a new generation of soul-winning preachers and revivalists. He wanted to return America to the days of the Great Awakening, when evangelical Christianity seemed to be at the very center of the nation's Manifest Destiny. He was on a mission to transform the continent and the world, a mission to save millions of lost souls by converting them to Christianity through the redeeming blood of Jesus. Rice yearned to return America to the days when evangelists such as Billy Sunday had preached in great, citywide revival campaigns for huge crowds, sponsored by most of the churches in a city.

An ever widening stream of publications by John R. Rice began to flow from the editorial offices of the Sword, from Bible tracts designed to be used by Christians in soul-winning to full-length commentaries on specific books of the Bible designed for use by pastors and Sunday School teachers, from reprints of sermons preached by famous fundamentalists to colorful pamphlets on controversial topics. In one such pamphlet, provocatively titled "Bobbed Hair, Bossy Wives, and Women Preachers," Rice explained that God had commanded women never to cut their hair, that God intended women to be subordinate to their husbands, and that women should never pastor churches.[*]

Rice was interested in cultivating and promoting a very specific type of preaching. It was preaching that pulled no punches. It was preaching that was sharp and clear, preaching that took a definite stand. It was preaching that could bring revival back to America. In 1940, one of his sermons titled "Evangelistic Preaching" appeared in *The Sword of the Lord*:

> Preach on booze. Preach on the scarlet sin, adultery.
> Some cheeks will turn red with shame, and some won't
> like it, but it will bring people to repentance. Preach on
> the dance, tell people it is rotten as sin. Tell people they
> dance because they enjoy the lust, the deliberate
> inflamement of passion of the dance! They do! Preach
> on the movies made by vile, lewd people, holding up
> rotten moral standards, breaking down respect for
> marriage, pure love, hard work, God and the Bible.
> Preach against the Masonic Lodges. Preach against
> evolution and false cults. Preach on death, sin, Hell,

---

[*] The title of the pamphlet was attention-getting, though it might leave the mistaken impression that my grandfather was permanently grumpy toward women, which was not the case. He was surrounded by intelligent, talented, and well-educated women whom he dearly loved, and who doted on him—his wife Lloys and his six daughters among them.

judgment! Such preaching with boldness, with love, with tears, with scripture, with faith, will bring great revivals, will save hardened sinners.[140]

A few months after John R. Rice had arrived in Wheaton in the spring of 1940, Billy Graham registered for the fall semester at the college. Billy Graham was in Wheaton for several of the same reasons John R. Rice was there. Billy was only 22 at the time, a full 23 years younger than Rice. He had grown up in a Presbyterian church in North Carolina, and shared with Rice the full panoply of assumptions that most Southern fundamentalists carried—about race, religion, and politics. Both of Graham's grandfathers were Confederate veterans, and the only society he'd ever known was racially segregated.

Graham was at Wheaton because he loved revivals and soul-winning, and more than anything he wanted to be an evangelist following the path blazed by fundamentalist preachers such as Billy Sunday, Mordecai Ham, and John R. Rice. After preaching his first sermon at Florida Bible Institute, he had headed north to Illinois.

The two men met within the first year the two of them lived in Wheaton. They quickly formed a friendship. John R. Rice quickly became a mentor for the younger man. Graham was inspired by Rice's citywide revival campaigns and became an avid reader of *The Sword of the Lord*. He attended some of the first *Sword of the Lord* conferences on evangelism in the 1940s, and his first published sermons would appear in the pages of *The Sword of the Lord* after Billy graduated from Wheaton.

From the point of view of most Americans, Christian fundamentalism had virtually disappeared after the Scopes Monkey Trial. Fundamentalists were held up to scorn and derision for their supposed anti-intellectualism and intentional ignorance of science. Evangelists were money-grubbing shysters and sentimental hypocrites. Revivals were events where hellfire-and-brimstone fear mongers preyed upon the ignorance and credulousness of country bumpkins.

During the 1920s, fundamentalists had waged a great battle against modernism within the mainline Protestant denominations. The battlegrounds had included the various denominational conventions and governing bodies, the faculties of all the seminaries, divinity schools, institutes, and Bible schools, and most importantly, the field of public opinion. In all of these arenas, the fundamentalists had suffered defeats, and had withdrawn to lick their wounds and nurse notions of the Apocalypse and dreams of vengeance—or simply to carry on with their own more private work of separation from the modernists and perfection of their own orthodoxy.

Outside of the public eye, however, the fundamentalists were by no means finally defeated. Many individual fundamentalist leaders such as John R. Rice dug in to build their networks and resources and to create new forms of evangelism and outreach. Fundamentalist pastors built vital and growing churches, and fundamentalist evangelists began to use the still new medium of radio ever more effectively to build mass audiences. Fundamentalist and evangelical schools such as Wheaton College, Bob Jones University, and Moody Bible Institute nurtured a new generation of preachers, missionaries, deacons, and Sunday school teachers. The role of *The Sword of the Lord* and other journals and book publishers became ever more important as a way to develop and promote a shared fundamentalist understanding of Christian doctrine and the mission of Christians. Contrary to public expectations, the growth and development of fundamentalist Christianity was explosive during the 1920s and 30s, and fundamentalism was becoming much more deeply connected and influential.

As historian Joel Carpenter pointed out:

> The success of fundamentalism and other evangelical groups, which also grew rapidly, came at the very time that mainline Protestantism was experiencing decline...While fundamentalist missions and ministries grew, Southern Baptists gained almost 1.5 million members between 1926 and 1940, and the Pentecostal denomination the Assemblies of God quadrupled during the same period to total some two hundred thousand members. At the same time, almost every mainline Protestant denomination declined in membership, baptisms, Sunday school enrollments, total receipts, and foreign missions.[141]

Mainline Protestantism had reached its peak of influence as the religious establishment in America, and mainline churches were at the beginning of a decades-long decline. By contrast, fundamentalist and evangelical churches, which appeared to have become irrelevant for religious historians, were on the verge of a decades-long ascent toward mainstream respect and influence.

By the 1940s, fundamentalists had created a thriving and independent subculture outside of the dominant Protestant institutions—the churches, denominations, mission boards, colleges, and publications of mainline Protestant Christians. The new fundamentalist institutions were generally outside the knowledge of the American public. Fundamentalism had no real center and no consistent messages. Instead, there were many leaders, little coordination, and multiple messages. Many leading fundamentalists began to feel frustrated by their lack of unity, and began to believe there might be real value in some more formal organization. An inspiring model for such an organization was J. Elwin Wright's New England Fellowship, comprised of evangelical and fundamentalist leaders from various churches and denominational backgrounds who sustained a network that gave rise to friendships, conferences, collaborations, and meetings.

In April of 1942, over 140 leading fundamentalists met in St. Louis, Missouri to craft a plan for the new network. Virtually all the leading fundamentalists were there—William Ayer of Calvary Baptist Church in New York, Stephen Paine of Houghton College, Robert G. Lee of Bellevue Baptist Church in Memphis, Bob Jones Sr., William Bell Riley, and many others. Some of them were still members of the historic Northern denominations that had dominated the evangelical landscape before the World War, but many more were part of churches, networks, and fellowships far out of the mainstream.

As they considered their past isolation from each other and marginal impact on American culture, they confirmed that they agreed about essential Christian doctrines. They agreed about the mission of the church and how to interpret the Bible and how to understand the way Christians should act. They agreed that Christians should be "separate from the world" and refrain from collaborating with "liberals and modernists." They agreed that they had done the right thing in leaving the mainline Protestant denominations during the previous two decades. They were united around evangelical principles laid out in *The Fundamentals* thirty years earlier. And they began to see themselves as a unified movement of evangelicals. They were especially stirred by Harold Ockenga of historic Park Street Church in Boston, who "lamented that the cause of evangelical Christianity in America—once maintained by the united, corporate testimony of the established denominations—had been reduced to individuals and individual congregations. He challenged those single voices to put aside denominational differences for the sake of a more consolidated witness for Christ."[142]

The newly founded organization was named the National Association of Evangelicals (NAE). Despite their broad agreement, the founders still had some differences. Some of the more conservative fundamentalists declined to sign the call for the meeting because they were concerned that some of the other attendees were insufficiently pure in their opposition to modernism or liberalism in any form, or insufficiently enthusiastic about revivals.

However, as historian George Marsden has recounted:

> Almost no one seems to have regarded the formation of the NAE as a sign that "evangelicals" were now breaking from "fundamentalists" over the principle of separatism. There was not a practical distinction between fundamentalist and evangelical: the words were interchangeable. All involved in the NAE were frankly fundamentalists, and among fundamentalists only a minority would make separatism a test of fellowship... Some of the most militant fundamentalists, such as Bob Jones Sr., and John R. Rice of the influential *Sword of the Lord*, even joined the NAE.[143]

John R. Rice joined the NAE because he agreed with Ockenga's call for unity, and he was convinced—along with Ockenga—that the NAE could be a tool to bring big-time, mass revivals back. In November of 1942, Rice used *The Sword of the Lord* to organize his first national conference on evangelism, featuring some of the most prominent evangelical preachers in America. Much more than just another "Bible school," the conference was sharply focused on the tools and techniques needed to bring back old-time revivals. It wasn't simply a cheerleading session. Renowned revivalists taught how to organize a successful fundamentalist church, how to organize a successful revival meeting, how to set up a successful program in a local church to visit people in a neighborhood and invite them to a church for a revival meeting, and how to issue an invitation for people to come forward and get saved at the end of a revival sermon.

This Chicago conference was a hit, playing to a packed house and producing powerful forward momentum for the re-energized evangelical movement. The week after the meeting Rice summed up its accomplishments in an article in *The Sword* entitled, "Crowds, Great Messages, Life Dedications to Soul-Winning":

> The infidels say you cannot have great mass revivals because the people have become too intelligent to be moved by the fear of Hell... The modernists say that now the social gospel is the only thing that can fill man's needs... Fundamental pastors all over America side with

the infidels and modernists when they say we can no more have great mass revivals with hundreds or thousands saved, with whole cities shaken by gospel preaching and by the wonderful power of God...The idea that revivals are out of date is a slander against God, a vicious lie of Satan, and real Christians should hate that lie with all their hearts.[144]

Although it was still nine years before Billy Graham's first breakthrough mass revival campaign in Los Angeles, John R. Rice represented the emerging consensus among evangelicals about the importance of revivals and soul-winning. At the first full national convention of the NAE in 1943, Rice and his friends Bob Jones Sr. and H. A. Ironside were members of the committee that drew up the statement of faith for the new organization.[145] The NAE affirmed Rice's focus on revivals by setting up an Evangelism Commission designed to spark and support the burgeoning efforts to bring back large scale, citywide revival campaigns. Rice was a leading member of the commission, and James Murch's history of the NAE published in 1956 referred to Rice as one of the three leading evangelical revivalists of the 1940s, along with Hyman Appelman and Bob Jones Sr.[146]

Most evangelicals agreed with this focus on revivalism. In fact, revivals hadn't actually disappeared since Billy Sunday preached to pitifully small crowds in his last failed attempt to maintain the big-time revival spirit in the early 1930s. But they had disappeared from the sight of most Americans and were conducted only in single churches. Revivals were not the mass public events seen in past decades, sponsored by many churches across the spectrum of Protestant denominations. Big revival tents no longer appeared on vacant lots of cities across the country; tens of thousands of people no longer crowded into temporary plywood tabernacles to hear colorful hellfire-and-brimstone sermons by strutting, gesticulating, spirit-filled orators supported by every local Protestant church within hollering distance. The sawdust trail was a thing of the past.

John R. Rice's innovation of the 1940s—large scale, citywide, mass evangelism supported by many churches, revivals large and newsworthy enough to capture the attention of an entire city or region—was no innovation at all, but rather a throwback to a simpler and more deeply religious time in America. As Rice himself said, it was a deliberate attempt to revisit the extraordinary mass campaigns of Charles Spurgeon and Charles G. Finney in the mid-19th century, and of the revolutionary evangelicals Jonathan Edwards and George Whitfield and John Wesley during the Great Awakening of the 18th century.

Over the next six years, Rice made headlines by conducting this mass form of revival, known as union campaigns, in scores of cities across the U.S. and Canada, in such places as Everett, Washington; San Pedro, California; Waterloo, Iowa; Springfield, Missouri; Goshen, Indiana; Akron, Ohio; Winston-Salem, North Carolina; Moncton, New Brunswick, Canada; Chicago, Illinois; Buffalo, New York; and Cleveland, Ohio. A typical example was Seattle, where in November of 1946, the Seattle Evangelical Ministers Association, including over 60 churches, sponsored Rice's revival crusade in the Seattle Civic Auditorium and Moore Theater.

One of his largest revivals was held in Chicago in 1946 in the Chicago Arena. Along with his fellow campaigners, Bob Jones Sr. and Paul Rood, Rice spoke to almost 10,000 people at every service, every day for five weeks—an almost unheard of length for a revival in the 1940s or any other decade. The event was billed as the first "united evangelical campaign" since Billy Sunday had preached there in 1918. It was sponsored by 200 churches plus many other evangelical institutions, including Moody Bible Institute, Northern Baptist Seminary, Chicago Evangelistic Institute, Pacific Garden Mission, Youth for Christ, Christian Businessmen's Committee, Wheaton College, Lutheran Bible Institute, and Child Evangelism Fellowship.

Although the crowds for Rice's revivals were large by the standards of the 1940s, they were considerably smaller than the massive numbers that had turned out to hear Billy Sunday three decades earlier—before the Scopes Monkey Trial, before the publication of *Elmer Gantry*, and before the general and public disillusionment with revivalists. A significant difference was that Rice was typically sponsored only by the thin slice of evangelical churches, not by the broad swath of mainline Protestant denominations that had sponsored Sunday.

The very fact that Rice could hold successful union campaigns was impressive and surprising to many. But he wasn't satisfied with conducting his own successful revival campaigns. From 1945 on he organized an increasing number of Sword of the Lord conferences on soul-winning and revival across the country, bringing together thousands of fundamentalist leaders in a strongly aligned, deeply connected and growing revivalist movement. Rice launched a nationwide radio broadcast, the *Voice of Revival*, syndicated to hundreds of radio stations and featuring the Voice of Revival Choir, which included his six daughters and their husbands plus several *Sword* employees. When he was not traveling or speaking on the radio, he was writing and publishing scores of books and pamphlets which he marketed and sold through the *Sword* and in his many public events.

The United States had emerged from the devastation of World War II relatively unscathed and as the only clear winner. The country now confronted the second half of the 20th century with vast optimism for what some America political pundits dubbed "The American Century": an era of unchallenged military power, political superiority, and evangelical possibility. If America could rule the world, some reasoned, why should not its true religion, conservative and orthodox Christianity—the faith of its fathers, the only version of Christianity that could reasonably claim legitimacy as the true face of American Christianity—find favor with the masses of people around the world who would naturally equate the freedom and democracy offered by America with the salvation offered by Jesus as proclaimed by evangelical American Christians?

From the point of view of John R. Rice and most other fundamentalist leaders, the problem was that America itself was in need of salvation. To their eyes, the social convulsions associated with World War II had led to a cascade of immorality, lewdness, corruption, and sin unparalleled in American history. Hollywood movies depicted corrupt yet attractive lifestyles driven by lust and greed and untouched by Christian values or the message of salvation. Young people were being seduced by sex-drenched dancing and music. Skirts were hiking higher and higher, revealing ever more female flesh. Women were seeking power and independence equal to that of men, and divorce was becoming commonplace. The Devil was roaming the earth, "seeking whom he may devour."

God was calling Christians to a holy struggle against the forces of evil—and more than ever, Rice and other fundamentalist leaders believed, America was ripe for an old-fashioned mass revival, a return to the Great Awakenings of the18th and 19th centuries. And the results seemed to bear them out: within a few years of the end of World War II , John R. Rice's horizons had expanded dramatically, and so had those of the united evangelical Christian movement. The circulation of *The Sword of the Lord* had expanded rapidly from 30,000 in 1940 to 50,000 in 1946; by 1953 it would exceed 90,000.

The atmosphere in the offices of *The Sword of the Lord* was charged with excitement and a sense of global mission and large plans. *The Sword* seemed to be the epicenter of a universe of evangelical leaders, churches, and denominations, a network of earth shakers and movement builders on the leading edge of change.

Together with other key evangelical institutions such as Wheaton College, Bob Jones College (soon to be Bob Jones University), and the NAE, *The Sword* appeared ready to retake the ground lost for Christianity in the split with mainline Protestants in the 1920s. John R. Rice's global vision for Christian fundamentalism was embodied in the new International Commission of the National Association of Evangelicals. The commission was chaired by NAE president Harold Ockenga, and its membership included John R. Rice, Bob Jones Jr., and Billy Graham.

After leaving Wheaton College in 1944, Billy Graham had become the pastor of a small church outside Chicago, tried his hand at hosting a weekly radio program, and then become the first full-time evangelist representing an evangelical organization called Youth for Christ. The 27-year-old almost glowed with charisma and energy when he preached, and he appeared perfectly at home on the platform. Youth for Christ turned out to be the ideal venue for showcasing the talents of young Billy. "He would now serve the Lord onstage in a pastel suit, with shiny socks that appeared to glow in the dark, loud ties, and pomaded hair," reported Roger Bruns' biography of Billy Graham. "He would be backed by impresarios, girl trios, magicians, huge choirs, swing-band instrumentalists, and even a horse named MacArthur who would kneel at the cross and tap 12 times, signifying the number of Christ's apostles. One memorable performance added a sonata for 100 pianos."[147]

Graham traveled around the country, flying 200,000 miles in his first year alone and speaking to groups of young people in 47 states. The movement attracted large, youthful crowds who packed venues such as Madison Square Garden in New York. At Chicago Stadium, 30,000 attended a rally in which a thousand-voice choir held forth under a gigantic banner reading "Chicagoland Youth for Christ."[148]

By 1947, John R. Rice was ready to recruit Billy Graham as one of the speakers for a multi-city revival campaign set to visit every major town in North and South Carolina. The campaign itself was less than a rousing success, and *The Sword of the Lord* ended up $5,000 in debt for expenses, but John R. Rice was undeterred: not every experiment can be successful. In the wake of the campaign, Rice reported in the *Sword* that Billy Graham was "a powerful, spirit-filled, doctrinally sound young man." He began heavily endorsing and promoting Graham in the pages of *The Sword of the Lord*, and several of Graham's sermons were published in the *Sword*, helping him rise to prominence among hundreds of thousands of evangelicals long before he was well known in the rest of the world.

The two men called each other regularly and met in person whenever they could. They hit it off as friends as well as evangelical colleagues. Both were Southerners who had successfully made the journey from regional parochialism to the national stage of evangelical Christianity. Both considered that they had moved beyond the stereotypes and prejudices that marked their ancestors' more reactionary or racist proclivities and more limited points of view. Both saw themselves first of all as soul-winners and evangelists, and only secondarily as defenders of theological orthodoxy—though both would have said they shared the only correct interpretation of scripture.

In the autumn of 1949, the 31-year-old Billy Graham suddenly broke out of obscurity with a successful citywide revival in Los Angeles. In the first couple of weeks, Graham filled a big-top circus tent in downtown L.A. every night and established the meetings as a successful local event. Then the newspaper mogul William Randolph Hearst, seeing Graham as a compelling spokesman for his own views and believing Graham could spearhead a national anticommunist crusade, sent out a telegram to Hearst newspapers everywhere famously telling them to "Puff Graham!"

The result was a flood of prominent and positive articles in newspapers across the country. The crusade turned into a phenomenon lasting seven weeks, and almost overnight Graham became a national sensation. Within the next few years his audiences swelled to fill sports stadiums around the world, and soon Henry Luce had joined the chorus of acclamation and began to feature Graham regularly on the cover of *Time* magazine. In *The Sword of the Lord* John R. Rice exultantly reported on Graham's March 1950 crusade when 45,000 people crowded into the stadium at the University of South Carolina in Columbia, and ran a page one photo of the crowd, captioned "Governor Strom Thurmond estimated it was the largest crowd ever gathered for any event in the history of South Carolina." Rice headlined a Graham crusade in Houston in July, 1952, when 60,000 filled the Rice University stadium in Houston, and proclaimed it "the greatest Protestant assemblage in American history" and "the largest crowd ever to hear an evangelist."[149]

By 1952, John R. Rice was at the apex of his influence and leadership in the fundamentalist evangelical movement in America. The promotional copy for some of his many books and pamphlets read, "by John R. Rice, the 20th Century's Mightiest Pen." *The Sword of the Lord* was widely viewed as the leading journal of fundamentalism, and its approval and endorsement was crucial for any evangelist who wanted a successful career preaching in revivals almost anywhere in the country. Rice's many books collectively were selling millions of copies, and his

Bible tracts were published in scores of languages and distributed around the world in tens of millions of copies.

In September of 1952, Rice announced a cooperating board for the Sword of the Lord Foundation designed to be a who's who of the evangelical movement, tantamount to a national governing body for evangelicals. The board included the most prominent evangelical pastors, evangelists, college presidents, publishers, and broadcasters in the country: Billy Graham; Raymond Edman, president of Wheaton College; Pat and Bernie Zondervan, publishers; Louis Talbott, president of the Bible Institute of Los Angeles; Bob Jones Sr. of Bob Jones University; and Robert Cook, president of Youth for Christ.[150]

John R. Rice was ecstatic about the enormous success Billy Graham was having on the revival trail. But he'd apparently heard reports or warnings from other fundamentalists about Billy entertaining modernists and liberals on the platform with him or as members of the ministerial committees that sponsored Graham campaigns in various cities. Rice sent Graham a letter of inquiry into Graham's beliefs and associations before announcing his membership on the Sword cooperating board. In response, Graham reassured his friend and mentor of his fundamentalist orthodoxy: "Contrary to any rumors that are constantly floating about, we have never had a modernist on our Executive Committee, and we have never been sponsored by the Council of Churches in any city, except Shreveport and Greensboro, both small towns where the majority of the ministers are evangelical."

This exchange of letters between Rice and Graham was significant more for what was left unsaid than for what was said. The concern that both men were tiptoeing around was the issue of separatism. In addition to agreement on various doctrines that defined orthodox Christian belief, the struggle was over the need for true Christians to separate themselves—absolutely and completely—from anyone claiming to be a Christian who did not share belief in those fundamentalist doctrines. Genuine Christians could "witness" or preach to "lost people," but it was impermissible to do so in company with anyone who disagreed in any way with the doctrines held to be core to "orthodox" Christianity. Fundamentalists had waged bitter and heated struggles against fellow pastors, theologians, and religious writers who deviated in the most microscopic way from the doctrines proclaimed and explained in *The Fundamentals.*

Since the beginning of the 1920s, separatism had become a principle of fundamentalism more important than any of the doctrines proclaimed as orthodox by the fundamentalist network. Billy Graham continued to assure John R. Rice that they were in agreement on the fundamentals of the faith. However, for many fundamentalists, doctrinal purity was not enough if you might be united in spirit or association with a modernist who was theologically impure. If Billy Graham was to retain the friendship and support of John R. Rice, he would need to do more than espouse fundamentalist doctrine. He would have to be careful with whom he associated as he reached ever larger crowds for Christ.

Chapter 21
The Jim Crow Challenge

When I was 11 years old in 1961, my family moved to Shelby County, Tennessee. I was introduced to Mary Smith, the second Negro I had ever met (after Mr. Thurston the plumber, who came by the house of our next-door neighbor Mrs. Davis in Wheaton so she could keep the books for his business). Despite my family's relative poverty, my mom still had enough money to pay Mary to clean and iron our clothes each week. Mary was a short, skinny woman with straight, black, stringy hair, a deep country accent, and a shy smile. She wore an old gingham dress decorated with small blue flowers and an old black pair of shoes rundown at the heels. Her neck sported a grapefruit-sized goiter that I found endlessly fascinating.

I visited Mary's home just once, in my mom's company, to drop off a bag of clothes my brother Johnny and I had outgrown, for use by Mary's growing boy. We parked the car at the side of a country road and walked along a dirt path through cotton fields. Their home was a two room shack with a little front porch, and my mom hollered "Hello, Mary!" as we neared the door. She came out with her boy, Sam, who clung to her side and remained silent as our mothers passed a few minutes of polite conversation.

It's kind of bizarre, thinking back on it, how foreign and distant black people seemed to me, despite the fact that most folks who lived in Shelby County were black. I had no black friends and I saw no blacks in any social situation. I saw Negroes every day from the window of my school bus or at the drugstore or on the street when I rode my bike delivering the *Memphis Commercial Appeal*. But only white kids attended my school and only white families attended my church. No blacks entered the public library or anywhere else I went, except as janitors or cafeteria workers or maids. I don't recall even wondering why there was a separate "Colored Only" waiting room at my dentist's office or why every gas station in town had separate toilets for "White" and "Colored." I am ashamed to admit that I believed black people smelled bad and had low moral standards and that good Christian white people only associated with a few "good" colored people—despite the fact that I knew no Negroes firsthand. Isn't that remarkable? Where in the world did I get those strange ideas?

For his entire adulthood and throughout his public ministry in Texas, John R. Rice had avoided talking about the subject of race. He had never, by any published report or in the memory of any of his friends or family members or in any sermon in *The Sword of the Lord*, attacked or defended the institution of slavery or the subjugation of black people by white people.

He had never publicly supported or criticized the Ku Klux Klan. He had never defended, opposed, or even acknowledged the legacy of racial oppression in the South. He had never commented on the Jim Crow laws in Texas or preached on what the Bible might have to say about racial injustice. It would have been almost unthinkable for him to express an opinion about such matters. This was true first because his concentrated and only objective was to win souls to Jesus so they could be saved from a fiery eternity in the pit of a literal Hell. And secondly it was true because to do so—in the prevailing atmosphere of Texas and the fundamentalist movement nationally—would subject him to the most bitter and withering attacks from his own constituency. John R. Rice could not possibly offer a critique of racial oppression in the white South without destroying his own ministry and undercutting his movement's support for *The Sword of the Lord*. Even if he had been opposed to racial injustice, his Texas audience was not.

At last, in 1940, Rice found that he had enough distance from his Texas roots to express a limited critique of the Klan and the racial violence it espoused. During the late 1930s Rice, along with many other fundamentalist leaders, had advocated isolationism and expressed a pacifistic horror of all war. But in 1939 Germany divvied up Poland with the Soviet Union, and in the spring of 1940 Hitler launched a lightning-fast invasion of Denmark, the Low Countries, and Norway. The British army was defeated and trapped at Dunkirk by May. In June, Italy entered the war on the side of Germany, and Hitler invaded France, taking Paris in only five days.

Rice's previous opposition to the United States' engagement in another European conflict crumbled, and he moved rapidly to find the moral and scriptural justification for changing his position. In the process, he expressed his first public criticism of the Ku Klux Klan.

In a sermon published in *The Sword of the Lord* in June of 1940, Rice linked the war crimes of the Germans in occupied Europe with the racial crimes of the Klan. Both were the result of the sinful nature of humans everywhere:

> The present warring state of the world is a blazing indictment of the whole race. Mankind is an incurable race of sinners…There is no human remedy for the woes of the world. The overwhelming evidence is that every human being is inherently wicked, helpless and hopeless…does not know the way to peace by nature, and must be forever damned by his own sin…Nor can any nation in the world claim to be essentially different from those that are instigators of war…Other nations have their communism, their class hate, their wicked greed. Members of a labor union in America that would bomb a tailor shop for charging less than usual prices, destroy a truck and shoot the strike-breaker in a mill strike…who willingly commit themselves to murder, to sabotage—such men are not different in spirit and in heart than those who deliberately plunged Europe into war, or the Japanese who ravished China, or the Italians who massacred helpless Ethiopia. What difference is [there] in high-riding Ku Klux Klansmen in America who beat offending Jews or negroes or foreigners, [and] a German machine gunner, strafing refugees in Poland…? At heart, they are one.[151]

Although his critique of the Klan was almost buried in a general indictment of all wicked humans and a litany of crime and sins committed by evildoers ranging from homegrown Communist labor agitators to German soldiers, still…it was his first public and negative reference to the Klan.

A sensible inference is that John R. Rice was beginning to shift his thinking about the racial issues that plagued that South. The Klan had been largely discredited and emasculated for several years, and the crimes of the Nazis were beginning to be well known. Rice's own father, avowed Klansman Will Rice, had died 11 years earlier, and Rice probably no longer felt constrained by his father's disapproval, if he ever had. And he may have begun to feel that he possessed the moral authority and leadership credentials within the fundamentalist movement that would allow him to express some of his own tentative thinking about race.

In 1943 John R. Rice wrote and *The Sword of the Lord* published a little pamphlet titled "Lodges Examined by the Bible." The thesis of the pamphlet was that Christians should avoid being members of secret fraternal organizations such as the Oddfellows, the Masons, and the Ku Klux Klan. Rice disapproved of Christians joining a lodge that had non-Christian members. He objected to various bloodthirsty and murderous oaths that lodge members were required to take when they joined. He believed that religion as practiced in various lodges was not truly Christian but rather pagan and anti-Christian. Rice made a point of condemning lodges rather than lodge members. He added, "My own father was…an ardent Klansman. Whatever his mistakes in this matter he was an earnest Christian, a Godly man who had and deserved the profound respect of Christian people."[152]

Rice, however, further excoriated the Klan:

> There are many known cases where the Klan resorted to violence and some proven cases of assassination. While the Klan is now in general disrepute, it is only fair to remember that members of other secret societies took a leading part in the work of the Klan. That was the case of my father who was both a Mason and an Oddfellow and joined the Klan, also. My father told me of cases of violence by lodge action, which he justified. The spirit of vengeance is inseparably connected with the horrible oaths and penalties of the secret orders.[153]

The shift in Rice's thinking went beyond his view of the Klan, and included his personal relationship with at least one black person whom he knew as a friend and ally in his revival ministry. John R. Rice's daughter Joy Martin (my aunt) tells the story of her father's close friendship with Elbert Tindley, a black gospel singer who often performed in revival services with him during the 1940s. One evening in 1948 after a church service, John R. Rice invited Tindley to join the Rice family for dessert at a local ice cream parlor. When Tindley arrived with John R. and Lloys Rice and their six daughters, the owner of the ice cream parlor refused to serve Tindley and announced that blacks were not welcome in his store. Rice was fiercely indignant and led his family back out of the store, while announcing that he would tell other Christians not to patronize the store until the owner changed his policy.

All John R. Rice's thinking about race, however, was conditioned by the priority he placed on the struggle to save lost souls from the terrors of Hell. No political or racial issue could be so important. From his perspective, no dispute over any question of doctrine could match the importance of revival and the urgency of soul-winning.

In an article published in *The Sword of the Lord* in 1954 Rice said:

> There is a wicked, worldly philosophy that is coming into churches. We get the idea that the churches are to take care of Christians. They are not to do anything of the kind. Churches are to win souls. We get the idea that a preacher, a pastor, is called to take care of the church and shepherd the sheep, and to feed the flock. There is nothing like that in the Bible. That is a man-made philosophy that is of the Devil, not of God. What pastors are called for is to use the church and lead the church in soul-winning. What churches are called for is to win souls.[154]

This is the attitude that would condition his response to the Southern struggle for civil rights and social justice that loomed on the horizon in the 1950s. No question of racial justice could be allowed to subvert or contradict the struggle to win souls for Jesus. No one could truthfully claim to be a Christian and work to end the system of segregation in the South if that effort interrupted the work of evangelism or upset social peace.

The response of Rice's fellow Southerner Billy Graham to the system of segregation was markedly different. Early in Graham's career he seemed to embody fundamentalist positions as fully as John R. Rice—including the attitudes of most white Southern fundamentalists about race and segregation. In 1950, the summer after his breakthrough revival in Los Angeles when Graham had begun receiving intense press scrutiny and rapidly expanding crowds, he conducted a mass campaign in Atlanta. The services were fully segregated, and audiences were almost entirely white. Criticism erupted both in the North and South for what was perceived as Graham's racially tainted theology. A columnist for the Atlanta Constitution critiqued Graham's willingness to hold segregated services: "Will you preach, sir, on the sins of violent sectionalism and hatred, with brother pitted against brother?...And will you, in all humility, state your position on the greatest thorn in the brow of Southern clergymen...the puzzles of race, white supremacy and segregation?"[155]

Graham, however, was on a journey. In the course of his rise as an evangelist and public figure, he would leave behind the narrow conservatism and racial assumptions of many other fundamentalists in his native South.

Graham first spoke publicly about race in an interview that appeared in the *Jackson Daily News* during his first Mississippi revival campaign in 1952. Although he admitted to conforming to local custom by having segregated services, he declared: "There is no scriptural basis for segregation. The audience may be segregated, but there is no segregation at the altar...[and] none in the church...And it touches my heart when I see white stand shoulder to shoulder with black at the cross."

Graham took his first clear stand against Jim Crow laws a year later in his 1953 crusade in unambiguously segregated Chattanooga, Tennessee, when he personally removed the ropes separating the black and white sections of the audience. He later recalled telling two ushers, "Either these ropes stay down or you can go ahead and have the revival without me."[156]

After the 1954 Brown decision in the Supreme Court declaring public school segregation unconstitutional, Billy Graham finally formalized a strategic decision to end segregation in all future meetings, and from that time none of his future campaigns—in Nashville, New Orleans, Dallas, Louisville, Richmond, or any other Southern city—were segregated.

Despite ending the practice of racial separation in his own meetings, Graham continued to be cautious and diplomatic in his criticism of other fundamentalists who continued to wave the banner of segregation. Graham had taken his formal church membership in the First Baptist Church of Dallas, one of the wealthiest, largest, and most powerful churches in the Southern Baptist Convention. The pastor of First Baptist was W. A. Criswell, a segregationist firebrand. Criswell had first answered his calling to be a preacher in 1920 under the ministry of John R. Rice, and remained Rice's longtime friend.[157]

In February of 1956, Criswell swung through South Carolina on a speaking tour during which he defended segregation in every institution throughout society and declared that it was a system ordained by God. At one speech in Columbia, Criswell censured those who would integrate schools or churches as "a bunch of infidels, dying from the neck up." In company with many other fundamentalist leaders, he castigated the "spurious doctrine [of the] universal Fatherhood of God and brotherhood of man."[158]

Graham commented only that he and his pastor "had never seen eye to eye on the race question."

Within the next few years, Billy Graham struck a middle course in support of gradual racial change. He applauded the Brown decision and individual Christians who acted to pull down racial barriers. He was still reluctant, however, to endorse specific legal or legislative remedies for racial injustice. He called for Christians to take steps to improve race relations, but only on the voluntary basis of their Christian principles: "The church, if it aims to be the true church," said Graham, "dares not segregate the message of good racial relations from the message of regeneration, for...man as sinner is prone to desert God and neighbor alike." He encouraged a personal conversion to the message of love and salvation found in the words of Jesus. "Any man who has a genuine conversion experience will find his racial attitudes greatly changed." Finally, in a 1957 article in *Ebony* magazine, he called for a revival "to wipe away racial discrimination" and the sentiments of white supremacy.[159]

The *Ebony* article reflected an important shift for Graham that had implications beyond the issue of race relations. It appeared immediately after a massive and successful revival crusade in New York City. As historian Steven P. Miller reported: "The Graham team had made special efforts to appeal to African Americans (including inviting Martin Luther King Jr. to give the invocation at a service)...That crusade had also finalized Graham's rift with leading fundamentalists [especially John R. Rice], who were distraught by his willingness to associate with the liberal Protestants (as well as, one can assume, King). The official Crusade invitation had come from an affiliate of the National Council of Churches. Perhaps the break momentarily freed Graham to speak more candidly about social issues."[160]

Billy Graham and John R. Rice never disagreed publicly and directly with each other about racial segregation or social justice in the South. Instead, their public disagreement was over the issue of separatism—the requirement that fundamentalists separate themselves completely from modernism and liberalism. However, the shadow of race and the racial legacy of the South hung over every theological debate within the world of fundamentalism and evangelical Christianity. Ultimately, only by resolving any ambivalence they felt about the racial issue could evangelicals hope to exert any national influence.

Billy Graham's success in finding a way to move beyond the outmoded racial politics and strained racial theology of the Old South would be a model for the rise of the Religious Right and its leaders, including Jerry Falwell in the 1980s and 90s.

Chapter 22
The Uneasy Conscience of Fundamentalism

The year was 1956, and April in Wheaton was lush and luminous. The grass at Grandpa and Grandma's house was an electric green that seemed to sizzle in the sunshine. Red, orange, and yellow marigolds crowded around the front steps. Brilliant red geraniums erupted from pots on the porch railing. The closely bunched blooms on the tall lilac bushes along West Franklin Street produced an immodest and compelling scent, sweet yet astringent, that transfused and subtly altered the colors of the grass, the yellow house, the gray stone of the wall at the edge of the yard, my granddad's black Buick sedan in the driveway.

We were buzzing with excitement, because my grandparents were just back from spending a week with Billy and Ruth Graham at their new home in Montreat, North Carolina. On this Sunday afternoon after church, my aunts and uncles plus all of us Himeses—my mom and dad, little brother Johnny, and my two older sisters Lloys Jean and Faith— were over for Sunday dinner. I was six years old then, and we were the vanguard of a yet-to-be-born multitude of Rice grandkids. As the oldest male grandchild, I felt that I must be someone very special indeed.

The adults gathered around the big dining room table over fried chicken and biscuits, French green beans and Jell-O fruit salad, while my siblings and I were relegated to a card table in the kitchen, listening intently to my grandmother in the next room describe how they had driven along a winding road up the side of the mountain to reach the large and rustic log house where the Grahams lived.

"Edward R. Murrow from CBS was there this week interviewing Billy for his television show, and there were wires and lights and people all over the house. We had to be careful to stay out of the way when they were around," my grandma said. "They had a big fireplace, and a guest bedroom where we stayed, and someone had given their children an ice cream soda fountain!"

An ice cream soda fountain! I quickly developed a sense of profound injury. How dare God provide the Graham children with an ice cream soda fountain when I was not similarly blessed? All I knew about Billy Graham was that he was a famous preacher, though how in any remotely just world his children could possess an ice cream soda fountain was beyond my capacity to explain or imagine.

My sense of resentment toward Billy Graham built over the next few years as he and my granddad had a falling out over theological issues of which I knew little. From my granddad's sermons, I understood that Billy was associating with people my granddad called "modernists" and "liberals," who included assorted heretics, infidels, and Episcopalians. I was too young to understand any of the issues, and my granddad only criticized Billy with sadness and regret. Nonetheless, I came to feel that I had something personal at stake in this struggle. I had heard Granddad inveigh against atheists, communists, New Dealers, and Unitarians. I could only imagine that Billy Graham, if he were in disagreement with John R. Rice, must be one of these…whatever they were.

The split was gradual in its very nature, atmospheric rather than tectonic. It was difficult to tell at first that a split was taking place, in fact. Throughout the 1940s and into the 1950s evangelical Christians all seemed to be part of a united "fundamentalist" movement, and only slight variations in phraseology or emphasis were discernible.

In 1948, 30-year-old Billy Graham became president of Northwestern Schools in Minneapolis, a seminary that had been founded by William Bell Riley, the "grand old man of fundamentalism." Graham invited John R. Rice to be one of the featured speakers at the school's annual conference that fall, and then sent Rice a telegram announcing that Rice had been elected to a three-year term on the Northwestern Board of Trustees. In November of 1948, Graham was a featured speaker at the increasingly influential Sword of the Lord Conference on Revival and Soul-Winning, along with Bob Jones Sr., Bob Jones Jr., Bill Rice, Joe Henry Hankins, and others. The following year, Graham again invited Rice to be a featured speaker at his Northwestern conference, and soon after Graham traveled to England for one of his first mass revival campaigns. Rice reported in *The Sword of the Lord*:

> Dr. Billy Graham told me how, when he was preparing to go to England…he took many copies of *The Sword of the Lord* to a quiet retreat and there spent two weeks in earnest reading and waiting on God, that his heart and mind might be prepared for the glowing ministry which

God graciously gave, with thousands saved, in Great Britain.[161]

One of the first symptoms of malaise and dismay within the fundamentalist movement was the 1949 publication of Carl F. H. Henry's first book, *The Uneasy Conscience of Modern Fundamentalism*. Henry had graduated from Wheaton College and then taught theology at a fundamentalist seminary. He was one of the founders of the National Association of Evangelicals and served on its board for several years, and he would go on to help found Fuller Seminary and spend a dozen years as the first editor of Billy Graham's *Christianity Today*. In short, Henry was one of the leading theologians of the fundamentalist movement.

Henry titled his first chapter "The Evaporation of Fundamentalist Humanitarianism," and immediately threw down the gauntlet. Conservative Christians, he said, were feeling pretty good about themselves in 1947, and heady about their prospects. Mainline modernist Protestants had blown it in the first half of the 20th century, he wrote: "The modernist embarrassment is serious indeed. The shallow insistence on inevitable world progress and on man's essential goodness has been violently declared false. Not only sound Bible exegesis but the world events of 1914–1946 indict optimistic liberalism."[162]

Henry was right, of course, about the failure of liberalism to provide an effective answer to the immense disaster of the wars. The mainline denominations were theologically and historically bankrupt. If the triumphant United States had a state religion at the end of World War II, it was mainline Protestantism. The mainline denominations, however, were entering a steep, decades-long decline in members and influence. The religious liberals or modernists who had given up their "supernatural" beliefs for what fundamentalists called the "perfectibility of man" had been left holding an empty theological bag. "God" had been reduced to a set of pious euphemisms and smug hypocrisies. Worship had become rote and formulaic. Religious experience had been relegated to patriotic expostulations and pious sentimentality. The fundamentalists objected not only to the supposed "heresy" and "infidelism" of the mainline Protestants; they also believed that only fundamentalists offered a genuine religious experience—that is, a genuine experience of Christian conversion and redemption. In the eyes of the fundamentalists, the mainline Protestants were not even Christian; instead they were members of churches devoted to a kind of secularized, theistic, liberal philosophy.

Carl Henry looked at his fellow fundamentalists, however, and saw little to applaud. Evangelicals in the 19th century had been passionately involved in the struggles to end slavery, elevate the social status of women and children, and address the foundations of poverty. Henry noted in the 20th century, however, "the apparent lack of any social passion in Protestant Fundamentalism. On this evaluation, Fundamentalism is the modern priest and Levite, by-passing suffering humanity."

He summed up:

> The picture is clear when one brings into focus such admitted social evils as aggressive warfare, racial hatred and intolerance, the liquor traffic, and the exploitation of labor management, whichever it may be. The social reform movements dedicated to the elimination of such evils do not have the active, let alone vigorous, cooperation of large segments of evangelical Christianity. In fact, Fundamentalist churches increasingly have repudiated the very movements whose most energetic efforts have gone into an attack on such social ills. The situation has even a darker side. The great majority of Fundamentalist clergymen, during the past generation of world disintegration, became increasingly less vocal about social evils. It was unusual to find a conservative preacher occupied at length with world ills.[163]

Henry offered, he believed, a critique from the very center of fundamentalist doctrine. The fundamentalist, he said, holds that "the liberal, the humanist, and the ethical idealist share a shallow sense of the depth of world need and an over-optimism concerning man's own supposed resources for far-reaching reversal of even admitted wrongs." The core of the problem was that individual humans shared a sinful nature, and required the saving grace of Jesus. Nonetheless, Henry argued for the "social relevance of the gospel...A globe-changing passion certainly characterized the early church...Had it not been so, Christianity would not have been the religion of the then-known world within three centuries...A Christianity without a passion to turn the world upside-down is not reflective of apostolic Christianity."

Henry charged that "modern fundamentalism":

...does not challenge the injustice of the totalitarianisms...the evils of racial hatred, the wrongs of current labor-management relations, the inadequate bases of international dealings. It has ceased to challenge Caesar and Rome, as though in futile resignation and submission to the triumphant Renaissance mood. The apostolic Gospel stands divorced from a passion to right the world. The Christian social imperative is today in the hands of those who understand it in sub-Christian terms.[164]

The tension in Carl Henry's book was the tension between a fundamentalism that wanted to remain pure and orthodox, separate from "the world" and from any taint of unorthodoxy, and a fundamentalism that wanted to "win the world for Jesus and his kingdom." In practice, it was a very hard thing to try to do. Henry's prescription was a radical departure from the old-fashioned revivalism of John R. Rice and Bob Jones Sr., and represented one of the first public cracks in the façade of fundamentalist unity that had prevailed since the 1920s. Henry and other leaders of the NAE such as Harold Ockenga represented a trend that came to be called "new evangelicalism" to distinguish it from the "old fundamentalism."

In September of 1949, Jones expressed his concerns to Rice in a letter: "Just between you and me, the National Association of Evangelicals and other organizations have always tried to get everything we had to offer; and we always go all the way out; but when the time comes to coming out for us and our program, they always shy off."[165] In the wake of Carl Henry's book, the crack in the fundamentalist movement began to widen into a chasm, and soon the two sides were becoming more clearly differentiated. By the early 1950s, both Rice and Jones withdrew from various commissions and committees of the NAE, and by 1955 they were no longer active in the organization.

Billy Graham's revivals grew ever larger and more popular heading into the 1950s. Ironically, Graham's very success, which John R. Rice celebrated, brought the two men into conflict and triggered the historic split between traditional fundamentalists such as Rice and "neo-evangelicals" such as Graham and Carl Henry.

By the early to mid-1950s, Billy Graham's prominence and effectiveness as an evangelist, measured by the size of his crowds, the impact of his crusades on the public dialogue, and the numbers of people walking the "sawdust trail" to seek salvation or repent of sins, were astounding and historic. Graham started a crusade in London in March

1954 that was sponsored by over a thousand London-area churches, lasted 12 weeks, and drew a total audience of over a million. The crusade closed on May 22 with an evening service at Wembley Stadium that drew 120,000 attendees. The coverage of the crusade in *The Sword of the Lord* was extensive and entirely positive. One article celebrated that "No preacher in history has ever faced an audience as large as Billy Graham has at Wembley."[166]

The only ambivalent note sounded was John R. Rice's editorial noting the thousands of ministers from nonfundamentalist churches that sponsored and supported the crusade. "I am glad that the Church of England ministers attended the Billy Graham revival," said Rice. He added, wryly, "Most of them never heard that kind of preaching."

Hidden in *The Sword's* coverage was Rice's deepest fear—that Billy Graham might trade away his fundamentalist purity for larger crowds, greater public acclaim, and a more transitory impact. Sinners might walk down the aisle at a Graham campaign to proclaim their faith in Jesus, but if the next Sunday they were seated in the liberalistic pews of a modernistic church listening to an infidel providing an heretical exegesis of a passage in the Bible, the whole point of evangelical revivalism was being missed. When theological liberals and modernists showed up on the platform and in the list of sponsors for Graham, all the warning bells sounded for "separationists" such as Rice.

The conflict bubbled under the surface for a few years. Graham tentatively began to map out a new position, even as he provided assurances to Rice that he was still walking the straight and narrow path of fundamentalist orthodoxy. In 1954, Graham gave an address at Union Theological Seminary in New York, a bastion of liberal theology if there ever was one. When he was attacked by other fundamentalists for "selling out" and cozying up to modernists, John R. Rice published a spirited though conditional defense in the *Sword*: "Now Union Theological Seminary is a hotbed of infidelity. I think it would be a sin to encourage any student to go there. I would not dare to call any man who teaches there 'brother.' I think the school represents infidelity and not Christianity. But I would preach there if I had an opportunity and were allowed to preach clearly what God laid on my heart, as, I am sure, Billy Graham was."

Rice played a key role throughout the early and mid-1950s in retaining the support of most fundamentalists for Graham. Historian George Marsden wrote: "John R. Rice, who, through his newspaper *The Sword of the Lord*, with a circulation in the hundreds of thousands, was the most influential fundamentalist publicist of the era. [Rice retained ties with the National Association of Evangelicals], and while...others were attacking Graham for his association with Ockenga and his lack of militancy toward some modernists, Rice still backed Graham and helped keep most of fundamentalism solidly in Graham's camp." [167]

Billy Graham's success, however, was connected to his openness to new ideas and collaborations. He disliked the fundamentalist practice of violently attacking those who held slightly different interpretations of scripture. More and more, he tended to believe and preach that the fundamentalist demand for separatism was neither based in the Bible nor a good way to "win souls for Jesus." He believed it was possible to hew to fundamentalist doctrines—that the Bible was the inerrant word of God, that Jesus was born of a virgin, that humans were sinful and doomed to Hell without the saving grace of Jesus—while working with other Christians in an open-hearted, ecumenical style.

John R. Rice shared Graham's openness—to a point. Rice, a Baptist, had preached in city-wide revival campaigns sponsored by broad coalitions of churches that included Methodists, Pentecostals, and others with whom he had doctrinal disagreements. However, these churches all agreed on what Rice believed were the fundamental orthodox positions.

This created a serious problem for the friendship and partnership of Rice and Graham. Graham was defining a "new evangelicalism" that shared the basic principles of fundamentalism while opening itself up to cooperating with many religious leaders outside of the fundamentalist camp. Sooner or later, this meant that he would step outside the allowable boundaries set by fundamentalist orthodoxy. For some time, Graham performed a delicate and politically charged dance of theological association. Several times, Graham crossed a line and was publicly attacked by other fundamentalists. Rice would step up to defend Graham, and then would seek private assurances from Graham of his orthodoxy.

The apogee of their relationship came in April of 1955 when Graham invited Rice to join him for a week during his revival crusade in Scotland. Graham later remembered the Scotland crusade as one of the extraordinary events of his life, far larger in scope than the record-breaking London crusade of 1954. Total crowds reached over 2.5 million, and over 50,000 converts walked the aisles at the end of a service. Graham recounted individual stories:

> ...like the woman who told her hairdresser that she owed her new permanent to Billy Graham. Her husband, after being converted at the Crusade, brought home all of his paycheck instead of holding out much of it for drinking and gambling. Or like the cabby who was led to

Christ by my old friend John R. Rice, editor of *The Sword of the Lord* newspaper. Rice had enthusiastically participated in the Crusade for a week...When he got back he described his visit in the *Sword* as 'seven miracle days.'[168]

By the fall of 1955, Graham was walking a fine line between the two warring worlds of evangelical politics. He invited Rice to share the podium with him at a revival crusade in Toronto in October, but at the same moment was finalizing plans for a new magazine of evangelism to be called *Christianity Today*, which would be a direct competitor to *The Sword of the Lord* as well as to the mainline Protestant journal *Christian Century*.

In March, an article titled "Is Evangelical Theology Changing?" appeared in *Christian Life* magazine, suggesting a clear division between fundamentalism and evangelicalism. The authors recalled the colorful shenanigans of J. Frank Norris, Texas-based mentor of John R. Rice in the 1920s, and argued: "That's why to the man on the street fundamentalism got to be a joke. As an ignorant, head-in-the-sand, contentious approach to the Christian faith, it seemed as outdated as high button shoes." The article suggested Billy Graham as a model for evangelicals, and quoted Graham saying, "I can't call myself a fundamentalist." The article further said there was "an aura of bigotry and narrowness associated with the term [which Graham hoped was] certainly not true of himself."[169] The denouement of the struggle was by then obvious—apparently to everyone except Graham and Rice. In April of 1956, Billy Graham and his wife Ruth invited John R. Rice and Lloys Rice to spend a few days with them at their home in the mountains of North Carolina—the same visit that led to my own jealous discovery that the Graham children were proud owners of a soda fountain. The two men spent hours in conversation, and Rice recalled later that Graham offered passionate assurances of his orthodoxy.

Within weeks, however, the war was underway. Rice ran an article in the *Sword* characterizing Harold Ockenga and Carl F. H. Henry among others as: "doubtless honest, noble, good Christian men, but all of them are enlisted in a left-wing movement to bring in a 'new evangelicalism.' They sneer at fundamentalists...and talk about 'the reactionary anti-scholasticism' of the fundamentalists of the past generation." He further attacked new evangelicals for "playing down fundamentalism and the defense of the faith, to poke fun at old-time fundamentalists, and to quote with glowing terms of appreciation the weighty pronouncements of infidel scholars."

In July came the first public notice of Graham's new magazine *Christianity Today*. The inaugural editor chosen by Graham was Carl Henry, the author of *The Uneasy Conscience of Modern Fundamentalism*, the book that had first opened the divide between fundamentalists and neo-evangelicals.

An avalanche of letters from outraged fundamentalists flooded the offices of *The Sword of the Lord* in Wheaton, attacking Billy Graham and demanding to know when the *Sword*'s editor would pull the plug on his partnership with Graham, who was now clearly (to many fundamentalists) in league with the Antichrist and doubtless an infidel himself

In November, Rice ran an article in *The Sword of the Lord* titled, "Which Way, Billy Graham?" announcing that Billy Graham had resigned from the Cooperating Board of the Sword of the Lord Foundation because he disagreed with the paper's doctrinal platform. In the spring of 1957, the *Sword* announced it could not endorse or support Graham's planned autumn revival crusade in New York City because it would be held under the auspices of the Protestant Council of New York, a large mainline Christian group of over 1700 churches that included few if any fundamentalists, but many modernists and liberals.

In later years, Rice explained that he had broken with Graham only after much struggle and soul-searching:

> I talked with Dr. Graham again and again about the danger of yoking up with modernism. Again and again he assured me that he had vowed to God he would never have a man on his committee who was not right on the inspiration of the Bible, the deity of Christ, and such matters. I visited Dr. Graham in his own home in Montreat, North Carolina, by his invitation, and we talked earnestly on such matters. Again and again we have talked by long distance telephone sometimes as long as thirty minutes. At his own request, we sent him *The Sword of the Lord* air mail, week after week, in his tour around the world. I wrote him in great detail on matters where I thought he was wrong. And all the time I defended him openly and publicly, excusing his mistakes, until he openly declared he had decided to keep company with modernists and put them on his committees and to go under their sponsorship. Then I was compelled, in order to be true to Christ, to come out openly against that compromise. [170]

The New York campaign was all that Graham hoped it would be. The crowds were massive, packing the 18,000 seats of Madison Square Garden virtually every night for over three months, dominating the radio and television airwaves nationally, and benefiting from a cascade of media attention internationally. Over two million people witnessed Graham's preaching, and untold millions more saw or heard the broadcasts. By the fall of 1957, Graham was arguably the most famous American on the planet. But his success came at a deep personal cost. Graham said in his memoir, *Just As I Am*:

> ...painful to me was the opposition from some of the leading fundamentalists [who] had been among our strongest supporters in the early years of our public ministry. Their criticism hurt immensely, nor could I shrug them off as the objections of people who rejected the basic tenets of the Christian faith or who opposed evangelism of any type. Their harshness and lack of love saddened me and struck me as being far from the spirit of Christ. The heart of the problem for men like...John R. Rice was the sponsorship of the Crusade by the Protestant Council of New York [which] they contended included many churches and clergy who were theologically liberal and who denied some of the most important elements of the Biblical message It was not the first time [they] had raised their objections to my growing ecumenism, of course, but the New York Crusade marked their final break with our work.[171]

The split between fundamentalism and evangelicalism was a watershed event in the history of Christian Protestantism in the United States.

On one hand, it signaled the re-emergence of an evangelical movement on the national stage for the first time since Billy Sunday had dominated the headlines with his massive citywide revival campaigns before and during the Great War and before the disaster of the Scopes Monkey Trial. In the wake of World War II, an American empire dominated the world economically, politically, and militarily. Billy Graham seemed to represent a fourth pillar—the dominant influence of an American religious movement. The "sawdust trail" at Graham's New York Crusade seemed also to be a triumphal procession for 20th-century evangelicalism.

On the other hand, the split highlighted the continued isolation of Southern fundamentalists such as Bob Jones Sr. and John R. Rice—and their many millions of Southern followers—from the American mainstream. Fundamentalists continued to inhabit the wilderness of the American political landscape, powerless to affect public policy or even influence the public understanding of God, morality, and faith.

After 1957, Southern fundamentalists were even more isolated. Within 12 months, *The Sword of the Lord* had received a barrelful of protest mail from subscribers disgruntled over the paper's criticism of Billy Graham, and the *Sword's* subscribers had declined by over a third from 106,000 to 66,000. The world of evangelicalism quickly bifurcated, as partnerships dissolved, friendships went awry, doors closed, and people took sides. The conference center in Toccoa, Georgia where Sword of the Lord conferences on revival had been held for 13 years was suddenly no longer available. Rice's friendships with well-known radio preacher Charles E. Fuller and many other evangelicals were suddenly severed.

In one camp were the neo-evangelical schools and institutes such as Wheaton College and Fuller Theological Seminary, and publications such as the new *Christianity Today*. In the other camp were the diminished ranks of the fundamentalists, most prominently led by *The Sword of the Lord* and Bob Jones University.

In December of 1958, Bob Jones Sr., Bob Jones Jr., and John R. Rice held a conclave in Chicago attended by all the remaining prominent fundamentalist leaders. Together, they pledged never to participate in any future evangelistic effort sponsored by anyone not fully in agreement with the "cardinal doctrines of orthodox Christian belief."

In effect, Billy Graham was written out of the fundamentalist movement, and the fundamentalists themselves were back in the wilderness.

Chapter 23
Segregation and Separatism

> *"For the word of God is quick, and powerful, and sharper than any two-edged sword, piercing even to the dividing asunder of soul and spirit, and of the joints and marrow, and is a discerner of the thoughts and intents of the heart."*—Hebrews 4:12

I was 13 years old when cracks began to appear in my world. It was 1963, and I was a skinny, desultory, and intimidated member of the Mighty Trojan Marching Band of Millington Central High School, an all-white public institution. I sat on the rear bench seat of a yellow school bus on a Friday evening as we drove through a Negro neighborhood in Memphis on our way to play a football game with another all-white school. I clutched a battered baritone horn in my lap and adjusted my ill-fitting black wool uniform, redolent with the Friday night sweat of generations of band members before me, and straightened the deteriorating loops of gold braid adorning my shoulders.

Black children played in the hard-packed dirt yards of the tin-roofed, unpainted row houses we drove past, and their elders sat in rocking chairs on their front porches overlooking the scene as dusk fell and the bluish glow of mercury streetlights suffused the street. In the seats in front of me, the other boys in our band cranked open the windows, stuck their heads out, and began screaming at the children and the elderly Negroes on their porches: "Nigger, nigger, nigger! Yard apes! Baboons!" On the front seat of our bus, seated next to the driver, was our teacher and band director, Mr. Nersesian, a short and swarthy Armenian known as a killer disciplinarian with a wooden paddle taller than he and drilled with holes to better suck back the flesh of an offending buttock on an energetic backswing. Mr. Nersesian kept his eyes steadfastly trained on the road ahead, ignoring the screaming boys behind him.

I slunk down in my seat, ashamed and cringing in my Trojan uniform. I hated what they were saying and doing, but they were bigger, louder, and more self-confident than I was, and I was afraid to object.

A few weeks later, I stood in the hallway outside the door of my eighth grade English class. A dozen feet away from me the first black children ever to attempt to integrate my school, a boy and a girl, stood with their backs against the wall next to the drinking fountain. Between us, ranging up and down the hallway was a mob of several score of my classmates, many of them hollering "Nigger! Nigger! Go home, niggers! Go back to the jungle!" Boys from my class came out of the restroom with little plastic sandwich bags full of urine, hurling their bags at the black children.

I was rooted to my spot, crying uncontrollably, straining to see the black children through my tears, noting the terror in their dark eyes and how they held onto each other and how the boy shifted his body and held up his hand to ward off the missiles thrown at them. I had never been so conscious of my sinful nature, of my cowardliness, of my uselessness. I knew my silence made me as guilty in the sight of God as my classmates.

Billy Graham and John R. Rice, born a generation apart, were both Southerners, products of a segregated and deeply religious society. Ostensibly, they had parted over the religious issue of separatism. Rice praised Graham for preaching the gospel, but criticized Graham for preaching the gospel in the company of modernists and liberals.

Embedded in the heart of the Southern fundamentalist understanding of separatism, however, was the dark, unspoken issue of race—a topic never raised directly between the two men in public. Their conflict over race, racial segregation, and racial justice was clearly visible in their contrasting public statements, but never publicly acknowledged by them or any of their followers.

John R. Rice had arrived at adulthood at the end of the Great War, just as fundamentalists and modernists began to engage in a bitter theological dispute for control of denominations, seminaries, and congregations. He began his evangelistic career at the beginning of the vast Negro diaspora from the farms and plantations of the rural South to the factories and mills of the urban North, and at a time when it was unthinkable to most white Southerners that blacks and whites might ever vote together, go to school together, or attend church together.

Billy Graham arrived at adulthood in the wake of World War II. It was a moment of American political and military triumph when American fundamentalists sensed the possibility of a new Great

Awakening, a grand re-awakening of the revival impulse. They saw opportunities to convey the gospel to millions of unsaved sinners both in America and around the globe. Graham began his evangelistic career when millions of young men and women, black and white, were turning their attention, after the vast and bloody battles of the war, to the making of a new society. It was a time when anything might be thought possible, and much could be demanded. Change was in the air, and the first new battles of the civil rights movement were fought immediately after the war. Segregation would be ended, and soon. A new generation had arrived on the scene.

Billy Graham had held integrated revival meetings throughout the South since his Chattanooga campaign of 1953, and had expressed open support for the aims of the civil rights movement even earlier. But Graham decided to kick it up a notch for his 1957 New York Crusade. He hired Howard Jones, a black pastor from Cleveland, to lead an outreach campaign to the black community. He held mass rallies in Harlem and Brooklyn, recruited two preachers who were close friends of Martin Luther King Jr. as campaign leaders and advisers, and spoke publicly about the need for social justice and racial reconciliation. Jones recalled:

> When Billy approached me to join him in New York, it was more or less understood that white Christians worshiped with white Christians and black Christians worshiped with black Christians. Our evangelical churches seemed to believe that Heaven too would be "separate but equal." We recited the Lord's Prayer and prayed: "Thy will be done on Earth as it is in Heaven" but then proceeded to bow at the altar of Jim Crow. Talk about being countercultural; what Billy did was radical. There's no getting around it. He weathered the barrage of angry letters and criticisms. He resisted the idea of pulling the plug on the whole thing and playing it safe. There was never any hesitation on Billy's part. He remained faithful to his convictions.[172]

On July 18, Graham invited Martin Luther King Jr. to deliver the opening prayer at Madison Square Garden, thus signaling his solid support for King. "A great social revolution is going on in the United States today," Graham said in his introduction. "Dr. King is one of its leaders, and we appreciate his taking time out of his busy schedule to come and share this service with us tonight." In his benediction, King called for liberation from "the dungeons of hate" and "the paralysis of crippling fear," for "a warless world and for a brotherhood that transcends race or color."[173]

On August 29, just two days before the end of the extraordinary New York revival, Dwight D. Eisenhower signed the 1957 Civil Rights Act, a guarantee of voting rights for all and the first civil rights legislation passed by Congress since Reconstruction. South Carolina senator Strom Thurmond (a trustee for Bob Jones University) attempted to protect racial segregation by mounting the longest filibuster conducted by a single senator in the history of the Senate.

On September 23, Little Rock, Arkansas became the next flashpoint of the civil rights movement when Governor Orval Faubus ordered the National Guard to prevent a group of nine black students from enrolling at Central High School. When mobs of white segregationists gathered to threaten the students, President Eisenhower ordered thousands of paratroopers, National Guardsmen, and U.S. Army soldiers to guarantee their right to enroll.

The reaction of John R. Rice to Little Rock was radically different from Billy Graham's response to Martin Luther King and the aims of the civil rights movement. In his sermon "Negro and White," Rice charged that "Violent agitation goes on to stop segregation," and the agitation was carried out by "the socialists, the communists, the professional and paid Negro leaders, and politicians who hope to gain votes, raise enmities, hurl epithets, threaten force, and incite hate."

Previously, he said, the Supreme Court had held that "separate but equal facilities for white and colored people were a fair and just solution." But in the *Brown v. Board of Education* decision, the court, "largely influenced by the New Deal and left-wing thought has changed its stand. Has the Supreme Court a right to change the meaning of the Constitution or of laws passed by Congress which originally meant something else? Has the Supreme Court a right to intervene in purely state matters?"[174]

Rather than calling for the white citizens of Little Rock to show Christian love toward the black students, Rice mocked "the wholly selfish and political attitude of the NAACP radical leaders, by socialists and communists, by modernist 'do-gooders' who have no other gospel but questions of race and pacifism and labor unions." He continued:

> The nine Negro children were selected by the National
> Association for the Advancement of Colored People,
> and on their instructions and to make a public issue..
> wholly for political and propaganda purposes...and not

for the good of the students themselves, attempted to transfer to Central High School…The Negroes already had a high school equally as good, newer and less crowded…To force integration, President Eisenhower called out units of the 101st Airborne Division to Little Rock, who took over somewhat as "occupation troops." Citizens were barred from certain streets. Some [whites] were clubbed in the head by soldiers. The nine Negro students went to Central High School.[175]

From Rice's point of view, he was sincerely taking a moderate and even-handed position, calling to task "extremists" on both sides of the civil rights struggle. "Race hatred is wrong," he concluded. "It is just as wrong when stirred up by Negro newspapers against white people as it is when stirred up by white people against Negroes…It is just as wrong when stirred up in a church by a modernist infidel preacher as it is when it is stirred up in the South by an over-zealous defender of southern white womanhood and the status quo."

However, Rice went on to say that while Jim Crow laws ought to be abolished, "many things are worse than these, and most intelligent people would prefer to have Jim Crow laws than to have unrestrained intermarriage between the races." The problems with integration were practical, Rice believed. Negroes were "not inherently inferior"; however, Negroes were unfortunately "not morally advanced" compared to white people. For example, Rice said, "Some years ago in Atlanta, Georgia…a check proved that venereal disease was 10 times as frequent among Negroes as among white people…Now suppose that the question of whether white people and Negro people should use the same swimming pools in the parks of Atlanta comes up. Do you see any reason why intelligent and kindly white people would prefer that Negro people have their own parks and swimming pools and white people use different parks and swimming pools? I think any parent can see that it is not merely race prejudice to prefer that."

Rice saw himself as an "intelligent and kindly" moderate on racial issues, and in some sense he could truly claim that he could "see both sides of the issue." He pointed out that both of his grandfathers had served in the Confederate Army during the Civil War. His father had been born into a slave-owning family, proudly remembered the Lost Cause, and was a prominent Klansman in Texas. He recounted proudly that he had "worked with colored people and sometimes employed colored people. I have preached in Negro churches. I had Negro choirs to sing in my [segregated] church." However, he said, "My viewpoint is not a typical southern viewpoint. I have lived in the North for eighteen years…I have an intimate knowledge of southern white people and understand their viewpoint, and since I love and respect colored people and have worked with them often, I think I can deal without prejudice as a minister of God with the great principles and problems of race segregation."

Having laid the basis for his claim to sympathy for colored people, Rice proceeded to devote his entire argument to defending white people:

> Southern Christians are generally Bible believers and are generally in constant daily touch with Negro people and treat them kindly…The South is not against being kind to colored people. They are simply against the dictatorship from the North. They are against the Supreme Court taking over the rights and authority of the states. They have genuine problems to solve in their relations with colored people; these problems are much more serious than outsiders know, and the problems cannot be solved so easily as by simply repealing Jim Crow laws.[176]

By contrast, Rice said, "Negro ministers, unfortunately have…very often had a bad influence. The Negro minister [Martin Luther King Jr.] in Montgomery, Alabama, who led in the organization of a Negro boycott of the buses, led that fight, unfortunately, not as a Christian trying to make good Christians and to lead in Christian understanding between the races. He led that boycott as a modernist and a socialist who was more concerned about racism than he was about Christianity, I fear."

From the vantage point of several decades later, it is difficult to imagine the mindset that would allow white Southern fundamentalists to believe such things about King, so elevated is he in our collective esteem. Moreover, our current notion of King as a saint, leading a struggle against injustice and combating hatred with love and nonviolence, has obliterated our collective memory of the controversies King embodied and took part in during the 1950s and 60s.

Part of the explanation for John R. Rice's obliviousness to the evils of racial injustice is provided by African-American author Joy DeGruy Leary in her landmark 2005 book, *Post Traumatic Slave Syndrome: America's Legacy of Enduring Injury and Healing*. Leary described how former slaves and their descendants continued to experience the damage inflicted by slavery as a permanent traumatic injury for generations after the end of slavery. The aftermath of slavery was a continuing powerlessness, a pervasive sense of being disrespected, a lack of opportunity, and an internalized self-hatred taught to each new generation of black children. The consequences of slavery for the descendants of slaves included poor physical and mental health, difficulty in creating healthy families and relationships, and self-destructive impulses.

Moreover, although the Thirteenth Amendment had declared that "neither slavery nor involuntary servitude, except as a punishment for crime whereof the party shall have been duly convicted, shall exist within the United States," the Congress took a hands-off attitude toward actually enforcing the Amendment. The Southern states responded by creating a host of laws and practices effectively designed to outlaw life in freedom for black people. As historian Douglas Blackmon wrote: "By 1900, the South's judicial system had been wholly reconfigured to make one of its primary purposes the coercion of African Americans to comply with the social customs and labor demands of whites."[177]

Slavery in law had been abolished, but slavery in fact continued until after World War II, and was accomplished and supported through violence, brutality, imprisonment, torture, denial of civil and human rights, and enforced poverty. The keystone of slavery in its new guise was the system of convict labor, which entrapped hundreds of thousands of black men in a permanent state of terror and involuntary servitude, and which kept the entire black community in a state of quiet, fearful resignation. "It was a form of bondage distinctly different from that of the antebellum South," said Blackmon, "But it was nonetheless slavery—a system in which armies of free men, guilty of no crimes and entitled by law to freedom, were compelled to labor without compensation, were repeatedly bought and sold, and were forced to do the bidding of white masters through the regular application of extraordinary physical coercion."[178]

Joy DeGruy Leary emphasized that for the descendants of the slave owners, the legacy of slavery is an acute, social denial of both historical and present-day racism that has become pathological. She said: "The root of this denial for the dominant culture is fear, and fear mutates into all kinds of things: psychological projection, distorted and sensationalized representations in the media, and the manipulation of science to justify the legal rights and treatment of people. That's why it's become so hard to unravel."[179]

For John R. Rice, it proved to be impossible to acknowledge the consequences of slavery, because to do so would be to admit to his family's collective participation in a moral crime. For Southerners generally, it was easy to acknowledge the moral problem of slavery, and to remember the end of the institution with relief. But it was difficult to acknowledge the continuing damage created by slavery's legacy because to do so would imply that they—that we, the white descendants of the slave-owning class, culture, and economy—shared guilt for a continuing moral failure.

The legacy of slavery in the South for the children of the slaveholders was indeed bitter and overpowering. It clouded the emotions and distorted the perceptions of all those who grew up within its stench. And John R. Rice had grown up inside the reality-distorting field of segregation and racial injustice. As Joy DeGruy Leary said: "Unfortunately, many European Americans have a very hard time even hearing a person of color express their experiences. The prevailing psychological mechanism is the idea, 'I've not experienced it, so it cannot be happening for you.'"

John R. Rice believed that Southern blacks had made steady upward progress with the help of good white people for a century since the end of slavery, despite clear evidence to the contrary, and he seemed incapable of hearing black people say that the system that had enslaved black people was still in place, still denying Southern blacks basic human rights. He was, unfortunately, far more concerned with protecting social peace than with undoing social injustice.

In August of 1955, Emmett Till, a 14-year-old black Chicago youth, visited a small town in the Delta country of Mississippi. The teenager entered a country store where a white woman accused him of whistling at her. Within a day Till was dead, so savagely beaten that it was beyond the ability of his mother to recognize her son. Two white men were arrested: Roy Bryant, the husband of the white woman, and his brother, J. W. "Big Milam." An all-white jury quickly found the defendants not guilty, and they were released. The two men immediately provided an interview for *Look* magazine in which they openly admitted to and bragged about committing the crime. Their admission was published along with horrifying photos of Till's body revealing what they had done to him before his death.

Big Milam said:

Well, what else could we do?...I'm no bully; I never hurt a nigger in my life. I like niggers—in their place—I know how to work 'em. But I just decided it was time a few people got put on notice. As long as I live and can do anything about it, niggers are gonna stay in their place. Niggers ain't gonna vote where I live. If they did, they'd control the government. They ain't gonna go to school with my kids. And when a nigger gets close to mentioning sex with a white woman, he's tired o' livin'. I'm likely to kill him. Me and my folks fought for this country, and we got some rights. I stood there in that shed and listened to that nigger throw that poison at me, and I just made up my mind. "Chicago boy," I said, "I'm tired of 'em sending your kind down here to stir up trouble. Goddam you, I'm going to make an example of you—just so everybody can know how me and my folks stand."[180]

According to John R. Rice, the not guilty verdict was perfectly understandable. Responsibility for Till's murder lay with the NAACP and other "race agitators," and not with the white men who in fact killed him. Rice preached that:

Emmett Till, a Chicago Negro lad, a man in size and appearance, visited relatives in Mississippi, and boasted that he had had white women in sex relationships. Urged on by other young Negroes, he went into a store conducted by a pretty young married white woman, seized her bodily, embraced her, and asked her for a date. His boasting continued. His body was found in the river. The accused husband of the insulted wife was tried for murder but was found not guilty. In the South, leading men in the government and out have banded themselves together to avoid what they think would result in intermarriage and the mongrelization of the race and the breakdown of all the Southern standards of culture. I have no doubt that this agitation caused the death of Emmett Till. That colored boy, who attempted to embrace and to make a date with and to seduce the young married white woman, was spurred on by widespread feelings, a cocky attitude agitators have cultivated among colored people. Remember, it was down in the delta country in Mississippi, where a white woman dare not walk the streets alone at night or go anywhere alone at night because of the animosity and the standards of the large Negro population. On the part of colored people, all this agitation makes for bad incidents. It makes for cases of murder and rape. It makes for some rare cases of vengeance and cases in which offended white men, even good men, take the law in their own hands.[181]

In any case, for John R. Rice any question of racial justice paled in importance beside the critical nature of his evangelistic mission. If the stakes are as high as eternity, and the roots for any problem can be found in the sinfulness of the human heart, then people had no business messing around with smaller matters related to social improvement, he believed. "If there is a place of eternal torment where damned souls cry in vain for water amid the flames they cannot escape forever, it is the most alarming and terrifying fact in the universe!" said Rice. "The very possibility that such a doom may await a sinner is so shocking that no other question can compare with its importance. How can today's feasting or hunger, clothing or nakedness, honor or infamy, pleasure or pain compare in importance with a million years of pain, torment of body, mind and conscience?"[182]

When Rice acknowledged problems with the South's Jim Crow laws and expressed his opinion that they should be abolished—someday—he was actually taking a relatively progressive, though carefully nuanced, stand compared to many of his fellow Southern fundamentalists. In 1960, his close friend and ally Bob Jones Sr. published a small pamphlet titled *Is Segregation Scriptural?* in which he proposed to demonstrate that God had ordained the Southern system of segregation in the pages of the Bible:

> God never meant for America to be a melting pot to rub out the lines between the nations. ... for a man to stand up and preach pious sermons in this country and talk about rubbing out the line between the races—I say it makes me sick...The trouble today is a satanic agitation striking back at God's established order. ...Now, you colored people listen to me. If you had not been brought over here and if your grandparents in slavery days had not heard that great preaching, you might not even be a Christian, you might be over there in the jungles of Africa today, unsaved. But you are here in America where you have your own schools and your own churches and your own liberties and your own rights, with certain restrictions that God Almighty put about you—restrictions that are in line with the word of God.[183]

By contrast, in his sermon *Negro and White* published in 1958, John R. Rice said: "People of all races are members of the same human family. We are blood brothers...so whether Caucasian, Mongolian, or Negro, all races alike are descended from Adam and Eve...Everybody alive on the earth now descended from Noah and his three sons. Racial differences are incidental. We are one race of beings and all alike have the blood of Adam and the blood of Noah in our veins." He quoted the apostle Paul's letter to the Romans in which Paul told how God offers salvation alike to all, and punishes sin alike with all, concluding that "there is no respect of persons with God who views all His children, both black and white, as equals in his sight."[184]

Rice set aside the racial legacy of his family and their traditions in that sermon. He called his listeners to an understanding of the American project that would someday include all those who had been left outside, left behind, or otherwise crushed beneath the boot of Southern extremism and racial oppression from the time of slavery. Although he carried the curse and sin of racism within him, he also carried with him his belief in the Constitution and democratic government. Rice said:

> Every person is equal before the law. One is not kept from citizenship because of his race or his previous condition of servitude. The Negro has a right to vote just as well as the white man. The Negro has a right to run for office and try to be elected, just the same as a white man. Both may fail; in every election more people fail to get elected then get elected. But everyone has the same right. Before the courts of the land every person is equal... It is true that in particular instances there are miscarriages of justice, there is discrimination...but, thank God, in principle we in America hold that every person is equal before the law. And all of us ought to insist that colored people have the same rights before the law as white people, and vice versa. Race hatred is wrong.[185]

Although Rice's earthly racial and political ideas drove him away from the struggle for justice in the South, the heavenly core of his faith was just enough to also drive him away from the Klan and his father Will Rice's racial politics, and to leave him open to the claims of black people for justice on earth. His opposition to integration was oddly conditional. He upbraided the civil rights demonstrators for breaking the law, while acknowledging the inevitability and justice of racial integration—in some spheres. He thought it would be okay for adult whites and blacks to work together, but not okay for black and white children and teenagers to go to school with each other where they might become confused and develop sexual attachments. He acknowledged that "godly colored people, born again, would be in Heaven," but he guessed that Heaven itself might be segregated because "we may prefer to be with those we know than with those we do not know."[186]

His quarrel was with what he saw as the impatience and intemperance of the demonstrators, but he claimed that, ultimately, he had no quarrel with their cause. Like Thomas Jefferson, he lived in ambivalence. He decried the racist society in which he lived, and believed that someday Southerners would find a way past their racism to social equality with black people. At the same time, he feared the tumult and dislocation he saw as the price of social change.

The opposition of fundamentalist preachers and leaders to the civil rights movement was deeply connected to their historic separatism. They believed in an inerrant Bible that had been inspired by God, and they also believed that God explicitly ordained the separation of the races. The claims of the civil rights marchers were an affront to their interpretation of the Bible, and not just to their racial beliefs.

The extreme, angry, and impassioned rhetoric of fundamentalist preachers in the 1950s and 60s echoed J. Frank Norris's and John R. Rice's bombastic attacks against modernists and liberals in Protestant denominations in the 1920s and 30s. In the 1960s, Rice conflated modernists and "socialistic" civil rights demonstrators, and attacked them both using the same language. In 1964, he claimed that "although religious infidels boost him as a Christian, Dr. Martin Luther King has openly declared that he does not believe the Bible. He is not a Christian in the historic sense of holding to the great essentials of the Christian faith, he is a 'minister' who doesn't preach the gospel, doesn't save souls."[187] In a 1965 sermon titled, "Sow to the Wind, Reap a Whirlwind," Rice condemned "modernist preachers" who had given up evangelism for social justice, and demanded that churches return to "the old-fashioned gospel instead of the newfangled social gospel, the United Nations, the National Council of Churches, sit-downs, pickets, strikes and law-breaking."[188]

Other fundamentalists attacked the civil rights movement with vitriol equal to Rice's, and also using language from the battle for separatism. California fundamentalist G. Archer Weniger published a sermon in *The Sword of the Lord* in 1962 in which he insisted that Martin Luther King Jr. was a "pro-communist" and a "modernist" who denied Hell as "a place of literal burning fire," and was "by this definition…an apostate."[189]

Noel Smith, editor of the *Bible Baptist Tribune*, claimed that "the most strutting, merciless, brutal enemy the Negro ever had on this earth is the Negro," and that "self-discipline, responsibility, energy, persistence, sound judgment, and pride in their surroundings, are foreign terms" to blacks.[190]

In the mid-50s, another Southern fundamentalist began to weigh in on racial matters. 23-year-old Jerry Falwell founded the Thomas Road Baptist Church in Lynchburg, Virginia in 1956. Two years he later took the warpath against the Supreme Court's *Brown v. Board of Education* decision to desegregate public schools with a sermon titled "Segregation or Integration: Which?" "If Chief Justice Warren and his associates had known God's word and had desired to do the Lord's will, I am quite confident that the 1954 decision would never have been made," Falwell preached. "The facilities should be separate. When God has drawn a line of distinction, we should not attempt to cross that line…The true Negro does not want integration…. He realizes his potential is far better among his own race." Falwell claimed that integration "will destroy our race eventually. In one northern city," he said, "a pastor friend of mine tells me that a couple of opposite race live next door to his church as man and wife."[191]

By the mid-1960s, Falwell was beginning to shift his thinking about race, however, and was no longer directly attacking the objectives of the civil rights movement. Instead, he was rejecting the call of Martin Luther King, Jr. that Christian leaders of all colors become involved in the political process and take a stand on the side of social justice and civil rights. "Preachers are not called to be politicians, but to be soul-winners," Falwell said in a 1964 sermon titled "Ministers and Marches."[192] "We have a message of redeeming grace through a crucified and risen Lord. The message is designed to go right to the heart of man and there meet his deep spiritual need. Nowhere are we commissioned to reform the externals. We are not told to wage war against bootleggers, liquor stores, gamblers, murderers, prostitutes, racketeers, prejudiced persons or institutions, or any other existing evil as such. I feel that we need to get off the streets and back into our pulpits and into our prayer rooms." He also questioned "the sincerity and intentions of some civil rights leaders such as Dr. Martin Luther King Jr., Mr. James Farmer, and others, who are known to have left-wing associations. It is very obvious that the Communists, as they do in all parts of the world, are taking advantage of a tense situation in our land,

and are exploiting every incident to bring about violence and bloodshed."

Six weeks after King's assassination in the spring of 1968, *The Sword of the Lord* published a postmortem assault on King by an Alabama pastor titled, "Dr. Martin Luther King Died by the Lawlessness He Encouraged." Bob Spencer charged that King's movement was "anti-Christian" because "Jesus was not and is not a 'revolutionary,'" and claimed King was a liberal who had "rejected the cardinal tenets of Biblical Christianity for the heathen philosophy of Mahatma Gandhi."[193]

For many in the fundamentalist movement, however, continued support for segregation simply was not a defensible or sustainable position. A national consensus continued to develop throughout the 1960s that segregation was morally wrong. Especially in the wake of the Selma to Montgomery march in 1965, most Americans concluded that responsibility for the violent upheaval in the South lay with white Southern segregationists, and the system of segregation constituted a grave social injustice that ran counter to the principles on which the country had been founded, and counter to the teachings of Jesus.

My uncle Walter Handford became the pastor of the prominent Southside Baptist Church of Greenville, South Carolina in 1965. Handford was a native of Seattle and a graduate of Wheaton College, where he met his wife, my aunt Elizabeth Handford Rice, one of the six daughters of John R. Rice. Handford had been the assistant editor of *The Sword of the Lord* when he lived in Wheaton, and brought a broader perspective to his new job as a fundamentalist pastor than many others who were raised in the South or were members of his "whites-only" fundamentalist church. Handford recalled that in 1965 Greenville "had a great deal of racial black/white tension. The public schools were under a Supreme Court integration order...This was the Deep South. No doubt about it: blacks were not welcome at white churches."[194]

Handford remembered a process of profound change in his church. "Our bus ministry jumped. One Sunday morning one of our Sunday school bus drivers phoned and said, 'When we arrived at the pick-up point in a housing development, there were five black children waiting along with the others. What should I do?' This was not a question I could give my people the opportunity to decide. I do not believe we ought to give an opportunity to vote when it is a clear, important, Biblical and moral matter. 'Bring them along. We are not going to send missionaries to Africa and refuse to reach blacks in Greenville.' Soon the bus attendance became largely black."

Handford's decision to invite blacks to attend a white fundamentalist church in the late 1960s was highly controversial and created deep divisions, causing some members to leave the congregation. A few years later, the church's decision to change its policies on segregation across the board met an even stiffer challenge when a white man and his black wife came forward on Sunday morning to join the church.

Handford wrote:

> I had to decide in those few minutes as they walked down the aisle how I would handle it...[then] I announced their names along with the names of others who had come for membership. 'How many vote to receive them?' I knew that inter-racial marriage was the thing most feared by whites in the South, so I did not ask for a negative vote. When the couple went out with a deacon for the customary interview, I said, 'What you have just witnessed is troubling to many, I am sure. On Wednesday night I will address what I believe the Bible teaches about mixed racial marriage.' We had a large crowd to hear that Wednesday night message. I said, 'This problem is not a Bible problem. It is a very real social problem. But we are not going to keep sincere Christians from our fellowship, regardless of their color.' Galatians 3:28 says, 'There is neither Jew nor Greek, slave nor free, male nor female, for you are all one in Christ Jesus.' Then I told them about Aaron and Miriam confronting Moses because he had a black wife, and how God made Miriam a leper because of her criticism. I said, 'I don't want to get leprosy and I doubt if you do, either!'[195]

Handford's stand was especially fraught with risk because Greenville, South Carolina was the home of Bob Jones University (BJU), the leading fundamentalist school in the country, which remained fully segregated and formally opposed to "miscegenation" or any other "mixing of the races." A sizable percentage of the members and leaders of Handford's Southside Baptist Church—including Sunday school teachers, deacons, and other volunteers—were connected in some way to BJU.

The following week, the school's president, Bob Jones Jr., announced in the school's chapel service that any BJU student, faculty, or staff member would be fired or expelled if he or she continued to attend Southside. Membership and attendance at the church instantly plunged by more than a third as the Bob Jones community responded to the threat. It took a few more years before Southside could rebuild membership rolls and attendance to equal its level before the tempest with Bob Jones Jr.

For his part, Jerry Falwell temporized for years before taking a similar stand to end the segregated policies in place at Thomas Road Baptist Church. "In my adolescence and young adult years I don't remember hearing one person speak of the injustice of segregation," Falwell wrote in *Strength for the Journey* in 1987.

> To the contrary, all my role models, including powerful church leaders, supported segregation. I have never once considered myself a racist. Yet, looking back, I have to admit I was one. Unfortunately, I was not quick enough or Christian enough or insightful enough to realize my condition until those days of tumult in the 1960s. But believe me, it wasn't the Congress or the courts that changed my heart. [The] demonstrators, in spite of their courage, didn't move me to new compassion on behalf of my black brothers and sisters. The new laws and the loud protest marchers may have helped to enforce the change and to speed it up, but it was God's still small voice in my heart that was the real instrument of change and growth for me.[196]

God's still small voice spoke at precisely the right moment and the right decibel level to have a profound impact on Jerry Falwell's career. His Thomas Road church opened its doors to the first black members within a few weeks after the assassination of Martin Luther King Jr. in April of 1968, and the number of attendees immediately began to climb—though no more than a small percentage of the new members were black. His wife Macel Falwell recounts, "Having crossed that color barrier, Thomas Road membership exploded. Between 1968 and 1970 the church outgrew the 1,000 seat sanctuary that we'd built in 1964. Our architect found a set of historic old church plans designed, but never built, by Thomas Jefferson. Expanding those basic plans, we built a sanctuary that could seat 3,200 people...June 28, 1970, was the first service in the new sanctuary."[197]

The new members were almost entirely white. And Thomas Road continued to be an overwhelmingly white church, its services still practically segregated by long habits of relationship and association.

Nonetheless, it became clear that many whites were getting beyond their intransigent opposition to the moral message of the civil rights movement. They welcomed a preacher who could leave the old racial categories behind in search of a more inclusive—and more Christian—fundamentalist message.

John R. Rice's quandary was the historic conundrum of American fundamentalism. Planted in the hills of Appalachia by the righteous individualism of Scots-Irish Presbyterians, nurtured by the need to find Biblical justification for slavery, inspired by the noble myth of the Lost Cause, hunkered down into a permanent defense of the indefensible, fundamentalist Christians were confronted with a question: how was it possible to map the love of Jesus to racial wrongs? That challenge, they came to realize, was insurmountable. This was the key issue. And unless fundamentalists developed the capacity to confront the problem of race, they would never exert influence in any national debate about any other moral issue.

Chapter 24
Consolidating the Fundamentalist Base

*"The sword of the Lord is filled with blood, it is made
fat with fatness, and with the blood of lambs and goats,
with the fat of the kidneys of rams: for the Lord hath a
sacrifice in Bozrah, and a great slaughter in the land of
Idume'a. And the unicorns shall come down with them,
and the bullocks with the bulls; and their land shall be
soaked with blood, and their dust made fat with fatness.
For it is the day of the Lord's vengeance."* —Isaiah
34:6-8

By the time I graduated from high school in 1968 I had traveled far
from my fundamentalist roots. I hated going to church, stopped talking to
anyone in my family, and descended into a deep pit of self-righteousness
and suicidal despair. I held my granddad and his religion responsible for
most of the sins and crimes of the world, to which I believed I was
acutely sensitive. I watched Walter Cronkite reporting on the nightmare
of the Vietnam War and nursed my feelings of continual outrage at the
crimes being committed by my country. I wrote reams of angry poetry,
nihilistic short stories, and pretentious essays. I grew my hair and
affected a uniform of baggy sweaters and blue jeans. I smoked Tareytons
and worked for Eugene McCarthy's campaign for president. On Saint
Patrick's Day I got drunk on two pitchers of green beer, smoked several
fat brown cigars, came home at midnight, rousted my dad to unlock the
kitchen door for me, passed out in the La-Z-Boy recliner in the living
room, and then woke up an hour later vomiting all over myself.

In the spring of my senior year, my parents ordered me to apply for
admission to attend Bob Jones University, a fundamentalist school. I
refused, and announced that I would attend the University of Wisconsin
in Madison, known as a hotbed of radical protest. In desperation, they

gave me an early graduation present of a weekend trip to visit the Bob Jones campus in Greenville, South Carolina. I arrived on campus two days after the assassination of Martin Luther King Jr., in the midst of a wave of violent demonstrations in hundreds of cities and towns across the country. After my brief glance at Bob Jones's cloistered and racially segregated campus, I returned home to announce that my plans were unchanged. That fall I enrolled at Madison and almost immediately threw myself into organizing and leading demonstrations against the war, against racial injustice, and against any other kind of oppression I could imagine or discover. I quickly developed a new fundamentalist faith to replace my old fundamentalist faith.

Predictably, as I moved into the radical opposition I became a cautionary tale, an oft-repeated anecdote for the sermons of my grandfather, who was mightily disturbed by the turmoil of the 60s. All Hell had broken loose, quite literally, John R. Rice believed. America had left its fundamentalist faith behind, and the hippies and radicals, revolutionaries and yippies, infidels and rebels, had overthrown common sense and the proper authority of Christian leaders. It was time for Americans to take back their country from Marxist rabble-rousers such as me.

Granddad referred directly to me in a national radio address:

> I know a young man from a pastor's home, a young man of great brilliance, well-raised. But he went to Wisconsin University (sic). They taught him to become a follower of Karl Marx. And, although he said he did not believe in violent communism, yet he became a Marxist and said so. And all the energy and ambitions and ideals and dreams seemed to have fled away. He became a dropout and unsure and uncertain, with no plans for the future, and the ruin of all a godly mother and father had hoped for in that godly home."[198]

In another published sermon, he concluded that my life went so thoroughly off track because my mother had failed to spank me enough when I was a child:

> I know a family where, among four children, the older boy was always given preference. He was Momma's pride and joy…He is the only one of the family who is not a good Christian. He early sought liberal friends, espoused the doctrines of Karl Marx. What I saw long

ago and foretold has come to pass. A child who is not punished for his sin and not held accountable as he ought to be is likely to go wrong.[199]

I had gone about as far wrong as John R. Rice thought I could possibly go.

In 1940, John R. Rice had moved his family and *The Sword of the Lord* from Texas to Wheaton in order to expand his base. Establishing his headquarters in the evangelical center near Chicago would help him to solidify the *Sword's* practical and spiritual leadership of the fundamentalist movement. Not incidentally, all six of his daughters had attended Wheaton College and all six married fine young men, all alumni of Wheaton College, whom Rice would refer to as his "preacher boys."

But Wheaton was no longer the center of fundamentalism. The principal institutions of the fundamentalist world in Wheaton, including the headquarters of Youth for Christ and the National Association of Evangelicals plus Wheaton College, were now part of the neo-evangelical world. Rice found himself isolated practically and organizationally from his closest evangelical neighbors, and isolated geographically from his closest theological neighbors, the thriving fundamentalist community in the Bible Belt.

In June of 1963, Rice moved the offices of *The Sword of the Lord* to Murfreesboro, Tennessee. Along with the staff, the rest of the Rice family—daughters and sons-in-law, aunts and uncles, cousins and grandchildren—migrated back down South from Wheaton over the next few years. The six Rice sons-in-law ended up taking pastorates or teaching positions at fundamentalist churches or colleges in the Carolinas, Georgia, Virginia, Texas, or Tennessee. Soon, the Rice clan was, geographically speaking, a Southern family once again.

Moving back down South wasn't just a defensive move for Rice. The South, with its thousands of fundamentalist churches and church networks, its fundamentalist Bible conferences, colleges, campgrounds, publications, and personalities, was where the overwhelming majority of grassroots fundamentalists lived and drew breath, worked and worshipped. In the South was concentrated a wide spectrum of fundamentalist Baptist networks such as the Southwide Baptist Fellowship, the many fundamentalists with wide influence remaining inside the Southern Baptist Convention, and, of course, schools such as Bob Jones University in Greenville, South Carolina, and Tennessee Temple University in Chattanooga. In addition, by moving to Murfreesboro John R. Rice could be a neighbor of his half-brother, evangelist Bill Rice, who ran the Bill Rice Ranch, a sizable, thriving Christian retreat center and summer Bible camp outside Murfreesboro. The South provided a base for building the fundamentalist movement.

John R. Rice was doubtless disappointed at his split with Billy Graham. From Rice's point of view, Graham had violated the principle of separatism. He had strayed across the line that should forever divide orthodox Christians from their enemies in "the world"—liberals and modernists, infidels and heretics who dominated the mainline Protestant denominations and Catholic institutions. In addition, it saddened him to lose a friend and close ally in whose evangelistic accomplishments and growing prestige he rejoiced.

The split signaled further isolation from the mainstream for Rice and the fundamentalist movement, at least temporarily. In this way it was similar to the split between fundamentalists and mainline Protestants in the 1920s. The earlier split had helped fundamentalists define themselves as a separate movement, and forced them to withdraw from the mainline denominations, churches, and seminaries they had failed to capture. But it had also spurred them to create their own fundamentalist institutions. Over the next three decades, the fundamentalist movement grew deeper roots and developed a vibrant subculture with a shared understanding of Christian doctrine and a common focus on separatism.

The new split, by contrast, signaled the beginning of an attitude of more aggressive engagement with the immorality and secularism that John R. Rice and other fundamentalists believed pervaded postwar American culture. Beginning in the 1920s and 30s many other fundamentalists had retreated into a complete and purist "separatist" reaction against involvement by Christians in the secular world of politics and political action. However, Rice, since the beginning of his career had championed the involvement of fundamentalists in the political process. At the side of J. Frank Norris, he had barnstormed against Catholic, Democratic Al Smith running for president against Herbert Hoover in 1928. He had called the New Deal a communist plot to destroy the moral fiber of America, and deemed Franklin Roosevelt an unwitting tool of Joseph Stalin. He had castigated "the liquor interests" and called for criminalizing the teaching of evolution in the public schools, and assaulted conscientious objectors during World War II as rebels against God and tools of totalitarians.

The turmoil of the 1960s seemed to support Rice's message that America was in desperate need of returning to its fundamentalist and Christian roots. Millions of people marched in the streets to demand voting and other civil rights for Southern blacks. Riots and demonstrations marked rebellions against poverty and racial discrimination in cities everywhere. College students marched against the war in Vietnam on thousands of campuses. Young people were developing longer hair and shorter tempers, and their parents reacted with a complex mixture of bewilderment and umbrage. The very structure of American society seemed to be crumbling with the disappearance of "respect for authority": the respect of children for their parents, of women for their husbands, of the black masses for the intentions of their white Southern rulers, of young draft dodgers and draft card burners for the boards of old men who wanted to send them off to fight an unpopular war.

Rice resurrected an argument first made by evangelicals in the mid-19th century known as Christian Americanism. This was the idea that American colonists from Europe had been guided by the hand of God and their Christian faith to found "a city on a hill," in the words of Puritan John Winthrop, which could be a beacon of righteousness for the rest of humanity. In this view, the framers of the Constitution had been providentially guided to create a nation that could walk in the light of God. For some 19th century evangelicals, America had a unique covenant similar to the promises God had made to the Jews. Americans were the new "chosen people," and would retain God's favor as long as they followed God's commands. Preaching on America's supposed Christian origins and heritage was a way of calling America to repentance.

In 1966, Rice published a pamphlet titled "War in Vietnam: Should Christians Fight?"[200] He explained that God frequently used wars to punish the wicked. He noted that the Old Testament God many times "led his people into war, and then gave them the victory" over their enemies. He argued that just as God sent the people of Israel to destroy the evil Amalekites and Philistines, America had a "holy and righteous cause for war" to stop the murder, torture, and persecution perpetuated by the forces of Godless communism. He wrote: "When America goes to war, where it is clearly right, and where our armies would be carrying out the command of God, that sacred commission He has given the nations of the earth to enforce law and order and bring criminals to justice, then American boys should obey the government. If they be called for war they should, in my humble opinion, go boldly, go without malice or hate, but prayerfully and lovingly determine to do what is necessary." Rice condemned war resisters or draft dodgers for revealing their "wicked hearts" in refusing to obey government officials who were serving as God's ministers on earth, and he demanded that they be prosecuted to the fullest extent of the law.

Resistance to the authority of the American government, Rice explained, was resistance to the express command of God. Patriotism was essentially equivalent to righteousness. He never went so far as to advocate a theocratic state, but he melded politics and religion in a way that made very clear what side of any political issue he believed God was on. God had been very clearly opposed to the New Deal "socialism" of Franklin Roosevelt, and God was equally opposed to the Great Society "socialism" of Lyndon Baines Johnson. God was definitely in favor of capitalism and just as definitely opposed to government programs to alleviate poverty or ameliorate working conditions in factories. God was wroth over demands for civil, political, and employment equality by women. God was incensed in 1962 and 1963 when the Supreme Court banned state-sponsored prayer and Bible reading in public schools as a violation of the First Amendment prohibition against the state establishment of religion.

Fundamentalist ire over the banning of prayer in schools was ironic, given the origin of the First Amendment to the Constitution as a way of guaranteeing freedom of religion. The religious community in the 1700s with the most to gain by a separation of church and state had been the Baptists, a relatively small and powerless sect at the time of the American Revolution. Freedom of religion had been commonly understood as freedom to believe in any religion or none, and to be free of any religious coercion. For almost 200 years, a national consensus had prevailed forbidding any governmental "establishment" or promotion of religion. The consensus broke down remarkably in 1954 when Congress added the words "under God" to the Pledge of Allegiance so that it read "one nation under God, indivisible, with liberty and justice for all," and then in 1956 when Congress declared "In God we trust" as the national motto.

In the 1960s, the United States was torn between two countervailing tendencies. On the one hand, it was wracked with profound social changes forcing it to recognize the legitimacy of diverse cultures and divergent points of view. On the other hand, the country had slid rapidly towards a civic religion that declared belief in God to be part and parcel of patriotism. John R. Rice was in good—or at least popular—company when he declared in his pamphlet "God Bless America," "It couldn't be an accident that in these days God has raised up a nation and given us the freedom and the prosperity and the religious heritage that we have. It is the plan of God."[201] Rice believed that good Christian people "ought to be interested in every moral question, that is, interested as citizens and not only to preach the Word but to make a moral climate in America. That is everybody's business and is as much a citizen's business as it is the church member's business. So there ought to be laws, of course, against liquor, against dope, against sex sins, against pornographic literature and against sex education in the schools which is done by the immoral and openly anti-Christian crowd."[202]

For many fundamentalists, the notion that Christians ought to be involved in politics was nothing short of heresy. Ever since the 1920s, the crucial tenet of their faith, more than any doctrine found in the Bible, had been separatism. For many fundamentalists separatism had meant being separate from any potential non-fundamentalist allies in the political process, in addition to separation from modernists and liberals in prayer, evangelism, or any other religious practice. So John R. Rice's insistence that good fundamentalists should be active with other conservatives in political life was shocking and controversial. In scores of editorials, sermons, and articles published in *The Sword of the Lord* throughout the 1960s and 70s, Rice hammered away at the notion that Christians needed to be active and collectively powerful in a wide range of struggles: to support the war in Vietnam against "atheistic communism," to keep abortions illegal, to promote the death penalty, to oppose the teaching of evolution in the public schools.

In Rice's view, the core problem was not really political, that is, not a problem with government policies or social ills. It was not a "head" problem, but rather a "heart" problem. The root of social problems lay in the sinful nature of humans, who instinctively rebelled against the "authorities" that God had placed in charge of human institutions: the man in a family, the teacher in a classroom, a policeman on the street, the judge in a courtroom, the leader of a state. In a small pamphlet titled "The Home, the School, the Nation and Law and Order" published in 1972, Rice laid out the foundation of the philosophy that would inspire and guide the development of the Religious Right in the 1970s:

> In many, many cases the home will raise a bunch of rebels and criminals. Why? Because it starts out with a violation of the fundamental laws and vows, breaking obligations. When a wife does not obey her husband, she is lawless, she is a criminal, as far as the home is concerned. Children, then, won't respect their parents. Those same children will not respect the teacher at school. The same young people will hate the policeman on the corner, and these, when drafted, will want to burn draft cards or break any law they do not like, or flee to Canada to avoid serving their country. I am just saying that if wives are rebels and lawbreakers in the home, they break down the very fabric that makes good

citizens…They lead children into sin, and set a pattern of rebellion.[203]

The language Rice used was intentionally provocative and oppositional. His audience was not just fundamentalist Christians, but rather a broad spectrum of conservative Americans whom he believed were the majority of a Christian nation. He sought to rally them around what he believed were both traditional Christian and American values. He pointed a finger of blame at the "opponents of authority," at political liberals who were, as it happened, also religious liberals. These people were of two types, he said. One was "people who claim to be Christians but they do not believe the Bible is all inspired…The other people are openly infidels." Moral failings were strongly connected to political issues by a relationship of cause-and-effect:

> It is a sad thing that the people who take up for the murderer, and take up for the sex pervert, and take up for the kidnapper and the hijacker, are the same kind who want to murder unborn babies. They are for abortion. They are the same kind who call policemen pigs and think it is all right to break the law…Those kind of foolish people are liberals in their political life and liberals (if they have any) in religion. [204]

Rice was helping to lay ground for a profound shift in the thinking of many fundamentalists about the appropriateness of political action by orthodox Christians. The principle of separatism in religious affairs—in evangelism, in public prayer, in ecumenical outreach—still held, and required good Christians to hold others to the test of fundamentalist orthodoxy. However, it was perfectly permissible for conservative, orthodox Christians to unite in political action with others who had different points of view on certain religious issues.

Chapter 25
"I Am a Fundamentalist"

"And I will appoint over them four kinds, saith the Lord: the sword to slay, and the dogs to tear, and the fowls of the Heaven, and the beasts of the earth, to devour and destroy."—Jeremiah 15:3

I last saw my granddad alive in August of 1979, when he came to the city where I lived, Birmingham, Alabama, for a Sword of the Lord conference on revival and soul-winning. At the time, I was spending most of my days and nights producing and distributing revolutionary leaflets and newspapers in order to persuade the proletarian masses of Alabama to rise up and overthrow their capitalist and imperialist masters. I had so far failed in the attempt. I earned a meager living as a union welder at KB Southern Foundry to support my wife and daughter.

Granddad called me on the phone and asked me to go to dinner with him. He was frail and almost transparent, skinnier and shorter than when I had seen him at Christmas. He moved slowly and with great care, and when I picked him up at his hotel I went around the car to open the door for him. We ate a dinner of fried chicken and mashed potatoes, greens and cornbread at the Ensley Grill, a legendary establishment in a working class neighborhood near U.S. Steel. Our meal was awkward and conversation strained. He told me about my grandmother and I told him about Amber, his two-year-old great grandbaby. "Do you know I pray for you every day?" he asked with tears in his eyes, and I evaded the question and asked after his health.

He preached that night to a packed church of over a thousand people, telling story after story in his quavery voice, quoting a hundred Bible verses from memory. He wept repeatedly. When he had finished preaching and the crowd sang the final song, it took half an hour for him to reach the back of the auditorium where I stood by the book table that held more than 30 of the titles he had authored stacked ready for purchase. People crowded around him, touching his sleeve, hugging him, asking him to sign their Bibles. When he got to the table he asked me to pick two of his books as gifts from him, and I grabbed a couple at random.

I drove him back to his hotel and let him off at the front door. I shook his hand and he hugged me and kissed me on the cheek. He said, "Andy, I pray that God will bless you and bring you to himself."

I drove off in the darkness, crying, and I stopped by a dumpster in an alleyway and threw his books away.

I loved him more than I could say, and I hated him so fiercely.

But I hated myself even more.

By 1970, *The Sword of the Lord* was the most influential fundamentalist publication in America, with a growing list of 130,000 subscribers: preachers, Sunday school teachers, deacons, evangelists, and fundamentalist theologians. Over 20 regional Sword of the Lord conferences with thousands of attendees took place across the country that year.

On May 27, 1970, Bob Jones Jr. hosted John R. Rice in a laudatory ceremony on the campus of Bob Jones University, presenting him with "The Bob Jones Memorial Award for the Defense of the Scriptures." The award was given in memory of Jones's own father, Bob Jones Sr., because John R. Rice exemplified "evangelism, Biblical preaching, and the winning of souls to Christ." Jones said that *The Sword of the Lord* "has strongly stood for New Testament principles in affairs of the church," and had opposed "the compromise of scriptural principles." The words would soon come back to haunt Jones.

Rice believed it might finally be time to create an international movement of broad scope. In January, 1971 he called a meeting at Sword of the Lord Foundation headquarters in Murfreesboro, Tennessee for a global conference on evangelism. The conference was to take place in August of 1972, and the organizing committee included several of the most prominent fundamentalists in America. The legendary Bob Jones Jr. was a key leader, along with Lee Roberson, pastor of Chattanooga's renowned Highland Park Baptist Church, Earl Oldham from the World Baptist Fellowship, Bill Dowell from Bible Baptist College, and Jack Hyles, pastor of the massive First Baptist Church of Hammond, Indiana. Also present was the younger and relatively unknown Virginian Jerry Falwell.

Rice expected the call for this international conference to be signed by over 200 of the most prominent fundamentalist leaders in the country.

It would be preceded by several great citywide revival campaigns in major cities. The purpose of the World Congress on Biblical Evangelism, as it would be called, was "to stir revival fires, show how it can be done, to promote the fellowship without compromise of fundamental churches, pastors, and people in soul-winning; to bring sin-condemning, scriptural, aggressive revival with a moral revolution to America and the world."

Rice planned for the congress to be open to all true fundamentalists, and he expected it to be a positive demonstration of the importance of soul-winning. Rice intended to invite two prominent Southern Baptists, W. A. Criswell and Robert G. Lee, to speak at the Congress. Lee had been president of the Southern Baptist Convention three times and he and Rice had been close friends since 1938.

Right away, the planning committee broke down in a painful conflict. Bob Jones Jr. charged that Criswell and Lee were "compromisers and traitors to the cause of scriptural evangelism and, indeed, to scriptural separation all the way down the line." Further, said Jones, the congress needed to "contend for obedience to the word of God and oppose boldly those who, in the name of evangelism, disobey the word of God and build the church of the Antichrist." Jones specifically called out Billy Graham as the one who was building the "church of the Antichrist." He said that the only proper basis for fundamentalists to work together was to use every public occasion to attack Graham, whom he considered a danger to them all and to Christianity itself.

Rice and Jones disagreed about the very definition of separatism. Rice defined the term yet again in *The Sword of the Lord* in May of 1971: "You are not to have [a modernist] help translate the Bible. You are not to have him teach in your colleges. And you ought never to give a dime where he will get it as a matter of Christian service to God. If you do, you dishonor God and make a lie to all you preach."

Jones, however, proposed a more stringent standard of "secondary separationism." A good Christian, he believed, must go much further in separating from liberals and modernists, refusing to associate with anybody who was in any way associated with them. Billy Graham, said Jones, might falsely claim to be an evangelical Christian, a Bible believer, and a preacher of the word of God. But he was evidently a snake in the grass, an infidel, a traitor and apostate, an agent of the Antichrist. He should be exposed, condemned, and opposed at every possible opportunity. The duty of every fundamentalist to attack Billy Graham was more important, it seemed, than holding revivals or winning souls to Jesus.

All the planning for Rice's World Congress on Biblical Evangelism ground to a halt, and Rice and Jones opened a bitter public battle for the soul of fundamentalism. A flurry of sermons and pamphlets emerged from Bob Jones University, and a steady stream of articles began to appear in the pages of *The Sword of the Lord*. The struggle tore apart people who had been close friends and allies for decades.

Bob Jones Jr. resigned from the Sword Cooperating Board in 1971, which led to other losses of support for the *Sword*, as the schism within the fundamentalist movement deepened. Jones's replacement on Rice's board in late 1971 was Jerry Falwell. A second new board member was Curtis Hutson, the pastor of a fundamentalist mega church in Decatur, Georgia. Hutson would succeed Rice as editor of *The Sword of the Lord* in 1980.

As the terms of the debate became better known to the fundamentalist rank and file, the consequences of the split were radically different for Rice compared with his split with Billy Graham 13 years earlier. This time, Rice appeared to be fighting for a more "moderate" or mainstream fundamentalism, compared with an extreme position held by Bob Jones Jr. And the results of the split were all positive. Within the next three years, the circulation of *The Sword of the Lord* doubled, hitting almost 300,000. The fundamentalist movement went into hyper drive. Sword of the Lord conferences on soul-winning and revival were suddenly sold out, and demand was rapidly rising for more conferences, more books, more literature, more training classes.

In 1974, Rice held the first truly national week-long Sword Conference on Evangelism in Indianapolis, Indiana. Over 7,000 people thronged the auditorium and packed "how to" workshops on soul-winning, revival, evangelism, church growth, Christian living and service. Hundreds of exhibitors of Christian literature, films, and audio/visual equipment filled an exhibit hall, along with representatives from fundamentalist colleges and dozens of other evangelistic organization. In the following years the *Sword* held national conferences in Dallas, Atlanta, Detroit, Murfreesboro, and Birmingham, all following the same successful model.

The split between Rice and Jones seemed to push both men, along with their camps of supporters, in opposite directions: Jones in the direction of deeper isolation from mainstream American culture and politics, toward an ever more extreme separatist position in matters of religious doctrine, and a more stubborn and unyielding defense of racial segregation on the campus of Bob Jones University. Jones attacked Rice as a liar, a traitor and a sellout, accusing him of betraying his calling to defend the fundamentals of the faith and failing to attack those who sought to undermine and destroy Christianity. Jones published a pamphlet titled "Facts John R. Rice Will Not Face," which accused Rice of being "soft" on liberalism and claiming that his own father, Bob Jones Sr., had always harbored deep suspicions that Rice was a liability to the fundamentalist movement and not to be trusted as a true "separatist."

Rice responded with a book in 1975 titled *I Am a Fundamentalist*. Rice was 80 years old at the book's publication, and by that point had written almost 200 books and pamphlets published in over 60 million copies, in addition to publishing *The Sword of the Lord* for over four decades. His statement of fundamentalist positions and principles would be familiar to most of his readers. He began by listing several terms he would agree applied to him, but which he thought didn't go far enough. He was a conservative, he said, but more than a conservative. He was an evangelical, but wanted to be more precise in his terminology because many whom he considered to be modernists and infidels also claimed to be evangelicals. He was a Baptist, but was also sure that some Baptists didn't believe the Bible or care much about soul-winning, so he was certainly more than a Baptist. The only label he could fully embrace, he said, was fundamentalist.

Rice began by connecting fundamentalism with what he called "the fundamentals of the Christian faith, including the inspiration and thus the divine authority of the Bible; the deity, virgin birth, blood atonement, bodily resurrection, personal second coming of Christ; the fallen, lost condition of all mankind; salvation by repentance and faith, grace without works; eternal doom in Hell of the unconverted and eternal blessedness of the saved in Heaven." However, he also believed that fundamentalism meant "a vigorous defense of the faith, active soul-winning, great New Testament-type local churches going abroad to win multitude; having fervent love for all of God's people, and earnestly avoiding compromise in doctrine or yoking up with unbelievers."[205]

In the rest of the book, Rice took on various "popular misconceptions" about fundamentalists (for example, fundamentalists are not snake handlers or polygamists), and listed some things fundamentalists should not believe in (such as "speaking in tongues") or behavior they should avoid (fundamentalists should not be "hell-raising nuts").

In one chapter titled "Fundamentalists Should Love All Christ's Other Sheep," Rice focused sharply on the distress he had felt about the bitterness expressed by people who found themselves on opposite sides of the conflict over "secondary separationism." The title referred to a well-known Bible verse, John 10:16, in which Jesus said, "And other sheep I have, which are not of this fold: them also I must bring, and they shall hear my voice; and there shall be one fold, and one shepherd."

This phrase about Christ's "other sheep" was seldom quoted by combative fundamentalists who had historically been good at assigning "other sheep" to other doctrinal "folds" and then hurling exegetical and oratorical rocks at them. To the contrary, the phrase had been popular with modernists, mainline Christian ministers and ecumenical evangelicals such as Billy Graham. It was popular among people who wanted to explain that God's love and mercy covered all of humankind, and not just those who held rigidly to a narrow range of orthodox beliefs.

John R. Rice, however, used the phrase to encourage fundamentalists to leave behind the bitter internecine warfare that had erupted between himself and Bob Jones Jr. He gave examples of various people with whom he disagreed about some point of Christian doctrine or practice, and then said he thought Jesus wanted him to love them anyway. "God, give us hearts of compassion," wrote Rice. "Oh, some of us think we are so strong. Then let the strong bear the burden of the weak. Some of us think we are so wise and good! But God has chosen the weak things to confound the mighty. God loves the poor, the ignorant, and the lowly. How happy is the man who thinks not of himself but of others!"[206]

A chapter in the heart of the book was a virtual manifesto for the creation of the Religious Right. Titled "A Fundamentalist is a Good Christian Citizen," the chapter laid out all the reasons why good Christian fundamentalists needed to leave their political isolation behind and become engaged in the political process. First, Rice quoted Jesus's well-known observation that one should "render unto Caesar the things which are Caesar's, and unto God the things which are God's." This, he said, meant that a Christian's obligation to be a loyal, obedient, patriotic citizen, "even to an oppressive conqueror like Rome," was just as important as a Christian's obligation to worship God. A good Christian, said Rice, should obey all the laws, even laws he thought were wrong or oppressive. A Christian should vote, could run for office, and should support candidates in elections. A Christian should serve in the military when drafted, should support the death penalty, should oppose abortion, and should work to end the teaching of evolution.

He provided a long list of people and institutions he believed were working to tear down respect for law and bring about disorder and disrespect for authority. He blamed state universities "founded to advance learning and build the future of America, now turning out Marxists, anarchists and hippies and rioters." He castigated "the Supreme Court, the Warren Court, [which] aided along the decay in law and order and morality. It took the part of the filth peddlers; it overturned state laws against pornography; it set prisoners free who had been proved guilty of rape and murder." He criticized the news media, "usually left-wing or liberal, and usually pro-socialist," and attacked "left-wingers, hippies, Negro rioters (not all Negroes are rioters, of course), and college anarchists."

Finally, said Rice, fundamentalists are "on the 'far right' both in religion and in politics. *The Sword of the Lord* is for the old-time fundamentals of the Christian faith and we say so on the front page of every issue. We are for free enterprise, not socialism." He acknowledged that "Negroes should have…the same rights everybody has, to vote, to get a good education, to prepare for and get as good jobs as they can fit themselves for and secure in open and fair competition." But he added, "We are against the crowd that deliberately cultivated the hate and violence of the late Martin Luther King and the 'Civil Rights' demonstrations."

John R. Rice, while pointing toward the future Religious Right, was still stuck in the racial attitudes and rote language of the past, restrained by the fundamentalist politics and culture of the Old South even as he struggled to transform them. Unlike Billy Graham in the 1950s, he had been unable to see Martin Luther King Jr. as a prophet of God heeding the cry of the poor and the oppressed. Unlike Walt Handford and many other fundamentalist and evangelical Southern preachers in the late 1960s and early 1970s, he was unable to leave behind the century-old Southern narrative that had pitted white privileges against the upwelling movement for freedom and justice for all people in the South. Like Moses, he was able to see the Promised Land, but would not be able to go there before he died. It would take a Joshua such as Jerry Falwell to bring down the walls of Jericho.

Falwell, however, needed the authority of Rice's belief that fundamentalist Christianity could reclaim the historic American mainstream, and should reach out for profound influence in the religious and political life of the country. To do so, the fundamentalist movement would have to create a broad umbrella for probable allies who might support its conservative moral and political agenda.

The split with Bob Jones Jr. had helped cement a growing friendship between Rice and Jerry Falwell. Falwell called Rice the "titular leader of the fundamentalist movement," and by 1976, Rice was looking for ways to further promote Falwell as his successor. Rice published many of Falwell's sermons in the pages of *The Sword of the Lord,* and provided him a prominent platform at Sword of the Lord conferences.

Rice also decided to explore making a film that could provide a vehicle for Falwell while bringing more souls to Jesus. He contacted Ron Ormond, who lived a few miles away in Nashville, and who had become famous for producing a long string of low-budget Hollywood potboilers, mainly Westerns and horror flicks, over more than a quarter century. Most of Ormond's biggest hits had starred a former hairdresser named Lash Larue, named for the skill he exhibited as a cowboy dressed all in black and wielding an 18-foot-long bullwhip. They included such low budget classics as *Mesa of Lost Women*, starring Jackie Coogan as a mad scientist who assembles a race of scantily clad spider women with long fingernails, led by a gigantic tarantula, and whose horrific shenanigans are accompanied by what must be the most comically incompetent flamenco-guitar-and-piano soundtrack in the history of films.

Rice commissioned Ormond to produce *The Grim Reaper*, a religious horror movie designed to scare lost souls out of Hell. The film starred Jerry Falwell and evangelist Jack Van Impe as themselves and Ron Ormond's wife June as the witch of Endor, a character straight from the lurid pages of the Bible itself. *The Grim Reaper* was part of a 1970s genre of horror films that came to be known as "Christsploitation" flicks. It tells the story of a divided family. The mother and her younger son have accepted Christ as their personal Savior, and her boy is in training to become a preacher. His daddy is unsaved, as is the older son, whose career as a stock car racer comes to an end when he is mangled horribly in a terrible crash. The boy dies in agony, and is sent straight to the eternal flames of Hell. Daddy is tormented by guilt for failing to bring his son to Jesus, and tries to contact the boy with the help of a mystic (the witch of Endor), failing to realize Satan himself is using the witch as a conduit for communication. In the film's climactic moment, the father dreams a trip to Hell to visit his son.[*]

The makeshift masterpiece that resulted was shown in the basements of fundamentalist churches across America and introduced Jerry Falwell to countless thousands of new fans.

His film career aside, Falwell leapt to mainstream national prominence for the first time during the 1976 presidential campaign. Jimmy Carter had touted his evangelical credentials as a born-again

---

[*] My mother recalls that Ormond shot the film on location on my grandparents' farm outside of Murfreesboro, Tennessee. Just behind my grandparents' house was a second house where Mom and Dad were living at the time with my youngest sister, Joanna, while my dad worked in the *Sword's* shipping department. Just behind my parent's house was the barn and pasture. Ormond brought the flames of Hell to the silver screen by using a backhoe to dig a big pit out behind my granddad's barn, filling it with old tires and setting them on fire. My mother remembers continually having to shoo my sister Joanna away from the film production—especially from the scenes of the Devil and the stock car racer dancing around the flames of Hell—for fear that Joanna would suffer from nightmares.

Christian and publicly discussed his faith and history as a Sunday school teacher in a Baptist church in the small town of Plains, Georgia. In the last weeks before the election, an interview with Carter appeared in *Playboy* magazine. Famously, he admitted that he had "looked on a lot of women with lust. I've committed adultery in my heart many times," though he said he had never acted upon his lust. "This is something that God recognizes, that I will do and have done, and God forgives me for it. But that doesn't mean that I condemn someone who not only looks on a woman with lust but who leaves his wife and shacks up with somebody out of wedlock. Christ says, don't consider yourself better than someone else because one guy screws a whole bunch of women while the other guy is loyal to his wife."[207]

Carter clearly meant to say that all human beings were imperfect and that God's forgiveness was universal. However, John R. Rice heard his words quite differently, and accused him in *The Sword of the Lord* of pandering to pornographers and setting a poor example for young people. Despite Carter's claim to be a Christian, such a president could inflict great harm on the country. The only proper response for Christians was to turn out en masse and vote against him on election day.[208]

In agreement with Rice's critical reaction to Carter's unfortunate remarks, Jerry Falwell provided interviews to the *Washington Post* and the *CBS Morning News*. He also recorded two sermons on the subject scheduled to be broadcast on television right before the November election. Falwell told of his own reaction in a sermon titled "Seven Things Corrupting America" that appeared in *The Sword of the Lord* shortly after the election:

> Mr. Carter's forces began immediately contacting all of our television outlets, threatening that if they aired the programs they would be in violation of FCC rules and regulations. I immediately got Dr. John R. Rice, Dr. Jack Hyles, Dr. John Rawlings, and Dr. Bill Dowell together. We went to Washington and called a press conference at the National Press Club and I said, 'I resent anybody in Washington, or anybody trying to go to Washington, silencing and muzzling a preacher of the gospel from preaching his moral convictions.[209]

That press conference marked the beginning of the rise to national prominence of the Religious Right in America, and was Falwell's first step toward organizing the Moral Majority.

In 1979, John R. Rice published a collection of sermons Falwell had preached at Sword of the Lord conferences on soul-winning and revival throughout the 1970s, titled *America Can Be Saved!* Falwell's theme throughout the book was a 1976 Gallup Poll reporting that 34 percent of Americans claimed to be saved or born again Christians. "Those seventy-five million Americans, adult and below, are a mighty force of God in this generation if properly taught, trained, and disciplined," said Falwell. "I look on us preachers as that army of mobilizers and spiritual organizers who have to go out like the labor union and find them and bring them into our camp, teach them the Word of God, train them in the way of God, and set their souls on fire."[210]

Falwell's words were unsettling to readers and listeners who had grown up believing that Christians had no business dabbling in the dirty business of secular politics. For many fundamentalists, separatism required separation from "the world" in every possible way, in politics as well as in entertainment, education, and religion. He pushed them toward an ecumenical fundamentalism that would have a secular impact. In his sermon "A Day of Many Solomons," Falwell urged his colleagues to

> ...rebuild a nation. For too long, we have sat back and said politics are for the people who live in Washington, business is for those on Wall Street, and religion is our business. But the fact is, you cannot separate the sacred and the secular. We need to train men of God in our schools who can go on to Congress, can go on to be the directors of the largest corporations, who can become the lawyers and the businessmen and those important people in tomorrow's United States. If we are going to turn this country around, we have to get God's people mobilized in the right direction and we must do it quickly.[211]

The timing of Jerry Falwell's jeremiad *America Can Be Saved!*— printed on the presses in the basement of the Sword of the Lord building in Murfreesboro—coincided with a press conference Falwell called in April of 1979. Prompted by Republican operatives Paul Weyrich, Howard Phillips, and Richard Viguerie, Falwell and others (including Tim LaHaye, a Rice ally who co-wrote the *Left Behind* novels) announced the founding of the Moral Majority. The organization was designed be a "pro-family" political movement, declaring war on abortion and homosexuality, demanding the return of state sponsored prayer to public schools, and demanding the return of "traditional family values" to Washington.

In June of 1979, Falwell and his partner Elmer Towns flew to Murfreesboro to ask for John R. Rice's support for the founding of the Moral Majority and the expansion of Liberty University. The success of the Moral Majority, especially, would require activating every possible network of fundamentalist activists, donors, and supporters. For Falwell, the most valuable network available was the mailing list of *The Sword of the Lord*, which contained over 300,000 names of fundamentalist pastors, deacons, evangelists, and teachers.

Their pitch to Rice was a simple request that he turn over the mailing list for a massive evangelistic effort to double the size of Liberty University and to support the launching of the Moral Majority which Falwell had announced two months earlier. Rice's response was direct and immediate: "Of course we can help. Do you want the names today?"[212]

Falwell and Towns returned to Lynchburg carrying several metal canisters protecting spools of computer tape that contained *The Sword of the Lord* mailing list. By November of the 1980 presidential campaign, that initial list would expand to over two million names of supporters of the Moral Majority. Over 100,000 evangelical pastors, conservative rabbis, and Catholic priests would be members. The organization would claim to raise over $70 million to support its efforts on behalf of Republican presidential candidate Ronald Reagan, and would conduct church-based voter registration drives to mobilize 8.5 million new voters.[213]

In 1965, Bob Jones Jr. had said that Billy Graham "is doing more harm in the cause of Jesus Christ than any living man" by failing to condemn modernists and "leading foolish and untaught Christians, simple people that do not know the Word of God, into disobedience to the Word of God."

In 1980, Bob Jones Jr. called Jerry Falwell "the most dangerous man in America as far as Biblical Christianity is concerned."[214] Falwell's great sin was his political collaboration with nonfundamentalists— Catholics, Jews, evangelical and mainline Christian conservatives—in the Moral Majority. Ironically, the success of the Religious Right would rest on the capacity of fundamentalists such as Falwell and Rice to appreciate and celebrate diversity.

Chapter 26
Jesus Has Other Sheep

"And, behold, one of them which were with Jesus stretched out his hand, and drew his sword, and struck a servant of the high priest's, and smote off his ear. Then said Jesus unto him, Put up again thy sword into his place: for all they that take the sword shall perish with the sword."—Matthew 26:51-52

John R. Rice had continued working into his 80s for several hours almost every day, writing and publishing more books, continuing to edit *The Sword of the Lord*, traveling and speaking in conferences across the country. But he was moving with more care and deliberation, resting more and working less.

Rice's grandson and namesake, my brother John Himes, was speaking at churches around the U.S. as he prepared to go to Japan as a Baptist missionary, but he made sure to return to Murfreesboro, Tennessee as often as he could. John reported that our granddad developed a stock answer to the question, "How are you?" His full answer was, "Not bad for a man of my size, age, weight, disposition, doctrinal position and previous condition of servitude!" As conditions dictated, he varied his answer. When his doctor once asked him how he was, he answered, "Pretty good, for a man of my size, age, weight and disposition. Mother (his wife, Lloys Rice) says I can change my disposition!"

Regardless of his disposition, he suffered a minor heart attack, and then was slowed down by a second heart attack in April of 1980. John Himes was back for a visit to Murfreesboro when Rice was in the hospital. He found our granddad in good spirits, though clearly weary of being ill and putting up with all the discomforts and inconveniences of hospital care.

John reported:

> A day or two after he entered the hospital my mother
> and I went again to visit him. We had a good time of
> fellowship and talk. He mentioned the discomfort of
> needles in his arm from the heart monitor and one or two
> other things, then told us about the nurse who had come
> to take a blood sample. "I asked her if she wanted to
> earn a quarter," he said with a smile. "When she asked
> how, I told her to go stick that needle in the doctor
> instead of me!"
>
> One day a nurse slipped a thermometer into his mouth
> while he dozed. He woke, and with a hurt tone, said,
> "You're trying to put one over on me!" Once while the
> nurses fooled with an oxygen tube, trying to get it into
> his nose just right, he quipped, "I need my nose to hold
> my glasses on!"
>
> He was especially bothered by the restricted-liquid diet
> they put him on. One day he said to his physician, Dr.
> Garrison, "Someday you're going to find a cave full of
> old men, all dried up!" On another day, while I was
> reading the paper, he proclaimed solemnly, "Someone
> ought to write an article about how they don't let old
> men with heart attacks have the water they want."[215]

That April, John Himes saw a profound sense of peace in our
granddad. He was a man who had spent a full and rich time on this earth,
and he was consciously preparing himself for the end of his life, which
would come several months later. John stayed with him for many hours
in the hospital, reading to him, chatting, and listening to his reflections
and ruminations.

"At one point," said John:

> Granddad lay still for awhile, and then began to quote
> "Crossing the Bar," a poem about death by Tennyson,
> his favorite poet. He rose up and looked at me and said
> very distinctly. "Johnny, Tennyson said…" and then
> repeated what he could say of the poem:
>
> Sunset and evening star,

And one clear call for me!
And may there be no moaning of the bar,
When I put out to sea,

But such a tide as moving seems asleep,
Too full for sound and foam,
When that which drew from out the boundless deep
Turns again home.

Twilight and evening bell,
And after that the dark!
And may there be no sadness of farewell,
When I embark;

For tho' from out our bourne of Time and Place
The flood may bear me far,
I hope to see my Pilot face to face
When I have crossed the bar.

"After that effort," said John Himes:

He began to look off into space. Indeed, it was as if he really was hearing "one clear call" from Heaven. I'll ask him someday what his thoughts were then. A little later a nurse came in to give him medicine. He looked at her, and in great simplicity began to quote the first two stanzas from "Crossing the Bar."

Lying back in bed, he slept once more. Occasionally he awoke, once to sing softly, "Jesus, Jesus, Jesus: Sweetest name I know!" then lapse in silence. The head nurse came in once, and he asked her to sing. She confusedly said that she didn't know what to sing, so Granddad looked at me and said, "What do you think she should sing?" We talked it over, and I told the nurse that he had been singing about Heaven earlier, so, at her suggestion, we sang a duet of "Heaven came down and glory filled my soul!"[216]

In August of 1980, John R. Rice was nearing his 85th birthday when he preached for almost the last time to an audience of several hundred fundamentalist preachers at the National Sword of the Lord Conference in Atlanta, Georgia. Rice was frail and weak, able to walk and stand only with difficulty, and lacking the strength and stamina for speaking much longer than 20 minutes or so. He decided to offer some parting wisdom to the assembled preachers, encouraging them to act with compassion toward each other and others with whom they disagreed. He was wheeled to the pulpit and then stood with difficulty. He was distressed by the spirit of discord and division that had afflicted fundamentalism since his split a few years earlier with "ultra-fundamentalists" such as Bob Jones Jr.

The text he preached from was John 10:16: "Other sheep I have, which are not of this fold: them also I must bring, and they shall hear my voice; and there shall be one fold, and one shepherd."

Rice spoke in quiet, emotional tones, breaking into tears several times, his voice shaking as he clung to the podium:

> Jesus said, "I have other sheep!" The truth is there are a lot of other people who are God's people and they're my people too…What about all those others, the people you don't like very much? Do you love the people of God who don't see things like you do? How about Billy Graham? I love Billy Graham. I pray for him every day. About once a year at Christmastime I get a letter from him, and he says, "Brother Rice, you and I preach the same gospel, though we don't always agree on methods." Would you rather Billy Graham was on the Lord's side than not? There're some folks who criticize me, or they just don't like me very much. Well, the truth is that if they knew as much about me as I know there'd be more to criticize than there is…I'll say this: I'm a member of the family of God, and I'm a friend of everybody who's in the family of God. I read recently that Pope John XXIII wrote out a wonderful meditation, and he said, "Lord, I'm that prodigal son who said he wanted to come home from the hog farm to his father." He said, "Lord, I'm that publican in the temple who prayed, Lord, be merciful to me a sinner." And my heart went out to him and I said, "Amen!" When I get to Heaven I'm going to put my arm around him! Would you be glad to see someone saved who doesn't agree with you? Wouldn't it be good for all of this crowd to get to loving all God's people? In John chapter 13, Jesus

said, "A new commandment I give unto you, that ye love one another; as I have loved you, that ye also love one another. By this shall all men know that you are my disciples, if you have love one to another." Of course, Jesus meant you and your little buddy, didn't he? No he didn't! He meant the rest of 'em too. If you're going to love like a Christian, you've got to love everybody Jesus loves. You know, when I get to Heaven, I'd sure hate to be so I couldn't say howdy with anybody who's also in Heaven. The scripture says love everybody, and I'm gonna do it.[217]

Rice had planned at the end of his sermon to ask his audience to join in singing "The Family of God," a song well loved by many evangelicals. Written by Bill Gaither, the lyrics were about loving all of God's children: "I'm so glad I'm a part of the family, the family of God…" He'd had some cards printed up with the words of the song, and a pledge he wanted all those present to sign, promising to love everyone Jesus had loved.

Unfortunately, the meeting was under the control of Curtis Hutson, the man Rice had chosen to succeed him as editor of *The Sword of the Lord*. Hutson was more extreme and "separatist" in his beliefs than Rice, and he was afraid some of the fundamentalists present would conclude that John R. Rice had gotten weak in both his mind and his separatism. Hutson collected the cards and forbade anyone to pass them out.

Later, Rice sat in his wheelchair with three of his daughters and wept with disappointment and sadness. He felt that his last public effort to leave a legacy of compassion to guide the movement he had helped to create had been defeated by Hutson's refusal.[*] A spirit of discord, disdain, and disapproval that fundamentalists had incubated against liberals and modernists, in the end, and particularly on that day, boomeranged to poison the relationships among fundamentalist allies.[†]

---

[*] I heard this story from my aunt Libby Handford, a daughter of John R. Rice who was with him that day.

[†] Rice's words in 1980 echoed Billy Graham's words in 1960, in the wake of John R. Rice's split with Graham over the evangelists' supposed cooperation with modernists. Graham admitted that his concept of the church had become less narrow: "During the past 10 years my concept of the church has taken on greater dimension. 10 years ago my concept of the church tended to be narrow and provincial, but after a decade of intimate contact with Christians the world over I am now aware that the family of God contains people of various

In December of 1980, John R. Rice wrote his last letter to be sent out to family members along with his thousands of friends at Christmas:

> I still, from my arm chair, "preach" in great revival campaigns. I still envision hundreds walking the aisles to accept Christ. I still feel hot tears for the lost. I still see God working miracles. Oh, how I long to see great revivals, to hear about revival crowds once again! Talking about revival in a Christmas letter to friends? It would be no Christmas to me without the sense of the breath of God upon me still, weak and frail as I am. I want no Christmas without a burden for lost souls, a message for sinners, a heart to bring in the lost sheep so dear to the Shepherd, the sinning souls for whom Christ died. I will have the comfort and company of my faithful wife, my sweet girls' arms around my neck, grandchildren to be proud of and to hear tell of their plans for God's service; I will give and receive presents and surprises, and carols will be heard the day long, along with feasting and fellowship with family and workers. All this will be sweet, of course. But may food be tasteless, and music a discord, and Christmas a farce if I forget the dying millions to whom I am debtor; if this fire in my bones does not still flame! Not till I die, or not till Jesus comes, will I ever be eased of this burden, these tears, this toil to save souls.[218]

John R. Rice died in Murfreesboro, Tennessee on December 29, 1980. At his funeral four days later, I made the first notes that led, three decades later, to the writing of this book.

---

ethnological, cultural, class and denominational differences." (Billy Graham, "What 10 Years Have Taught Me," The Christian Century, Feb. 17, 1960)

Part V
Revisiting the Fundamentals

Chapter 27
Reframing Fundamentalism

My apostasy from faith in the communist revolution emerged full-blown when I was 30, in the spring of 1980, though it had been incubating for a few years. It was truly a loss of faith, and my Maoist religion had been accompanied by parallels to many of the practices or embellishments of the little Baptist churches where I had grown up. My Maoist scriptures had been the works of Marx, Lenin, and Mao Zedong rather than the Bible. My weekly tabloid newspaper of choice had been the *Revolutionary Worker* rather than *The Sword of the Lord*. My church was any place where two or three proletarian revolutionaries were gathered in the name of overthrowing the bourgeoisie.

I had left my fundamentalist God behind at the age of 17, because I simply couldn't recognize that image as God anymore—an elderly white male God who lived in a golden city beyond the sky, who apparently liked white people better than black people, who ordered women to be subservient to men, who supported the war aims of the United States in Vietnam, who created us in his image but then consigned the vast majority of humanity to suffer the torments of the damned forever in a literal lake of fire.

In the end, I left Maoism because its secular version of God was no more meaningful to me. My Marxist scriptures were fairly successful at explaining world history in the 19th century and before, but they had failed to predict or explain the disasters of the 20th, and had been used to justify a series of horrific crimes against humanity, from Stalin's carefully planned starvation of millions of Russian peasants to the killing fields of Cambodia. Finally, I was beginning to recognize that I had traded in one form of fundamentalism for another, equally rigid, dogmatic, and wrongheaded.

My first response was to register to compete in a motorcycle race, with no preparation or racing experience—which turned out to be a neatly disguised and nearly successful attempt to kill myself. In July of 1980, as my granddad entered his own final decline toward death, I showed up at the starting line of a dirt bike race known as a "hare scramble" in the Georgia woods twenty miles north of Marietta. I was mounted on a monster green Kawasaki four-stroke 250cc enduro bike and dressed in leathers, boots, helmet, and a plastic chest protector, none of which did me any good. Just 30 yards from the starting line, I lost control going down a steep hill and stopped a tree with my chest at about 45 miles per hour.

Several men dragged me up the hill and laid me out to recover in a plastic and aluminum lounge chair. I was covered with mud and blood, gasping for air, and in much pain, but when various bystanders asked me how I was doing, like a good Baptist boy I said, "Oh, don't worry about me, I'll just rest for a bit and I'll be fine." After a while, I noticed the pain was increasing geometrically, and my abdomen was swelling, so I asked someone if they could please find me a doctor. As I lay on a table at a nearby rural clinic, fighting to retain consciousness and enduring more pain than I imagined possible, I had a sudden sensation of bonds being loosed, of the pain letting go. I felt euphoric and lighthearted, happier than I could remember being for years. I noted two nurses fluttering around me like doves, and heard one of them say, "We've got no pulse! He's not breathing anymore!" Then I was floating blissfully near the ceiling, looking down on the three of us, my own body stretched out, still smeared with mud and blood, my eyes open, staring at nothing.

Shortly, the nurse said, "Ok, we've got plasma going in," and I rushed back to my body, to the overwhelming pain and to a feeling of extreme disappointment. An ambulance carried me through a rain-drenched night to the hospital in Marietta, where a surgeon took me apart to discover I had no spleen left and was bleeding to death internally.

I woke up the next morning to the sun streaming in the hospital window, and a feeling of utter exhilaration. I had literally died and been born again. I had seen something like a heaven, and felt the presence of something like God.

By the time my granddad died six months later, I had begun a new journey to discover or define whatever it was I had glimpsed in that clinic as I lay dying, and what it all meant. Thirty years later, I am still working on the problem, but I think I've made a little progress in defining the question that matters. Here are some versions of that question: What is at the core of your life? What is it that guides all your thoughts and actions? What do you truly trust in? What is the ground of your being?

These are all forms of the same question: What is fundamental to you?

It's a pretty good question, after all, the sort of question you ask when confronted with the ultimate existential conundrum. We would do well to ask that question of ourselves fairly often. Most of us know how to ask how our pocketbooks are doing, or what kind of hair day we are having, or how our careers are progressing, or what our children or parents, partners or friends want from us, or how we are going to pay the bills, or what we are going to have for dinner. But we find it easy to ignore the fundamental question.

A century ago, in some sense the original Christian fundamentalists were asking a fundamental question. The core impulse that gave rise to fundamentalism was a healthy one: rediscover and cherish the essence of Christianity. In 1909, A. C. Dixon and R. A. Torrey and their fellow writers, in a series of booklets titled *The Fundamentals: A Testimony of Truth*, sought to minimize harsh rhetoric, bitter infighting, and bad feelings within the Christian community by focusing attention on what they called several fundamentals of the faith, five of which were recognized as crucial by fundamentalists: the virgin birth, the inerrancy and divine inspiration of the Bible, the need of sinners for atonement, Jesus's death and resurrection, and the miracles attributed to Christ (some conservatives listed instead the imminent second coming of Jesus).

Notably, the fundamentalists chose those five doctrines to emphasize because evangelical conservatives were embroiled in a bitter doctrinal dispute with evangelical liberals and modernists—not because for them those five doctrines constituted the only or even necessarily the most important Christian doctrines. For example, arguably, a fundamental doctrine, for any Christian, would be the doctrine of the Trinity, which has been at the core of Christian teachings for 17 centuries. And another fundamental doctrine would have to be the doctrine of salvation through faith by grace, first proclaimed by Martin Luther to be the very heart of the Protestant Reformation. Strikingly, the five "fundamentals" include no reference to the actual ministry of Jesus on earth; nothing about Jesus feeding the hungry or healing the sick; nothing about Jesus love for the poor, the meek, and the outcast; nothing about his declaration that peacemakers will be called the "children of God;" or his opposition to the political and religious rulers of his time.

Asking the fundamental question, however, requires something other than listing a set of doctrines, placing a check mark next to each one we claim to believe in, and then moving on with our lives, confident that we've taken care of our "salvation." As the second chapter of James says, "Thou believest that there is one God; thou doest well: the devils also believe, and tremble."

It is helpful to remember that the concept of belief has evolved considerably since Jesus's day. Since the beginning of the scientific revolution in the 17th century, *belief* has come more and more to mean "intellectual assent or agreement." American Christian fundamentalists were trying to list the doctrines they believed all Christians ought to agree with. However, the original Greek word in the New Testament was *pistis*, which meant "faith," or trust, loyalty, and commitment. When Jesus was asking his followers for *pistis*, he meant they should engage with the mission he proclaimed on earth, which included loving God and treating their neighbors as themselves, giving to the poor, feeding the hungry, leading compassionate lives, and seeking justice—in short, creating the beloved community on Earth that reflected God's presence. Well-known author Karen Armstrong has noted:

> When the New Testament was translated from Greek into Latin by Saint Jerome (c.342-420) *pistis* became fides ("loyalty"). Fides had no verbal form, so for *pisteuo* Jerome used the Latin verb *credo*, a word that derived from *cor do*, "I give my heart." He did not think of using *opinor* ("I hold an opinion.") When the Bible was translated into English, *credo* and *pisteuo* became "I believe" in the King James version (1611). But the word "belief" has since changed its meaning. In Middle English, *bileven* meant "to praise; to value; to hold dear." It was related to the German *belieben* ("to love"), *liebe* ("beloved"), and the Latin *libido*. So "belief" originally meant "loyalty to a person to whom one is bound in promise or duty."...During the late seventeenth century, however, as our concept of knowledge became more theoretical, the word "belief" started to be used to describe an intellectual assent to a hypothetical—and often dubious—proposition. Scientists and philosophers were the first to use it in this sense, but in religious contexts the Latin *credere* and the English "belief" both retained their original connotations well into the 19th century.[219]

The older and traditional meaning of belief was connected in the Bible with the Hebrew word *miqra*, which meant a holy calling or convocation. Belief was about what or who you trusted. Belief was the program of action you followed, the practice, rituals, and readings that characterized your faith. So the answer to a truly fundamental question has to go much deeper than a list of "beliefs."

For me, the death of my grandmother Lloys Cooke Rice in 1989 was a profound shock propelling me to deeply consider the fundamental question. Gram, as I called her, had a perpetually joyful spirit. She greeted everyone she met with compassion and cheerful affection. Through all my years of difficult struggle with my family, she displayed nothing but acceptance and uncritical regard for me. She was a key reason I returned to Murfreesboro, Tennessee every Christmas season of my life no matter where I lived or what I was up to. Over 1,000 people showed up at Gram's funeral, and I am convinced that every one of them sincerely believed she was the best friend they had.

When I got on the plane to fly back to Seattle after the service, I began to cry, and I cried all the way home. The stewards and my fellow passengers kept looking at me with concern and offering me tissues, and they must have been convinced I was going through a mental breakdown or profound existential crisis. When I got home I continued to cry for days, huge wracking sobs that struck me at the most embarrassing moments—while sitting in meetings, ordering coffee, or buying groceries.

When I finally calmed down and was able to reflect, I realized that my Gram was the only person in my life who had truly loved me unconditionally. She was the only one who had never condemned me, never argued with me, never judged me. She was the only person who offered me absolute and boundless love no matter how stupid, arrogant, dogmatic, or contemptuous I was, no matter how ridiculous my haircuts got or how far I strayed from other people's ideas of proper comportment and deportment. Perhaps the harshest criticism she offered was to tell me I really ought to shine my shoes more often because *other* people would judge me too quickly and unfairly.

I began to wonder, What would my life be like if I started trying to show other people the same unconditional love my Gram showed me? What if I acted that way toward my family members, my daughter, my friends? What if I acted that way toward fellow employees, toward neighbors, toward total strangers?

I began a series of experiments to transform my relationships with everybody in my life. The idea of God was way too big for me to consider at the time, so I set out to embody Gram's love in my life.

Quite frankly, I still find this an incredibly hard thing to do. I found that my feelings and behavior often don't match up. For example, I didn't like or love either of my parents very much after struggling with them for a quarter century. I am sure they thought I was a pretty big jerk in addition to being a world-class prodigal son. However, they were getting old themselves and soon needed a lot of help from me. Figuring out how I could treat them as if I loved them, with all the respect and affection they were due, was a hard struggle. Eventually, I began to feel that maybe I did love them after all, a little bit, and my emotions began to conform to my actions.

In its simplest and most elemental form, the energy that drove the development of fundamentalism was at the heart of the teachings of Jesus of Nazareth. A scribe asked Jesus the fundamental question: "What commandment is the foremost of all?" His response was: "The foremost is, 'Hear, O Israel! The Lord our God is one Lord; and you shall love the Lord your God with all your heart, and with all your soul, and with all your mind, and with all your strength.' The second is this, 'You shall love your neighbor as yourself.' There is no other commandment greater than these."

Jesus's words, read carefully and in context, make it clear that the test of whether I am following these two commandments is not whether I am experiencing the proper emotions, not whether I feel good about my neighbor, or like my neighbor, or even know my neighbor. The true test is whether I allow the spirit of God to transform me and to transform how I act toward my neighbor.

How can that impulse to ask the fundamental question help to generate a profoundly healthy response to the challenges facing America and the world in the 21st century? Globalization has forced us to confront an extraordinarily diverse world that is undergoing massive change at a pace unimaginable to our parents or grandparents. The very ground on which the structure of 20th-century fundamentalist theology and politics was built has crumbled into sand. The reason for which modern fundamentalism was created—in opposition to modernism and liberal theology—has been swept away in the avalanche of new ideas, in new dialogue between different faith traditions.

By the early 21st century, the most profound consequence of globalization and the culture of the Internet has been an expansion of our understanding of who our neighbors are. Ideas and influences can travel around the world and touch the lives of millions within seconds. Your closest "neighbor" might be male or female, young or old, gay or straight, living 3,000 or 10,000 miles away, Christian, Muslim, Jewish, Buddhist, Hindu, agnostic or not, spiritual but not religious, literate or not, mountain-dweller or plains-dweller, rural or urban or suburban. At

ne, you may have never met or spoken to the people who live
right next door to yours on a quiet street in your hometown.

Your neighbor might be a young man from Saudi Arabia who
decides one day to strap on a bomb and blow himself up on an airliner,
or a Dutch newspaper editor who decides to publish a cartoon offensive
to Muslims, or a man named Madoff who built a pyramid scheme to
defraud investors of over $18 billion, or a 13-year-old girl rescued from
the rubble of a Port au Prince building nine days after the 2010
earthquake in Haiti. Your neighbor might be a friend on Facebook, or
someone you follow and who follows you on Twitter, or someone you
met when she commented on your blog, or someone living in Florida
from whom you purchased a flowerpot on eBay.

What does it mean to "love your neighbor?" Jesus recounted a
startling parable about a Jewish man traveling from Jerusalem to Jericho
who was beaten and robbed of his clothes and money by bandits and left
to die by the side of the road. Seeing him, respectable travelers who were
part of the religious establishment passed him by and went on their way.
But a Samaritan stopped and had pity on the man. Samaritans were
despised by the Jewish establishment of that day, viewed as enemies,
ceremonially unclean, socially outcast, heretical in their beliefs. Yet the
Samaritan stopped, bound up the man's wounds, took him to a nearby
inn, and nursed him through the night to make sure he could recover.
This Samaritan, said Jesus, was the one who truly displayed the love of
God.

Accordingly, the test of "loving your neighbor" is showing
compassion for someone you might naturally be inclined to hate or fear
or despise—not someone who is your natural ally or blood kin or fellow
citizen. A fundamentalist Christianity worthy of the name will be a
fundamentalism that pours out the love of God for all humanity, without
judging or despising or holding back in the slightest. It will be a faith
that seeks to transform the world in the image of a God of love who
cares for the poor and the outcast, the disregarded and the deranged, the
sick, the hungry, and the desperate. Fundamentalism that recalls the
unearned grace proclaimed by Jesus will be open-hearted, generous,
kind, and hopeful, and will seek the Kindom (a term I use consciously,
not a typo) of God on earth.

In 1986, Bob Jones University Press published *In Pursuit of Purity:
American Fundamentalism Since 1850* by David O. Beale, a BJU
professor. In the first sentence of the first chapter, Beale defines his term:
"Ideally, a Christian Fundamentalist is one who desires to reach out in
love and compassion to people, believes and defends the whole Bible as

the absolute, inerrant, and authoritative Word of God, and stands committed to the doctrine and practice of holiness."[220]

I don't question Beale's sincerity or his desire to have people believe that fundamentalism is all about love and compassion, and his words are eloquent. My own definition of fundamentalism was set by my grandfather, who was genuinely motivated by his compassion for lost souls and a desire to help doomed sinners avoid spending eternity in the lake of fire. Beale's book provides a number of positive examples of leading fundamentalists who he said exemplified love and compassion, including Texas Baptist preacher J. Frank Norris. Beale mentions that Norris's nickname was the "Texas Tornado," but fails to note that the nickname referred to his vicious attacks on Catholics, Jews, and blacks, as well as many other Protestants with whom he had theological or doctrinal disagreements. Any of the targets of his vitriol would have had a hard time assessing Norris as a man of compassion or love.

Unfortunately for David Beale, the historical record over the past century is that fundamentalism is complicated. On the one hand, a core motivation of fundamentalists has been a love for God and a desire to keep lost sinners out of what they believed to be a fiery hell. Fundamentalists have cared deeply about finding and proclaiming the heart of Jesus' message of love and redemption. On the other hand, fundamentalism has been bound up with self-righteousness and contempt for others. Some fundamentalists have used their religion to justify slavery, defend racial injustice, promote intolerance, enforce the subjugation of women, deny human rights to gays and lesbians, and force their views on others. "Holiness," in the history of Bob Jones University where Beale teaches, has historically meant racial segregation and stalwart defense of myriad racial injustices, has meant dismissive revulsion against people of other faiths, has meant contempt for the poor and for efforts to end poverty and hunger. It is difficult to see how the "holiness" claimed by Bob Jones University in the past was related to the holiness espoused by Jesus.

By the late 20th century, however, it was evident that the Christian universe had entered a period of crisis and profound reconfiguration as deep and transformative as any in the 2,000-year history of the church. Charismatics and Catholics, evangelical and mainline Protestants, pastors and priests, laymen and laywomen, living room assemblies and megachurch congregations, theologians, philosophers, preachers and poets have all been drawn into a web of thoughtful reconsideration of what it means to be a Christian in a globalized, postmodern world. Some Christians have even seen this shift as a self-conscious movement, and have thought of themselves as part of an "emergent church," thus institutionalizing the language of change.

Fundamentalists have not been immune from this trend. In the 21st century, it's almost impossible for people in the South or anywhere else to maintain ideas about race, religion, or politics that we inherited without questioning in the 19th or 20th centuries. The Southern Baptist Convention, for example, was firmly in the hands of fundamentalists in 1995 when it finally acknowledged that:

> Our relationship to African-Americans has been hindered from the beginning by the role that slavery played in the formation of the Southern Baptist Convention; and many of our Southern Baptist forbears defended the right to own slaves, and either participated in, supported, or acquiesced in the particularly inhumane nature of American slavery; in later years Southern Baptists failed, in many cases, to support, and in some cases opposed, legitimate initiatives to secure the civil rights of African-Americans. Racism has led to discrimination, oppression, injustice, and violence, both in the Civil War and throughout the history of our nation.[221]

Likewise, Bob Jones University, long known as the last major Southern educational institution holding onto the old Southern tradition of racial segregation, at last apologized in 2008 for its past defense of racist policies and attitudes:

> For almost two centuries American Christianity, including BJU in its early stages, was characterized by the segregationist ethos of American culture…we failed to accurately represent the Lord and to fulfill the commandment to love others as ourselves. Though no known antagonism toward minorities or expressions of racism on a personal level have ever been tolerated on our campus, we allowed institutional policies to remain in place that were racially hurtful.[222]

Clearly, change is in the air, and younger generations of fundamentalists and evangelicals are considering how their Christian practice might be a truer and more radical reflection of their Christian faith. At stake is the very definition of a Christianity driven more by praxis than by doctrine, more inspired by the life and spirit of Jesus than by arcane doctrinal disputes.

In *Almost Christian*, Kenda Creasy Dean discusses the conclusions of the National Study of Youth and Religion (NSYR), a massive survey conducted in 2003—2005 on how young people understand and express their religious faith. The core finding of the study was that although 75 percent of all young people call themselves Christian, and about half say religion is important in their lives, the vast majority are "incredibly inarticulate about their faith, their religious beliefs and practices, and its meaning or place in their lives." When the survey asked for details, many of the young people backed away from the conversation or described views that their own churches viewed as heretical.

Most young people, said Dean "worship at the church of benign whateverism." They largely mirror their parents' religion, guided by a vague and inoffensive set of doctrines that could be summed up as "Moralistic Therapeutic Deism," a religion that has a superficial resemblance to Christianity but shares none of the radical and transformative properties of a faith that matters. As Moralistic Therapeutic Deists, young people believe that: a god exists who created and orders the world and watches over life on Earth; God wants people to be good, nice, and fair to each other; the central goal of life is to be happy and to feel good about oneself; God is not involved in their lives except when they need God to resolve a problem; and good people go to Heaven when they die. [223]

Such a faith has a kind of social utility, because it encourages young people to go along in order to get along with their peers, thus reducing social friction. But it's a faith that means very little, a faith we can quickly discard as soon as it makes anyone else uncomfortable. It's a faith based on liking other people and wanting other people to like us. But it's a faith that has little in common with the radical and unconditional love taught by Jesus.

I wonder if Moralistic Therapeutic Deism has become so entrenched, displacing Christianity, because we no longer have a vision of God that works for us. For many, God seems to have retreated from a postmodern world. As a child, the image of God I developed was a reflection of my times, my place, my community, and my culture—male, white, Baptist, Republican, and American—and looked a lot like my granddad. When I decided I couldn't believe in that God anymore, I adopted a replacement god who looked and talked a lot like Karl Marx or Mao Zedong. Both of my original images of god shared some characteristics with the Big Giant Head on the 90s television show *Third Rock from the Sun*. The Big Giant Head, played by William Shatner, was the ultimate patriarchal dictator, an angry, performance-based deity issuing edicts and commandments from time to time, most of which were ignored by his alien underlings on Earth.

The problem with the Big Giant Head notion of God is that it is an idol, constructed by us humans from our need to have a God that is a distorted image of ourselves. God becomes a tool we use to help us feel good about ourselves and to judge people who are not like us. This is how we can claim that God loves America more than other nations, or that God wants this or that politician to be defeated in the next election, or that God is on my side in this war and not on yours.

God, however, is an ineffable mystery, beyond human comprehension. Paul emphasized in Acts 17 that God for all of us is the "Unknowable God," neither male nor female, neither Jew nor Gentile, neither a member of our religion or someone else's, neither straight nor gay, not simply another being, no matter how powerful. Rather, God is the ground of all being. As Paul said: "For in him we live, and move, and have our being; as certain also of your own poets have said, for we are also his offspring. Forasmuch then as we are the offspring of God, we ought not to think that the Godhead is like unto gold, or silver, or stone, graven by art and man's device."

I have a friend named John who grew up on an island off the coast of Florida. His metaphor for God, beautifully expressed, is an ocean. We are the fish in the ocean, he says, living and dancing in and below the waves, drinking and breathing God. The currents in the ocean are the Holy Spirit, moving us here and there through our watery universe, teaching us to swim, training us to lift a fin here and twitch our tails there, waking us up to love for each other, living within God and discovering God within ourselves.

Chapter 28
My Post-fundamentalist Family

In the spring of 2009 I conducted an Appreciative Inquiry of my fundamentalist family. I went back to Chattanooga, Tennessee with my daughter, Amber, for a special visit. Chattanooga is where lots of my relatives live—my mom and her four surviving sisters (all of whom were born in Texas) and their husbands (all of whom they met while attending Wheaton College). These Rice family elders all spent a lifetime in Christian service—pastors, evangelists, teachers, musicians, parents, writers, counselors, and speakers, all grew to maturity within the fundamentalist world, and all are now retired and in their 70s or 80s.

The "unconditional positive questions" I asked them all, in hours of conversation, were: "Over your lifetime as a Christian, how has your capacity for compassion expanded? How has your appreciation grown for other points of view? What have you learned about the philosophy of love taught by Jesus?"

They all told me how they had grown less judgmental over time, less certain of their own perfect understanding and better able to hear the voices of others. They told me how they had come to appreciate diversity both among Christians and beyond their Christian community. They related how their ideas about race, politics, religion and culture had evolved over time, how they had come to love people whom previously they had dismissed or of whom they had disapproved. They told me how they had become more able to open their hearts to others, more humble as they tried to be followers of Jesus, more capable of expressing unconditional love for others.

My aunts and uncles generally haven't shifted their beliefs in the essential doctrines that defined the fundamentalist movement—inerrant Scripture, the virgin birth, the curse of sin and need for blood atonement, the resurrection, and the second coming—however, when I asked my aunts and uncles whether they still considered themselves

ˈs," I was surprised when they all said "No, of course
ked why, one of my aunts said, "You know, those people
be 'fundamentalist' nowadays wouldn't want to be
___ with us, either! They're what Daddy (John R. Rice) would
have called, 'ultra-fundamentalists,' arrogant and self-righteous, very
sure of themselves." A key part of their response, then, was that the term
"fundamentalist" had been damaged by some people who used it to
describe themselves, yet who displayed a lack of Christian love for
others.

The term fundamentalist has been highly charged by its history;
slapping labels on people based on their beliefs is a poor way to begin a
dialogue and seldom leads to any agreement or wise insights. I have
found that generalizations don't help me understand anyone better, and
often stand in the way of my learning. Many fundamentalists I know are
gentle and humble people who are beautiful models of Christ-like
behavior—including especially my own brother John, a fundamentalist
missionary to Japan who is one of the sweetest and kindest people I
know.

But I suppose that "ultra-fundamentalist" attitude is what John R.
Rice was struggling against when he preached on "Jesus's Other Sheep"
a few months before his death, and when he emotionally echoed the
words of Billy Graham two decades earlier. In some sense, I believe, my
grandfather had evolved by the last few months of his life to the point
where he might be considered a "post-fundamentalist," or at least quite a
different type of fundamentalist than how he began. At the very end of
his life, John R. Rice focused on what Jesus said were the true
fundamentals of faith: loving God and loving your neighbor as yourself.

Here, then, can be found the essence of Christianity. Loving God is
first of all about transforming yourself, internally, so that you can honor
the living presence of God both within yourself and manifested in the
world beyond you. Loving your neighbor is first of all about
transforming the world around you through building a loving
relationship with all living things and with the earth itself.

Jesus viewed his own ministry on earth as a call to radical
compassion. As he said in the Gospel of Luke, "The Spirit of the Lord is
upon me, because he hath anointed me to preach the gospel to the poor;
he hath sent me to heal the brokenhearted, to preach deliverance to the
captives, and recovering of sight to the blind, to set at liberty them that
are bruised, to preach the acceptable year of the Lord." Following Jesus
evidently requires much more than orthodoxy or platitudes about love. It
requires orthopraxy: placing Christ's incarnation of love and justice at
the center of your life and Christian practice.

John Wesley, the most eloquent, prolific and influential evangelist of the Great Awakening in 18th-century England, elaborated on the second commandment in a sermon titled "The Way to the Kingdom." He said:

> *Thou shalt love*—thou shalt embrace with the most tender goodwill, the most earnest and cordial affection, the most inflamed desires of preventing or removing all evil, and of procuring for him every possible good—*thy neighbor*—that is, not only thy friend, thy kinsman, or thy acquaintance; not only the virtuous, the friendly, him that loves thee, that prevents or returns thy kindness; but every child of man, every human creature, every soul which God hath made, not excepting him whom thou hast never seen in the flesh, whom thou knowest not, either by face or name; not excepting him whom thou knowest to be evil and unthankful, him that still despitefully uses and persecutes thee: Him thou shalt love *as thyself*, with the same invariable thirst after his happiness in every kind; the same unwearied care to screen him from whatever might grieve or hurt either his soul or body.[224]

In the spirit of appreciative inquiry, here is what I have learned from my post-fundamentalist family: Honor truth. Love well. Live your faith. As Jesus said in Luke 12, "Seek ye the kingdom of God, and all these things shall be added unto you."[225]

Glossary

Note: Except where otherwise noted, glossary definitions are from *Theopedia: An Encyclopedia of Biblical Christianity*, and are under the Creative Commons Attribution 3.0 Unported license. More information on this license is available at http://creativecommons.org/licenses/by/3.0/.

amillennialism. The view in Christian eschatology which states that Christ is presently reigning through the church, and that the "1,000 years" of Revelation 20:1-6 is a metaphorical reference to the present church age, which will culminate in Christ's return. It stands in contrast to premillennialism, which states that Christ will return prior to a literal 1,000-year earthly reign; and postmillennialism, which states that Christ's return will follow a 1,000-year golden age ushered in by the church.

Arminian. A school of theology based on the teachings of Dutch theologian Jacob Arminius, for whom it is named. It is perhaps most prominent in the Methodist movement and found in various other evangelical circles today. It stands in contrast to Calvinism, with which it has a long history of debate. Arminians as well as Calvinists appeal to various Scriptures and the early church fathers to support their respective views; however the differences remain—particularly as related to the sovereignty of God in salvation and the ideas of election and predestination.

Baptist. A term referring to churches and denominations within Protestant Christianity that emphasize a believer's baptism by full immersion, which is performed after a profession of faith in Christ as Lord and Savior. A congregational governance system gives autonomy to individual local Baptist churches. Groups of Baptist churches are sometimes associated in organizations for purposes of missions and other common goals while retaining their local autonomy. Notable Baptist organizations include: Southern Baptist Convention, General Association of Regular Baptist Churches, and American Baptist Association.

Calvinism. The theological system associated with the reformer John Calvin that emphasizes the rule of God over all things as reflected in its understanding of Scripture, God, humanity, salvation, and the church. In popular vernacular, Calvinism often refers to the Five Points of Calvinistic doctrine regarding salvation, which make up the acrostic TULIP: Total depravity, Unconditional election, Limited atonement, Irresistible grace, Perseverance of the saints. In its broader sense, Calvinism is associated with Reformed theology (and with the belief that souls are predestined to go to Heaven or Hell).

deism. The belief that God has created the universe but remains apart from it and permits his creation to administer itself through natural laws. Deism thus rejects the supernatural aspects of religion, such as belief in revelation in the Bible, and stresses the importance of ethical conduct. In the 18th century, numerous important thinkers held deist beliefs. (*The American Heritage® New Dictionary of Cultural Literacy,* 3rd ed., Houghton Mifflin Company, 2005.)

dispensationalism. A theological system that teaches biblical history is best understood in light of a number of successive administrations of God's dealings with mankind, which it calls "dispensations." It maintains fundamental distinctions between God's plans for national Israel and for the New Testament Church, and emphasizes prophecy of the end times and a pre-tribulation rapture of the church prior to Christ's Second Coming. Its beginnings are usually associated with the Plymouth Brethren movement in the U. K. and the teachings of John Nelson Darby.

ecumenicalism. A movement or effort promoting unity among Christian churches or denominations. In a more general sense, it may also refer to movements promoting worldwide unity among the various religions through greater cooperation and improved understanding. The idea is normally expressed in its adjective form, ecumenical, in terms such as "ecumenical thinking," "ecumenical activities," or "the ecumenical movement."

Enlightenment. Generally refers to the 18th century intellectual and philosophical developments in Europe. The Enlightenment movement advocated rationality as the sole criteria for establishing an authoritative system of ethics, aesthetics, and knowledge. The intellectual leaders of this movement regarded themselves as courageous and elite, and viewed their purpose as leading the world towards progress and out of a long period of doubtful tradition, full of irrationality, superstition, and tyranny (which they saw resulting from the "Dark Ages").

eschatology. The study or discussion of the "end times," a popular term used when referring to various interpretations of the Book of Revelation and other prophetic parts of the Bible, such as the Book of Daniel and various sayings of Jesus in the Gospels concerning the timing of Christ's Second Coming and the establishment of his kingdom. There are various views concerning the order of events leading up to and following the return of Jesus and the significance of these events.

Evangelical, evangelicalism. Evangelicalism is a wide-reaching definitional "canopy" that covers a diverse number of Protestant groups. The term originates in the Greek word *evangelion*, meaning "the good news," or, more commonly, the gospel. During the Reformation, Martin Luther adapted the term, dubbing his breakaway movement the *evangelische kirke*, or "evangelical church"—a name still generally applied to the Lutheran Church in Germany. In the English-speaking world, however, the modern usage usually connotes the religious movements and denominations which sprung forth from a series of revivals that swept the North Atlantic Anglo-American world in the 18th and early 19th centuries. (From *The Institute for the Study of American Evangelicals.*)

fundamentalism. Christian fundamentalism refers to the movement that arose mainly within American and British Protestantism in the late 19th and early 20th centuries, led by conservative evangelical Christians in reaction to modernism and liberalism in the mainline denominations. This movement included not only denominational evangelicals (such as the Princeton theologian J. Gresham Machen), but a growing breed of premillennial and dispensational independents such as D. L. Moody, R. A. Torrey, and the independent Bible college and Bible church movement. Taking its name from *The Fundamentals* (1910-1915), a 12-volume set of essays designed to combat liberal theology, the movement grew by leaps and bounds after World War I. The term "fundamentalist" was perhaps first used by Curtis Lee Laws, a British journalist for the *Watchman-Examiner*, in 1920 to designate those who were willing to do "battle royal for the fundamentals."

inerrancy. The view that when all the facts become known, they will demonstrate that the Bible in its original autographs and correctly interpreted is entirely true and never false in all it affirms, whether that relates to doctrines or ethics or to the social, physical, or life sciences. (P. D. Feinberg, "Bible, Inerrancy and Infallibility of," *Evangelical Dictionary of Theology,* 2nd ed. Walter A. Elwell, ed. [Baker Academic, 2001], 156).

liberalism. Theological liberalism, sometimes known as Protestant Liberalism, is a theological movement rooted in the early 19th-century German Enlightenment, notably in the philosophy of Immanuel Kant and the religious views of Friedrich Schleiermacher. It is an attempt to incorporate modern thinking and developments, especially in the sciences, into the Christian faith. Liberalism tends to emphasize ethics over doctrine and experience over Scriptural authority. While essentially a 19th century movement, theological liberalism came to dominate the American mainline churches in the early 20th century. Liberal Christian scholars embraced and encouraged the higher biblical criticism of modern Biblical scholarship. Protestant liberal thought in its most traditional incarnations emphasized the universal Fatherhood of God, the brotherhood of man, the infinite value of the human soul, the example of Jesus, and the establishment of the moral-ethical Kingdom of God on Earth. It has often been relativistic, pluralistic, and nondoctrinal.

mainline churches. A term used to describe the main traditional Protestant denominations in the U. S. as differentiated from and on the theological left of evangelicalism. These denominations are viewed as having adopted more liberal theologies and open stances to new ideas and societal changes while maintaining traditional practices regarding their public gathering and church polity. They tend to be influenced by higher Biblical criticism, increasingly open to the ordination of women, and less dogmatic regarding issues such as homosexuality and abortion. In general, mainline churches are less focused on doctrine.

Methodist. A Christian movement founded by John Wesley in 18th century Britain. Largely (but not exclusively) Arminian, it exists all over the world today. The United Methodist Church, the largest Methodist denomination, is the third largest denomination in the United States (after the Roman Catholics and Southern Baptists).

modernism. The worldview ushered in by the Enlightenment. The Enlightenment provided a new guardian of truth to replace the church—science. Modernism therefore proffered the idea that mankind, armed with rationalism and science, is able to access absolute truth and make unlimited progress toward a better life for itself. Therefore, at its core, modernism is a celebration of human autonomy.

postmillennialism. Teaches that the millennium is an era (not necessarily a literal 1,000 years) during which Christ will reign over the Earth, not from a literal and earthly throne, but through the gradual increase of the Gospel and its power to change lives. After this gradual Christianization of the world, Christ will return and immediately usher the church faithful into their eternal state after judging the wicked. This is called postmillennialism because, by its view, Christ will return after the millennium. (*The Blue Letter Bible*, http://www. blueletterbible.org/, accessed November 27, 2010).

premillennialism. Teaches that the Second Coming will occur before a literal 1,000-year reign of Christ from Jerusalem upon the Earth. In the early church, premillennialism was called *chiliasm*, from the Greek term meaning "one thousand," a word used six times in Revelation 20:2-7. This view is most often contrasted with postmillennialism, which sees Christ's return after a golden "millennial age" where Christ rules spiritually from his throne in Heaven, and amillennialism which sees the millennium as a figurative reference to the current church age. (Premillennialist theology framed the *Left Behind* series of novels by Tim LeHaye and Jerry Jenkins.)

Presbyterian. Refers to a branch of Protestant denominations derived from the Reformed churches of the Reformation, which have a presbyterian form of church governance. Presbyterian churches are historically Calvinistic in theology. Presbyterianism traces its institutional roots back to the Scottish Reformation, especially as led by John Knox. There are many separate Presbyterian churches around the world. Besides national distinctions, Presbyterians also have divided from one another for doctrinal reasons, especially in the wake of the Enlightenment.

reformed theology. Generally considered synonymous with Calvinism and most often, in the U. S. and the U. K., specifically associated with the theology of the historic church confessions such as the Westminster Confession of Faith.

Bibliography

Anderson, Ken. "Konvicted: How Dan Moody Destroyed the Klan in Texas." *The Alcalde* (July/August 2000), republished in *Utopia*, University of Texas in Austin. Accessed February 23, 2007. http://utopia.utexas.edu /articles/alcalde/moody.html?sec=texas&sub=laws.

Armstrong, Karen *The Battle for God*. New York: Ballantine Books, 2000.

———. *The Bible: A Biography*. New York: Grove Books, 2007.

———. *The Case for God*. New York: Alfred A. Knopf, 2009.

———. *A History of God*. New York: Ballantine Books, 1993.

———. *Jerusalem: One City, Three Faiths*. New York: Ballantine Books, 1997.

Bass, Diana Butler. *Christianity for the Rest of Us: How the Neighborhood Church Is Transforming the Faith*. San Francisco: HarperSanFrancisco, 2006.

Bates, David Keith, Jr. "Moving Fundamentalism toward the Mainstream: John R. Rice and the Reengagement of America's Religious and Political Cultures." PhD diss., Kansas State University, 2006.

Bawer, Bruce. *Stealing Jesus: How Fundamentalism Betrays Christianity*. New York: Crown Publishers, 1997.

Beardsley, Frank. *Religious Progress Through Religious Revivals*. New York: American Tract Society, 1943.

Bell, Rob. *Jesus Wants to Save Christians: A Manifesto for the Church in Exile*. Grand Rapids, MI: Zondervan, 2008.

Bergen, Doris, ed. *The Sword of the Lord: Military Chaplains from the First to the Twenty-First Century*. Notre Dame, IN: University of Notre Dame Press, 2004.

Bickel, Bruce, and Stan Jantz,. *I'm Fine With God: It's Christians I Can't Stand*. Eugene, OR: Harvest House, 2008.

Bobrick, Benson. *Angel in the Whirlwind: The Triumph of the American Revolution*. New York: Simon and Schuster, 1997.

Borg, Marcus J., and John Dominic Crossan. *The First Paul: Reclaiming the Radical Visionary Behind the Church's Conservative Icon*. San Francisco: HarperOne, 2009.

Borg, Marcus J. *The Heart of Christianity*. San Francisco: HarperSanFrancisco, 2003.

————. *Reading the Bible Again for the First Time*. San Francisco: HarperSanFrancisco, 1989.

Bready, J. Wesley. *England Before and After Wesley*. London: Hodder & Stoughton, 1938.

Bryan, William Jennings. *The Bible or Evolution?* Murfreesboro, TN: Sword of the Lord Foundation, 1965.

Carpenter, Joel A. *Revive Us Again: The Reawakening of American Fundamentalism*. New York: Oxford University Press, 1997.

Carse, James P. *The Religious Case Against Belief*. New York: Penguin Press, 2008.

Clapp, Rodney. *Johnny Cash and the Great American Contradiction: Christianity and the Battle for the Soul of a Nation*. Louisville, KY: Westminster John Knox Press, 2008.

Conder, Tim and Daniel Rhodes. *Free for All, Rediscovering the Bible in Community*. Ada, MI: Baker Books, 2009.

Cox, Harvey. *The Future of Faith*. San Francisco: HarperOne, 2009.

Dark, David. *The Gospel According to America*. Louisville, KY: Westminster John Knox Press, 2005.

————. *The Sacredness of Questioning Everything*. Grand Rapids, MI: Zondervan, 2008.

Dean, Kenda Creasy. *Almost Christian: What the Faith of Our Teenagers Is Telling the American Church*. New York: Oxford University Press, USA, 2010.

Dinnerstein, Leonard. "Leo Frank Case," The New Georgia Encyclopedia. Accessed March 22, 2007. http://www.georgiaencyclopedia.org/nge /Article.jsp?id=h-906

Dollar, George W. *A History of Fundamentalism in America*. Greenville, SC: Bob Jones University Press, 1973.

Domke, David. *God Willing?: Political Fundamentalism in the White House, the "War on Terror," and the Echoing Press*. London: Pluto Press, 2004.

Dorsett, Lyle. *Billy Sunday and the Redemption of Urban America*. Grand Rapids, MI: Wm. B. Eerdmans Publishing Co, 1991.

Ehrman, Bart. *Jesus Interrupted: Revealing the Hidden Contradictions in the Bible*. San Francisco: HarperOne, 2009.

Falwell, Jerry, Ed Dobson, and Ed Hindson. *The Fundamentalist Phenomenon: The Resurgence of Conservative Christianity*. New York: Doubleday, 1981.

Fellman, Michael. *Inside War: The Guerrilla Conflict in Missouri During the American Civil War*. New York: Oxford University Press, 1989.

Gossett, Thomas F. *Race: The History of an Idea in America*. Dallas: Southern Methodist University Press, 1963. 243.

Grainger, Brett. *In the World But Not of It: One Family's Militant Faith and the History of Fundamentalism in America*. New York: Walker and Company, 2008.

Grant, Michael. *Jesus: An Historian's Review of the Gospels*. New York: Charles Scribner's Sons, 1977.

Hankins, Barry. *God's Rascal: J. Frank Norris & The Beginnings of Southern Fundamentalism*. Lexington, KY: University Press of Kentucky, 1996.

Harding, Susan Friend. *The Book of Jerry Falwell: Fundamentalist Language and Politics*. Princeton, NJ: Princeton University Press, 2000.

Hazleton, Lesley. *Jezebel: The Untold Story of the Bible's Harlot Queen*. New York: Doubleday, 2007.

———. *Mary: A Flesh-and-Blood Biography of the Virgin Mother*. New York: Bloomsbury, 2004.

Hedges, Chris. *Losing Moses on the Freeway: The 10 Commandments in America*. New York: Simon and Schuster, 2005.

Henderson, Jim, Todd Hunter, Craig Spinks. *The Outsider Interviews: A New Generation Speaks Out on Christianity*. Ada, MI: Baker Books, 2010.

Himes, John R. *The Making of a Soul-Winner*. Murfreesboro, TN: Sword of the Lord Publishers, 1979.

Howe, Daniel Walker. *What Hath God Wrought: The Transformation of America. 1815-1848*, New York: Oxford University Press, 2007.

Hunter, James Davison. *To Change the World: The Irony, Tragedy, & Possibility of Christianity in the Late Modern World*. New York: Oxford University Press, 2010.

Hunter, Todd D. *Christianity Beyond Belief: Following Jesus for the Sake of Others*. Downers Grove, IL: Intervarsity Press, 2009.

Jones, Tony. *The New Christians: Dispatches from the Emergent Frontier*. San Francisco: Jossey-Bass, 2008.

Keller, Timothy. *The Reason for God: Belief in an Age of Skepticism*. New York: Dutton, 2008.

Kinnaman, David, and Gabe Lyons. *Unchristian: What a New Generation Really Thinks About Christianity and Why It Matters*. Ada, MI: Baker Books, 2007.

Knitter, Paul. *Without Buddha I Could Not Be a Christian*. Oxford, UK: Oneworld Publications, 2009.

Lamont, Anne. *Traveling Mercies: Some Thoughts on Faith*. New York: Anchor Books, 1999.

Leary, Joy Degruy. *Post Traumatic Slave Syndrome*. Milwaukie, OR: Uptone Press, 2005.

Leonard, Bill. *Baptists in America*. New York: Columbia University Press, 2005.

Lesher, Stephen. *George Wallace: American Populist*. New York: Addison Wesley, 1994.

Lewis, CS. *Mere Christianity*. San Francisco: HarperOne, 1952.

Lichtman, Allan J. *White Protestant Nation: The Rise of the American Conservative Movement*. New York: Grove Press, 2008.

Long, Christopher. "The Handbook of Texas Online: Ku Klux Klan." Accessed February 23, 2007. http://www.tsha.utexas.edu/handbook/online /articles/KK/vek2_print.html.

Lyons, Gabe. *The Next Christians: How a New Generation Is Restoring the Faith*. New York: Doubleday, 2010.

Mackenzie, Don, Ted Falcon, and Jamal Rahman. *Getting to the Heart of Interfaith*. Woodstock, VT: Skylight Paths, 2009.

Macy, Joanna. *Widening Circles*. Gabriola Island, BC, Canada: New Society Publishers, 2000.

————. *World as Lover, World as Self*. Berkeley, CA: Parallax Press, 1991.

Marks, John. *Reasons to Believe: One Man's Journey Among the Evangelicals and the Faith He Left Behind*. San Francisco: HarperCollins, 2008.

Marsden, George. *Fundamentalism and American Culture*. New York: Oxford University Press, 2006.

————. *Understanding Fundamentalism and Evangelicalism*. Grand Rapids, MI: Eerdmans Publishing Co., 1991.

Marsh, Charles. *God's Long Summer: Stories of Faith and Civil Rights*. Princeton, NJ: Princeton University Press, 1997.

McLaren, Brian. *Everything Must Change: Jesus, Global Crises, and a Revolution of Hope*. Nashville, TN: Thomas Nelson, 2007.

————. *A Generous Orthodoxy*. Grand Rapids, MI: Zondervan, 2004.

————. *A New Kind of Christianity: 10 Questions that are Transforming the Faith*. San Francisco: HarperOne, 2010.

————. *The Secret Message of Jesus*. Nashville, TN: W Publishing Group, Thomas Nelson, 2006.

McVey, Steve. *Grace Walk: What You've Always Wanted in the Christian Life*. Eugene, OR: Harvest House, 1995.

Mencken, H.L. Quoted in "History on Stage." Accessed March 30, 2008. http://www.historyonstage.com/viewpage.aspx?ID=78.

Miller, Steven P. *Billy Graham and the Rise of the Republican South*. Philadelphia, PA: University of Pennsylvania Press, 2009.

MLK Online. Accessed March 30, 2008. http://www.mlkonline.net.

Monaghan, Jay. *Civil War on the Western Border, 1854-1865*. Lincoln, NE: University of Nebraska Press, 1955.

Moneyhon, Carl. *Texas After the Civil War: The Struggle of Reconstruction*. College Station, TX: Texas A&M University Press, 2004.

Moore, Howard Edgar. "The Emergence of Moderate Fundamentalism: John R. Rice and The Sword of the Lord." PhD diss., George Washington University, 1990.

Nicholl, Armand M. *The Question of God: CS Lewis and Sigmund Freud Debate God, Love, Sex, and the Meaning of Life*. New York: Simon and Schuster, 2002.

Noll, Mark. *The Civil War as a Theological Crisis*. Chapel Hill, NC: University of North Carolina Press, 2006.

O'Flaherty, Daniel. *General Jo Shelby: Undefeated Rebel*. Chapel Hill, NC: University of North Carolina Press, 1954.

O'Reilly, Mary Rose. *The Barn at the End of the World: the Apprenticeship of a Quaker, Buddhist Shepherd*. Minneapolis, MN: Milkweed, 2000.

Pagitt, Doug. *A Christianity Worth Believing: Hope-Filled, Open-Armed, Alive-and-Well Faith*. San Francisco: Jossey-Bass, 2008.

Pagitt, Doug and Tony Jones. *An Emergent Manifesto*. Ada, MI: Baker Books, 2007.

Palmer, Parker J. *A Hidden Wholeness: The Journey Toward an Undivided Life; Welcoming the Soul and Weaving Community in a Wounded World*. San Francisco: Jossey-Bass, 2004.

———. *Let Your Life Speak*. San Francisco: Jossey-Bass, 2000.

Price, James D. *King James Onlyism: A New Sect*. Chattanooga, TN: James D. Price Publisher, 2006.

Putnam, Robert D. and David E. Campbell. *American Grace: How Religion Divides and Unites Us*. New York: Simon and Schuster, 2010.

Rahman, Jamal. *The Fragrance of Faith*, Watsonville, CA: The Book Foundation, 2004.

Rahman, Jamal, Kathleen Schmitt Elias, and Ann Holmes Redding. *Out Of Darkness Into Light: Spiritual Guidance in the Quran With Reflections From Christian and Jewish Sources*. Harrisburg, PA: Morehouse Publishing, 2009.

Reece, Erik. *An American Gospel: On Family, History, and the Kingdom of God*. New York: Riverhead Books, 2009.

Rice, Chris. *Grace Matters: A True Story of Race, Friendship, and Faith in the Heart of the South*. San Francisco: Jossey-Bass, 2002.

Rice, John R. "God Save Young America." Murfreesboro, TN: Sword of the Lord Publishers, 1972.

———. *The Home—Courtship, Marriage, and Children*. Wheaton, IL: Sword of the Lord Publishers, 1945.

———. "The Home, the School, the Nation, and Law and Order." Murfreesboro, TN: Sword of the Lord Publishers, 1972.

———. *I Am a Fundamentalist*. Murfreesboro, TN: Sword of the Lord Publishers, 1975.

———. *Is God a "Dirty Bully"?* Wheaton, IL: Sword of the Lord Publishers, 1958.

———. "Lodges Examined by the Bible." Wheaton, IL: Sword of the Lord Publishers, 1943.

———. *Prayer—Asking and Receiving*. Wheaton, IL: Sword of the Lord Publishers, 1942.

———. *Revival Appeals*. Wheaton, IL: Sword of the Lord Publishers, 1945.

———. *The Rice Reference Bible*. Nashville, TN: Thomas Nelson Publishers, 1981.

———. "The Ruin of a Christian." Wheaton, IL: Sword of the Lord Publishers, 1944.

———. "The Scarlet Sin." Wheaton, IL: Sword of the Lord Publishers, 1946.

———. *Songs of John R. Rice*. Murfreesboro, TN: Sword of the Lord Publishers, 1976.

———. *The Soul-Winner's Fire*. Wheaton, IL: Sword of the Lord Publishers, 1941.

———. "War in Vietnam: Should Christians Fight?" Murfreesboro, TN: Sword of the Lord Publishers, 1966.

————. *We Can Have Revival Now! Annual Lectures on Revival at Bob Jones University*. Wheaton, IL: Sword of the Lord Publishers, 1950.

————. "What is Wrong With the Movies?" Grand Rapids, MI: Zondervan, 1938.

————. *When Skeletons Come Out of the Closets!* Wheaton, IL: Sword of the Lord Publishers, 1943.

Robinson, Marilynne. *Gilead: A Novel*. New York: Farrar, Straus, and Giroux, 2004.

Rollins, Peter. *The Orthodox Heretic*. Orleans, MA: Paraclete Press, 2009.

Rubart, James L. *Rooms: A Novel*. Nashville, TN: B&H Publishing Group, 2010.

Sandeen, Ernest. *The Roots of Fundamentalism: British and American Millenarianism, 1800-1930*. Chicago: University of Chicago Press, 2008.

Schaeffer, Frank. *Crazy for God*. Cambridge, MA: Carroll & Graf Publishers, 2007.

Schwartz, Regina. *The Curse of Cain: The Violent Legacy of Monotheism*. Chicago: University of Chicago Press, 1997.

Sheldon, Charles Monroe. *In His Steps: "What Would Jesus Do?"* Chicago: Chicago Advance, 1896.

Sifton, Elizabeth. *The Serenity Prayer: Faith and Politics in Times of Peace and War*. New York: Norton, 2003.

Sine, Tom. *Ceasefire: Searching for Sanity in America's Culture War*. Grand Rapids, MI: Eerdmans Publishing Co, 1995.

Smallwood, James, Barry Crouch, and Larry Peacock. *Murder and Mayhem: The War of Reconstruction in Texas*. College Station, TX: Texas A&M University Press, 2003.

Strout, Elisabeth. *Abide with Me*. New York: Random House, 2006.

Sumner, Robert L. *Man Sent From God: A Biography of Dr. John R. Rice*. Grand Rapids, MI: Eerdmans Publishing Company, 1959.

Sweeney, Jon M. *Born Again and Again: Surprising Gifts of a Fundamentalist Childhood*. Orleans, MA: Paraclete Press, 2005.

Tarico, Valerie. *The Dark Side: How Evangelical Teachings Corrupt Love and Faith*. Seattle, WA: Dea Press, 2006.

Taylor, Barbara Brown. *Leaving Church: A Memoir of Faith*. San Francisco: HarperSanFrancisco, 2007.

Tickle, Phyllis. *The Great Emergence: How Christianity is Changing and Why*. Ada, MI: Baker Books, 2008.

Tippett, Krista. *Speaking of Faith*. New York: Viking, 2007.

Torrey, R. A., A. C. Dixon, Louis Meyer, eds. *The Fundamentals*. 2 vols. Ada, MI: Baker Books, 2003.

Turner, Matthew Paul. *Churched: One Kid's Journey Toward God Despite a Holy Mess*. Colorado Springs, CO: Waterbrook Press, 2008.

Walden, Viola. *John R. Rice, the Captain of Our Team: A Biography by his Personal Secretary for 46 Years*. Murfreesboro, TN: Sword of the Lord Press, 1990.

Waldman, Steven. *Founding Faith: Providence, Politics, and the Birth of Religious Freedom in America*. New York: Random House, 2008.

Wallis, Jim. *God's Politics: Why the Right Gets It Wrong and the Left Doesn't Get It*. New York: HarperCollins, 2005.

———. *The Great Awakening*. San Francisco: HarperOne, 2008.

Wallis, Jim and Joyce Hollyday. *Cloud of Witnesses*. Maryknoll, NY: Orbis, 1991.

Warren, Rick. *The Purpose-Driven Life*. Grand Rapids, MI: Zondervan, 2002.

Webber, Robert, ed. *Listening to the Beliefs of Emerging Churches*. Grand Rapids, MI: Zondervan, 2007.

Wiesenthal, Simon. *The Sunflower: On the Possibilities and Limits of Forgiveness*. New York: Schocken Books, 1998.

Willard, Dallas. *The Divine Conspiracy: Rediscovering Our Hidden Life in God*. San Francisco: HarperSanFrancisco, 1998.

Wright, N.T. *Surprised by Hope: Rethinking Heaven, the Resurrection, and the Mission of the Church*. San Francisco: HarperOne, 2008.

Wright, Robert. *The Evolution of God*. New York: Little, Brown, 2009.

Yaconelli, Mike, general ed. *Stories of Emergence: Moving from Absolute to Authentic*. Grand Rapids, MI: Zondervan, 2003.

Yancey, Philip. *Rumors of Another World: What On Earth Are We Missing?* Grand Rapids, MI: Zondervan, 2003.

———. *Soul Survivor*. Colorado Springs, CO: WaterBrook Press, 2001.

———. *What's So Amazing About Grace?* Grand Rapids, MI: Zondervan, 1997.

Young, Wm. Paul. *The Shack*. Newbury Park, CA: Windblown Media, 2007.

Index

Notes

[1] Hans Johnson and William Eskridge, "The Legacy of Falwell's Bully Pulpit," *Washington Post*, http://www.washingtonpost.com/wp-dyn/content/article /2007/05/18/AR2007051801392.html (published May 19, 2007, accessed September 15, 2010).

[2] Transcript of the tape recording of the funeral service for John R. Rice in the Rice Family Papers, a collection of letters and other personal documents in the possession of Jessie Rice Sandberg.

[3] George Marsden, *Understanding Fundamentalism and Evangelicalism* (Grand Rapids, MI: Eerdmans Publishing Co., 1991) vii.

[4] Collin Hansen, "Pastor Provocateur," *Christianity Today*, September 2007, http://www.christianitytoday.com/ct/2007/september/30.44.html?start=1

[5] David Kinnamen, *Unchristian: What a New Generation Really Thinks About Christianity* (Ada, MI: BakerBooks, 2007), 35.

[6] Quoted in David E.Stannard's "Death and the Puritan Child," *American Quarterly: Special Issue; Death in America,* 26, no. 5, (December 1974, 456-476, http://www.jstor.org/stable/2711885 (accessed November 25, 2010).

[7] "Scotch-Irish American" *Wikipedia*, http://en.wikipedia.org /wiki/Scotch-Irish_American (accessed January 31, 2009).

[8] Malcolm Gladwell, *Outliers* (New York: Little, Brown, 2008), 167.

[9] Steven Waldman, *Founding Faith* (New York: Random House, 2008), 101.

[10] Ibid, 102, quoted in Lewis Peyton Little's *Imprisoned Preachers and Religious Liberty in Virginia* (Lynchburg: J.P. Bell, 1938).

[11] James Madison, *Memorial and Remonstrance Against Religious Assessments*, 1785, *We the People*, http://religiousfreedom.lib.virginia .edu/sacred/madison_m&r_1785.html (accessed November 29, 2010).

[12] "Samuel Doak," Wikipedia, http://en.wikipedia.org/wiki/Samuel_Doak (accessed January 31, 2009).

[13] Quoted in Benson Bobrick's *Angel in the Whirlwind*, (New York: Simon and Schuster, 1997), 314.

[14] Richard B. Drake, *A History of Appalachia* (Lexington, KY: University Press of Kentucky), 88.

[15] "The Emancipator," *Tennessee Encyclopedia of History and Culture,* http://tennesseeencyclopedia.net/imagegallery.php?EntryID=E017 (accessed January 31, 2009).

[16] "The Emergence of the African American Church," Library of Congress exhibit "Religion and the Founding of the American Republic," http://www.loc.gov/exhibits/religion/rel07.html (accessed January 31, 2009).

[17] "Featured Biography: Oliver Anderson," Missouri State Parks, http://www.mostateparks.com/lexington/oliveranderson.htm (accessed April 9, 2009).

[18] Harrison Anthony Trexler, *Slavery in Missouri, 1804-1865* (Baltimore, Md. Johns Hopkins Press, 1914).

[19] Waverly Missouri Arts Council, "Early History of Waverly," http://www.waverlyarts.org/ (accessed April 4, 2008).

[20] "John Brown—abolitionist)," *Wikipedia,* http://en.wikipedia.org/wiki /John_Brown_(abolitionist) (accessed November 29, 2010).

[21] "Victor Hugo's letter to the London News regarding John Brown," *Wikipedia,* http://en.wikisource.org/wiki/Victor_Hugo's_letter_to_the_ London_News_regarding_John_Brown, (accessed February 1st, 2010).

[22] Perry Miller, *The Life of the Mind in America from the Revolution to the Civil War* (New York: Harcourt, Brace, and Word, 1965), 46.

[23] Mark Noll, *The Civil War as a Theological Crisis* (Chapel Hill, NC: University of North Carolina Press, 2006), 27.

[24] Ibid, 21.

[25] Jeremiah 47:6, King James Version.

[26] Genesis 9:25-27

[27] Philemon 15:16

[28] Colossians 3:22, 4:1

[29] Gardner Shattuck, "Faith, Morale, and the Army Chaplain in the American Civil War" (Notre Dame, IN: University of Notre Dame Press. A chapter in *The Sword of the Lord*, 2004), 111.

[30] Increase Mather, quoted in Mark Noll's *The Civil War as a Theological Crisis* (Chapel Hill, NC: University of North Carolina Press, 2006), 41.

[31] Ibid, 44.

[32] "Civil War Music: God Save the South," Civil War Preservation Trust, http://www.civilwar.org/education/history/on-the-homefront/culture /music/god-save-the-south/god-save-the-south.html (accessed May 12, 2010).

[33] Jay Monaghan, *Civil War on the Western Border* (Lincoln, NE: Bison Books, 1955) 185.

[34] Bowen Kerrihard, *America's Civil War: Missouri and Kansas, HistoryNet.com,* March 1999, http://www.historynet.com/americas-civil-war-missouri-and-kansas.htm/2 (accessed November 29, 2010).

[35] *The Battle of Warrensburg,* The American Civil War, http://www.mycivilwar.com/battles/620326b.htm (accessed March 28, 2009).

[36] Quoted in Michael Fellman's *Inside War: The Guerilla Conflict in Missouri* (New York: Oxford University Press, 1989), 68.

[37] "General Order No. 11," *Wikipedia*, http://en.wikipedia.org/wiki /General_Order_%E2%84%96_11_(1863) (accessed March 21, 2009).

[38] Quoted in Michael Fellman's *Inside War: The Guerilla Conflict in Missouri* (New York: Oxford University Press, 1989), 78.

[39] Ibid., 80.

[40] Daniel O'Flaherty, *General Jo Shelby: Undefeated Rebel* (Chapel Hill, NC: University of North Carolina Press, 1954), 232.

[41] Richard McCaslin, *The Handbook of Texas Online*, http://www.tshaonline .org/handbook/online/articles/GG/jig1.html (accessed April 9, 2009).

[42] James Smallwood, Barry Crouch, and Larry Peacock, *Murder and Mayhem: The War of Reconstruction in Texas* (College Station, TX: Texas A&M University Press, 2003), 40.

[43] T. R. Fehrenback, *Lone Star: A History of Texas and the Texans* (New York: Collier Books, 1985).

[44] United States census, 1870.

[45] Carl Moneyhon, *Texas after the Civil War* (College Station, TX: Texas A&M University Press, 2004), 95.

[46] Ibid., 176.

[47] Harry Haynes, "Biography of Dr. Burleson," *The Life and Writings of Rufus C. Burleson* (Waco, TX: Published by Georgia Jenkins Burleson, 1901), 433.

[48] Kelly Pigott, "Fannin County," *The Handbook of Texas Online* http://www.tshaonline.org/handbook/online/articles/FF/hcf2.html (accessed April 9, 2009).

[49] Rice Family Papers, a collection of letters and other personal documents in the possession of Jessie Rice Sandberg.

[50] Robert L. Sumner, *Man Sent From God: A Biography of Dr. John R. Rice* (Grand Rapids, Michigan: Eerdmans Publishing Company, 1959).

[51] Charles. M. Sheldon, *What Would Jesus Do?* (Chicago: Advance Publishing, 1898), 15.

[52] Ibid., 19.

[53] Jack B. Rogers and Robert E. Blade, "The Great Ends of the Church: Two Perspectives," *Journal of Presbyterian History* 76 (1998), 181-186.

[54] J. Wesley Bready, *England Before and After Wesley* (London, UK: Hodder & Stoughton, 1938), 201.

[55] Ibid., 229.

[56] Dorinda Outram, *The Enlightenment* (New York: Cambridge University Press, 1995), 43.

[57] Reported in conversation with John R. Rice's daughter Jessie Sandberg.

[58] Robert L. Sumner, *Man Sent from God* (Wheaton, IL: Sword of the Lord Publishers, 1959), 29.

[59] Ibid., 30.

[60] Lyle Dorsett, *Billy Sunday and the Redemption of Urban America* (Grand Rapids, MI: Eerdmans Publishing Co, 1991), 48.

[61] Matthew 13:42

[62] *Autobiography of John Stuart Mill* (Utilitarianism.com: 1873), http://www.utilitarianism.com/millauto/ (accessed November 28, 2010).

[63] John R. Rice, *Is God a Dirty Bully?* (Wheaton, IL: *Sword of the Lord* Publishers, 1958).

[64] Reuben A. Torrey, *How to Obtain Fullness of Power* (Ada, MI: Revell Company, 1897), 32.

[65] "The Coming of the Lord: The Doctrinal Center of the Bible," *Addresses on the Second Coming of the Lord*. December 3-6, 1895, 82. Quoted in George Marsden's *Fundamentalism and American Culture* (New York: Oxford University Press, 2006), 55.

[66] Leonard Dinnerstein, "Leo Frank Case," *The New Georgia Encyclopedia*, http://www.georgiaencyclopedia.org/nge/Article.jsp?id=h-906 (accessed March 22, 2007).

[67] Ibid.

[68] Ibid.

[69] Ibid.

[70] Ibid.

[71] Benjamin Capps, *Sam Chance* (New York: Duell, Sloan and Pierce, 1965), 35.

[72] A. C. Greene, *Sketches from the Five States of Texas* (College Station, TX: Texas A&M University Press), 94.

[73] Howard Edgar Moore, "The Emergence of Moderate Fundamentalism: John R. Rice and *The Sword of the Lord*" (unpublished PhD diss., George Washington University, 1990), 34.

[74] Lyle Dorsett, *Billy Sunday and the Redemption of Urban America* (Grand Rapids, MI: Eerdmans Publishing Co, 1991), 98.

[75] Shailer Mathews, *The Faith of Modernism* (New York: Macmillan, 1924), 22-23.

[76] Quoted in George Marsden's *Fundamentalism and American Culture* (New York: Oxford University Press, 2006), 148.

[77] *World War 1: A Call to Arms*, Encyclopedia.com: http://www.encyclopedia .com/doc/1G2-3468300599.html (accessed February 22, 2010).

[78] Edward J. Larson, *Summer for the Gods: The Scopes Trial* (New York: Basic Books, 1997), 32.

[79] George Marsden, *Fundamentalism and American Culture* (New York: Oxford University Press, 2006), 150.

[80] Ibid, 158.

[81] Ibid, 161.

[82] Ibid, 159.

[83] Barry Hankins, *God's Rascal: J. Frank Norris & the beginnings of Southern fundamentalism* (Lexington, KY: University Press of Kentucky, 1996), 50.

[84] Ibid, 52.

[85] Ibid, 53.

[86] Ibid, 31.

[87] Joseph Hocking, *The Sword of the Lord* (Boston: Dutton and Co., 1909), 325.

[88] R. A. Torrey, *The Power of Prayer and the Prayer of Power* (New York: Cosimo Publishing, 1924), 185.

[89] William Bell Riley, *Christian Fundamentals in School and Church* (April-June, 1922), 4-5.

[90] T. T. Martin, *Hell and the High School* (Kansas City, MO: Western Baptist Publishing Co., 1923), 164-165.

[91] *New York Times*, quoted in Jackson Lears's *Rebirth of a Nation* (New York: HarperCollins, 2009), 187.

[92] Bradley J. Longfield, *The Presbyterian Controversy: Fundamentalists, Modernists, and Moderates* (New York: Oxford University Press, 1991), 68.

[93] William Jennings Bryan, "The Bible or Evolution" (Wheaton, IL: Sword of the Lord Press, 1942), 9.

[94] Ibid., 28.

[95] Ibid.

[96] John R. Rice, "Leaving All for Jesus," The *Sword of the Lord*, April 11th, 1952.

[97] John R. Rice, *The Soul-Winner's Fire* (Chicago: Moody Bible Institute, 1941), 32.

[98] John R. Rice, *Lodges Examined by the Bible : Is It Sinful for a Christian to Have Membership in Secret Orders?* (Findlay, OH: Fundamental Truth Publishers, 1943), 45.

[99] Howard Edgar Moore, "The Emergence of Moderate Fundamentalism: John R. Rice and *The Sword of the Lord*." (PhD diss., George Washington University, 1990), 48.

[100] Barry Hankins, *God's Rascal: J. Frank Norris and the Beginnings of Southern Fundamentalism* (Lexington, KY: University Press of Kentucky, 1996), 161.

[101] Christopher Long, "Ku Klux Klan," *The Handbook of Texas Online,* http://www.tsha.utexas.edu/handbook/online/articles/KK/vek2_print.html (accessed February 23, 2007).

[102] Ken Anderson, "Konvicted: How Dan Moody Destroyed the Klan in Texas." *The Alcalde* (July/August 2000), republished in *Utopia*, an online project of the University of Texas in Austin. http://utopia.utexas.edu/articles /alcalde/moody.html?sec=texas&sub=laws (accessed February 23, 2007).

[103] Mordecai Ham, quoted on various websites connected with the "Christian Identity" movement of extreme right wing Christian fundamentalists who claim Ham as their inspiration. For example, see: http://www.christianidentitychurch.net /world_ends_tomorrow.htm, where Thomas Robb praises Mordecai Ham as a great revivalist while lambasting Billy Graham as a "stooge of Satan."

[104] Bruce Clayton and John A. Salmond, *Debating Southern History* (Lanham, MD: Rowman & Littlefield Publishers, November 1999), 31.

[105] Lyle Dorsett, *Billy Sunday and the Redemption of Urban America* (Grand Rapids, MI: Eerdmans Publishing Co, 1991), 117.

[106] Ibid.

[107] Harry Emerson Fosdick, "Shall the Fundamentalists Win?" *History Matters* web site, http://historymatters.gmu.edu/d/5070/ (accessed November 6, 2010).

[108] Doug Linder, *William Bell Riley* (Kansas City: University of Missouri Kansas City School of Law, 2004), http://www.law.umkc.edu/faculty /projects/ftrials/conlaw/releyw.html (accessed November 28, 2010).

[109] Edward J. Larson, *Summer for the Gods: The Scopes Trial* (New York: Basic Books, 1997).

[110] Matthew Chapman, *Trials of the Monkey: An Accidental Memoir* (New York: Picador, 2001), 217.

[111] H. L. Mencken, quoted in *History on Stage*, http://www.historyonstage .com/viewpage.aspx?ID=78 (accessed March 30, 2008).

[112] *Elmer Gantry Study Guide*, http://www.bookrags.com/studyguide-elmer-gantry/intro.html (accessed November 20, 2009).

[113] John R. Rice to Lloys Cooke, March 21, 1921, Rice Family Papers, a collection of letters and other personal documents in the possession of Jessie Rice Sandberg.

[114] David Keith Bates, "Moving Fundamentalism toward the Mainstream," unpublished PhD diss. (Kansas State University, Manhattan, KS, 2005).

[115] Walter Lippman, *A Preface to Morals* (New York: Macmillan Co., 1929), 31.

[116] John R. Rice, "Why I Am a Big F Fundamentalist," *The Fundamentalist* (March 2, 1928), 1.

[117] Ibid., 3.

[118] Barry Hankins, *God's Rascal: J. Frank Norris & The Beginnings of Southern Fundamentalism* (Lexington, KY: University Press of Kentucky, 1996), 163.

[119] Ibid., 165.

[120] Robert L. Sumner, *Man Sent From God: A Biography of Dr. John R. Rice* (Grand Rapids, MI: Eerdmans Publishing Co., 1959), 70-71.

[121] John R. Rice, "Lodges Examined by the Bible" (Wheaton, IL: Sword of the Lord Publishers, 1943), 25.

[122] Nolan Thompson, "Sherman Riot of 1930," *The Handbook of Texas Online*, http://www.tshaonline.org/handbook/online/articles/SS/jcs6.html (accessed November 30, 2009).

[123] John R. Rice, quoted in Howard Edgar Moore's "The Emergence of Moderate Fundamentalism: John R. Rice and *The Sword of the Lord*" (PhD diss., George Washington University, 1990), 68.

[124] Ibid.

[125] John R. Rice, *The Soul-Winner's Fire* (Wheaton, IL: Sword of the Lord Publishers, 1941), 5.

[126] J. Frank Norris's letter to Louis Entzminger, November 4, 1932, Rice Family Papers, a collection of letters and other personal documents in the possession of Jessie Rice Sandberg.

[127] Roger Burns, *Billy Graham* (Westport, CN: Greenwood Press, 2004), 9.

[128] "God's Billy Pulpit," *Time Magazine*, November 15, 1993, http://www.time.com/time/magazine/article/0,9171,979573-3,00.html (accessed August 7, 2009).

[129] "World War 1 casualties," Wikipedia, http://en.wikipedia.org/wiki /World_War_I_casualties (accessed August 13, 2009).

[130] William Vance Trollinger, *God's Empire: William Bell Riley and Midwestern Fundamentalism* (Madison, WI: University of Wisconsin Press), 72.

[131] Ibid., 74.

[132] Bill Leonard, *Baptists in America* (New York: Columbia University Press, 2005), 48.

[133] Ibid.

[134] Barry Hankins, *God's Rascal: J. Frank Norris & The Beginnings of Southern Fundamentalism* (Lexington, KY: University Press of Kentucky, 1996), 88.

[135] Ibid.

[136] John R. Rice, quoted in Howard Edgar Moore's "The Emergence of Moderate Fundamentalism: John R. Rice and *The Sword of the Lord*" (PhD diss., George Washington University, 1990).

[137] Ibid.

[138] Wyeth Willard, *Fire on the Prairie*, (Wheaton, IL: Van Kampen Press, 1950), 29.

[139] "Wheaton College," *Wikipedia*, http://en.wikipedia.org/wiki /Wheaton_College%28Illinois%29 (accessed November 19, 2009).

[140] John R. Rice, quoted in Howard Edgar Moore's "The Emergence of Moderate Fundamentalism: John R. Rice and *The Sword of the Lord*" (PhD diss., George Washington University, 1990).

[141] Joel A. Carpenter, *Revive Us Again:The Reawakening of American Fundamentalism* (New York: Oxford University Press, 1997), 31.

[142] "History of NAE," National Association of Evangelicals, http://www.nae .net/about-us/history/62 (accessed April 25, 2010).

[143] George M. Marsden, *Reforming Fundamentalism: Fuller Seminary and the New Evangelicalism*, (Grand Rapids, MI: Eerdmans Publishing Co., 1987), 48.

[144] John R. Rice, "Crowds, Great Messages, Life Dedications to Soul-Winning," *The Sword of the Lord*, Volume 9, #19 (November 20, 1942)

[145] John R. Rice, *I Am a Fundamentalist* (Murfreesboro, TN: Sword of the Lord Press, 1972), 15.

[146] James DeForest Murch, *Cooperation Without Compromise* (Grand Rapids, MI: Eerdmans Publishing Co., 1956), 49.

[147] Roger Bruns, *Billy Graham, a Biography* (Westport, CN: Greenwood Publishing Group, 2004), 23.

[148] Ibid., 24.

[149] John R. Rice, "Billy Graham Houston Campaign" (*The Sword of the Lord*, July 4, 1952).

[150] John R. Rice quoted in Howard Edgar Moore's "The Emergence of Moderate Fundamentalism: John R. Rice and *The Sword of the Lord*" (unpublished PhD diss., George Washington University, 1990).

[151] John R. Rice, "War: Wickedness and the Certain End of Civilization" (*The Sword of the Lord*, Volume 6, #48, June 21, 1940).

[152] John R. Rice, "Lodges Examined by the Bible" (Wheaton, IL: Sword of the Lord Publishers, 1943), 25.

[153] Ibid., 27.

[154] John R. Rice, quoted in Howard Edgar Moore's "The Emergence of Moderate Fundamentalism: John R. Rice and *The Sword of the Lord*" (unpublished PhD diss., George Washington University, 1990).

[155] *Atlanta Constitution.* Quoted by Steven P. Miller, *Billy Graham and the Rise of the Republican South* (Philadelphia, PA: University of Pennsylvania Press, 2009), 21.

[156] Ibid., 28

[157] "Biography of W. A. Criswell," Sword of the Lord Foundation, http://www.swordofthelord.com/biographies/CriswellWA.htm (accessed April 25, 2010).

[158] Quoted by Steven P. Miller, *Billy Graham and the Rise of the Republican South* (Philadelphia, PA: University of Pennsylvania Press, 2009), 39.

[159] Ibid., 43.

[160] Ibid., 43.

[161] John R. Rice, "Billy Graham Winning Thousands in England" (*The Sword of the Lord*, February 28th, 1947).

[162] Carl F. H. Henry, *The Uneasy Conscience of Modern Fundamentalism*, (Grand Rapids, MI: Eerdmans Publishing Co., 1947), 1.

[163] Ibid., 3

[164] Ibid., 39

[165] Bob Jones Sr. to John R. Rice, September 19, 1949, quoted in David Keith Bates's "Moving Fundamentalism Toward the Mainstream" (unpublished PhD diss., Kansas State University, Manhattan, KS), 117.

[166] John R. Rice, quoted in Howard Edgar Moore's "The Emergence of Moderate Fundamentalism: John R. Rice and *The Sword of the Lord*" (unpublished PhD diss., George Washington University, 1990).

[167] George M. Marsden, *Reforming Fundamentalism: Fuller Seminary and the New Evangelicalism*, (Grand Rapids, MI: Eerdmans Publishing Co., 1987), 159.

[168] Billy Graham, *Just as I Am* (San Francisco: HarperOne, 1999), 103.

[169] "Is Evangelical Theology Changing?" *Christian Life,* March 1956; Quoted in Howard Edgar Moore's "The Emergence of Moderate Fundamentalism: John R. Rice and *The Sword of the Lord*" (unpublished PhD diss. at George Washington University, 1990), 244.

[170] John R. Rice, *Earnestly Contending for the Faith* (Murfreesboro, TN: Sword of the Lord Publishers, 1965), 304-305.

[171] Billy Graham, *Just as I Am* (San Francisco: HarperOne, 1999), 302.

[172] Harold Myra and Marshall Shelley, "Jesus and Justice," *Christianity Today*, June 24, 2005, http://www.christianitytoday.com/ct/2005/juneweb-only/52.0c.html?start=2 (accessed December 1, 2009).

[173] Billy Graham, quoted in Steven P. Miller's, *Billy Graham and the Rise of the Republican South* (Philadelphia: University of Pennsylvania Press, 2009), 66.

[174] John R. Rice, "Negro and White," *Is God a "Dirty Bully"?* (Wheaton, IL: Sword of the Lord Publishers, 1958), 143.

[175] Ibid.

[176] Ibid., 155.

[177] Douglas A. Blackmon, *Slavery by Another Name* (New York: Doubleday, 2008), 7.

[178] Ibid., 4.

[179] Joy DeGruy Leary, "Post Traumatic Slave Syndrome," *In These Times*, http://www.inthesetimes.com/article/2523/ (accessed December 2, 2009).

[180] William Bradford Huie, "The Shocking Story of Approved Killing in Mississippi," *Look Magazine* article in American Experience, http://www.pbs.org/wgbh/amex/till/sfeature/sf_look_confession.html (accessed December 2, 2009).

[181] John R. Rice, "Negro and White," *Is God a "Dirty Bully"?* (Wheaton, IL: Sword of the Lord Publishers, 1958), 151.

[182] Fred Barlow, *Dr. John R. Rice, Giant of Evangelism* (Murfreesboro, TN, Sword of the Lord Publishers, 1983)

[183] Bob Jones, Sr., *Is Segregation Scriptural?* (Greenville, SC: Bob Jones University Press, 1960), 22.

[184] John R. Rice, "Negro and White," *Is God a "Dirty Bully"?* (Wheaton, IL: Sword of the Lord Publishers, 1958), 148.

[185] Ibid., 148.

[186] Bill J. Leonard, "A Theology for Racism: Southern Fundamentalists and the Civil Rights Movement" (Stauffenburg Press: essay in *Southern Landscapes* edited by Badger, Edgar, and Gretlund, 1996), 168.

[187] John R. Rice "Editor's Note," *The Sword of the Lord*, August 19, 1964.

[188] John R. Rice "Editor's Note," *The Sword of the Lord*, September 24, 1965.

[189] G. Archer Weniger, "Martin Luther King, Negro Pro-Communist," *The Sword of the Lord*, November 9, 1962.

[190] Noel Smith, "Martin Luther King," *Bible Baptist Tribune*, November 17, 1967, quoted in Bill Leonard's *Baptists in America*, (New York: Columbia University Press, 2005), 195.

[191] Jerry Falwell, quoted in Max Blumenthal, "Agent of Intolerance," *The Nation*, May 16, 2007, http://www.thenation.com/doc/20070528/blumenthal (accessed December 12, 2009).

[192] Jerry Falwell, "Ministers and Marchers," (Lynchburg, VA: LBC Liberty Archives, 1956).

[193] Bob Spencer, "Dr. Martin Luther King Died by the Lawlessness He Encouraged" (*The Sword of the Lord*, June 14, 1968).

[194] Walter Handford, *Finding New Ways to Communicate the Everlasting Gospel* (Greenville, SC: self-published, 2008).

[195] Ibid.

[196] Jerry Falwell, *Strength for the Journey* (New York: Simon and Schuster, 1987), 295.

[197] Macel Falwell, *Jerry Falwell: His Life and Legacy* (New York: Simon and Schuster, 2008), 103.

[198] John R. Rice, *The Home, the School, the Nation, and Law and Order* (Murfreesboro, TN: Sword of the Lord Publishers, 1972), 9.

[199] John R. Rice, *God in Your Family* (Murfreesboro, TN: Sword of the Lord Publishers, 1971), 214.

[200] John R. Rice, "War in Vietnam: Should Christians Fight?" (Murfreesboro, TN: Sword of the Lord Publishers, 1966).

[201] John R. Rice, *God Bless America!* (Murfreesboro, TN: Sword of the Lord Publishers, 1973).

[202] John R. Rice to Larry Kauffman, October 4, 1973, Rice Family Papers, a collection of letters and other personal documents in the possession of Jessie Rice Sandberg (Chattanooga, TN).

[203] John R. Rice, *The Home, the School, the Nation and Law and Order,* (Murfreesboro, TN: Sword of the Lord Publishers, 1972), 5.

[204] Ibid, 22.

[205] John R. Rice, *I Am a Fundamentalist* (Murfreesboro, TN: Sword of the Lord Publishers, 1975), 10.

[206] Ibid., 111.

[207] Robert Scheer, "Jimmy Carter: A Candid Conversation with the Democratic Candidate for the Presidency," *Playboy*, November, 1976.

[208] John R. Rice, "Editor's Notes: A Shock for Christians," *The Sword of the Lord*, October 15, 1976.

[209] Jerry Falwell, quoted in Susan Friend Harding, *The Book of Jerry Falwell* (Princeton, NJ: Princeton University Press, 2000), 128.

[210] Ibid., 126.

[211] Jerry Falwell, *America Can Be Saved.* (Murfreesboro, TN: Sword of the Lord Publishers, 1978).

[212] Dirk Smillie, *Falwell Inc: Inside a Religious, Political, Educational, and Business Empire* (New York: MacMillan, 2008), 85.

[213] Wikipedia, "Moral Majority," http://en.wikipedia.org/wiki/Moral_Majority (accessed December 15, 2009).

[214] Mark Taylor Dalhouse, *An Island in the Lake of Fire: Bob Jones University, Fundamentalism, and the Separatist Movement* (Athens, GA: University of Georgia Press, 1996), 108.

[215] John Himes, "Last Memories of Grandpa John R. Rice" (unpublished story sent to author Andrew Himes by his brother John Himes).

[216] Ibid.

[217] John. R. Rice, "Other Sheep." Transcription of an audio CD of the August 1980 sermon, distributed by Sword of the Lord Publishers, Murfreesboro, TN.

[218] Letter from the author's own family files.

[219] Karen Anderson, *The Case for God* (New York: Alfred A. Knopf, 2009), 86.

[220] David O. Beale, *In Pursuit of Purity: American Fundamentalism Since 1850* (Greenville, SC: Bob Jones University Press, 1986), 3.

[221] Southern Baptist Convention, "Resolution on Racial Reconciliation on the 150th Anniversary of the Southern Baptist Convention," http://www.sbc.net /resolutions/amResolution.asp?ID=899 (accessed November 7, 2010).

[222] Bob Jones University, "Statement About Race at BJU," http://www.bju .edu/welcome/who-we-are/race-statement.php (accessed the web, November 7, 2010).

[223] Kenda Creasy Dean, *Almost Christian* (New York: Oxford University Press, 2010), 14.

[224] John Wesley, "The Way to the Kingdom, Sermon 7," *The Sermons of John Wesley, 1870 Edition*, Global Ministries of United Methodist Church, http://new.gbgm-umc.org/umhistory/wesley/sermons/7/ (accessed November 29, 2010).

[225] Luke 12:31, King James Version.